Black Woman Walking

For Peter

BLACK WOMAN WALKING

A Different Experience of World Travel

Maureen Stone

BeaGay
Publications

Copyright © Maureen Stone 2002

First published in 2002 by BeaGay Publications
Suite 171
89 Commercial Road
Bournemouth BH2 5RR

Distributed by Gazelle Book Services Limited
Falcon House, Queen Square
Lancaster, England LA1 1RN

British Library Cataloguing in Publication Data
A catalogue record for this book is available from the British Library

ISBN 0-9541179-0-5

Typeset by Amolibros, Watchet, Somerset
This book production has been managed by Amolibros
Printed and bound by T J International Ltd, Padstow, Cornwall, UK

But what of those travellers who never write? How far have gender, class race and sexual orientation circumscribed the literary expression of the art of travel? In the history of travel, just as of a broader nature, how far have the writings of men, drawn from particular backgrounds and outlooks, and underpinned by an imperial imperative, foreclosed the construction of a meta-thesis of individual expression and self-identity?

Hall, D and Kinnaird, V (1996), A note on women travellers
in Kinnaird and Hall (eds)
Tourism, a Gender Analysis, Wiley, London

CONTENTS

ACKNOWLEDGEMENTS

I wish to thank my friend Annette Brice for her untiring interest, and her constant nagging. I also wish to thank Professor Lourdes Arizpe of the Centro Regional de Investigaciones Mulitdisciplinarias Universad Nacional Autónoma (CRIM) de Mexico for permission to use the picture of a woman walking en la zona de Flora from *Cultura y Cambio Global: Perceptiones Sociales sobre la Deforestación en la Selva Lacondona* (CRIM, 1993). Thanks to my friend Pearl Eintou Springer for kind permission to use her poem "Bois" (There are no men) from *Shades of I-She,* The Collective, Diego Martin Trinidad, 1997. Thanks are also due to that tireless campaigner for fair play for the self-publisher Johnathon Clifford without whose helpful advice and information on self-publishing, my manuscript might have fallen into the wrong hands. A special thanks to my husband Peter for our many walks, and for his patience, quiet support and encouragement, which helped me to carry on when I was least inclined to.

A BIOGRAPHICAL
SKETCH

In a book about women travellers yet to be written, but hopefully to be published in the year 2020, the following entry will appear for Maureen Stone, a black woman sociologist, traveller and hiker:

> In previous books about women travellers black women did not appear, most notably in Jane Robinson's (1996) *Wayward Women: A Guide to Women Travellers*. Robinson did not mention Nancy Prince's *A Narrative of the Life and Travels of Mrs Nancy Prince – A Black Woman's Odyssey Through Russia and Jamaica* (1853); nor Mary Seacole, and her *The Wonderful Adventures of Mrs Seacole in Many Lands*, (1857). Black women travellers were ignored by white women writers and publishers. This ensured that black women's voices remained silent and their stories continued to be hidden from history. This also meant that the role of black women in travel books and tourist literature could remain one of service: as servants, whores and as exotic objects of cultural curiosity. We hope that this entry on Maureen Stone will mark a departure from that racist tradition, and will herald the inclusion of black woman's travel stories in mainstream literature.

> Maureen Stone was born in 1942 during the Second World War, the sixth child in a family of seven, and the war was responsible for Mr Rawlins not having been in Barbados when his sixth child, and second girlchild, was born. In those days most black Bajan families were poor, and those with lots of children were that much poorer. As the intended last child of the family Maureen was given the name Augusta for her absent father. From birth she was sickly, with a huge head and not much more. Her mother was told by the doctor to take the

child home and "Make her comfortable." As a midwife Mrs Rawlins knew that this doctor-speak meant that her child was unlikely to survive.

Many years later Maureen used to tell the story of how she overheard a friend of her mother (who had just returned to Barbados from the USA) asking after the "poor child" who had been so sick when she had left the island many years before. Her mother pointed to the teenager, busily talking on the phone, and said: "Look! There she is, always on the phone." Mrs Rawlins had seen the circumstances of her child's birth as a challenge, both to her faith in God and her nursing skills. And by a combination of God's will, her nursing skills and mother's love the child survived. But she was not a fine specimen and did not walk competently until she was almost three years old. When her father returned to Barbados and saw her for the first time, he was not at all impressed with his "last child". Within a year of his return, they had produced another "last child" a boy, who was in every way a much finer specimen.

Maureen was not a conventionally bright child and did not gain entry to any of the Barbados government high schools. But she did complete secondary schooling and left with results adequate for higher education. After leaving school she worked as a trainee journalist, before joining the civil service as an assistant librarian. At the age of twenty, and with no other prospect of obtaining a university education, she applied for and was awarded a scholarship to study at Calcutta University West Bengal India. On arrival in India she was sent to a Bengali -speaking women's college, where her presence caused quite a disturbance among students who had never before seen a black i.e. African woman. She quickly arranged a transfer to another women's institution where English was the medium of instruction and Roman Catholicism was the religion – Loreto College – where many years earlier Mother Theresa had started her saintly career.

And so for three years this agnostic Caribbean woman of Exclusive Plymouth Brethren background attended a Roman

Catholic College in India, ran by Irish nuns. During these years she met and started walking and hiking with Peter Stone. They married in 1965, settled in England and had two children, and it is where she began her professional career. First she trained as a social worker at the London School of Economics where she was remembered for having asked an interesting question. During a session on Freudian psychology the lecturer explained that a dream about an umbrella was really a dream about a penis. Maureen innocently enquired whether the converse was also true and a dream about a penis was really about an umbrella.

After a short career in social work in 1975 she joined the sociology department at the University of Surrey, where she is remembered for having completed her PhD thesis in record time – three years' part-time as against a national average of ten years. Her thesis, published in 1978 under the title "The education of the black child", caused a major stir in education circles around the world and brought her much unwanted attention. She left university teaching in 1983 to work as a freelance academic, and in 1998 she was appointed Visiting Professor at the University of Bournemouth, Dorset.

As a child Maureen had been slow to walk, as an adult she made up for this late start by walking and hiking all over the UK, and all over the world. Travelling, walking, listening, being robbed here, befriended there, always on the receiving end of some story. She observed the many worlds around her with the trained eye of a western sociologist, enriched with insights from her "Third World" Caribbean childhood and her education and experiences of the East. Out of these rich and varied cultural, social and life experiences came her book *Black Woman Walking: A Different Experience of World Travel*, which was published in 2002.

Reader, please note that the author and publisher of the book in which the above biographical sketch is due to appear has yet to be found – any volunteers?

1

THE SOCIOLOGY OF WALKING

Why black women don't hike

In Britain the overwhelming majority of ethnic minority communities are in cities. Judy Ling Wong, director of the Black Environment Network (BEN) invites Ramblers to help them break down the invisible barriers that prevent them enjoying the countryside.

> Wong, Judy Ling (1997), "Just Like Us", in *Rambling Today,*
> *Magazine of the Ramblers' Association,* Spring 1997, London

Walking is declining so much that within a generation, few people are likely to do more than move from the front door to the car. The Pedestrian Policy Group claims that the average distance walked has fallen by a fifth over the last 20 years.

> Illman, J, "Getting a leg up in life", in the *Guardian,*
> London, 16th July 1996

IT WAS in Africa that human beings first stood up and walked, so black women have been walking for a long time. The first woman ever to walk was black; the anthropologists who discovered her remains gave her the name Lucy. Lucy is thought to have been the mother of all modern human beings. The reason why human beings stood up and walked had to do with getting a better view. Since that time people have discovered that almost any other form of transport gives a better view and as a result, in most parts of the world where people have a choice, walking has given way to other forms of transport.

1

I am happy to be following in Lucy's footsteps and to be walking, not only in Africa but wherever in the world I find myself. This is the reason why walking, and experiences connected with walking, is one of the main themes of this book. It is true that other forms of transport do get a look in, but travel by foot provides a unique means by which my world is shared with others. Other forms of transport come a poor second to my walks. So I begin with a more or less sociological analysis of the activity of walking – walking for pleasure and walking from necessity. As a way into this I use the example of white and black women walking in Africa. The poor African woman walks from necessity, the middle-class European woman walks from choice. To understand more about women's choices and lifestyles, we look at how women spend their time. I must stress from the outset that I am not writing a sociological treatise: this book is primarily about my own experiences of travel and walking in many parts of the world. The walks and the travels present me with the opportunity to be involved in other people's lives, and to observe and comment on various issues of our day.

We start with a picture of a young English woman walking in central Africa – in fact walking as if her life depended on it. She is on a journey that will take her *On Foot Through Africa* (Campbell, 1994). She is walking from the Cape to Cairo, and nothing less will do. Who is she, and why is she doing this? The lady is Ffyona Campbell and her walk through Africa is but a small part of her round-the-world walk: she is a very serious walker. As she walks she tries to be nice to the locals. In spite of the pain of her blisters, the plague of flies and her weakness from diarrhoea, she manages to smile at them in what she hopes is a friendly way. Sometimes these efforts pay off and local women walk along with her for a short while, and she enjoys a brief interval of woman talk.

For the most part the black women ignore the young white woman. At times Fyona senses something like hostility, especially when the African women call out to her in their own language – a language that she can't understand. The African women appear to be calling her names, but she can't be sure. She decides that she must find out the meaning of a particular word that they seem to repeat. Eventually she finds out that the African women are calling her "silly" for walking when she doesn't have to. These African women are not impressed by Ms Campbell's marathon, though it is different with Sir Ranulph Fiennes. According to *his* introduction to *her* book, Ffyona Campbell is "the greatest walker of them all".

A world of difference separates the view of the African women and that expressed by Fiennes, who cannot praise highly enough what others dismiss as a pointless activity. In the rich white European world of Campbell and Fiennes people can choose if and when to walk. This is the difference between Ffyona Campbell's walk and the walking of the African women she passes on her way across the continent. When Ms Campbell has completed her walk around the world she may put up her feet and choose never to walk any further than to the bottom of her garden. Yet those African women will still be walking to the well for water, and walking to work in the fields, and almost always will be carrying babies on their backs. Walking is declining in Europe, but not in Africa.

At about the same time that Ffyona Campbell is doing her great walk across Africa, in Zimbabwe in southern Africa, two black women are walking along a road in Hwange National Park, heading for the tourist lodge forty-three kilometres from the main road, where the bus dropped them at 9.30 in the morning. It is 2.30, and they have been walking ever since. They are returning from a visit to their village, to join their husbands who work at the lodge. They are each carrying two suitcases, and an assortment of other bags and packages, as well as the inevitable baby on each back. Unless they get a lift from a car or lorry it will be 5.30 or 6 p.m. before they reach their destination. They are not "great walkers" in the style of Ms Campbell; they are just two African women going about their normal business, in the course of which they may walk forty-three kilometres or more. They think nothing of it. It's all in a day's work.

Could there be a wider gulf than the one that separates the world of Ms Campbell from that of these African women? The English woman chooses to walk as a way of achieving her personal goals. She walks empty-handed and with all kinds of backup and support. Unlike the African women walking in the Hwange National Park, and the ones she passes on her walk through Africa, Ffyona Campbell's walk is not part of her normal life. When the sun was too hot, and the flies too persistent, Ms Campbell could cheat and take a lift in her support truck, which apparently from time to time she did. Her belated admission of "cheating" added to media interest and almost certainly increased the sales of her book. For the two African women walking, weighed down with children and other heavy loads, relief might come in the form of a lift from a passing motorist. Lifts are rare. I know. I too have walked in the hot sun of Africa and have been passed by numerous cars, without so much as a glance. I was just another black woman walking in Africa.

3

On that occasion however, here in the Hwange National Park, the two women were in luck. My husband Peter and I were also headed for the lodge, and we offered them a lift. The car became full to overflowing, what with them, their children, and all their considerable stuff. I marvelled at their strength, endurance and patience, for after all they were walking over forty kilometres, with the contents of a small house and two babies, as if the most natural thing in the world.

So far, the word "walk" or "walking" has been used to describe widely differing activities, reflecting different ways of life and different values. The first use of the word was to describe a walk across a continent, Ms Campbell's *On Foot Through Africa*. This is followed by the story of the walk of two African women in the Hwange National Park. These two women were walking forty-three kilometres to their home, carrying two children on their backs, and a lot more in their hands and on their heads. The difference represented by these two accounts is fascinating, and it seems to me that the physiological process of actually walking is their only common factor. As a black woman, who is a sociologist and who is now free to choose when to walk and when not, I am thoroughly absorbed by what I have come to think of as "the sociology of walking", by the way in which a natural process has become, in so-called advanced societies, an industry, round which has grown up a set of meanings and values that most people who *have* to walk cannot understand or relate to.

I hope that a brief sociological analysis of the phenomenon of "walking" as depicted in the above scenarios will help set the scene for what is to come. Hiking, i.e. walking for pleasure is about choice, and choice is linked to power and control. Those with power can exercise control over resources and can exercise choice – whether to walk around the world or around the village. Whether to go for a great walk across Africa, or simply go by aeroplane. One thing is clear – when power was being handed out, women in general and black women in particular were way behind in the queue. What with having to carry the baby on her back, and having to tend the fire and get the water and cook the meals and feed and service the men, by the time she was able to join the queue, most of the power was gone. So while two African women walk forty-three kilometres in the midday sun, carrying baskets in their hands, babies on their backs and bundles on their heads, one young European woman walks across Africa, and indeed, across the world, for pleasure, personal development, or just because "it's there".

In each instance the different perceptions of walking and the role that walking fulfils is the difference between black and white, poverty and riches, north and south. In the rich white countries of Europe and North America walking has become part of the leisure industry, marked by designer clothes and walking-boots that cost as much as a poor black family in Africa might survive on for a year. Among the reasons for walking in the so-called "developed" world are these: to improve health, to gain or to maintain fitness, to fight the flab, and to ward off heart disease. In order to "go for a walk" people may drive many kilometres in a car. This is simply one of the many choices associated with an advanced lifestyle. In this context, walking becomes highly stylised, structured and controlled; so that one adult can ask another in all seriousness "Have you been walking long?" The question is not about the length of time a person has actually been "walking" as in putting one foot in front of the other. The questioner is trying to find out how long the other person has been taking part in an organised, structured activity also called "walking". In this activity participants wear specific types of clothing, walk certain distances and if required take part in inane conversation, usually with the same opening line: "Have you been walking long?"

The rambling movement in Britain actually has its roots in intellectual socialism and working-class activism, as Raphael Samuels so convincingly shows in his posthumous book on this subject, *Island Stories: Unravelling Britain*. Walking in the countryside for fresh air and self-improvement was a central part of left-wing ideas, as Raphael Samuels puts it:

> Hiking was a mass enthusiasm of the 1930s, it was promoted by an array of now forgotten organisations, such as the Workers Travel Association. Rambling in the 1930s was a cause, and it was fought for on occasions by direct action, most famously in the mass trespass on Kinder Scout in The Peak District.

Samuels, R (1998), *Island Stories: Unravelling Britain*, Verso, London

Samuels goes on to document the importance of "fresh air" to the intellectual labour movement. The reasons for my interest in this quest for "fresh air" will become clear later in this chapter, when I write about my own first feeble attempt at walking for health. I just want to quote one bit more from Samuels' book, where he explains that

The idea that fresh air made better people had been vigorously canvassed by housing reformers for three generations

Samuels, R, *Island Stories*

The British working classes were to be improved by a good dose of walking and exposure to fresh air. How far all this now seems from Rohan trousers and Basher boots!

As with any recreational activity walking, or hiking, reflects the needs and interests of those taking part. The American poet Robert Frost used to engage in what he called "talk-walkings". These were long walks during which he had long conversations with others or monologues with a companion. He found that walking gave him the opportunity to be both reflective and discursive. I feel much the same way, except that, as will be amply demonstrated later, I tend to listen. So the label "listening-walks" probably fits my experiences better. Before I turn to my own travels and the walks and experiences I've had in various parts of the world, I want to look more closely at some of the issues that affect and determine the way we women spend our time. I am not interested in writing a sociology textbook or a women's studies reader. What I am prepared to do is use ideas and theories that seem helpful in explaining or describing my own social reality, and the observations and experiences of people and events over a lifetime. I will do this via the sociology of leisure, women's travel and gender tourism.

The sociology of leisure, women's travel and gender tourism

The image of Ffyona Campbell on foot through Africa is not typical of women of her class and background or of women anywhere in the world. Not many young white women walk across Africa or even across fields in their own countries. In contrast the image of black women burdened with bundles and babies is very much more typical of black women's life experience and general situation anywhere and everywhere in the world. A very wide gulf separates the experiences of life and walking for the two sets of women. About the female population of the world we know that:

Women are half of humanity. They do two-thirds of the world's work. But they earn perhaps one-tenth of the world's income.

United Nations Statistics 1979, United Nations, NY

Most of the work women do is not paid for at all and is not even counted as part of the world's wealth.This unpaid work never ends: bearing, nurturing and educating children; home making; caring for the sick and elderly; farming for subsistence, fetching and carrying wood and water. Yet most economists define such women as "economically inactive".

It is obvious why women in all societies, especially in poor and so-called "developing" countries have little time for leisure. Leisure is the reward for hard work and enterprise. Poverty is the reward for being "economically inactive". In *Women's Leisure – What Leisure?*, published in 1990, Eileen Green argued that the average British woman generally has very little leisure time, and that what leisure time she does have is tightly controlled and regulated. Green asserts that

> even a cursory glance at the historical and contemporary experiences of leisure reveal not surprisingly, that leisure has not escaped the intervention of power or politics: –

> Not only is leisure divided along lines of class, race, gender and sexual orientation, and more, but leisure must also be seen as an area of life where these divisions are negotiated, redefined and reproduced.

> Green, E, Hebron, S and Woodward (eds) (1990) *Woman's Leisure – What Leisure?*, Macmillan Education, Basingstoke, UK

Green goes further and states that the very concept of "leisure" cannot be construed as "innocent" of the influence of power and politics. She argues that this means that where women do have access to leisure, their freedom to pursue and enjoy leisure activities is circumscribed by a number of factors.

> Her employment status and income level, her family situation, and most important of all her status as a woman in a particular society.

Green says that until we place women's leisure in the social and political and economic context of women's lives we cannot understand the issues. The concept of leisure was itself a by-product of the industrial revolution, and the separation of "work" from "home". Historically certain activities were considered suitable for women; these included dancing, walking, and church-going – those activities that were respectable. Religion and religious activities were safe areas for women's involvement. According to National Survey Data 1995:

> Today in the UK, the most popular leisure activities engaged in by women are watching TV, reading, and doing home-based tasks.

We must agree with Green's conclusions about women's leisure activities, when she says that:

> The leisure activities which women do most frequently... are those which can be done at home, that can be done in the bit of time left over from doing other things, or can be easily interrupted... the activities which do not require expensive equipment or facilities... they rarely challenge stereotyped assumptions about the 'nature' of women as wives, mothers or daughters; and they are safe and demand little expenditure of energy. In short, women's pattern of recreational activity is entirely predictable, given the structural and normative context of their lives.

English women of any social class do not routinely go on foot through Africa, or even on foot through England. Like the Victorian women travellers, Ffyona Campbell is not a typical product of her society; walking is not generally a very popular activity among women. It is not an activity women feel able to do on their own, and anyway recreational walking for women carries specific risks and dangers. Not all women experience the same degree of danger or the same levels of risk. As in all else class, race and economic status play a part in the perception of risk and in the response to danger. As a black woman walker, in addition to all the risks that confront other women walkers, I face the problems and hassles of encounters with neo-fascists, racists and patronising white people, male and female. I have already outlined some of Eileen Green's ideas and arguments about women and leisure in today's Britain. I return to Green's writings for further analysis. Green has argued that access to and use of leisure facilities is determined by class, race and gender; women are viewed as a "problem" by the leisure industry, which is male-dominated and controlled. Green's "leisure industry" includes academics who study and research these matters, and who assume that women

> either had the same experiences as men, in which case there was no need to study them, or else they were anomalous and messed up the research findings.

These comments suggest that the problem starts with the very conception and definition of "leisure"; and I would argue that as there is no agreed definition of work, there can be no agreed definition of leisure. In any field and track competition, but in sports generally, there are many images of black women and men. Are these images of work or leisure? Whatever the definition of "work" and leisure" it is clear to me that most women have too much of one (work) and too little of the other (leisure). Are the many images of black sportswomen pictures of leisure or of work?

There is a problem of perception regarding black people and leisure (see my earlier quotation from the Spring 1997 issue of *Rambling Today*, the magazine of the Ramblers' Association [RA]). Now let us look more closely at Judy Ling Wong's article, called "Just Like Us". It begins thus:

> Many ethnic minority groups hail from the countryside of their country of origin, yet arrive in Britain to be trapped in the concrete jungles of inner city estates. Abruptly, an instant family tradition of having no contact to the countryside is created.

Ms Wong does not provide us with any sources in relation to the views expressed: her views are simply presented as received wisdom. Ethnic minority people are presented as incapable of making the same choices as anyone else, so we must be the target of this or that project, and we must be rescued from inner city jungles and introduced to the countryside – whether we like it or not. So there! Thanks to Ms Wong and the BEN the English countryside will be integrated. It was with an equal measure of amusement and amazement that I read this article by a woman whose name and photo suggest ethnic Chinese origin. The writer continued to explain how daunting it is to be an ethnic minority in the countryside, observing that:

One has to be able to laugh off being stared at, and accept the pressure of curiosity.

Ms Wong also has advice for the members of "the main population". She writes:

The presence of ethnic minority groups in the countryside does not only involve adjustment and learning on the part of ethnic persons, but also on the part of the main population... The most important skill for relating successfully with ethnic groups is to be able to relax in communication with them.

Ling Wong, Judy, "Just Like Us"

As a black woman walker I feel patronised by Ms Wong's article. Ms Wong's views seem to say as much about herself as about those whose views she comments on and implicitly condemns. From where I stand, or walk, there is not much to choose between these two sets of opinions. Black women compete in sports world-wide, but the image of black women in leisure and recreational activities is one predominantly of service. This has been brought home to me in diverse ways and in diverse countries, for now I will give two examples that I hope will enlighten and entertain.

The first story is from my adopted country and the second is from my country of origin. First to Dorset in England and then to Barbados in the Caribbean. I am out with my local ramblers' group for a Sunday walk in Dorset, which will last the best part of the day, and during it we will cover some thirty kilometres. After many years of living in Surrey, and walking with the Staines ramblers, I have recently moved to Dorset and this is my first walk with this group. I am of course the only black person in the group and I can sense that there is a lot of curiosity about me. In due course one of the men sidles up to me and in the classic rambler opening gambit asks me: "Have you been walking long?" to which I reply, "Ever since I stopped crawling!" This merits a small smile and a compliment on my sense of humour. Now that "Dorset man" has established I am possessed of a sense of humour, he feels safe to begin his interrogation. He is anxious to establish the reasons for my presence in the group, and wants to know whether I am an overseas student. My reply is negative. I am giving nothing away, so he decides that I must be a nurse. I say, "Wrong again, I'm not a nurse." His reaction to this is very interesting: "You must be a nurse, every black girl I've met in Dorset is a nurse." I am only a tiny bit amused to find myself described as "a girl"; and I tell him that I am sorry to disappoint him but this is one black girl in Dorset who is not a nurse. Having said this I walk on ahead of him and make a point of avoiding any further conversation with anyone.

Later on in that same year on a Sunday afternoon hike in Barbados I had an uncanny experience, almost exactly the same conversation with a Bajan man. We were half-way through the hike and we stopped for a rest and a talk. I was sitting on the grass next to a very fat man who had been panting all along the way and seemed in danger of collapsing at any moment. He was obviously as curious about me as I was about him, and as soon as he regained his breath he started to question me. The first thing he wanted to know was whether I lived in England. I answered in the affirmative, which was not enough. He had to know exactly where in England. When he heard that I lived in Dorset he wanted to know whether I also walked in Dorset. Then he wanted to know what I did for a living, with that question again, "Are you a nurse?" I made no effort to hide my irritation: "Do I look like a nurse? Are you a doctor?" Very quietly he responded to my outburst. It seemed that he was indeed a doctor, and he'd thought that I must be a nurse because – wait for it – most of the black girls he knew who went to Dorset were nurses. So there. As it happens I am the only woman in my family who is not a nurse, but I did not mention this to "Bajan man" or to "Dorset man". I shall reserve this piece of information for my third encounter of this kind.

What do these two encounters signify? Well for me the same thing, as it happened that both men found the picture of a black woman walking a challenge. It was something that required explanation, whether in Dorset, Worthing, England or Worthing, Barbados. These experiences have helped develop my knowledge and understanding of the sociology of walking, and of people's perceptions of black women walkers.

I have been walking in the British countryside for more than thirty years, and my experiences are not reflected in Ms Wong's writings. I have also walked in Asia and in China, and I would state categorically that the level of curiosity, including punishing stares, bears no comparison to anything one is likely to experience in the UK, or Europe. In Asia the colour black has even more negative connotations than it has in Europe – of this I have no doubt. It therefore interests and amuses me to see an ethnic Chinese woman, identifying with "blackness", and lecturing to white people on how to treat "ethnic minority people" in the countryside. Maybe I will try for a career advising the Chinese on how to treat black people, walking or studying in China. Or maybe I will start in Africa with a guidebook for African women on the proper response to white women walking across their continent. I will start off by telling them that they must engage in "relaxed communication" with their white sisters, and not to dismiss her great walk as "silly".

To a more serious note. It is well known that people who have escaped from poor rural backgrounds are not over-keen to rush back to the countryside for recreational purposes. This is true whether they be ethnic minorities or just plain human beings. Where communities of people have migrated to the metropolis from rural countries, it is not surprising to find a transitional stage through which such communities pass, before succeeding generations rediscover the joys of the countryside. So the British countryside will increasingly and inevitably reflect the diversity of the British population in spite of Ms Wong's best efforts. That is not to deny that black people may encounter prejudice and racism in the countryside as elsewhere, for such is the reality of life. But there is also the possibility of a very positive social encounter and above all the certainty of an enjoyable walk. I found Ms Wong's article very limited and patronising; in particular I balk at the possibility of being engaged in "relaxed communication". I can't imagine anything more likely to spoil a walk.

There are serious social issues concerning gender, class and race in the leisure industry generally, and access to the countryside in particular. What do we get? The Ramblers' Association marginalizes black people and "ethnic minorities" to a one-page "Forum" article. The academic discipline of sociology, which will not or cannot deal with black people, except as social problems, does little better. So the everyday life experiences of black people in general and black women in particular have remained untold. If white women were "hidden from history", black women were and still are for the most part invisible. Nowhere is this more clearly demonstrated than in the leisure industry, where black women feature almost always in the supporting role of maid or waitress. Green has questioned whether "leisure" is even a meaningful concept for women, and I am inclined to agree with her that the concept of leisure is of limited use in discussing most women's life experiences. The very concept of leisure must involve the exercise of choice; and as such cannot be a meaningful concept for most women in the world. Even those women who are economically independent may find their choices limited by a variety of personal and social factors. Furthermore leisure is not high on their agenda, because in common with women everywhere their own needs and interests come a long way behind those of other family members.

In my experience many middle-aged and single people, especially women, join walking groups out of loneliness, in search of social contact and companionship. The walk itself is a means towards an end. Such people not only welcome, but also actively seek out any opportunity to talk. I don't know how many times I have listened to tales of death, divorce and separation, the birth of babies, the leaving home of teenagers. All human life is there on a ramble, if you want to listen and share in it. Peter dismisses all this "chattering" and is not too keen on group walks. Depending on mood, I quite like group walks and at times the conversations can be very interesting and informative. But there are times when talk is an intrusion, and it takes a lot of confidence to be able to say to people eager for conversation that all one wants at the moment is a quiet walk. One Saturday afternoon, walking a stretch of the Thames path with a group of London ramblers, I found myself walking next to a woman, walking for a while without either of us speaking. Then she broke the silence and explained that she "felt like a quiet walk today". I replied, "You and me both."

The two of us did not know each other at all, but we continued walking, without feeling threatened or uncomfortable by the silence. At the end of the walk we did chat for a few minutes before going our separate ways. No problem. Many people live a lifetime together without being able to tolerate silence, and are compelled to fill it. If I don't feel like talking I simply strike out and outpace the talkers, or chatterers, as Peter describes them. It does not bother me at all what people make of this, I am there only for the walk. Perhaps my indifference is due to the fact that I have not had the benefit of instruction from Ms Wong and the BEN. So instead of doing what is expected of a black person walking in the English countryside, I simply please myself – just like anyone else. Oh dear.

There is a group of young women unencumbered by children and with money to spend, and for them the concept of leisure is a very meaningful one. Go to any gym and you will see them. In America there is a new magazine called *Heart and Soul*, which is all about health and fitness for African American women. In its May 1997 issue it invites its readers to "Celebrate Black Health & Fitness Week". This magazine has many images of young black women and is full of good advice on health and fitness, and represents the first attempt by black women to impact on this world of leisure. I do know that it is therefore an over-simplification to present the issue of gender and leisure as a black and white matter. The issues are black and white, but they are also a lot more things as well, more complex and difficult than a simple colour classification would suggest. It is time to turn our attention to women travellers. We start with wayward women, and needless to say they are all white.

Wayward Women?

Jane Robinson called her book on women travellers of the nineteenth and early twentieth centuries *Wayward Women*. Not because these women were "wayward" in the sense of wanton or feckless. Their waywardness consisted in their willingness to stray from what was generally accepted behaviour for their sex and class at that time. Enloe summed up the position of these women travellers admirably in her description of the challenge they represented to the accepted notion of womanhood, as they took on themselves the identities of "adventurer" and "explorer".

Both labels were thoroughly masculinized. Masculinity and exploration had been as tightly woven together as masculinity and soldiering. These audacious women challenged that ideological assumption, but they have left us with a bundle of contradictions.

Enloe, C (1989), *Bananas, Beaches and Bases: Making Feminist Sense of International Politics*, Pandora, London

Hall and Kinnaird (1996), writing on "gender tourism", noted that until recently there was hardly anything written specifically for or about women travellers. They observed that of late there had been, and comment that

Led to something of a bookshelf ghettoisation: guides for women are often found on the travel book shop shelf next to those for 'other', 'minority' and 'specialist' groups such as vegetarians.

14

It is difficult to understand how women who are more than half of the human race can be classed as a "minority". I have just located myself at least three times in the above classifications: firstly as a woman; second as an ethnic minority; thirdly as a vegetarian. How many points does one have to score before being counted as a person?

Women travellers form part of what Hall and Kinnaird describe as the "commodisation of egotism" and women's travel writing represent "marginal voices in marginal texts".

> Marginal voices in marginal texts succumbing to... the lure of high and mystical places.

Places such as Tibet, Kashmir, Bhutan and Nepal

> have provided contexts of high mystical places through which (European) women travellers have pursued their discourses.

Jan/James Morris (1956/1992) who has written both as a man and a woman, presents an interesting perspective on women's travel, if only because s/he represents both viewpoints. Davies et al (1986) in *Half the Earth – Women's Experience of Travel Worldwide* provide a feminist perspective on women's travel and do try to be more inclusive, but European feminist writing has a long way to go before it can be said to give even a glimpse of everywoman's experiences of travel worldwide.

Books such as *Half the Earth – Women's Experiences of Travel Worldwide* offer a feminist perspective on women's travels, but are written for white women travellers.

Gender tourism – white woman power

There are other women from the north, with time and money, who do not want the adventures and challenges of the "traveller", but yet want to go to exotic places. These are tourists. Some feminist women are worried about being tourists, feeling uncomfortable in a relationship of power over black and brown sisters, and they are not sure how to behave. They want to be nice to the natives, and do not want to act within the same constraints of what they call the "patriarchy".

Feminist choice itself is controlled. The global patriarchy, through book publishers, and the media, guide their choices on destinations, and so on. In the countries that the European feminist visits the local patriarchy rules supreme, and the visiting sisters cannot afford to offend them. So they are caught in a triple-bind from which there is no escape. As Cynthia Enloe (1989) explains in her attempt to make feminist sense of international politics:

> No matter how good the feminist intentions, the relationship between the British woman on holiday and the working women of Portugal seems to fall short of the international sisterhood.

If that is true of Portugal, how much more so of Zimbabwe, Bhutan, India! As Enloe says, it is virtually impossible to find a postcard expressing sisterhood rather than exploitation, because the fact of the holiday itself demonstrates the relationship of power between women tourists and poor women. The development of mass tourism in Europe and America from the 1960s opened up the tourist market to ordinary men and women. The majority of women tourists are not concerned with feminist issues. Another image of women in tourism is the one reflected in what has come to be known as "sex tourism". South East Asia, in particular, has developed as a target destination for paedophiles. The image of black women presented in the tourist and anthropological literature is worthy of study in itself, when invariably black women are serving or selling themselves or their countries. It is rare to see a picture of a black woman tourist or anthropologist: we are never consumers or social commentators. Sceptics may do their own research by studying the tourist literature, looking at travel TV and reading *National Geographic* and similar publications.

At this point I cannot resist the temptation of talking about my missed opportunity to contribute to the development of tourism in Barbados. I was twelve, rising thirteen, and not being a conventionally "bright" child I had failed the exam that would have secured me a place at a grammar school. Many of my friends' education had been completed when they left elementary school, and it seemed that the same fate awaited me. I overheard my parents having a discussion about my future. My father had no doubt about what should be done:

> "There is a new hotel opening in Hastings, they will want maids, send the girl there," he said.

> My mother replied: "Mr Gibbons is opening a new school, I want to send her there."

> My father asked, "Where is the money to come from?"

My mother had no idea, but she would manage somehow. The conversation between my parents ended with my father disclaiming any responsibility for the decision to send me to secondary school. That was how I became one of the first intakes at the Washington High School, and not one of the first maids at the new hotel. If things had gone the other way, I might well by now have made my way to the role of housekeeper or similar, in the process making what I hoped would be a significant contribution to the development of tourism in Barbados, instead of just writing about it.

The story did not end there. Many years later my mother, who was very disappointed with my rather casual approach to dress, chided me with these words: "What's the use of being a PhD if you are going to dress like a maid?" Was there a hint of regret there? My mother's comments were very understandable in the social context of Barbados, where dress is very much linked to status; and for me to be "dressed like a maid" must have seemed to her like a rejection of everything she had worked so hard to achieve.

What is the point of all this? I am attempting to put women's experience of walking in some sort of context. How come some women can walk around the world and other women walk with babies on their backs, and baggage in their hands until they reach home, where their real work actually begins? What do these two types of walking women have in common? To sum up the different types of white women, who figure in this scenario, first you have the travellers and adventurers. Then there are professional women, writers and anthropologists who study and observe the native women as they walk with their bundles and babies. Then there are the women tourists whose main interests are having a good time as cheaply and comfortably as possible. This group of women has the choice about whether and when they walk; they are "economically active" and the concept of leisure is "meaningful" in their lives. In the countries they visit, these women come into contact mainly with women who are working as maids, nannies and other servants. Those women may be "economically active", but, unlike the visiting sisters, their choices are severely limited, and they have very little time for leisure. They do not walk for pleasure.

The women in the first group are almost always white and those in the second almost always non-white, black, and brown. There are always some exceptions, but that is the general picture. The very concept of travel and the word "traveller" have come to be associated with a particular type of person, usually white, and almost always male. Yet there are people for whom travelling is a natural part of life – Gypsies and other nomadic and semi-nomadic people. There has been a process by which certain activities, e.g. "walking" and "travelling", have become identified with certain clearly defined groups, and outside these groups these activities don't count. But things are changing, as we shall see.

A brief history of hiking in Barbados

My own method of identifying the status of a country as it moves from under-development is the number of local people who walk for recreation or health reasons. Together with the microwave oven, video recorder, increase in car ownership, and other trappings of "progress", walking for pleasure is a good indication that a country has or is soon to acquire "developed" status. Barbados today reflects that change. Time was when people laughed at us and considered us eccentric for walking when we had a car. Now everyone seems to be walking or hiking. I have previously written about my introduction to recreational walking, in the extreme heat and humidity of Calcutta. In 1966 when Peter came with me to the Caribbean for the first time, we naturally began walking and exploring the countryside. I had never walked like this in Barbados, so it was a new experience. We had some tricky moments, in that sometimes people who could not understand what we were doing accosted us. The idea of "just walking" was simply outside their own experience. Walking in the countryside on his own, Peter had a few unpleasant experiences, mainly because people could not understand what he was doing walking across their fields, or close to their homes. This was Barbados in 1965.

In the Barbados of 1997 everything has changed. No one is curious if you are out walking the countryside, no one laughs at you and asks what's wrong with the car. Everyone is into "healthy lifestyles" and "hike Barbados" has arrived. I do not know what was involved in the process of change, or when these changes began. I have heard that the Barbados National Trust (BNT) was mainly responsible, but it seems to me that the changes I have observed extend well beyond this small group. I am a member of the BNT and from time to time we do go on their walks, and I have written elsewhere about an experience during one of these walks. As the economic and social profile of Barbados changes, the pattern of life and of death also changes. This means that Bajan people will have to develop lifestyle changes as an antidote to the diseases that come with what is called progress. This means more local people are walking for pleasure and for health.

Even so the recreational walking that the BNT encourages does not touch the majority of Bajans. Recreational walking is in itself a minority sport, with its rituals and ways of behaving, which does not suit everyone. What Barbados needs is for people to walk as a natural part of their life, not something you have to dress in special shoes for or drive to a specific place to take part in. Barbados needs a more walker-friendly environment, more sidewalks/pavements so that walkers do not walk in fear of their lives. In St James I was encouraging a friend to walk the short distance from her home to mine, and as we set off I suggested that we face the on-coming traffic. She wanted to know why? As the traffic thundered past, threatening to mow us down, I gave what I considered an appropriate response. I told her that we should face the drivers, so that "if in spite of our best efforts the bastards kill us, they will be haunted by our faces for rest of their lives!" After that she faced the traffic.

Death by inconsiderate and selfish car drivers did seem a real possibility at that moment; not surprisingly my friend continues to go by car even for very short journeys. It is easy to see why people in Barbados prefer to drive or take a bus for comparatively short distances. I was almost killed walking back from posting a letter. I was forced to flatten myself against a wall as a car-trailer thundered past at great speed, indifferent to my fate. In Barbados safe walking is walking for pleasure, which means having access to a car or willingness to travel by bus. Although there have been changes in attitude to walking, unfortunately it is still not possible to walk safely as part of normal Bajan life.

I have given my own version of the history of walking for health and pleasure in Barbados. There is another story. In 1994 the BNT, the Duke of Edinburgh award scheme, and the Barbados Heart Foundation produced a *Hike Barbados Guide*. This guide outlined the history and development of hiking in Barbados thus:

> They (the hikes) started in 1983 with 11 persons participating and by 1988, sometimes over 400 persons were hiking. In 1988 the Barbados Heart Foundation became a co-sponsor. The number of hikers continues to grow every year, so in 1991, afternoon hikes were started to accommodate those who did not want to rise early or who normally go to church.

> *Hike Barbados! Guide* (1994), Barbados National Trust, Duke of Edinburgh Award Schemes, Barbados Heart Foundation, Barbados

Short and sweet, and surprisingly on this occasion no mention was made of the fact that the BNT hikes have included such notables as Prince Edward! I have been walking and hiking in England for over thirty years and royalty have never, to my knowledge, graced an RA hike. Once more Barbados leads the way for England to follow! The truth is that the RA has a much more political role in the UK than the BNT – and in any case British royalty do not need to join public hikes in the UK, when they own land many times the size of Barbados.

Black women don't hike

> The walk from St David's to River Salle was a long and arduous one. It was best started early. Queenie was still half-asleep when they left. But the way Cousin walked sleep didn't stay around for long. It departed with a frown and an irritated yawn. Queenie pushed the straw hat more firmly over her head, held the cloth bag securely on her shoulder, and kept running to keep up.

> Collins, M (1985), "The Walk" in her collection *Short Stories*,
> Rain Darling, London

Merle Collins' short story "The Walk", set in Grenada in the Caribbean, is about a walk undertaken by Queenie, a young girl and her cousin. The walk took eight hours, and when eleven-year-old Queenie had completed her mother's business she

> would leave again with cousin Liza, or whoever else happens to be making the trip to St Davids. The one thing that remained to haunt her was the knowledge that the return trip would have to be made in the darkness, when the sun was down, and when those who had to walk always made their journeys.

Merle Collins illustrates the difference between those who walk for pleasure, and those who have no choice but to walk. I myself started out in the former group but over the years I have moved closer to the latter, so my own experience includes both types of walking.

This is where my story proper begins, so let me explain my choice of that subheading, "Black Women Don't Hike". One Sunday evening I got a phone call from a sociologist colleague, who said he had been ringing me since morning. He obviously wanted to speak to me urgently and was not impressed when I said I had been out hiking. His response amused rather than irritated me, as he dismissed walking for pleasure, i.e. hiking, as a "white middle-class activity" and ended by telling me in no uncertain terms that "black women don't hike!" I smiled and asked the question, "When will I ever learn to conform to the white male sociologist stereotype of the black woman?"

Many years later I recalled this exchange as I read Trudier Harris on the black American woman's experience of being labelled:

> Called Matriarch, Emasculator, and Hot Moma. Sometimes Sister, Pretty Baby, Auntie, Mammy and Girl. Called Unwed Mother, Welfare Recipient and Inner City Consumer. The Black American has had to admit that while nobody knew troubles she saw, everybody, her brother and his dog felt qualified to explain her, even to herself.
>
> Harris, Trudier (1982) *From Mammies to Militants*, Temple University Press, Philadelphia, USA

In fact my sociologist colleague was wrong about black women and hiking and about the social origins of organised walks in Britain. Walking/hiking in the UK was not historically a "middle-class" activity, in fact the history of the struggle for open access to the countryside and the "freedom to roam" is part of working-class history and folklore. But as walking/hiking has been taken over by the leisure industry, so its image has changed, and without your Brasher Boots and Rohan gear you cannot be considered a serious walker.

Black women do hike – walking and me

I was not telling the exact truth when I told the guy in the Dorset ramblers that I had been walking ever since I had stopped crawling. The truth is that I don't think I ever crawled as such. I was born in Barbados, the sixth of my parents' seven children. I was such a poor specimen when I was born that the doctors gave up hope and told my mother to "make me comfortable". That is doctor-speak for "she's not going to live". My mother did not give up as easily as that, and because of her "tender loving care" and what she called "the Lord's will", I survived. But I was not very strong and for the first two and a half years

21

I more or less sat in a box looking at the world. I would probably never have bothered to walk if Gladys, who worked for my mother, did not every now and again take me out of the box and stand me up and shout at me to "walk". Eventually it worked and I walked. There was also a story about a bone, but I don't recall that bit, and anyway I'm now a vegetarian, so I can't believe that a bone played a significant part in getting me on my feet.

As I write this, it occurs to me that, after a working life spent in social work and education, as a practitioner, teacher and researcher, with quite intimate knowledge of the major theories on child development and such, I can't help but be amused when I think of my own development. The two activities that have given me the most pleasure and brought most rewards to my life – walking and reading – were both attained in the most unorthodox way. When I was about four, my father decided that I should be able to read so that I could take my turn at reading from the Bible during the morning family prayers. We were raised as Plymouth Brethren – Garrison Keeler's childhood had nothing on mine! My father's approach was simplicity itself. He read me a passage from a children's story book, then told me that when he returned home next Thursday (I'm sure it was a Thursday) he wanted to hear me read the whole story, without any help. I was very afraid of my father and I knew that I had to do exactly as commanded. When he returned home the next Thursday, I read him the story. This was the same man who when I was twelve or so thought that I should be a maid in a hotel rather than go to secondary school. Life is full of these little contradictions, though I am not sure that my father would recognise his behaviour towards me as contradictory. "By rights" as we say in Barbados, meaning it stands to reason, "by rights" my father's approach should have put me off reading for life. It had exactly the opposite effect, and I became a compulsive reader. So I'm glad that my father knew nothing about reading and child development – otherwise I might have turned out illiterate.

My childhood experience went from being faced with an early death to walking at two-plus and reading by age four. Not, I think, a typical developmental profile. My mother put it all down to "the Lord", and felt very strongly that of all her children, I was the one who had the most reason to be thankful to God. In fact I was the one to reject the idea of religion and God from very early on, at least from the time I could think and reason for myself – which was probably soon after my father started me off reading.

Although I had started off as a weakling, the runt of the litter, my mother's methods had been extremely successful in strengthening both my lungs and my legs. During our stay in Bhutan we went for a weekend hike in the mountains. After walking all day in sub-zero temperatures we arrived at the "tourist lodge", where we were to spend the night. We had been surprised when we'd been told that we could stay there for nothing, and once we got there we understood why. The lodge was nothing more than an old house that had fallen into disrepair and was more or less open to the elements. We were more than 4,000 metres up in the mountains, and for two nights we slept on the freezing stone floor in our sleeping bags. I wondered then what had become of Mrs Rawlins' delicate little girl child. For health reasons, for "fresh air" to strengthen my lungs, I went on to walking out of necessity – to get to school and back four times a day. But I loved it. And the best and most enjoyable of these walks would be after it had rained. We would take off our shoes, or pumps as we called them, and we would walk in the warm, muddy puddles: bliss! Unless you were told off or got "some licks", I can't remember being caught, and I never got many licks at home. But my love of walking and of the sea did get me into trouble at school at least once.

On that occasion my class was taken on an outing, I think it was to the Barbados museum. After the visit we were left to find our own way home. My friends and I walked by way of Bay St, and as we passed by the sea I suggested that we "had a dip". We were very hot, and I loved the sea. We had a dip, but someone saw us and we were reported. This was a Friday. On the Monday morning after school prayers the headmistress spoke of a very serious matter she had to deal with. She said that Maureen Rawlins had persuaded others to join her in disobedient behaviour, and so on and so forth. I didn't take everything in, but I do recall her referring to me as an "influential child", then qualifying this with "and I don't mean that she gets influenza easily!" I could see where this was leading to, and I was not happy.

Eventually there came the command for me to come up onto the platform, where I received, among other humiliations, "a good licking". I think I must have been around seven or eight at the time. Not long ago in Barbados, more than forty years on from this incident, I went into Holetown, shopping with my friend, and as we walked back along the beach, the same thing happened. I got hot and suggested that we go into the sea for a dip. We were fully dressed. In we went, and this time no one reported me, and no public humiliation followed. My friend and I agreed that it was good to "let the child in us come out". My friend is from Trinidad, and Trinidadians are noted for having a more fun attitude to life than we, rather staid, Bajans. Later in the day, I mentioned this incident to a Bajan school friend who had been a teacher. She left me in no doubt of her strong disapproval, as she said with horror, "You did what?" as if I had stolen the crown jewels or something. I was just very glad she was not in a position to punish me.

When I was growing up in Barbados, my mother was the only woman in our village who regularly took her children to the beach, and we walked. We would set off early in the morning, when walking to the beach was quite fun. We took food and spent the day enjoying. Walking back was another matter; we would be dead tired by then, exhausted from the sun and the sea. My mother would hitch lifts for one of us: "Mr So-and-so, could you give this little one a lift please… she is too tired." One of us, it was usually me, would be given a lift to some point along the way, where we would sit and wait until the others caught up, and so it would go on until we reached home. When I drive along these same roads now, I am amazed at how short the distances are – five, maybe six kilometres. But those memories are sweet and very precious.

My next experience of choosing to walk came when my nephew was born. I was twelve at the time. His mother, my sister, did not find mothering very interesting. She migrated to England soon after his first birthday, after which I more or less took over his care. For reasons that are not entirely clear to me even now, I decided it was important for him to be taken for a walk, so every morning we went out. He was quite a big child, and very heavy. I had to carry him and at twelve I was not all that big. We must have cut a fine picture. We attracted quite a few comments as I lugged him round the village, such as, "de baby nearly as big as she and she play she tekking he fe walks!" At least no one remembered my earlier expeditions, and no one reminded me of my quest for "fresh air". I kept on with our early-morning walks until my nephew was really too big to carry, by which time he could walk by himself.

When I went to secondary school I got a bike, and walking to school became a thing of the past. In fact it was not until 1963, when I met Peter in Calcutta, that walking, for pleasure, once again became part of my life. Peter had always been a keen walker, and he introduced me to "recreational walking". It was a common joke among our friends that I was the only woman who would go for a walk with Peter in temperatures of 120 degrees in the shade!

Whatever the truth of that, I remember my amazement and amusement when Peter had to toughen his feet in preparation for a Himalayan trek. His toughening-up regime consisted of soaking his feet in surgical spirit, which was supposed to harden the outer layer of skin and reduce the possibility of blisters. Never having had a blister in my life I neither understood nor appreciated just how important this would be on a trek lasting three weeks. It seemed weird to me that there were people whose feet were so soft that they had to be artificially hardened. Peter was equally amazed by the toughness of *my* feet, with no need for chemical baths there! All that barefoot walking had certainly paid off, and continues to do so, even now. My doctor once told me that I had "beautiful feet". I was quite taken aback, and she explained that it was very unusual for her to see feet unblemished by calluses, corns and other ravages of female footwear. It was just as well that my parents couldn't afford proper shoes. When I came to buy my own, except for some minor indulgences as a teenager, I always chose comfort over fashion.

After Calcutta I came to live in England. By this time I was a serious walker in my own right, and we traversed various and varied footpaths across the British Isles and parts of Europe. In 1990 Peter had a by-pass operation and as there were very few areas where I felt safe walking alone, I joined the Staines branch of the RA. In 1992 Peter and I rented out our house in Weybridge, and with my laptop computer and printer we set off on a round-the-world trip, in which we both anticipated doing a fair bit of walking. We did do a fair bit, but I also continued to work, thanks to the wonders of modern technology. It was quite exciting to receive the proofs of the child protection book in Zimbabwe, and a copy of the book itself in Canberra. I continued with my research consultancy while I was travelling; and I also kept notes and collected material for the book that one day I hoped to write.

Black woman walking – travels and experiences around the world

Put simply, this book is about today's world as seen through the eyes of a woman who is black, who is interested in people, and who enjoys travelling and walking. I find myself feeling part of and identifying with the women, especially the poor and dispossessed women in the worlds

I pass through. When I visit Zimbabwe, as a guest of the government and of the British Council, I am a sociologist from England, an honoured guest. When I go on my own I am just another black woman in Africa. This contradiction is inherent in my life as an academic and as a black woman. It does not matter whether I am in Europe, Africa or wherever in the world. I move between these very different worlds with confidence and curiosity, sustained by what I like to think of as my sense of humour.

I have walked with my friend in Africa as she carried the water from the well on her head. She completely refused to believe me when I said that I too used to carry water home from the standpipe, in exactly the same way, and flatly refused my offer of help. I am sure I could still carry water on my head if I had to. I walked with the Staines ramblers in Surrey, from the start of the group, until we moved to Dorset in 1995. Each experience brings value and interest to my life. To walk in Africa is something entirely different from walking in Europe. All over Africa are tracks where people walk day and night, not for exercise or because they are concerned for the environment, but because they have to. Walking away from war zones in Sudan, Zaire or Rwanda, or to the well to get water, is part of Africa's daily life.

In Africa and South America women walk many kilometres with babies on their backs and goods in their hands (see cover picture of a South American Indian woman walking). It's nothing for women to walk twenty or even thirty kilometres carrying extremely heavy loads. I am interested in the sociology of walking, and in observing the changes that happen when people become comfortable enough to be able to afford to walk for pleasure. Walking has brought me in touch with people and places that I would otherwise have missed or passed by. These experiences have touched on all aspects of life, including politics and personal relations. There is a view that personal relationships are largely a reflection of cultural influences, and the economic and social arrangements of each society. The tensions between men and women, including family violence and the sexual and physical abuse of children, can then be explained as a phenomenon arising from these factors. As I have travelled in many countries, and heard the same stories over and over again, I begin to wonder and to question. From the worldscape of the global village, to my own tiny island of Barbados, I have brought together the problems and issues that have interested, fascinated and challenged me as I travelled, walked and worked in various parts of the world.

The widespread failure of marriage on the one hand, and the strength and endurance of friendship on the other, are the things that have impressed me most. As I have travelled and walked and talked with women in different countries and from very different backgrounds, I have heard the same stories time and time again. From the hills of the Himalayas to the plains of Africa to the Australian outback, the drama is the same, and it is only the cast that changes. I have tried to provide a different view on the issues that affect the lives of women in different cultures and countries around the world today, and only incidentally to break the Eurocentric and mainly male-dominated monopoly in this field.

On the political scene the themes of dispossession and the anger and pain of the dispossessed are constant and enduring throughout the world. From Africa to Australia, from New Zealand to Hawaii, to North America (Canada and the USA), people press for their rights to land and for their culture to be restored. In Victoria Falls, a bus driver asked me whether I was from America. I said yes, thinking that was near enough. He said, "You are one of those that were kidnapped and taken away." I said no, we were not kidnapped, we were sold. He denied this and insisted that we were kidnapped from Africa by the whites, then added for good measure, "Now we want you back." I know my history and I know the difference between being sold and being kidnapped. Am I one of the dispossessed, or am I an observer? I think I may be both, for is there any reason why I can't be both? If I have been dispossessed, do I want to be, in the words of the bus driver, "taken back"? I don't think so.

Another inescapable theme in today's world is child abuse. On the day I left England to go on our round-the-world tour, I handed to the printers the draft of a book that was a training manual designed to assist with decision-making in child protection work. As I handed over the disc and rushed to the airport – it was that close – I felt such overwhelming relief that I could leave child abuse behind me. Yet this was not to be, for within hours of arriving in Zimbabwe I was in a discussion with a friend and colleague about another former colleague who was suspected of sexually abusing boys in his care. This was how my year of travel started, and how it continued, for in every country, with the exception of Bhutan, the subject of child abuse, sexual and/ or physical, surfaced. Emerging as an important issue in plays, TV documentaries, and chat shows and in the newspapers; and last but not least in conversation, it was a subject impossible to escape. I want to discuss this further through some of the stories I was told and observations I made.

War is not an explicit component of this book, though everywhere I have walked and travelled people seemed to be at war in one sense or another. In Europe in 1992 there was "ethnic cleansing"; in Kenya "ethnic clashes"; in India the unending caste warfare, communal strife and tribal wars; and of course there was the genocide in Rwanda. War, drought, famine, wherever you are in the world you are never far from one or all of these. Where are the women in all this, whither the sisterhood? Is there something uniting women across the world, regardless of race, economic and social circumstances? Is the experience of simply being a woman something that can unite people across these barriers?

Then there is "the environment", another pervasive theme, together with "globalisation" and "Americanisation". No thinking person can hope to escape confronting these aspects of contemporary life. Is there a difference in the approach of the East? Will the world be saved by the "lotus" of India, or be consumed by the Chinese "dragon"? Perhaps Australia will provide the answers, being neither east nor quite west. And what of Mother Africa – how can we ease her pain and suffering? Let me say now that I have no answers. I like walking, talking and listening to people and being, for a time, a part of their world.

More images of... women walking in Africa

This book began with images of women walking in Africa, the first being of Ffyona Campbell, a young English woman who explains why she is going "on foot through Africa" in the following exchange:

Driver: "Why are you doing this?"

Walker: "Because I said I would."

Driver: "Who did you say it to?"

Walker: "Myself."

Campbell, F (1994), *On Foot Through Africa*, Orion, London

Through a brief exploration of ideas about leisure and women, we saw that this young woman was neither typical of her class nor of her gender.

Let us now turn to another picture of a woman walking in Africa, this time a black woman returning from the well.

> A minute ago I came from the well…. My body was weary and
>   my heart tired.
> For a moment I watched the stream that rushed before me
> And thought how fresh the smell of flowers,
> How green the grass around it.
> And yet again I heard the sound of duty
> Which ground on me – and made me feel aged
> As I bore the great big mud container on my head
> Like a great big painful umbrella.

> Rungano, Kristina (1984), "The Woman" in *A Storm is
> Brewing,* Zimbabwe Publishing House, Harare

When "the woman" reaches her home she finds that while she has been toiling in the field, her husband had been out drinking, and now wants food, sex, and sleep. She pleads to be excused from the sex, but she is not, and says of her husband, "You beat me and had your way." She hates him for a while but in the morning all is well again: "For isn't it right that woman should obey, love, serve and honour her man?"

"The woman" in the poem has no time to stand and stare; she cannot possibly enjoy the walk back to her village with the "big painful umbrella on her head" – and the child in her belly. There is no time to rest, for as she is about to complete one task she hears the sound of duty calling her to a new set. In her world, walking is like everything else, a painful duty.

Walking has put me in touch with many people and places throughout the world; as I have walked and travelled I have had many and varied experiences. The walks, travels, and experiences and observations are presented through letters, stories and discussions. These images of women walking in Africa, and the different worlds that these images represent – the rich white world of Europe, and the poor black world of Africa – remain with me always. I know that I belong to both of these worlds and to neither. I move between these and other worlds, seeing the similarities and the differences; what unites and what separates. These worlds are not always separated only into black and white, by the differences between Europe and Africa. There is, after all, a lot of Europe in Africa and increasing amounts of Africa in Europe

– both literally and figuratively – as day by day the world becomes ever smaller.

This book offered me the opportunity to reflect on some of the issues and problems that have concerned me in both my personal and professional life. My interest in people and society, and my love of walking, came together, as I hiked and travelled around the world. Walking was the most significant single factor: walking influences more than anything else the kind of people one meets, and therefore the kind of the experiences one has.

2

SISTERS UNDER THE SKIN?

On friendship and sisterhood in the global village

CHAPTER ONE presented different and contrasting images of African women: first there was "Lucy", perhaps the very first woman ever to walk this earth. Another image was of African women through the eyes of a European woman walker, Ms Campbell, as she passed them by on her marathon walk across Africa. The African women were not amused or impressed by Ms Campbell. In fact they thought her silly for walking when she didn't have to. After that I mentioned my encounter with two women in Zimbabwe who were walking more than forty kilometres carrying babies on their backs and assorted baggage in their hands. Then there were the middle-class and professional African women who treated their maids like slaves. And, finally, there was "the woman" in Kristina Rungano's poem – the woman who walks to the well and returns tired and weary carrying the water on her head in the sure and certain knowledge that she must be ready to provide food, sex, and finally be a punch bag for her lord and master, otherwise known as her husband. This chapter presents a very different image of African woman – here we meet the middle-class African woman relaxing in the sauna. But let me start at the beginning.

In October of 1993 the round-the-world tour that Peter and I had been enjoying came to an abrupt end. One day we were walking in the Banff National Park and the next we were on a plane bound for Heathrow airport. On arrival in England I barely had time to recover from my jet lag before I was off again, this time bound for Harare. I had been summoned there to sort out our son. But when I arrived I found he did not want to be "sorted out". I was caught between a stone (literally!) and a hard place. I could use coercion – withdrawal of financial support – to force my son to return to the UK, or I could accept his decision to remain in Harare. Instead of making a decision I went to Bulawayo to visit friends and to marvel at the Victoria Falls once again. While at the falls I took the opportunity to go white-water rafting on the Zambezi. The river was in full flow and our guides left us in little doubt that we were engaged in a potentially dangerous exercise. The raft I was in capsized twice and on each occasion I was tossed about like in cork in the water. All that tossing about left me bruised, my body ached and even walking was difficult and painful.

As soon as I arrived back in Bulawayo I sought the comfort of the sauna. I went in search of solace – to heal my body and my soul: too much walking, too much white-water rafting – too much worrying about my son. I felt completely exhausted both emotionally and physically. When I arrived at the sauna there was one other person there, but she soon left, and just as I was beginning to enjoy having the sauna all to myself, about four or five black and brown women joined me. They came in at the same time, but were not together. And so the peace and quiet was exchanged for the usual woman-talk, which any other time I would have welcomed. Soon one of the women remarked that there was a very offensive smell in the room. The others agreed, and that awful, rancid smell became the focus of their attention.

Each one of them hazarded a guess as to what it might be. I was silent. I was wrapped up in my own thoughts about the situation awaiting me in Harare. The women continued talking about the smell and speculating about its origins. Eventually they decided that it was the smell of burnt urine. I still maintained my silence, knowing that as long as I remained mute I was just another African woman. As soon as I spoke it would be clear that I was a stranger, an outsider. I listened to the discussion; then the women came to another decision – someone must have thrown the pee on the sauna. Their collective reaction to this idea was immediate: "How awful, what a disgusting thing to do, who would do such a thing?" This question required an answer, and the answer came, only a black woman would do such a thing. Sighs of regret and shame that "our people" are always letting us down. Black people just do not know how to behave.

After that I found it impossible to maintain my silence any longer. I swallowed hard and spoke: "Actually... it was a white girl who threw pee or whatever it is on the sauna; we were here together and I saw what happened. She seemed a bit strange. I think she may be sick or something. She seemed to have a problem." All the women turned and stared at me. They seemed stunned and perplexed so I went on to tell them exactly what had happened in the sauna prior to their arrival. I told them that the white girl had sat rocking backwards and forwards, smiling and muttering to herself. That there had been a white plastic cup next to her and, that as she got up to leave, she walked slowly up to the fire and emptied its contents onto the sauna, smiling all the while. I told them how I had tried to ignore the horrible smell, hoping it would go away after a while. When I had finished telling my story, there was a hush. This silence was soon filled with questions about my identity and my reasons for being in Zimbabwe. The matter of the pee was soon forgotten, as I became the focus of attention. This was the inquisition I'd been trying so hard to avoid, as my intervention revealed me as a stranger in their midst.

All this talk did nothing about the smell, which still persisted, and we were all now very uncomfortable. At last someone volunteered to do something. This lady went off to find an attendant. The attendant came and did some mopping up, but she could do nothing about the smell. She could not mop the sauna fire! By this time I'd had enough; it was time for me to leave. I had not experienced the healing glow of the sauna. If anything, I was more fraught when I left than I had been when I arrived. The white girl's behaviour reminded me of my son's problems and of the reasons why I was in Zimbabwe. Not only had I been unable to escape, however briefly, from my own personal problems; but somehow I had become embroiled in the social problems of a post-colonial African society, and the impact of historical oppression and contemporary racism on a group of African sisters.

Reflecting on it later, I did not feel at all good about what had happened in the sauna that afternoon. I felt angry and dissatisfied with myself for opening my mouth. Why had I not remained silent? Why did I always want to "explain things"? Why not leave people alone to think what they want to think? Was it my mission in life to go around putting people right about who had peed where? What difference would it make anyway? Those African women had been so confident that only a black woman would behave so badly, but I'd shattered their perceptions by telling them the truth: that the pee was not after all black-woman pee. They had not considered that any woman black or white or whatever, who behaved in that way, might be in need of help.

Those women in that sauna in Bulawayo had so internalised the negative views of black women, of themselves, that they were incapable of considering any other explanation for such unusual behaviour. They would never have thrown pee on the sauna themselves, because they could never behave like that. Yet, according to them, somewhere in the town of Bulawayo there was a black woman who had done this horrible thing, and in so doing had let down all the other black women. This woman, whoever she was, had shown that African women could not be trusted to behave properly in the sauna. It had been impossible for them even to entertain the idea that the guilty person might not be an African or a woman of any colour, but a white woman.

Most African women do not spend their time in the sauna, most African women have no leisure time, and even if they did they certainly would not have the money. In fact most women living in tropical countries would not be have the money, the time or the inclination to use the sauna; going to the sauna is an activity mainly associated with the cold countries of Northern Europe. I have quite a wide experience of sauna use, having been to saunas in many parts of the world. The women in the sauna that day in Bulawayo were all middle-class professionals, or wives of men who fitted this profile. The pee-throwing white woman would not need to be categorised by class; in Africa it is enough just to be white. If a mentally disturbed black woman had gone to the sauna it is unlikely that she would have been allowed in. But no one would think to question the behaviour of a white woman or to deny her access to the sauna. The African women, when they considered the matter, looked at it purely as an act of vandalism, and not as possibly the result of a disturbed mind. They had seemed eager to blame the absent black woman, whereas the truth was of a very different hue. The racial politics of southern Africa did not allow those black women to believe a white woman capable of throwing pee onto the sauna, whereas they could easily see a black woman doing it. What hope of a sisterhood here?

A change of scene, a year or so on from this Bulawayo sauna experience. It is 1994, another sauna, another country. This time I am in Staines in Surrey and I am with a white sister who is recovering from a severe mental breakdown. We have come to the sauna to relax and to chat. And what happened? No prizes for guessing – we are soon joined by a very disturbed black sister. The sister is really in difficulty, she is in constant conversation with herself, and every so often laughs out loud. It is pretty much the same as that other woman in that other sauna in that other country. It is also a pattern of behaviour that I was very familiar with at the time, and from which the sauna offered a temporary escape. Or so I hoped. I can tell that my friend is finding the whole experience disturbing and threatening: perhaps the woman's behaviour is a reminder of her own recent experience. I suggest that a walk might be more relaxing, and so we desert the sauna and our mad black sister for the banks of the Thames.

I feel quite sure that there are many sisters out there who would have handled both these sauna situations more skilfully, and more sensitively than I did. Every time I have thought about it since, I have been forced to acknowledge to myself the inadequacy of my response, and my failure to live up to some idea of sisterhood that I carry within myself. The idea of "sisterhood", which I constantly question, and quite often deny, clearly exerts a subtle, but powerful influence over me.

This seems a good point at which to look at the whole question of sisterhood more closely. I start in another country, in another context, and with a different approach. I come at it by way of my what I call an "almost" poem: "The Sister House-Sitter". Peter and I were in a tourist minibus in San José, Costa Rica, when these words more or less came into my mind. I must have been thinking about this white American woman that I had met a few days earlier. Many North Americans live in Costa Rica in what appears to be a state of perpetual paranoia; they build grand houses, which are then fortified with all sorts of electric, electronic, animal and human defences. On their annual pilgrimage to North America, in addition to their usual defences, they employ house-sitters. I had gone to the supermarket with an American guy who was staying in the same low-budget hotel as we were.

On the way back from the supermarket, my companion mentioned that we had to stop by at the American Legion to give a woman a lift back to the hotel. The car, a Volkswagen Beetle, was already quite full with the two of us plus our shopping. I quietly wondered to myself where the newcomer would sit. I soon found out. She was waiting for us in the road outside the Legion, and she and all her worldly goods with her, including her cat. Crowded into that small space we seemed to get close rather quickly, and were soon exchanging personal details. She had been working as a house-sitter in Costa Rica for fifteen years. At that moment she was at a loose end, as there were no houses to be sat, and she had nowhere to go. So, in exchange for her keep, she was moving into the grotty apartment that we were hastily vacating.

The next day I sat in a mini bus on the way to see a volcano and wrote about the sister-house-sitter as I'd come to think of her; but the file containing the original composition went missing and when I returned to Dorset I re-wrote it.

The Sister House-Sitter

In San José Costa Rica I met the sister house-sitter.
She told me that she had made a very good career from
    housesitting.
She said this as she sat crammed into the back of the
    Volkswagen
Beetle with her cat in a wire-basket, and all her worldly goods
Stuffed into plastic bags.

I asked how the cat took to the changes.
"No problem" she replied "He loves changing homes
And making new friends"
Was she still talking about the cat?
I'd lost the tread of our conversation,
Thinking about the career prospects of housesitting.
No time to find out, we had arrived at Linda Vista
Where she and the cat would soon occupy the space
Made vacant by our leaving.
Had the sheets been changed?
Did it matter to a seasoned house-sitter?
It was time for me to go.
There were hugs and promises to "keep in touch"
As the sisterhood of white American reached out to embrace
    me in instant friendship
We parted. But my interest in the house-sitter remained
I liked the way she described her work as fulfilling
Challenging, rewarding.
Giving her independence and autonomy.
Not at all like a glorified servant
Forever packing, forever moving on
Sometimes with no house to sit, no place to be
For fifteen years she had worked as a house-sitter
She was now at the peak of her career. Okay?

I did meet the sister house-sitter once more before we left Costa Rica, but this time there was no talk of the career prospects in house-sitting. This time she was working in the hotel to pay for her keep; she had replaced the lowly paid black woman hotel worker with her free white labour. I knew that the black sister was a single parent with a child to support, whereas the sister-house-sitter had only her cat. I could see the plight of both these sisters, and I could no more blame the white one for "taking" the black one's job, than I could blame myself for bringing about the situation in the first place.

It was my decision to move from that hotel that had triggered the changes, which resulted in the sister-house-sitter moving in. The black sister had begged me not to move, telling me that she would lose her job if we left. In my halting Spanish I had tried to explain to her the inconvenience living in an apartment with virtually no curtains, not having any towels, trying to cook in a kitchen with hardly any cutlery or other equipment, and having to use a toilet without a door. She tried her best to improve things, and brought us lots of towels, some knives and forks, and she hung a sheet in front of the toilet door. But she could do nothing about the exposed electric wires in the bathroom. So we had to leave. Our leaving meant that there was accommodation available for the homeless house-sitter and her cat. So I was to blame for putting a black sister out of work.

For me this story of the white house-sitter and the black hotel maid contains many elements of the social and economic factors affecting the relationship between black and white women. Another very sad example of market forces is the replacement of black and brown prostitutes and mail-order brides from Africa and Asia, with white women from Eastern Europe and the former USSR. In each and every walk of life where there is competition between black and white women, almost always the black woman comes off the loser. It was no different with the white sister-house-sitter and the black hotel maid. In fact they were both big losers competing and fighting over scraps. The sister house-sitter had to survive until the next house needed a sitter. These two women were competing at the lowest end of the social and job scales; there was no room for sisterhood, as it was merely a question of survival. Higher up the social and job scale, the problems there show even greater tensions between women. Issues of power and control also impinge on and highlight the political and class nature of the relationship between women as much as between men and women. The politics of power knows no gender and "Third World", non-white mistresses can be even more cruel and demanding than their white European and American sisters. The sisterhood of power belongs with the mistresses, whatever their colour or ethnicity; the maids share in the sisterhood of poverty and oppression.

I have heard that in Malawi the coloured and black middle-class treat maids and other servants worse than the colonialist ever did, where servants have to approach literally on bended knees. In Zimbabwe, the maid problem takes on a somewhat different aspect: maids as substitute wives. In the Harare newspapers there was constant coverage of this maid/wife dilemma. This is the problem that arises when the husband starts sleeping with the maid, and explains that since the maid does most of the tasks associated with being a wife, he is simply extending her role to include a few more. It is the wife's fault for bringing another woman into the home – so is it any wonder that the poor men are confused? It is not unusual to see letters along these lines, written by men to the newspapers justifying their behaviour. In Zimbabwe the working woman employs a maid in order to release her from the burden of housework and to help with child care. An unintended consequence of this is to confuse her husband into thinking that he has an additional wife. Poor man.

In the Caribbean maids are also badly exploited, are over-worked and paid very little. I have sat at a dinner table in the Caribbean and listened to middle-class black women talk about their "maid problem" in almost exactly the same words as, years before in Calcutta, I'd heard expatriate European women discuss their "servant problem". In one of the Caribbean islands I was once a guest of left-wing academics, whose maid was heavily pregnant. During my stay she was given a Friday afternoon off to go to the antenatal clinic. I was amazed to observe that over that whole weekend no one did any washing up, except me, as I always wash up as I go along. The family kept every single cup, plate, glass, spoon, and all the kitchen utensils that they used from the Friday midday until the Monday morning, when the maid returned. On the Monday she stood in front of the sink piled high with washing-up, with her swollen legs and big belly. When I saw her standing there I volunteered myself and the two of us did the washing-up together.

The behaviour of my friends towards their maid disturbed and puzzled me. I could not understand how people with "socialist beliefs and values" could treat another human being like a slave. Outside the home they were radicals, inside the home they were slave masters. I was confused and uncomfortable. In my search for enlightenment I once raised this maid business with Bernard and Phyllis Coard. I asked them whether they had formed any views on the situation of female domestic labour in the Caribbean. At the time the Coards were both university lecturers at the UWI in Trinidad. In raising the subject of maids, and of domestic servants generally, I made the mistake of telling the story of how I myself had once almost ended up as a maid myself. This clearly identified me as someone with an axe to grind, whose analysis could not be taken seriously.

Bernard later became deputy prime minister and Phyllis minister for women's affairs in the People's Revolutionary Government of Grenada. Following the murder of Maurice Bishop and the American invasion of Grenada, Bernard and Phyllis were imprisoned and are currently still there. Bernard and I are in fact related, as his mother and mine were half-sisters. Even so Bernard and I came from different islands and very different social backgrounds: my family were the poor relations to his. Phyllis belonged to the Jamaican plantocracy, so there was an even wider gulf between her and me. But I believed that we all wanted the same thing: social change and a more equal society in the Caribbean. At that time I still had a lot of affection and respect for Bernard. So I listened as he explained the economics of the "trickle down" effect, and told me that it was more or less the social duty of the middle-classes (people like themselves) to employ maids. I explained that I did not have any problem with the idea of "employment". But I was very concerned about the harsh and inhumane working conditions of female domestic workers. Bernard demurred; he had nothing to say about such matters, such details were dismissed as "women's business". But Phyllis was happy to offer a more complete explanation, which amounted to her saying that the problem was really my own. She used Freudian "anal-retentive" personality theory to explain that I was "over-identifying" with maids; she also commented that I would never understand these things until I was able to let go of my past. I was left totally bemused by this conversation, for neither Bernard nor Phyllis had answered my questions and concerns about the exploitation of female domestic labour in the Caribbean. Instead the issue had been personalised and the focus of attention shifted onto my personality. I took my usual philosophical view – and decided that "you can't win them all".

But I don't learn that easily! On another occasion, in another Caribbean island, I got into a discussion along the same lines as the one with the Coards. This time I got an even more interesting response. My middle-class Caribbean sister turned the attack on me, and pointed out that I also employed a "maid" in England. We both knew that the employment practices and conditions of work extending to my "mother's help" in Shepperton, England were vastly different from the oppressive and exploitative conditions under which maids in the Caribbean work. For example, her own maid started work at six in the morning and never finished before seven or eight at night, sometimes even later. The maid had Sundays off, but had to return on Sunday night, at a reasonable hour, in order to be on time for Monday morning. Although she spent most of her time at work, the maid was not allowed visitors, for fear of attracting thieves and other undesirables. As a result the maid has no real social or family life. Back in middle-class England my part-time mother's help worked a total of about fifteen hours a week.

My Caribbean sister, in arguing that the employment of another woman in the home, whatever the working conditions or terms of employment, is oppressive and exploitative, seems extreme to me. When I employed a mother's help I was a full-time mother, full-time worker, and a part-time student, and if anyone needed help in the home I certainly did. What was important to me was the relationship between the two of us – my mother's help and myself. In fact we were just two women helping each other out. She had been unwilling to accept her premature rejection by the labour market, and by helping me she could remain physically active and socially engaged. Unlike my friend's maid and her sisters in other parts of the poor world, money was not the main reason my helper worked. In many poor countries maids are often the only breadwinners in a family, with many people depending on their earnings, and with many mouths to feed.

It hasn't been like that in England for the past seventy years or so. But that I was in an interesting sociological situation there can be no doubt. At times it bordered on the farcical. One was when a friend of my mother's came to visit from Barbados. This old Bajan woman had been used to employing maids and she immediately related to my helper on the same basis, for example in calling her by her surname, without any title. This caused problems, and I was forced to tell her to address our helper in a formal way, "Mrs", as we all did. She tried, but old habits die hard, and we were all very relieved when her visit ended. She had been so conditioned to address anyone employed in the home as a servant that she found it impossible not to do so. People who are familiar with the colour stratification and consciousness of Caribbean society will appreciate the significance of this story and see the funny side of it.

It is also important to acknowledge that power in the mistress-maid relationship is not completely one-sided. A social worker in one of the Caribbean islands described it as "warfare". As my informant saw it, maids have little choice but to wage guerrilla tactics against their employers. They are poorly paid and exploited. My own observation is that maids have several ways of balancing the score: sometimes they may succeed in taking over the master and in becoming the mistress themselves. A black Latin American sister told me that her friends and family had warned her not to employ an Hispanic maid because she would soon replace her as the mistress. She went ahead and took the risk, feeling it was important to her status to have an Hispanic maid. Maids may also have other more dangerous ways of seeking revenge: they may use the children of their employers for sex themselves or make them available to others. I have heard from social workers in many countries of sexual abuse of children by maids (and other servants) and their associates. A common complaint of the mistress is that the maids steal foodstuff or short-change them in other ways. While these women worry over being robbed of trifles, their own children may be exposed to untold dangers and robbed of their precious childhood. This too is a part of the sociology of contemporary life, and of the experiences of childhood in postmodern society around the world.

In Puerto Rica I met an academic sister who employed someone she described as "her slave", in order that she could be free to pursue her role as a feminist activist. I have seen many such situations in which the concept of sisterhood was equally unsustainable, but was nevertheless used, often serving to obscure or to confuse the main issue. On one occasion, when I was contributing to a workshop on women working with girls, I confronted the issue of the sisterhood. The participants were teachers, social workers, youth workers, and probation officers – people whose job it was to try and control difficult and troublesome girls and young women. I challenged the way some of them approached their work, in a spirit of what they called "sisterhood".

I accuse these professionals of exacerbating the confusion these young people already suffer. The use of terms such as "sisterhood" to gloss over the very wide differences in status, and the power relationship between professional and client is deceitful and misleading. My contribution was not warmly received; many people felt that the sisterhood offered an opportunity for women collectively to demystify traditional roles, and to bridge the gap that divides the client from the professional. They rejected the view that this scenario still leaves power and control with the professionals.

I thought then, and I still think now, that these professional women were being disingenuous, through their failure to acknowledge the reality inherent in their role and status. In the search for an alternative way of relating, it is tempting for women to slip into a comforting view of female relationships, based on sisterhood and solidarity between women. Whether with respect to troubled young women in England or the competition between a white American house-sitter and a black Costa Rican woman for work and a place to live – the question is the same: can there ever be a real "sisterhood" between women in the world today? Rich white/brown/black/yellow women have their sisterhood. And poor white/brown/black/yellow women theirs. There are Muslim sisterhoods, and Christian sisterhoods. It strikes me that there are many varieties of "sisterhoods" made up of all types of sisters. It is quite likely that from time to time the membership of these different groups may overlap – usually but not always through misfortune: the experience of war, rape, incest, divorce. And then there may be a bonding of some kind, and briefly these desperate women may indeed experience some kind of sisterhood. See Stacey's (1985) "Big White Sister Needs Help" for some insights into racism in the women's movement.

Friendship and sisterhood – what's the difference?

For African American and White Women who never interacted as children, attending college and sharing dormitory rooms may provide a crash course in getting to know women of the other race… But wherever it is that White Women and Black Women first come into regular contact, some will be able to form lasting relationships, others will run into conflict, hampered in their ability to get along by swirling undercurrents of racial inequality and social segregation.

Wilson, M and Russell, K (1996), *Divided Sisters Bridging the Gap Between Black Women and White Women*, Anchor Books, NY

Friendship has typically been seen as the most idiosyncratic form of personal relationship... friendship between women lies at the heart of what has been called a female world of love and ritual.

O'Connor, P (1992), *Friendship Between Women: a Critical Review*, Harvester Wheatsheaf, NY

I am interested in women's friendships specifically, and how the idea of friendship differs from or is part and parcel of the idea of sisterhood. Friendship is voluntary and social, whereas being sisters is primarily biological. Where and why did the expression "sisters under the skin" come from? Why do we never hear of "brothers under the skin"? We hear instead of "blood brothers". As I understand it the feminist idea of sisterhood as currently defined emerged from the women's liberation movement, was borrowed from African-American thought, and in terms of political allegiance identifies its adherents as radical. Just as all biological sisters are not necessarily friends, so too with the sisterhood, for sisters may be allies rather than friends. Sisterhood does not preclude friendship – but it does not necessarily include it either. "Sisters" can be very hateful and nasty to each other.

It seems to me that sisterhood, and the question as to whether we women are "sisters under the skin", is usually only discussed and debated with reference to white and black women in general and the American or European context in particular. This presumes that all non-white women are indeed "sisters under the skin" and that there is no need to debate or question this. I can say only that the gulfs separating my African sisters often seem to me as wide if not wider than between women of different races but who share the same nationally – e.g. black and white American women.

I have listened with utter amazement as women who appeared to be close friends explained to me (each at different times) why they could never be a close friend of a person in this or that ethnic group. I had mistaken sociability for friendship. Black people of the Diaspora are not generally aware of the significance of African ethnicity; we concentrate on blackness as the single, unifying factor. This is inherently a response to white racism, which presents us with a one-dimensional, simplistic, limited and mistaken view of Africa and of ourselves. In England a black child hearing a radio report on the genocide in Rwanda asked, referring to the Hutus and the Tutsis, "Which is the white one?"

For me, the development of friendships with my African sisters was one of the most challenging and disturbing aspects of my experience of Africa.

I want to explain my own use of the word "sister". In the Plymouth Brethren people called each other brother and sister, so much so that I am told that at my mother's funeral my father referred to her as "our departed sister". So the label "sister" obviously meant more to him than the label "wife". I grew up with the notion of sister as a word. All the women around me called each other sister, yet they were not, as far as I could see, the least bit sisterly towards each other – if the term "sisterly" is meant to imply feelings of affection, kindness and consideration. At that time in Barbados the Plymouth Brethren had a good number of local white members, and they too were sisters and brothers, even though the social and economic gap, which divided them from their black brothers and sisters, was unbridgeable.

There I was saddled with all those artificial "brothers" and "sisters". What about the real ones? My relationship with my brothers will be examined later; right now I want to focus on women – on my sisters. I do have one biological sister. We cut now to Bhutan (Bhutan is a kingdom in the Himalayas situated between India and China). It was towards the end of my visit there, and my friend, her daughter and I went out for a last meal together. No sooner were we seated than my friend asked me, in a tone that suggested this was a question she had been preparing for me: "Why do you never talk about your sister? In all the time we have known each other, you've hardly ever mentioned her." I was silent for a while, the question having caught me off-guard. My response, when it came, was slightly irritated: "I thought we'd come out for a nice evening. Why do you want to spoil things?"

I was not allowed to get away with that, and she persisted with her questions; she really wanted to know about my sister and me. I gave her the only response I could. I told her that all my life I had viewed my sister with an equal mixture of fear and fascination. I always tried to keep a safe distance between her and me – for this purpose the Atlantic Ocean would be considered just about appropriate. All my attempts to develop a relationship with my biological sister had invariably ended badly and always with me in the wrong. Now, I am content to accept the limits of biology. I told my friend that I was much closer to her than I could ever be to my "real" sister, and added that I didn't know why we are wasting precious time talking about unimportant things.

So we left it at that. I can't help smiling to myself as I write this, for I do find it a bit amusing. There we were, a black Caribbean agnostic woman and a Hindu Indian woman in Bhutan, which is a Buddhist country, affirming our friendship by contrasting the emotional ties that bind us with my biological link to another woman who is now a stranger to me.

What then is friendship? Who is a friend? Is friendship between women really, as O'Connor (quoted above) would have it, "At the heart of a female world of love and ritual"? When we are telling people about our travels, Peter always says of me, "Maureen has friends all over the world and we have visited most of them." Sometimes I wonder what he means, and speculate on the meaning and nature of these friendships. I do know many people. What I am not sure about is just when this changes to friendship, and whether it matters. There are so many levels on which relationships can and do develop, if we are not being deeply philosophical, then I suppose Peter is right, I do have friends all over the world. Each relationship is different, has a different significance and quality. Susie Orbach's (1998) analysis of women's friendships, *Between Women: Facing up to Feelings of Love, Envy and Competition in Women*, comes much closer to the truth of female relationships. Women's friendships simply reflect the tensions and problems of everyday life, and the marvel is the strength and endurance of such relationships in the face of these challenges. Duck (1983) offers an explanation for the endurance of life-long friendships. In *Friends for Life: The Psychology of Close Personal Relationships* Duck explores the meaning and significance of friendship, and explains as a kind of social investment a way of ensuring that we have people around to help us cope with life's traumas. As women generally have so little financial investment, is it hardly surprising that we should have major social investments, especially in friendships with other women? This does not mean that such relationships are uncomplicated or problem-free, but these very factors may add to the richness of the friendship – if it survives.

There is a generally accepted view that males and females have very different experiences and expectations of friendship. It seems that most women have at least one intense emotional relationship with another women – often described as "a best friend". Men on the other hand tend to have group friendships centred on activities, and do not generally share emotions, confidences and expressions of feelings. This

gender difference appears to be the major one in friendship patterns –
even more important than race or class.

When I was very young I did have a "best friend", but she passed the
exam to go to grammar school and I failed. That was the end of our
friendship. Her mother considered that I was no longer a suitable friend
for her daughter. In 1994 I returned to the village and walked around,
exploring old haunts, quietly taking everything in and reliving bits of
my childhood. I walked the length of the road in which we used to live
and as I passed my former best friend's house, without thinking I
stopped and knocked on the front door. I knew that the family had
long since moved away to one of the new terraces that have grown up
in Barbados, so I'd called to pass the time of day with the new occupants.
To my surprise my erstwhile "best friend", who recognised me even
though we had not seen each other in almost forty years, answered the
door. I was invited to lunch with her and her mother, the two of them
having returned from the terraces to live in the village. They preferred
village life. I had not eaten meat in more than twenty years, but I was
unable to decline her meal of liver with cou cou (a Bajan speciality)
and salad. It seemed I was a small child again, except that this time I
was acceptable company and could not risk jeopardising that. I pushed
the liver to the edge of the plate and explained that I did not normally
eat lunch. After lunch her mother retired and the two of us talked like
old friends again, and when we parted we vowed to keep in touch, but
we have not seen each other since.

Having failed the eleven plus, or whatever the exam was, I ended up
in a very second-rate private secondary school, where I had three close
friends. At Loreto College in Calcutta I also had three close friends,
but we were never a group. To return to my school days in Barbados,
and those three "best friends" – one died in Nigeria, one lives in
Barbados, and the other in the USA (she went there the year we both
turned sixteen). Two years ago I met the latter, and this was in fact our
first meeting in more than thirty-five years. We did not connect.
Although there is no longer the same closeness with the other one,
when we do meet my feelings of affection, warmth and interest never
fail to be reawakened. I know of many women who have remained
friends with people they were at nursery school with. Some of these
friendships cover periods of between forty and sixty-five years. I
sometimes wonder what these friendships really mean – are they are
nothing more than the habits of a lifetime, or something more
meaningful? It is not the kind of question one can put to people?

In my own life, I must say that I do find it interesting – and just a bit satisfying – to reflect on the fact that my college friendships have been so enduring. I don't question the significance of these friendships. The fact that they have lasted is enough for me. In 1962 the Loreto College girls and I were from very different worlds. I recall with only a slight amount of the pain that I felt at the time, one of my Hindu friends, a Brahmin, being told off by one of her upper-class Muslim friends for being so friendly with someone like me. I would say that the bridge that divided me from my Indian sisters was as wide as any that has ever separated womankind. My Indian friends came from very privileged backgrounds, and belonged to the Indian intellectual class. We were very unlikely friends.

In their book, *Divided Sisters Bridging the Gap Between Black Women and White Women*, Midge Wilson and Kathy Russell, based on their research findings, argue that friendships between black and white American women are subjected to such great social and political pressures that it is very difficult for these relationships to survive.

On the face of it my Indian friends and I had far less in common than the black and white American women who were the subject of Wilson and Russell's study, and surely were "divided sisters". In spite of all this these friendships have stood the test of time, while other relationships have blossomed, faded and died. It has been suggested that friendship is the relational genre of the future, and that marriage will survive only if it is based, not on true love, but on true friendship.

The idea of "true friendship" takes me back to my childhood. When I was growing up in Barbados we children had a way of defining different kinds of friends: a regular friend was "just a friend", but a real friend was a "true true friend". It is a characteristic of Bajan dialect to emphasise by repetition.Not very long ago I was sitting with a Bajan friend in her garden, cooling out when I must have made some mention of one of my Indian friends. My Bajan friend must have found these Indian relationships perplexing, and she now took the opportunity of asking me, "Is she really your true true friend?" This question, put in this way, took me right to the playground at St Giles Girls' School, when I was about eight or ten years old, with one best friend and several "true true friends". When I stopped laughing, I said that although she might find it hard to believe, yes, that person is really my "true, true friend". There is a lot of tension between Indian and African people and I think my Bajan friend was expressing doubts about the validity of such friendships. I now think that her choice of words "true true friend" was meant to deflect the underlying racism.

Another Caribbean sister of mine was not so subtle on the Indian-African issue. She literally bombarded me with facts and information showing what bad news Indians are for Africans. I tried to escape it by going to the loo, but even there it continued, and not even the sound of our joint peeing could drown the sound of her voice. "You won't believe what they are capable of," she said, preparing to give me another example of Indian duplicity and cunning. I knew that I would have to confront her, and I did. I told her that I did not like racism in any shape or form, and that I was not prepared to listen to her racist ranting any longer. She denied that it was racism to "speak the truth", but after that was silent on that issue. That was a long time ago. Over the years her experience and views have changed, and are now, I think, very much more balanced.

In Mombassa, Peter and I stayed with one of my Loreto College friends. It was quite obvious as we went around that it was unusual to see African and Indian women together. My friend and I went to one of her friends for a swim. The only Africans around were servants, and I could sense their look of bewilderment when she showed up with me. Through her I met a Muslim teacher, and went to a Hindu wedding, while she herself is Roman Catholic. The great divide was not religion, as it had been and still was in India, but race. Africa brought about a unity among Indians that would be impossible to achieve on the sub-continent itself. These rich and varied experiences of the wider world help me to understand and accept the views of my African sisters and their attitudes towards my Indian sisters. But it is not easy.

Feminism is another uniting or disuniting feature of modern women's lives. I don't want to spend a lot of time going over old ground. I would rather stick with the theme of friendship and bring in the feminist one as necessary. I am certainly not going to come out against feminism. I generally support many of the things that feminists and the women's movement have fought for. But I do not like labels; labels bring packages with them. From the time I rejected the Plymouth Brethren and their absolutist teachings, I have been unable to accept any other such package. That does not mean that labels have not been attached to me: following the publication of my book on black education in Britain, I was labelled as both Marxist and a reactionary! I took this to mean that I was getting something right.

I did not like it at all when one of my friends of very, very long standing described me as "a strident feminist". Let me try to tell the story. I am visiting my friend whose husband has just left her. We are sitting on her bed talking about the men and women, children, marriage – the usual woman talk. My friend mentions that another mutual friend had diagnosed the recent failure of her marriage as being due to her feminist views. She then gives me her verbatim account of her response to the charge of being a feminist. "I said to her, don't confuse me with Maureen, it's Maureen who is the feminist, she never irons Peter's shirts, I used to iron twenty shirts a week, I always left my feminism in the office." I could not believe my ears! I listened in silence as she went on about feminism being all well and good "in its place", but that when it came down to it she had always put her man first. I thought that I too had always put people before ideas, but clearly I had failed to get this across to my friend. When Peter and I were first married I did the ironing as I'd seen countless women do, and it was Peter who, coming in one evening from work and finding me tired and irritable from doing this told me that ironing was a pointless activity, and that I should stop doing it. I was more than happy to oblige, and after that I ironed only the essentials. When I became a worker and a student we employed a mother's help, who ironed everything in sight, including socks and underpants! When, after ten years, she retired, it was business as usual in our home, with me doing the minimum amount of ironing.

I did not tell any of this to my friend; in fact I said nothing in my own defence. I was totally bemused by the conversation and by her view of me, also I did not want to add to her problems by quarrelling with her. But I had not recognised myself in her description of me. I also had this feeling of having been weighed in the balance and found wanting. We had never as far I could recall discussed ironing our husbands' shirts, and I had not been aware that this was a criterion against which my worth as a wife would one day be judged. As a result of this conversation I went into a frenzy of ironing, but it did not last long; though I do now try to make a point of ironing the really crumpled shirts. More important than her views of my situation was the way my friend's attitude highlighted the conflict, confusion and contradictions around women's roles and feminism. Is it possible, as my friend seems to think, to separate one's life into little chunks, being an "office feminist" between nine and five and "the little woman" after work and at weekends?

I have had more than my fair share of relationships that I think illustrate the concept of "divided sisters" in relationships between black and white women. I will now provide a selection of some of these experiences, which I hope will be helpful in showing the range and complexity of such relationships. I once had a white female friend; all our previous association had been in contexts in which I now realise she saw me as just like herself, but black. Then, when she visited me in Barbados, she did not know me. The feeling of non-recognition was completely mutual. Her suspicion and mistrust of local people was almost pathological, to the point where, instead of buying drinks herself when it was her turn, she wanted to give me the money because she was afraid of being robbed! The price-list for the drinks was clearly displayed in the stall, so there was really no question of being over-charged. And even so, what was a few pence to her? Our friendship came under enormous pressure, and it became clear to me that it had reached its shelf life or sell-by date, and every other indication of its being over. Nothing was said, but we both knew that it was the end of our friendship. We became divided sisters; our friendship ended because in the context of Barbados society she either became a different person or showed her true self.

My next example of racial undertones in a black-white friendship and sisterhood concerns a work-related experience. I am not sure if this story is about friendship or patronage, but I will tell it anyhow. Since 1975 I have worked as an academic in England. In 1983, fed up with the changes in higher education, I left what was then Plymouth Polytechnic and is now Plymouth University, to become self-employed. About a year or so after this I received a call from a very high-profile feminist, left-wing female academic, who until then I might have regarded as a kind of friend. My friend and colleague had called to offer me a "proper job", a half-time lectureship in race-relations or something like that – or something that she clearly regarded as suitable to my status as a black woman academic.

When I reacted to her offer with less than enthusiasm, she informed me that the freelance world was a very cold one, and that I could not afford to refuse her offer. I gritted my teeth, thanked her and said that I would think about it and come back to her within a few days. This woman had known me for many years, first as a student, then as a colleague. She was well aware of my areas of interest, which did not include race relations. Why then this "friendly approach"? What did she know about my finances? What made her think that I was not in a position to refuse her offer? What would happen when I did refuse it?

Was she threatening to "white list" me? Or were her comments a simple display of her arrogance?

These were the terms in which I considered her approach, trying to tease out what was behind it. I finally came to the conclusion that this enlightened, socialist, feminist "sister" had got into a situation of completely believing her own rhetoric. She assumed that it would be impossible for me to work as a black woman academic outside the protection of the university system. So she had set out to rescue me from the coldness of the freelance world, which she knew would be both racist and sexist. She would find me a nice safe job in race relations where I would be appropriately placed and would do no harm. The irony was that her actions showed her to be not only racist but also anti-academic. My left-wing feminist friend and colleague clearly did not accept me as a full member of the academic community – she wanted to place me in the pigeon-hole that she had made for me, where I would be safe as her "race relations expert". I was enjoying the freedom of self-employment and I had no intention of returning to the intrigues and pressures of university life. My reply would be "Thanks but no thanks".

I typed two letters on my word-processor. In the first I was completely unrestrained, and told my socialist sister exactly what I thought of her and her job offer. In the second I politely thanked her for the offer, but said that I did not want to return to university employment "at any price". I kept both letters for a day, then I posted letter number two. I feel quite sure that my big white-sister remained ignorant of the true significance of this event. As far as she was concerned she had only tried to help this poor black sister (me), who had been too proud or too stubborn, to accept her help. Did I reject the hand of friendship or a poison chalice? I think the latter, and since that then, every time I see Professor Hilary Rose on TV providing a feminist perspective on some issue of the day, I either smile quietly to myself – or laugh out loud.

My next story of black-white friendship is somewhat salacious, and would not be out of place in a tabloid newspaper. I tell this story, not only because it illustrates the potential strains that race can place on a friendship, but also because I think that it is really worth telling.

The story begins at a funeral. After the funeral I am driving myself and one of the relatives of the deceased back to the house for the usual social gathering that takes place on these occasions. It is winter and my mind is fixed on the road and on the dear departed, who was someone I knew and liked a lot.

As we are driving along, out of the blue the lady, my good friend's sister, turns to me and tells me that she wants to make me an offer. I am constantly being made offers: many years, at least two, separate this from the first. I know that the lady and her husband are business people, but I cannot see what that has to do with me. Still, you never could know! "What sort of offer?" I ask. Her reply went something like this: "You may have noticed that X [her husband] is interested in you." "No," I said, "I've noticed no such thing." I had actually, but I wasn't going to let on. She continued: "Well, he is very interested in you. As a matter of fact he wants to go to bed with you." "I don't sleep around," I said, "we are strictly monogamous." She: "I know, that is why I am asking you. I will make it worth your while. We are talking big money." I: "No, I don't think so, you'll have to try elsewhere." By this time we have thankfully reached the house. I cannot face going in, I cannot face my friend and what has just passed between her sister and me. So, I send my apologies, turn around and drive off. Back to work, back to the real world.

Some months on I raised the matter with my friend. I had to know whether she knew about it and whether she had been a party to the whole thing. I had waited for a safe time to bring it up; now, as we drank our cups of tea and remembered the deceased, I asked whether she had been surprised that I had not come back to the reception. She said that they had expected me but she understood that something had come up. I said nothing came up, except what was said to me on the way here. Of course she was all ears, so I told her more or less what I have recounted here, exactly what happened that day. I waited for her reaction. "We must keep this from Y [her husband's name]," she said. I understood immediately what she meant. Like me she was from a large family, and the one thing you do not want is a spouse holding you responsible for what your siblings do, and bringing it up every time there is a quarrel.

We agreed on that, and for good measure I volunteered not to tell my husband either. Then my friend outlined the following scenario. "Those two," she said, "have been together since childhood. Now he is getting bored and she wants to manage things to make sure that she knows what is happening, and that she is in control. She has always been the same; she must be in charge. She is worried that if she doesn't organise something for him, he will go off with someone else, a prostitute or something. I know how her mind works. She would see nothing wrong in what she said to you – and she believes in money, she believes that everyone has a price. That's her. It would never occur to her that she had insulted you or upset you in any way. She wouldn't give a thought to anything like that."

I said: "Even at her grandmother's funeral?"

"That won't have bothered her. She is very practical. She would take the opportunity when it came. We don't know how long she had been thinking of it, and waiting for the chance to get you alone."

We never mentioned the subject again, and when many years later, at a wedding this time, I met her sister and the husband, we passed the time of day and chatted like everyone else. All the same I couldn't help wondering just how big was the "big money" she had been prepared to pay me – and had she ever succeeded in finding a black lover for her husband? I'll never know.

I have had other experiences where white sisters married to black or other non-white men have tried to draw me into some kind of "special relationship". Two English women come to mind immediately: one was an extremely devout Catholic, and the other had converted to the Muslim religion in order to marry her husband. In both of these marriages, religion was of central importance, and I completely failed to see the common ground between them and me that they were claiming. I felt insulted and patronised by their efforts to form an alliance with me based on what I considered to be very spurious grounds. In contrast to their marriages my own marital relationship is based on our common agnosticism.

I will finish this section with another "almost" poem. It is meant to tell the story of what it feels like to have a treasured friendship fragment under the impact of new experiences.

A goodbye walk with a white sister

> Your whiteness meant nothing to me
> Until my blackness became important to you.
> And this changed perception of ourselves
> Opened up a hole into which went our affection,
> Our friendship and our sisterhood.
> We'd walked and talked
> In several parts of the world, and you were to me
> "Just another sister", only more so.
> Because unlike many sisters you were
> Or seemed to be, an ideal walking partner.
> Never needing to chatter.

But a good conversationalist when required.
In English villages we rambled or strolled
In quiet companionship.
Experiencing the excitement of being lost,
And the relief of finding our way.
We were okay together
Even in Asia, walking in the foothills of the great Himalayas.
And in the forest and scrubland of Australia –
Is Australia Asia?
I can't ask you, too tricky that one.
Australia was more challenging,
But still we remained firm friends.
And then we were in my neck of the woods.
My "Beautiful, beautiful Barbados,
Gem of the Caribbean Sea."
Where you see me with new eyes: white eyes.
And I see you with new eyes: black eyes.
What do we make of each other?
I can't answer for you, but I knew
Even as we walked from Holetown to Speightstown,
That this would be our last walk together.
That we have come to the end of our road.

Teaching white sister a lesson

My final anecdotal account of my own experiences of friendship and sisterhood is probably the one I find most difficult to think of and to write about. In some ways it places me in the same sort to dilemma as the white sister in so-called mixed-marriages, who assume some sort of bond with me. I can either stay silent and leave them with their illusions, or I can speak out and let the situation develop, as it will. Mostly I stay silent – for why bother?

But in the story I am about to relate I did not stay silent, as the sisterhood reached out to embrace me in complicity, and I spoke out. I am not a complete coward – am I? Let me start at the beginning – or even before.

As I struggled to find a way into this difficult tale, I saw this headline in *The Times*:

WOMEN MPS REVEAL SEXISM OF MEN ABOUT THE
HOUSE. POLLY NEWTON REPORTS ON ACCUSATIONS
OF CRUDE AND REPULSIVE SUGGESTIONS AND
GESTURES

The Times, London, 10th December 1997

The article continued to report on the behaviour of male MPs in
the British House of Commons, accusing them of using gestures and
body language calculated to humiliate and insult their female
colleagues; giggling at any mention of breast or pregnancy and making
crude and repulsive remarks about the women in the House.

Of all the arguments and discussions I've had in my life, one in
particular stands out – the one that was brought to an untimely end
when the man I was arguing with stopped talking, smiled and made a
comment about the size of my breasts. We had not been discussing
breasts. Whatever the subject of discussion, he had lost the argument
and instead of accepting this he decided to shift ground and to remind
me that I was only a woman. I was really hurt and disappointed, especially
as he was someone I had known for a long time and had always regarded
as a friend. (We are still on the way to the main story, and it is obvious
I am finding it hard work, so I'll get on with it.)

In the early to mid-1970s there was a group of people with whom I
was friendly, mainly black, though there were a few, as one might say,
white hangers-on. Among these was a woman, middle-class, intellectual,
quite good-looking, definitely bossy. I noticed her absence and asked a
black sister, "What happened to so-and-so, I haven't seen her around
recently?" I was totally unprepared for the response that my innocent
question elicited. Talking in a mixture of patois and English the sister
replied along these lines: "Didn't you hear wa' happen to she? How de
boys dem rape she?" I'd heard nothing, so I asked what had happened.
This is the story.

This white sister was at a meeting where she was the only woman
present among a group of black men. Throughout the meeting she
kept interrupting and trying to "take things over". The brothers told
her time and again to "keep out of black-people business", and that
they would ask for her contribution when they wanted it. The white
sister had been unable to follow this advice or warning, and had kept
on "interfering". Then one of the brothers got up from the table and
beckoned her to follow him into one of the bedrooms of the house

where the meeting was taking place. According to my informant, the woman did not object to this, as "she fancied him anyhow". But as he finished with her she realised that this was only the beginning, as all the men present took turns at "raping she". The sister finished by saying with obvious satisfaction: "Dat will teach she to interfere in black-people business, dese people dem too pushy."

I was deeply shocked and distressed by what I had heard, and it took me a little while to compose my thoughts. When I eventually spoke, I said something like, "I can't go along with that, I can't accept that, that is not the way to settle an argument." The smile froze on her face. I worried about her reaction; for perhaps she would condemn me as an Auntie Tom and sentence me to Coventry? But, all she did was to ask me to explain myself. I tried to. She said nothing in response, but many, many years later she referred to the incident, only obliquely, then thanked me for what she described as the "position" I had taken on that matter. I couldn't help noting that this time she did not speak in dialect.

From male MPs behaving badly to their female colleagues, to an old friend losing an argument and responding by being sexist to me, to black brothers gang raping a white sister who thought she could teach black people how to deal with racism – it is easy to see how situations like Rwanda and Bosnia develop and how rape can so easily become an instrument of terror and of war. But even in our suffering we women are far from being united in sisterhood. Some women may delight in or ignore the suffering of other women – the enemy, the "other". I had reacted spontaneously to the story of the rape of the white sister: I had really resented the assumption that I would share in my black sister's pleasure that the white woman had been "taught a lesson". Tutsi and Hutu women encourage and rejoice in the rape and killing of the women of each community, as do Muslim and Hindu women and women in the different communities of the former Yugoslavia, and so on wherever there are wars and ethnic and other conflict.

I will never forget a conversation I had with a Muslim girl at Loreto College, following the first of many "communal clashes" that occurred in Calcutta during the time I lived there. This girl who looked so sweet and inoffensive in her beautiful sari, and who, until then, I had assumed to be Hindu, assured me that she hated Hindus and that she would personally kill Hindus if she ever got the chance. She spoke quite quietly and calmly. We sat in our classroom surrounded by Hindu girls: we could have been talking about anything! There was nothing to suggest that killing Hindus was the subject of our conversation.

Another memorable conversation was one I had with the mother of one of my Hindu friends. Over lunch my friend's mother had boasted that during "partition" (the splitting of the sub-continent into India and Pakistan), she had gone around Calcutta in a Hindu gang killing Muslims. I asked her about something that had puzzled me for a long time. How had they been able to identify Muslims? She explained that they killed only men, and Muslim men were easy to identify. "We simply pulled down the dhotis with one hand and slashed them with the other." Many years later her daughter told me that this story had been an idle boast, and that her mother had never killed anybody. Well, even if she was right, and I do have my doubts, it still speaks volumes to me that her mother should have chosen something like that to make an idle boast about.

The oneliest MA in de island

In writing this book I have generally tried to avoid the use of personal names, and I have now fallen into a habit of style that I found quite difficult when I started out. Now, when I am free to use someone's name, I feel constrained and find that I have to justify to myself my reasons for the change. I am obviously not fully convinced that this change is necessary, so I will see how things go. This final story about my experience of friendship takes me back to my school days in Barbados.

In the autumn of 1997 I came across a diary that I had kept during the year 1958–59. It was very revealing and very surprising. The events I am about to recount took place a couple of years after that diary had been written. I was by then in the sixth form of the Modern high school doing "A"-level History and English. One of my classmates was someone I shall refer to as K. She was exemplary in every way, and was head girl. I was not exemplary in any way, but later on I became deputy head girl. K was a Christian and, although I did not yet have the courage to declare myself an unbeliever, it was well known that I had a very questioning and cynical attitude towards religion. I made no secret of the fact that religion did to not have much to offer me, because as far as I could see belief in God seemed to be based on fear of the devil. Fear of hell fire and love of milk and honey did not seem to me a sound basis on which to make such a great commitment.

K and I argued or discussed religion quite a bit, and one day she challenged me to attend a revivalist meeting. She said that I could not help but be moved or even "saved", because the American preacher was a very powerful speaker. She belonged to the Pentecostal Church and she was utterly convinced as to the literal truth of the Bible as interpreted by that church. I accepted her challenge and went along to the meeting. I was amazed at what I saw. I'd been used to the quiet, calm, boring, one might even say dignified Plymouth Brethren; and I'd also from time to time ventured a peek at the Pilgrim Holiness church near us. On these occasions I had enjoyed the hymn singing, hand clapping and tambourine playing, and had listened in amazement to the "confessions" shouted aloud with vigour, not whispered in shame. But I had never seen anything like this revivalist meeting: as the white American preacher launched into his sermon, members of the congregation shouted and screamed and rolled about on the floor. One woman fell to the ground in what appeared to me to be a fit of ecstasy, wriggling about and groaning all the time. Soon someone brought a white sheet, obviously kept for such eventualities, and covered her up. K and I stood side-by-side. She was swaying gently, singing along and clapping from time to time, but remained upright.

At the end of the service we walked home in the moonlight. It was a full moon, and very bright. K inquired gently of me what I thought of the service and the meeting. I knew that it meant a lot to her and I did not want to offend her, but at the same time she had issued me with a challenge. Instead of answering her directly I asked about the behaviour of the congregation. "What did it mean?" She explained that those people had "been possessed by the Holy Spirit" and had been "talking in tongues". I wanted to know why all the white people had been sitting sedately on the platform, gently fanning themselves, while the black people were rolling about on the floor screaming and carrying on. "Didn't the white people get the spirit too?" I asked. Patiently she explained that not everyone present would get the spirit at that time. So I inquired whether during the two weeks of the revival meeting any of the people on the platform, i.e. the all-white leadership, had rolled about on the floor? She had to admit that none of them had. I wondered why "the spirit" had been so selective about whom it possessed, and left it at that. Too soon we were almost at the point of my turn-off for Bridge Road, with K's home in Bank Hall in the opposite direction. We said goodnight and parted. Never again did either of us mention this episode.

After a year or so we left school and went our separate ways. Then in the late 1960s, during one of my visits to Barbados, I was invited to a

Christmas party and told that an old school friend of mine would be there. It turned out to be K. I was really pleased and excited to meet up with her, as we hadn't met or been in touch since school days. Unfortunately the occasion was not a happy one for me. As soon as we arrived K came and sat with Peter and me, then spent an hour or so in the most bitter attack on my personality. It was done in a low-key way, with her smiling most of the time. At one point she asked Peter whether he realised the type of person he was married to, and whether he had ever seen me take a person apart! Peter smiled and nodded. I sat there stupefied by this completely unexpected and unprovoked character assassination by someone I barely recognised as the person I'd been at school with. K was now drinking and smoking, and acting every inch the woman of the world. It was evident that she had "seen the light", and that this light had led her away from Christianity.

Somehow I managed to steer the conversation away from my manifold faults and shortcomings and we discovered that we had both become welfare professionals. I expressed an interest in learning about welfare in Barbados and K invited me to visit her at her office. A few days later I went as arranged. Although I was indeed interested professionally, I was more interested in making contact with K. I wanted to see whether it was possible to restore some of the comradeship that I had thought characterised our earlier relationship. This was not to be. I was kept waiting for more than an hour. From where I was I could see K moving about in the office, but she never looked in my direction. After what seemed like ages someone came to inform me that due to an emergency K would not be able to see me. No alternative appointment was suggested. As a social worker myself I knew that it was very easy to arrange "emergencies", and my suspicions were confirmed when in the days that followed I heard nothing more from K. I was puzzled and a bit hurt by what had happened, but so what? I decided it was best to forget about it.

I don't recall the exact time differences between these happenings and what followed next – probably two or three years had passed. At that time we could afford to visit Barbados only every two or three years, and I always looked forward to receiving letters from "home". One morning the post brought me a letter from one of my old school friends. I opened it hurriedly and sat down to read her news. In the penultimate paragraph my friend wrote that she "was sure that I would be sad to hear of the death of my old school friend K, who had drowned in a swimming accident". I can still remember her exact words. At the time they'd seemed very formal, as she gave some brief details of the accident in which K and another person had drowned. Of the three people in the party there had been one survivor.

The one survivor was a close friend of mine, Chalmer St Hill, now alas also dead. When I next met up with him I was diffident about raising the matter, but he was able to speak quite freely about it, and told me exactly what had happened. One minute the three of them were standing in the water chatting, the next minute a wave "just came from nowhere" and knocked them over. They had been taken completely by surprise, for up to then the sea had been calm and there had been no waves in sight. He told me that he thought he had survived because he had not panicked. He had tried to keep calm and let the waves lift him and toss him about, and eventually the waves deposited him on the beach. The following Saturday afternoon he had gone back to the same beach as usual, knowing he had to do this, otherwise he would never go back to the sea again.

Some weeks later, during one of my solo walks somewhere in the countryside, possibly in St Philips, I fell into conversation with a young woman. The details are very hazy, but I do recall that she was studying for her "A" levels and that we had talked about exams and such. In answer to one of her questions I told her that I had done my "A" levels at Modern High School. The young woman wanted to know if I'd been at school with K, and when she heard that I had she went on to talk about her in the most glowing terms. She told me that K had got her MA abroad, and asked me whether I knew that at the time of her death she had been "the oneliest MA in de island". I listened in silence, touched by the young woman's sense of loss, but all the same I could not help being mildly amused by what appeared to be K's epitaph: "The oneliest MA in de island". I am writing this towards the end of the twentieth century and in Barbados MAs are two a penny, and the University of the West Indies (UWI) has just (in 1998) celebrated its fiftieth anniversary.

In the years since I have from time to time returned to these events and wondered about the reason why I inspired such strong negative feelings in someone I had until then regarded as a friend – not a close friend – but someone whom I certainly felt friendly towards. I still don't really understand what happened between K and me. I think that her view of me and her reactions to me in 1968 were based on her experience of me as the somewhat brash, perhaps a bit cock-sure sixth-former of 1959. When we met almost ten years later, I was still that same person she'd been at school with, but at the same time I was also a very different person. As indeed was K herself, for she had changed almost beyond recognition.

Ironically I found the religious K far more attractive, with her gentle smile, her patience, tolerance and good humour towards a questioning unbeliever. The new K had come closer to my own world view, but in doing this she seemed to have lost quite a lot. I don't think that at seventeen-plus I had been quite as objectionable as K made out, though I had a sharp tongue and I guess I did use my skill with words to my own advantage. And why not? She had the Lord on her side; I had to fight my own corner. I think that what she found unforgivable was the fact that I had anticipated her rejection of religion by several years. The bitterness of her attack on me suggested that she must have remembered my visit to her church and our conversation afterwards in a very different way from me. On the few occasions when I thought of the events of that night, I remembered them with almost romantic nostalgia. This story highlights something that has been a feature of other relationships of mine, when I have been amazed to discover extremely negative feelings where I had thought there was either indifference or neutrality.

Sisters under the skin – on what unites and separates woman-kind

At this point I want to move away from the anecdotal, to what I hope will be a more analytical approach to some of these issues. I will try and do this through the work of two North American women writers. There are two works of fiction, one by Alice Walker, *Possessing the Secret of Joy*, and the other by Edith Wharton, *The Mother's Recompense*. I am drawn to these books for several reasons.

My relationship with these two books is both interesting and complicated. I was introduced to Edith Wharton's work by one of my Indian sisters. We were spending a weekend in Birmingham, and as always I made my way to the Birmingham arts centre and specifically to the bookshop. I was in fact looking to buy a copy of Walker's book *Possessing the Secret of Joy*. I must pause to observe something, which has just struck me in connection with Walker's book, and a book called *The City of Joy* by Daniel la Pierre. Both of these books have the word "joy" in their titles, but they are devoid of any real joy. *The City of Joy* deals with poverty in Calcutta, and *The Secret of Joy* is about child abuse, or to be specific female circumcision in Africa. We will return to these books and these topics, but for the moment it is back to Birmingham, in the English midlands, and my quest to buy a copy of Walker's book.

My Indian sister-friend is very sophisticated and knowledgeable, and I think that throughout the time we've known each other she has tried in various ways, some more subtle than others, to cultivate these attributes in me. As the assistant and I were searching for Walker's book my friend took me away to another part of the bookshop, where the Wharton books were located. "Have you ever read Edith Wharton? What! Never heard of her! We can't have that. You must read *The Age of Innocence*," whereupon I was presented with a copy of the said book. In the meantime the attendant had located the one remaining copy of Walker's book, and I left the bookshop clutching both, together in the same bag. Walker and Wharton were sisters in that bag, if nowhere else.

What happened after that still puzzles me. When I returned home to Weybridge I placed both books on the shelf beside my bed. I intended to read them more or less straightaway. I couldn't get started. I couldn't decide which one to read first, and I therefore read other things – then I would pick up Wharton, or Walker, leaf through it, and return whichever one it was, unread to the shelf. Although I had not read any of Wharton's books I knew of her writing and of the film of the book that I had been given. I also knew very well the subject of Walker's book, as I had seen her on television talking about her work, and had heard her on radio, defending the book and herself for writing it. I identified with her, both as a black woman and as two people who, in our different ways, were trying to do something about child abuse. I through my research and professional activities, she through her writing. Still, I couldn't get started on reading her *Secret of Joy*.

This went on for what seemed a very long time, but must have been at least six months. Then one night I took Walker off the shelf and did not put her book down until I had read it to the end. After that it was easy to turn to Wharton. On reflection, and as I write this, I can understand my reluctance to read Wharton, for I was not sure that I really wanted to spend my time reading about turn-of-the-century New York high society. I thought of all the books in that bookshop that my sister-friend *could* have given me, and wondered why Wharton? Just because she gave me Wharton did not mean that I had to read her. Wharton is a good story-teller, and I am a compulsive reader, so once I eventually got started on the book, that was it. And a few years later at the St James branch library in Barbados, when I was looking for something to read, and saw a Wharton book, I had no hesitation in picking it up: it was *The Mother's Recompense.*

Having said that I had been puzzled by the gift of an Edith Wharton book by an Indian sister, I now reflect on the fact that I was introduced to Dylan Thomas by a group of Bengali amateur actors in Calcutta, and that my Welsh friend made me a present of *A Suitable Boy*, a story of modern middle-class Indian life by Vikram Seth. I should not have been surprised or puzzled by the Edith Wharton gift. Through the Bengali actors I learnt about Dylan Thomas and heard *Under Milk Wood* for the first time, and was instantly captivated. It was not as good as the BBC 1956 production with Richard Burton, but it was a great experience to sit in a flat in Park Street, Calcutta, India, and listen to the most beautifully written English, spoken with the nearest thing to a Welsh accent outside of Wales. Where else in the world would I have had such an education?

To return to present-day concerns. The fictional heroine of Wharton's book is clearly a bad mother who has abandoned her child. Indeed her actions are more typical of those of "an irresponsible welfare client". She has abandoned her child and left her home and her husband for another man. The link between Wharton and Walker is child abuse and neglect. Wharton writes about a woman who abandons her child. Walker writes about a woman who as a child experienced abuse in the form of female circumcision. In both the Wharton and Walker stories women are both perpetrators and victims. The heroine of Wharton's book, Kate, abandoned her child – thereby making her daughter a victim. Walker's heroine is made a victim by the old woman that had circumcised her. Then as an adult she returns and kills the old woman and in doing this makes the old woman the final victim.

Wharton's reviewers are far more concerned with heroines:

> Heroines were traditionally young, middle-class, beautiful
> and above all virtuous… chaste before marriage and faithful
> within it.

Wharton, E (1995), *The Mother's Recompense*, Virago, London

The only adjective missing from the above description is "white", and it was not necessary, since Wharton's world was naturally a completely white one. Let us pause to consider briefly the story. Kate, a white American middle-aged woman, is living in exile in Europe when she receives a letter from her only daughter, inviting her to return to the USA to live with her. Kate accepts the invitation and at first all goes well, until she discovers that her old lover, not the one she left her husband for, but another, younger man, with whom she had once been obsessed, is now involved with her daughter and that they intend to marry. Kate is horrified. She sees this union as offensive and unnatural, but she is powerless to stop it without, as it were, coming clean about her own involvement with the young man. She remains silent, almost, because she does reveal her secret to an old admirer, whose reaction convinces her that she is best off back in Europe. She promptly sets sail with her maid (of course), leaving her daughter none the wiser.

As to the title of the story, it would at first appear that the mother is recompensed. She is welcomed and rewarded by the child she abandoned. The two women have none of the difficulties of mothers and daughters who have lived together. They are like friends who can enjoy each other's company, until the mother tries to act as a mother, and to tell the daughter that her choice of a mate is not acceptable. Kate cannot rely on her role as a mother as the basis for her intervention; nor as a friend can she disclose the true reasons for the rejection of her daughter's suitor. That is her recompense, her reward for abandoning her child. She must return to the wilderness of exile.

In today's world Wharton's heroine would not have experienced such a major crisis, though her stay might attract the odd tabloid headline: DAUGHTER WEDS MOTHER'S LOVER. No big deal. Although Kate is a fictional character, her experiences typify and say something about a situation faced by women in all parts of the world. The problem of how to be "a good mother". Not many of us know what being a good mother actually means, and what is required of women in order to carry out this job adequately.

The African women in Alice Walker's story have the same problem, but they are much clearer about their role. A good woman, a good mother, must ensure that her daughters are circumcised. Alice Walker is an African-American woman, and the story *Possessing the Secret of Joy* is more or less based in Africa. In Wharton's world, Africa does not exist. Her America is almost completely white, except for an almost-white maid. This maid is fairly central to the story, not in herself, you understand, but because of being a black, sorry, "coloured" maid.

This came about because Kate went to the home of her ex-lover to plead with him to give up her daughter. A coloured maid answers the door. Subsequently when her daughter in desperation tells her that she too has been to Baltimore to her lover's home, and that she had seen only the maid, Kate asks her, "The coloured maid?" and gives herself away. Since the maid was the only non-white person to grace the story, it is not surprising that Kate remembered her so clearly!

Walker's treatment of her characters is altogether more complete. They, whatever their colour, are fully rounded people. The world she describes is one of richness and variety, good as well as evil. The heroine of Walker's book is a young black woman who is receiving psychiatric treatment for a problem that is causing her enormous psychic pain. She does not understand the nature of her problem, and all attempts to help her deal with it fail. This will persist until she realises that the problem is located deep within her memory, and has to do with the death of her sister as a result of circumcision. The location of the problem suggests its own resolution and she returns to the village to kill the old woman who performs these operations and who has become for her the symbol of oppression and control.

This killing of the old woman was regarded by many of Walker's African-American sisters as a great betrayal. That the health and freedom of a young black woman should require the slaying of the black mother-figure was seen as disloyalty. One can but wonder what these sisters make of Burundi, Zaire, Rwanda and other African tragedies, where a person's skin colour is a matter of mere detail. In her TV and radio interviews, Walker seemed almost indifferent to her attackers, holding to the view that female circumcision is dangerous and wrong. She stated that if she, through her writing, could save one girl child from such torture, she did not mind what abuse was heaped on her.

I have to admit that I find literature the most interesting and compelling way of examining the human condition. I would rather read *Under Milk Wood* than any number of social science books on the nature of Welsh village life. The academic woman researcher goes into the world of the poor, the minority and the dispossessed woman – to write about it and explain it to the rest of society. The white middle-class world of herself and her sisters is presented to us mainly through literature. It is not the world in which the anthropologist and the sociologist undertake their participant observation studies – it is the world they live in and they don't research themselves.

So are we women sisters under the skin? I have meandered around the question, told some stories, raised some issues, considered some problems and looked at a couple of books as a way of exploring the topic. I am left with the view that women do have similar problems, often hinging on their relationship with men and motherhood. But although women's problems may be similar in their origin, the way these problems are dealt with depends very much on the social and cultural contexts in which they occur. Even within the same society women from different social and economic backgrounds have different options in responding to, say, being raped and being battered. In traditional societies, custom and practice exert enormous control over women's lives. The things that unite women seem to be mainly negative: rape, poverty, child abuse, the pain of childbirth, the pain of being battered. In other words – always being a victim. On the other hand, wealth, power, social class, education and race separate women.

Nothing more dramatically illustrates this than the situation in Afghanistan, where the Taleban fighters supported by Pakistan arrived to liberate the country and to create a pure Islamic state. At that time Pakistan had one of the few women prime ministers in the world, but Ms Bhutto supported a regime whose main agenda is to return the condition of Afghan women to the Middle Ages. Women are forbidden to work, to leave the house without a male escort, to go to school or college. Women are beaten if they appear in the street with even a tiny bit of their faces showing.

Afghanistan is a country that has been at war for ages. Many women are widowed and have no men to escort them outside the house, and many families depend on women's work to survive. Male doctors cannot treat women, and women doctors are not permitted to work. In the face of such oppression, their Asian sister, the former prime minister of Pakistan, did not remain silent but actually supported the Taleban movement. The United Nations (UN) can organise as many Beijing-style conferences and have as many "days for women" as it wishes; but the real value it places on half the earth, i.e. women, has been clearly demonstrated by its indifference to the women of Afghanistan.

"I wonder what is the use of the conference in Beijing if afterwards the same organisation (the UN) are not saying a word about the violation of the most basic human rights."

Emma Bonino, European Commissioner for Humanitarian Affairs.

"West Leaves Afghan Women to Fate", in the *Guardian*, 12th October 1996

Another kind of sister-love

I can't close this chapter about friendship and sisterhood without mentioning another kind of love between women: a love that now dares to speak its name – and very loudly. When I was a social-work student on placement at Chiswick women's aid, men and women around Chiswick frequently taunted us by calling us "lessies". We were assumed to be lesbians. A group of women living and working as we did could only be lesbians. In fact, most of the women could not wait to get into relationships with men, and most of them were openly hostile to what they understood as feminism.

There was a time when I naively believed that lesbian relationships must be inherently superior to heterosexual ones, because I felt that love between women would be inherently more equal and less oppressive. But when I came to observe some of these relationships at quite close quarters, I was forced to abandon this view. The lesbian relationships I saw seemed to me nothing more than a different version of the same old story. They seemed to me to mirror that of male-female couples, one taking the male and the other the female role. There is a real contradiction here, the rejection of the female-role by the partner who takes on the male role. It seemed to me very odd that, in order for two women to love each other, one has to pretend to be a man. Then there is the "scene", aping the male homosexual world, with its cruising, sadomasochism and such. This gives the lie to the claim that lesbian love is the purest form of female love. I think that true friendship between women exemplifies the purest form of female love. Lillian Faderman's (1985) analysis of female relationships in *Surpassing the Love of Man: Romantic Friendships and Love between Women* offers some interesting insights into female relationships from quite another perspective.

During my student days in India in the 1960s, I went travelling with another overseas student, a white American girl who was spending a year in India. I've written elsewhere about my visit to Kashmir and of some of my experiences there; I am writing about me and this woman now because it fits here, I think. My friend and I arrived in Srinagar after five or six days of rail and bus travel, where we very soon found a houseboat and settled in. After a sumptuous meal we retired to bed. It was a lovely soft bed, and after almost a week without proper sleep I was happy to sink into this warm luxury.

As I was about to fall asleep I felt someone get into the bed with me and grab me, trying to hold me. I froze as I realised that it was my friend and travelling companion. I asked her what she thought she was doing and she replied that she just "wanted to be close to me". I said that I was tired and wanted to sleep and would she please get back to her own bed. She persisted in trying to get into my bed and in trying to get hold of me, so I threatened to scream. I told her in no uncertain terms that unless she left me alone I would start to scream at the top of voice. This had the desired effect and she went back to her own bed.

From this, for me safe distance, my companion cried and sobbed as she told me her story. She said that she had been "interfered with" by her stepfather, that her mother had found out, and as a result had sent her away to India. This year in India was supposed to help her get over what had happened, and also to keep her away from her stepfather. But she felt that she had been rejected and punished by her mother, she in her words was "lost and alone". I listened to her words and her tears, and said that I could not see how getting into my bed would help. I felt deeply resentful that this privileged offspring of white East-coast USA should try to use poor little black me from Carrington's Village, Barbados, to solve her problems. I felt that these were far removed from my world, were nothing to do with me, and I certainly was not going to let her into my bed at any price. So I waited until I was sure she was asleep before I felt safe enough to relax and fall asleep myself.

I need not have worried. Nothing like that ever happened again, and no mention was ever made of what occurred that night.

We continued our travels as planned. In Delhi we shared a hotel room with a night-club hostess who was also a singer. My friend and the singer made a lively twosome, always in the company of men and always appearing to have a great time. When we ran out of money my companion sent a telegram to the USA, and money came, presumably from the same stepfather who had been abusing her. At the end of our travels we parted on good terms and we continued to correspond off and on for some years.

Before and since that incident in Kashmir I have shared rooms and beds with sisters all over the world, but that experience in Kashmir was the only one of its kind. In India I frequently shared a bed with one of my Indian sisters, from necessity, but to this day when we are together we still share a bed from choice. Among my most touching memories is of a weekend in a French farmhouse, sharing the house and a huge feather bed with my Dutch artist friend. We would talk late into the night and then fall off into a dreamy sleep, only to find that it was soon morning. Then again I shared a bed with a very heavily pregnant sister, spending an almost sleepless night wedged against the wall trying not to bump into her enormous stomach. Her son was born weeks later.

The only other comparable experience to the one in Kashmir was when I rather foolishly went to the sauna with a lesbian friend, though that really does not compare, because a look was all it took to nip the potential problem in the bud. And I did not have to listen to any tearful stories of sexual abuse. Also the problem was partly of my own making, but I had regarded my lesbian friend in much the same way as I saw my friendship with my many brothers, as I called my male friends. Then I realised that I never go to the sauna with my male friends, so I never made that mistake again.

I will almost certainly be returning to this topic. My life has not been lived in neat compartments, and as I write of my travels and experiences, I tell my stories more or less as they "come up". This means that in another part of this book I may return to an old subject with a new story, or just to look at it again from different vantage point.

Summing up on sisterhood and friendship

Praful Bidwai has argued that the domination of the world by the capitalist market economy of the north has distorted our view of human geography and human history. It has led to a view of the world that is anti-nature, anti-woman and anti-south. She has called for the abandonment of the market economy of the industrial north in favour of a "nature-oriented, female-oriented South". Bidwai demands nothing less than

> A shift from urban to rural, industrial to agricultural, high-cost to low-cost, inorganic to organic, exotic to indigenous, processed to unprocessed, market to subsistence, quantitative

to qualitative, standardised to vernacular, individual to community, male to female, light-skinned to dark-skinned.

Bidwai, P (1989), "New Ground" in Mellor, M (1992), *Breaking the Boundaries*, Virago, London

Bidwai offers us a seductive vision of a world in which all the economic, social, political and environmental problems of the world are solved as a result of the changes she advocates. I wish I could buy into her belief system. Unfortunately the south is too busy copying all the evils of the north, plus developing their own inherited ones, to be able to offer any advance over the problems currently facing the world. A more interesting and honest account of women's situation in the south, and around the world, is provided in Anees Jung's *Breaking the Silence*, (UNESCO, 1997), which documents the common suffering and the survival of women in each and every part of the world.

The south is no less racist than the north. The treatment of women, and relationships between women, is no better in the south. Female circumcision, female infanticide, and bride-burning are but few of the additional hazards that women in the south have to face. The philosophy and values that are historically associated with the south have been shown to be as saleable and as dispensable as the rain forest. We delude ourselves if we look to the south for a new brand of sisterhood. That is why I cannot buy into the simple myth of sisterhood, even though I find the idea of sisterhood both attractive and necessary.

For these reasons I will continue to regard all the women in my life as my sisters. The concept of sisterhood as it applies in my life will be demonstrated in the collection of "Letters to my Sisters Around the World", which follow in the next chapter. There will be many other occasions in the course of this book where my own relationships with women will provide many practical examples of what sisterhood means to me. Some will perhaps be amusing, some may well be provocative and distressing, but I hope that if nothing else they will provide examples of sisterhood in the global village we call the world today.

3

LETTERS TO MY SISTERS
AROUND THE WORLD

THERE ARE some letters that I can never forget. They remain fixed in my memory, burnt into the brain cells. I received such a letter when I was living at 6 Nassir Uddin Road, Calcutta 16, West Bengal, India. It was from one of my high school friends. She was living in England, and had been at a party in Leeds or Leicester or somewhere, and met one of my brothers. Having got my address from him, she had written to surprise me. The letter started off really nicely, as she filled me in on the main events in her life, telling me about her nursing studies, then about her Nigerian boyfriend. Then she went on to say that she'd heard that I was courting an Englishman. The whole tone of the letter changed as she went on to warn me of the problems and difficulties I would experience if I married "that man". For one thing I would no longer be able to count her among my friends.

I was amazed that someone who now seemed so distant and removed from my world could take such liberties, and be so intrusive. At the same time I was slightly amused – my friend clearly had no idea of the nature of Indian society and what life in 1960s India was like for a black woman. Warning me about prejudice and racism in England! England had nothing to teach India about how to treat black people. I felt that after India I could live anywhere. At that time my idea was to move to West Africa from India. I had no fear of living in England. I did not hurry to reply to my friend's letter, but when I did I thanked her for her advice and added that I thought that if she married her Nigerian her life would be far more interesting and also more complicated than mine if I married Peter. I ended by saying that at the moment I was not interested in marrying anybody.

I never heard another word from my friend. Just that one letter, which changed forever the way I would remember and think of her. Long after I'd left Calcutta, and married "that man", and was living in Shepperton, and was a lecturer at Surrey University, I heard that my friend had indeed married her Nigerian, and had died during the Biafran war. I never heard any details, but snippets of news over the years left me in little doubt that her life had indeed been more interesting, more complicated and certainly shorter than mine. I kept her letter a long time, but when we moved from Shepperton to Weybridge that letter was among the stuff that went on the bonfire.

Letters have always been an important part of my life. The idea of writing these letters came to me on one of our walks. It was a rather windy September day and Peter had gone to explore the Portland Bill area of the Dorset coast. My thoughts were far away from Dorset; I was thinking about my Caribbean childhood. These thoughts were prompted by a telephone conversation I'd had a few days earlier with one of my friends from "back home". My friend had gone on and on about her feelings towards her mother. The conversation had upset and disturbed me, not least because, although invited to, I had avoided making any comments. I had made noises and uttered vague platitudes, all the while feeling hurt and very angry on behalf of the mother. Barrow's (1996) *Family in the Caribbean* and Clarke's (1957) *My Mother Who Fathered Me* provide an interesting sociological overview of Caribbean family life.

I really wanted to ask my friend about her father's role in her life, and to have an idea of what his share of the blame was. I did not have the nerve, so the question remained unasked, and I simply inferred that the absent father had done no wrong. Whereas the ever-present, ever-struggling mother had always been there and so could be blamed for everything. I listened speechless as my friend itemised, aged sixty-plus, and with bitterness that astounded me, the many ways in which her mother had failed her. How, as a school girl returning late from extra lessons, she never met her off the school bus if it was late: "She never met me off the bus from school even though she knew how I hated walking in the dark." Still there was no mention of her father. Presumably he had done nothing wrong, and nothing right; presumably he had done nothing at all. I said nothing at all. Later that week, as Peter and I walked along the coast, my thoughts returned to that conversation, and I began to consider how I might have responded differently.

Then the idea of writing a letter to my friend came into my head, and there and then I started drafting it. But even as I composed it in my head, I knew that it could never be posted, so I decided to add a chapter of such letters in this book. This is how I arrived at the idea of writing these "letters to my sisters". I felt that in these letters I would be able to express my views and opinions freely, and could, with relative safety, complete a whole lot of unfinished business.

Once I came to this decision I began to very feel good about using letter-writing as a means of raising issues and talking things over with my friends and sisters. Most of the sisters I have written to are, as often as not, apocryphal, being a person that I have created as the recipient of any particular letter. But some of the sisters are real enough. It does not matter which is which. And another thing: there is no structure or logic to these letters. The content of each is determined by the woman, real or imaginary, I am writing to. These relationships span my lifetime, from childhood to yesterday.

The writing of letters came originally from my wish to confront and be honest with a particular woman about a painful personal matter; but it was not simply "a personal matter", because for me it raised issues far beyond the purely personal. In Chapter Two I examined the idea of friendship and sisterhood, and I illustrated the discussion with some of my own experiences with women in many parts of the world. In these letters I have tried to broaden and deepen the debate on sisterhood and friendship in my version of the global village. The letters were composed and written between September 1996 and August 1997.

Letter to China

Dear Chinese Sister,

I know that it is a long time since you have heard from me. It is so hard to get someone to translate my letters into Cantonese and I did not want to put you to the trouble and expense of having to get the translation done at your end. But now I have decided to write to you and worry about the translation later.

The only news I seem to get about China is bad news. I always think about you when I read or hear news of your part of China. I do hope then that you are all right and wish that I could pick up the phone and call you. I could call you. I still have your number, but what could we say to each other? When we met face-to-face we had the help of the very limited vocabulary in the *Rough Guide,* and we managed to communicate. Just! How is your son? He must have completed his secondary schooling by now. Is he working in the restaurant, the hairdressing salon, or is he doing something completely different? Whatever his chosen career, please give him by best wishes for his success.

Did you tell him that you took a stranger, a black woman, to his room while he was at school? I hope he did not mind. I can still recall almost every detail of your apartment, even though my visit was so fleeting. Your son's room with his music centre, records and posters, the same as any teenager's the world over. I liked your apartment, and how, even on such a very hot day, it was so cool. When I mentioned to my friend in Hong Kong that I had visited a Chinese home, he was incredulous. He said that Chinese people never invited foreigners to their homes! He had never been invited to a Chinese home. I think that he found it all the more surprising as he had warned me of another Caribbean woman who had found her visit to China very distressing. She had been stared at and pointed at and made to feel very uncomfortable. In India during my student days I'd had much worse experiences than those, so I wasn't particularly bothered.

In fact I found the people in your country on the whole very friendly and very welcoming. Not only you and your friends at the restaurant, but people in the hotel, the school kids, and people we met on our walks. Except for Peter being robbed of all his money and his credit cards, we really had a lovely time in your country. And we both want to come again!

But the theft was a very traumatic experience. We had to report the matter to the police, and that was an experience in itself! We were sent from one police station to another. I think we visited three altogether, which does not sound like much, but when you are in a strange country, have just had all your money stolen, are struggling to make yourself understood, and you get sent from pillar to post… ! Let me just say that it is not enjoyable. To be honest, I don't think the police were very interested, but we had to report the theft for insurance purposes. Back in Hong Kong we were told that in the mainland, theft from tourists was becoming a big problem, and we were told about a thief who had been hanged for stealing from tourists. When I heard this I was quite glad of the police indifference to our theft. Although it had been upsetting at the time, we did not think that it warranted the death penalty! Joke.

We saw quite a lot of the police, considering we were there such a short time. Our second encounter with the police was at the hairdressing salon, after we had left you back at the restaurant. I am sure you must have heard all about the police raid from the others who were there. But I want to tell you about it myself. I want you to share the experience with me, as I saw and experienced it, okay? So forget, for the moment, what anyone else told you, as you read my version of what happened that day.

We left you in the restaurant and went with the "boss man" to the hairdressing salon. As soon as we arrived we were offered free beauty treatment. Peter accepted, but I demurred, being reluctant to trust my African hair to the tender mercies of a Chinese hairdresser. As Peter was receiving a shampoo and massage, the first (and possibly the last he has ever had), I was busy with Mi Li trying to master the words of a Beatles song. I was trying to help her sing "She loves you, yeah! yeah! yeah!" This was a real test of my teaching skills, but great fun. After the singing lesson I started playing the game of patience, which I'd been taught by Dajun the day before. I was just about to get it out when the door burst open and in came a group of armed policemen.

I continued with my game. But I slowed it down, as I didn't want to have to shuffle the cards and draw attention to myself. The police ignored Peter and me. But all the other people in the salon, except for the lady who was massaging Peter's head, were rounded up, packed in the police van, and taken away. Throughout all this I continued to play patience, and Peter's beauty treatment continued uninterrupted. Eventually both activities came to an end and we left the salon.

The next morning we turned up at the restaurant for breakfast as planned. We didn't know what to expect. Would things be the same? Would we see the same faces, or would there be new people? We needn't have worried, as our friend the "boss man" was there, you were there and so were all the others. Everything and everybody seemed just fine. After breakfast, the two of us, you and me, went shopping together. You bought me that tape, and took me to visit your home. The police raid was quite forgotten. The next day our other friend Dajun took us to the amusement park.

By the way – did you know that the one I call the "boss man" (because he seemed to own everything and everybody) suggested a swap? He probably thought that this would be quite normal for us decadent Westerners. But when I said, "No, not okay", very firmly he just smiled and took it in good part. At the time Peter had no idea of what he was suggesting, and why I was so firm in my refusal. Does this surprise you, or is it what you would expect from him? Thinking about it now, I suppose I should have been flattered. His wife/woman was young and very beautiful, as indeed he was too, so I suppose he was simply interested in a bit of variety. He did seem to have many females hanging onto him. I guess I was just not expecting to be propositioned in this way: anyhow my idea of an adventure has more to do with bus rides across Africa and white-water-rafting down the Zambezi than with husband swapping. I don't think it would be a good idea for you to mention this to him, okay?

There was no harm done. It was the very next day, the day before we were due to leave, that Peter was robbed. Please do not worry that being robbed will spoil our memory of China, we have been robbed in many places including Africa, Australia, India and Spain. We think of it as the price we pay for our style of travelling, using buses, walking, being with ordinary people in the countries we visit. When Peter's pocket was slit open and his wallet taken, we were on the bus back to our hotel. The hotel manager wanted to know why we had not taken a taxi. Why indeed!

So much happened to us during our stay in China that it is hard to believe that we stayed only a week. Thanks very much for the card, it was lovely hearing from all of you, and I hope you like the pictures. I have listened to the tape you gave me, and I like the music, though the words remain a mystery to me.

Once again let me thank you and your friends for making our stay in China so interesting and enjoyable, and I hope that one day we will meet again.

Until then etc.

Letter to my sister in former Yugoslavia

Dear Sister,

This is just a short note to let you know that I have remembered you, and that I hope you have survived all the upheaval of the past few years. I am hoping you are alive and well.

We met at the conference of social work teachers at Ljubljana in 1986 – do you remember? No, I don't expect you do. It might help if I say that I was the black one. Do you remember me now? Of course you do, now! I have remembered our conversation and thought of you often, for some reason it made a deep impression on me. We were talking as people do at conferences about this and that, and I then told you about my bus ride and the tension I felt when, in response to something that was said on the radio, the whole bus exploded in anger. I wanted to know whether you had any idea what it was all about. You shuddered, and said it was too awful and you did not know how it would end. Then you changed the conversation to focus on me. You wanted to know about the situation of blacks in Britain and how we were coping with the racism there. I don't know if you realised how frustrated I felt at the time. In the setting of a conference, with academic pretensions, I did not expect to be fobbed off in quite that way.

Then you turned the tables on me, and I became the subject of your own unhealthy curiosity. I put it this way because my questions about your country, Yugoslavia, came from a real situation, which I had been exposed to on the bus, and also from my knowledge of European history. Whereas it seemed to me that your interest in me and in my experience of racism in Britain was voyeuristic and opportunistic, and therefore unhealthy, you did not want to talk about Yugoslavia. You assume that I would welcome any and every opportunity to hold forth on racism in Britain. I hope that you understand now why my cold got worse and I had to go to bed. I was sick of being your "case study".

Well, as things turned out, I can now at last understand your reluctance to talk – where did/do you fit in the ethnic divide that is Yugoslavia today? Were/are you Muslim, Croat, Serbian or what? Were you "ethnically cleansed"? Was that what lay behind your refusal to talk? Did you see it coming? To answer the question, which I avoided before, here in Britain ethnic cleansing has not yet arrived. There is going to be a Scottish parliament and a Welsh assembly, so hopefully we may yet avoid ethnic cleansing. The Irish question is still outstanding. For black people racism in the UK is alive and "well", as it is, unfortunately, in so many parts of the world. I can't end this letter without telling you that I met one of your brothers in Oslo, a young refugee who had fled the war and terror of your land. He told me that he was happy enough in Norway, but he wanted to go home, as he did not like being a refugee. Meeting him reminded me of meeting you, and I wondered whether you too had become a refugee.

By the way, how is social work faring in your neck of the woods? Did it survive the fighting? If you ever receive this letter, please send a reply to

Your black sister in England.

PS! It is now the summer of 1998 and I still have your letter with me. So much has happened since I first wrote to you! I will give you the highlights: The Irish have stopped killing each other, and Northern Ireland has its assembly back again. In London the Stephen Lawrence inquiry is on in London. Stephen was a young black student who was killed by racists as he waited for a bus. The inquiry has shown up the massive racism in and incompetence of the London police. And another thing, we are celebrating the arrival of *The Windrush* on the shores of England. It is fifty years since that boat arrived here full of immigrants from the Caribbean. I do think that there is much to celebrate. And that is why I say that in spite of the institutional and other types of racism in Britain: I would rather be black in Britain today than Albanian in Kosovo, Tutsi in Rwanda or "untouchable" in India. I hope you understand my meaning.

MS

Letters to the Caribbean

Letter number one

Dear Sister,

I can't tell you how disturbed I was by our last telephone conversation. Although it was quite late, I had to go out for a long walk just to clear my mind and settle my emotions. I was all churned up. Let me tell you this mother-daughter thing is real dread!

Did I ever tell you about the research I did with young people leaving care? Well, girl, one of the most astonishing things I came across was the strong attachment and loyalty many of the young women felt for the mothers who had abandoned them. This was not a part of the study, but it was something that emerged and that struck me, and made me think. Have you read Edith Wharton's book *The Mother's Recompense?* In that story the mother is welcomed and loved by the adult daughter she abandoned as a child. I think of your mother as I think of mine, as among that generation of Caribbean women the likes of whom we will never see again. They loved, not with words like "being there for you" and empty gestures and hugs, they loved with their lives. They worked so very hard in such impoverished circumstances, with little if any personal fulfilment and happiness in their own lives. And what for? Why did they do it? They did it in order to give their children, especially their girl children, you and me, the opportunities they themselves never had. They worked hard to give us the chance of a better life. Did they succeed? Materially we are that much better off than they ever were, but in the things that really matter I am not so sure. What do you think?

It is almost physically painful for me to hear you speak about your feelings and attitudes towards your mother. I know that some people from our background, once we become educated and "middle-class", can feel ashamed of and reject our origins, and in particular are embarrassed by our working-class parents. I can't help wondering how much something like this may be influencing you, without your even being aware of it. I realise that this is a delicate topic, but after our last conversation I think I have your permission to venture into delicate areas.

We talked about therapy and whether it might be helpful, my dear. What can I say? I know you have the wherewithal to seek the help of the most expensive private therapist in Europe or North America, but apart from spending money what would that achieve? Very little, I would guess. Have you read *Possessing the Secret of Joy*, by Alice Walker? Well, the black woman in her novel had a sympathetic, gentle and understanding psychiatrist, but in the end she had to find her own answers. I am unwilling to suggest that you go local. You may get a sympathetic ear and maybe some cultural relevance, if you think that is important, but confidentiality may well be a major problem.

So what is the troubled black woman to do? We must do as our own mothers did. How many therapists do you think your mother has been to? Exactly. I think that you are judging your mother's child-rearing skills by the knowledge and practices, and by the standards of a different time and place. I have seen the same thing in my own family. And it hurt my mother deeply. No black Caribbean women of our generation have faced the social and economic problems that our mothers faced. If our mothers did nothing else, they saw to that. It seems to me that we should begin by accepting this fact, and after that, perhaps, if there is time, we may be able to work our way back to something more worthwhile.

I am sorry that I have nothing more to offer. I can only try to understand your feelings and your pain. And I can but hope that with time, your acceptance and tolerance of your mother may lead to a more satisfactory situation. I don't know which of your addresses to send this letter to, so it might end up posted in my handbag. So be it.

Until the next time.

PS What about your father, how come you never once mention him? Were you an immaculate conception or something? I guess that like so many Caribbean children your mother fathered and mothered you. And now she has got her recompense.

PPS Please believe me when I say that I really am trying to understand your problem, and that I hope that I am still,

Your friend etc.

Letter number two

Dear Sister,

What is Grenada like these days? I was told that after the American invasion it had become something of a "gay paradise". Is this still true? Was it ever true? It is such a long time since I have visited my mother's country, must be about more than twenty years. Time was when we were always in Grenada; we couldn't keep away from our beautiful spice island. Do you know that although my mother spent most of her adult life in Barbados, she never lost her Grenadian accent, and their way of speaking?

Still, I am glad she never lived to see the way her little island home was catapulted onto the world stage in 1983. I am sure she would have been very distressed at the thought of her nephew Bernard, on TV, half-naked and handcuffed. She would never have actually seen the TV pictures herself, since as you know the Plymouth Brethren are not allowed to watch TV or listen to radio. I have often wondered how all that went on would have affected the two sisters. Bernard's mother saw the whole thing as a CIA plot to discredit and bring down the People's Revolutionary Government (PRG), though my mother, her sister, would not have known what or who the CIA was. I know that she did not understand or support the PRG, which she saw as "communist". She did not understand communism either, except that she knew that it was "evil". So I think that she would have supported the American invasion. That I am sure would have put her at odds with her sister.

That would have been very ironic. My mother went against her beloved Brethren only in one respect, and that was in her friendships and family relations. She never gave them up. So to break with her only sister over politics would have been, well, as I said before, ironic. This is mere speculation, for the fact is she died before it happened, and was spared the pain and bewilderment that the rest of us went through, and will in my case at least continue to go through.

Do you know that it was more than a year after my mother's death that Bernard rang me to offer his condolences? He was passing through London on his way to somewhere or other, possibly Moscow. He did apologise that he had left it so long, due to "pressure of work"! I met Maurice once. Bernard and family were staying with us and Maurice came down to Shepperton and spent the best part of a day. At around three o'clock Maurice said that he would have to leave for another meeting in London. So I asked him when he would have something to eat? He didn't know, so I offered to cook them a meal. Bernard said that they only had ten minutes,

"Can you cook something in ten minutes?" This was a long time before stir-fry appeared on the supermarket shelves, but I had learnt to cook Chinese. I still have a picture of those two men, these two brothers, talking and eating pork-chops and fried rice with stir-fry vegetables, cooked by me in less than ten minutes! Now one of them is dead, and the other is in prison for life.

And I wait for the time when it will feel all right for me to visit my mother's country again. How I envy your being there!

That is all I have time for, or perhaps all I can cope with now.

Good luck, and good-bye.

Letter to a white Bajan sister

Dear Sister,

Do you know that the day before I met you, the day before our Sunday walk, I said to Peter, "If there is one group of people whose absence I won't notice if they all disappeared off the face of the earth tomorrow – it's white Bajans!" I remained and still remain unapologetic in the face of his strictures and his reminder of my humanist values. My reasoning is simple. Why should I be humanist to those who would deny *my* humanity? I saw on TV the other day a meeting between Palestinian and Jewish school children. After the meeting a little Jewish boy said of the Palestinian children that he was surprised to see how like him they were. I have to admit that had I been asked, I would have had a similar reaction to meeting you. But just like the meeting between the Jewish and Palestinian children, it changed nothing.

I was fascinated when you talked about your childhood with your strict grandmother who gave you "licks". I myself never knew my grandparents, but lots of my friends did, and their experience was similar to yours in the licks department. So I instantly recognised what you were saying and where you were coming from – a Bajan childhood! I once attended a sociology conference somewhere in England, and one of the English academics mentioned the Barbadian white community as one that was inaccessible to black academics. I think he meant to challenge me, as I was the only black academic actually present. I was happy to ignore his challenge, because I had no interest in the subject, and I just listened politely to his presentation, remaining mute. I can do this quite easily when the situation requires it.

This conference came back to me during the time we were walking. You remember how we broke away from the rest of the group? The leader was fat and slow, the rest of the group was just too slow, and so the three of us made off on our own: you, your niece, and me. Well, I really intended to make off on my own, but somehow we fell into the same pace and continued walking as it were together. I really liked it when you invited me to come to the church to see "the wedding of the year": the reason why you and many other family members were gathered in Barbados. A lot of money had been spent, so much planning and organisation had gone into it, and it was going to be spectacular. You to me: "If you're not doing anything come along to the church, I'm sure you'll enjoy it, it's going to be quite an occasion!" Me to myself: "I bet!"

I did not tell you then, but let me tell you now: I am not a person for "occasions", and even when I was a small child growing up in Carrington's Village, other people's weddings did not interest me. I have never in my life stood outside or inside a church to watch anybody getting married. I am the person who astonished people by turning down an invitation to lunch at the House of Lords on the grounds that I was too busy. Apparently, this caused great amusement and amazement among my colleagues. I still can't see what was funny. Do you remember when Princess Margaret visited Barbados, back in 1956, or whenever it was? All of us school children were herded to the garrison or somewhere for the royal visit. On the following Monday morning, I was punished in front of the whole school for disrespect. Do you know what this disrespect consisted of? Complaining about being made to sit in the hot sun for hours, to cheer somebody who didn't care about me.

The day the Windsors (Charles and Diana) got hitched, I organised a work-party to clear an overgrown patch in our back garden. I did this so that no one in my house had the time to consider looking at the TV. I heard later that many people in Barbados actually reversed their day so that they could be up to watch the wedding live on TV, and why not? Exactly. It's just that personally I am not interested in weddings. You could say I am not a "wedding person". I tell you this, not to impress, I know better that to imagine that the likes of you could ever be impressed by the likes of me. I tell you this simply to explain why there was never a cat in hell's chance of my going along to gape at the Barbados wedding of the year. Thanks all the same.

Another thing I liked very much was the way that, at our parting, you made sure you told me about your poor eyesight, and invited me to "call out and say hello!" if you ever passed me in Broad Street. You very much wanted me to know that you were not one of those white Bajans who would not be seen dead speaking to a black person in Broad Street. I was deeply touched by that. The only trouble is that, like yours (we are probably about the same age), my eyesight is also not as good as it used to be; and I would have exactly the same difficulty recognising you as you would have recognising me. So you need not have worried. One day, when we were still living in Surrey, I went into the Oatlands village newsagent. As I was leaving a woman stopped me and with a broad smile said, "It's so nice to hear a Bajan voice." Like you she was a white Bajan, and in Weybridge, Surrey, she was pleased to hear my voice. In Bridgetown, Barbados, it would have been a different story. I bet you can't guess how I reacted to her? I smiled at her, and said, "Is it?" and walked out. I play my own games and I choose my own playmates. Please note.

But Barbados is such an interesting place; so very small, yet able to contain so many different worlds. When these worlds do touch, and we, sometimes literally, "cross each other's paths", we are able to negotiate and manoeuvre in such a way as to leave with our separate worlds intact. That at any rate is how I see our meeting and the time we shared during that Sunday walk.

I do hope that you continue to enjoy your hikes, but if our paths should ever cross again, please don't invite me to watch any more weddings. Thanks all the same.

Letter to America

Dear American Sister,

Of all the American sisters I know, it seems odd that I should be writing to you at this time, but a letter to you is what is coming up in my head, so I will follow it through. You did promise to write to me and we exchanged addresses, at least I gave you *my* address. Did you forget to give me yours, or have I lost it? I think you did give it to me, but either way I can't find it now. Ah, now I remember it clearly. I wrote mine in your address book, you wrote yours on a piece of paper. Never mind, I'll continue writing; the bit of paper might turn up.

I am interested to know whether you are still taking that long bus ride down south to put flowers on your husband's grave. When we first got talking, in I think Houston, you seemed very convinced that this was an okay way to spend your holiday. But by San Antonio, you seemed to be having doubts. By the time we parted you did not seem at all sure that these visits would continue. You said that it depended on what happened during this present visit. If things went well, you would continue with your annual pilgrimage to your husband's grave. It must be very hard, going all that way to visit your husband's grave, each time having to accept in silence the rejection of his family.

You know I was really surprised when you told me that your husband had died of AIDS, contracted by drug abuse. That bus ride was really something else. We boarded at El Paso, and got off at Miami – during that time I glimpsed a slice of American life. It began with a story, which was very moving. It was shared with me in private, two black woman talking quietly together. I felt deeply for and with you, but I couldn't really understand how you could make such a pointless journey year in year out. I guess I am just not sentimental over death and all that, and I don't take any comfort at all from putting flowers on graves. Don't get me wrong, I can understand perfectly the reason why initially one would want to have a public display of mourning, and if the grave was nearby, yes, the odd flower at significant times would be a good token of remembrance. But to make a bus journey of three days each way, sometimes twice a year – suggests more than the need to mourn. Perhaps I am wrong, just don't get upset if I say anything out of the way. I don't mean to cause you any more pain.

What was the rest of your journey like? Ours was quite uneventful until we reached Florida, when a guy got on the bus. I think he would be called in American terms an "Anglo" or a WASP. He was married to a Latino from Central America. There is nothing, but anything, I don't know about that guy, his wife and his four children. He just held forth non-stop. The first thing we heard was how, as a Gringo, he was always being mistaken for the baby-sitter. He then had to explain this by telling us that he was married to a Latino, which he then had to explain, by regaling in long and minute detail the process of his meeting, courtship and marriage to his wife. After that we heard about the birth of each of his six children – the ones he baby-sat for. Then we had to hear about each child's experience of being bilingual. How after all these years of marriage to a Latino, he still couldn't speak Spanish very well, and so on and so on. There were bits of his story that did interest me, such as when he was talking about the kids' identity and their experience of racism at school.

The thing is that I found him such an unsympathetic person, that I listened with as much boredom to the bits that were of interest as I did to the rest. He was a lawyer, and I think his success must have rested on being able to "out-talk" everyone else. I wondered what his wife would feel if she knew that he spoke with such indiscretion about their family life. I felt sorry for her, but according to him she loved him devotedly, as he did her, so good luck to them and may she never be on the same bus as her husband!

Actually Florida was so unusual this time, it must have been our mode of transport – the bus. This long-distance ride took us down a very different route, in terms of our experience of the USA. Soon after the lawyer with verbal diarrhoea departed, a young African American mother and her daughter came on board. They were both very beautiful, but their relationship was ugly, *very* ugly. The mother's shouting and carrying on disturbed all the passengers (I wondered how our other bus driver, the one who put that man off for drinking, would have handled this problem). Then the situation deteriorated, and the mother started shaking and hitting the child, all the time shouting at her very loudly. I was very upset, I had been chatting with the mother and cultivating the little girl, hoping for the chance to give a little hint here and there; when and if an opening arose. The mother was speaking to the child of twenty-two months as though she were a grown woman, and seemed to have no idea of how to relate to a child.

Before an opportunity presented itself for me to say something, the bus driver told her that one of the other passengers, an elderly white woman, had left the bus to go and report a "child abuse incident" to the authorities. The mother and child had just re-boarded the bus, where the mother had just bought the contents of a small department store for her daughter. Her reaction to the news of the child abuse report made me very glad that I had held my peace. She became very abusive and angry towards the woman, and left us in no doubt that another, possibly violent incident would have occurred had the old white woman still been on the bus.

Things took another turn when she made me her confidante, explaining to me what a good mother she was and how much she loved her child, showing me with great pride the many purchases she had just made for her daughter. She was especially proud of the new Walkman, which meant that they now each had one. This meant that she could listen in peace to her music, without interference from the child. Of course, the baby would soon tire of this new toy, and would be punished for being ungrateful, as had happened earlier. It seemed to me that none of us did the right thing by the child: certainly not the mother. Neither me, nor the woman who had threatened to report the mother, had really helped. What would you have done if you'd still been on that bus? Would you have said something to that woman, or would you have kept quiet? She was quite a big woman, about your size. I have a feeling you would have handled it better than we did.

I hope you don't think that I am over-reacting in describing that incident as child abuse. Let me tell you something. I am not one of those people who can't tell the difference between giving a child a smack, and abuse. This mother was abusing her child, in a public place in front of thirty or forty other people – it made me wonder what she did when no one was looking.

That unfortunate and disturbing incident brought us almost to our final destination in downtown Miami. At the last but one stop, I bought a copy of the *Miami Herald*. The headlines screamed at me: SLAUGHTER OF THE INNOCENTS. Without reading any further, and still recovering from the earlier incident, I at once thought that it was "another American gone mad with a gun!". I read on, only to find that it was not an American but a Scotsman gone mad with a gun. Why it should make a difference I don't know, but it did. It may be that I do associate your country with a very high level of violence, where anything can happen. Scotland I think of in very different terms. Whatever the reasons, it was with a heavy heart, for the black child with the loving mother and the innocent white children of Dunblane gunned down by a frustrated paedophile and ex-scoutmaster.

That was journey's end, so far as the bus trip went, and I was glad of it.

Now that I have made contact, I hope you will feel able to write to me, and even if you are still visiting the grave and enduring the attentions of your hostile in-laws – what matters? So long as you find that it is worth your while, that is what counts. So go for it! Who knows, you may well meet your next husband on your next bus journey to your dead husband's grave! Have you seen the Spike Lee film about the group of brothers going on a bus journey to the million-man march? Do you think we black women should do one of our bus rides? It's a thought!

If you are still making that pilgrimage, I do hope that somewhere, some time, you will meet an AIDS-free man along the way! In the meantime, enjoy the bus rides. So long, Sister.

Letters to England

Letter number one

Dear Sister

Peace and love! That is how we used to greet each other, and also how we took our leave. "So long then, Sister, peace and love!"

Peace and love have been in very short supply for some time now. When did it start – with the killing of Walter, or did Grenada provide the turning point? Perhaps there was no turning point, just a gradual turning from peace and love to war and hate.

So what went wrong, then? How come the brothers ended up killing each other, and the sisters, strangers to each other, like you and me? What happened to the brotherhood, the sisterhood, the peace and the love? Was it all a sham? Was it always a sham? Was I the only one naive enough to believe in it?

You called me "sister" and I accepted you as such. You said "peace and love", and I replied in the same way, and meant it. I saw only what I wanted to see. So long then, Sister.

Peace and love!

Letter number two

Dear Sister,

We did turn up at the meeting place to give you a lift from Rotorua to wherever on the road you wanted to be dropped. We waited a while, but you did not show up. Mind you, it was raining very heavily, and we thought that you'd either got a lift direct from where you were staying, or had decided to wait for the rain to stop. I wasn't too bothered. I felt sure that with your blonde hair you wouldn't be stranded for very long. Along the way I have met many young English women/girls like you, travelling along hitching lifts, taking risks.

I still feel a bit sore about the one we teamed up with in Malawi. We had travelled together on the bus from Zambia and we ended up staying at the same place in Malawi. We agreed to share the cost of the taxi to the hotel, and paid up front, but by the next morning she had disappeared. I asked around and was told she had gone off with a man she met at dinner. I must say that her apparent recklessness and dishonesty amazed me. I guess that at heart I am still an old-fashioned Bajan girl – or it might simply be the legacy of the Plymouth Brethren.

I am writing to you from Pamplona in Northern Spain. Have you been here? I am attending a social work congress on, would you believe, "exclusion"! The congress itself provides the best demonstration of exclusion: non-white Europe has but one representative here – no prizes for guessing who that is. I will not bore you with any more about that.

What about you? Did you return to your butcher in Sydney or did you cut your losses and return to England? Whichever way I do hope you found the man of your dreams – or that the man in your life, the butcher, turned out to be the man of your dreams. I know you did not intend it to be so, but your account of your Sydney romance was truly amusing. It just occurred to me that you may have completely forgotten me, and be wondering who in the world this is writing to you from Pamplona in Spain, and going on about having waited for you in Rotorua. We were together on that day trip around the volcanoes, and towards the end of the day we got talking. I am sure there were no other black sisters on that trip, so if you think about it you are bound to remember me.

You were alone and I was alone, and I was interested in your views and experiences. I still almost laugh out loud when I recall your story of your affair with the butcher and your obsession, as a failed vegetarian, with the smell of meat. You actually asked me if you smelt of meat, and you did not seem very reassured by my answer – probably because I was holding back the laughter as I said, "No, I can't smell any meat." In fact the pervasive smell of hydrogen sulphide was so overwhelming that it blotted out the smell of not only meat but everything else. I had no idea, until you told me, that Sydney is, as you say, "the gay capital" of Australia, not that I had given the matter much thought.

What you said made sense to me. You told me that small-town Australia exports its gays to the big bad cities, and you quickly discovered that it would be very difficult for you to find a lover in Sydney. Every man you fancied turned out to be gay, so in the end you, a vegetarian, had to settle for a butcher. You changed and adapted and started eating meat again, but you remained very sensitive to the smell of it. So much so that you felt that it was driving you round the bend. The trip to New Zealand offered a welcome escape from the butcher, and I must say I know exactly what you mean about the smell of meat. This was something I myself was not prepared for when I stopped eating, but continued to cook meat for the rest of the family. Pork in particular was difficult, and I began to wonder whether this had something to do with the reasons why so many religions seem to prohibit the consumption of pork.

Unlike me, before meeting your butcher, you had been a committed vegetarian. You had very strong feelings about animal rights and the eating of meat; whereas I stopped eating meat for purely aesthetic reasons, because I simply did not like the way meat was produced and the taste of these products. Yet you were willing to abandon your strongly held views and principles, in your search for a man. The only man you could find who also wanted you was a butcher, so you became a meat eater. On such alliances is much human misery based. It seemed to me at the time that you were so uncomfortable with the whole situation that when I asked a very general question about how you found life in Australia, it all came pouring out. It was obvious to me that you are one of these women who feel incomplete without a man. Some women put the burden of making them "complete people" onto men. When they remain the same incomplete people, they then blame men for failing to achieve the impossible. This is just a general remark and is not intended to apply to you, but do you think that there is anything in it?

Your views and concerns about Australia were very personal, whereas mine were more general, political even. So much so that while I was there I avoided expressing any views at all. There was a lot of hype around Aboriginal land rights, and the papers were full of openly racist and alarmist stuff. Alongside this hysteria the most visible presence of the Aboriginals in the cities were drunk in the streets or propping up the bar. It was only in the Northern Territory that I got a glimpse of something else. Did you form any views on this or other social issues, or were you completely wrapped up in your bar work and your quest to find a suitable man?

Forgive me if I have intruded into this private world with my political preoccupation and concerns. I was feeling a bit self-indulgent, that's all. I could go on, but I feel that I've said enough. Perhaps the gulf between your preoccupation with finding a man and my concern with the tragedy of the Aboriginal is too wide? You tell me.

This is not a nice way to end a letter. It is an unsatisfactory ending, just like missing you at the meeting point and never knowing whether we were too early or you were too late or simply never turned up. Now I have got bogged down and can't think how to finish off, so I will just leave it at that.

Cheers for now.

Letter number three

Dear Sister,

Where are you this time, is it Zaire, Rwanda, or Burundi, or some other trouble spot? Which black woman or child are you rescuing, adopting fostering or feeding this time?

I have wondered what it must be like to be rescued/fostered/ adopted/sponsored/fed (strike out whichever does not apply) by you – as of now my chances of finding out are somewhat limited. I do not quite fit the profile of one of your victims, do I? Is that why you have not responded to my phone message or my fax? Or is it that we have both been travelling and have missed each other? I somehow doubt this simple explanation.

I know that there is a category of white woman who lives by "doing good" to black women and children, and can relate to black people only by means of their good works. Are you one of these? I did wonder when you told me about your four or was it five adopted African daughters, and that does not include the ones you have sponsored. I know that I am in no position to criticise, because I have never adopted, fostered, sponsored or otherwise rescued anyone at all.

My problem is with the motivation of people like yourself, because I can't help wondering how much real good is achieved by your "good" works. Okay, so you save some lives, but so what? In the end we all have to die, it is just a matter of sooner rather than later. If I could put myself in the place of one of those little black girls you are so keen to rescue – I would say, leave me alone! At least that is what I would say now.

Would you believe what happened just after I wrote that paragraph? Just my luck! A social worker asked me about my attitude towards Romanian orphans being adopted by British families. I heard myself say that, "If I were a Romanian orphan living in an orphanage, and a someone came along and said would you like to come and live with me in England, I would reply eagerly yes please!" I think that the social consequences of large-scale relocation of Romanian children to the UK and elsewhere in Western Europe, is vastly different from the plight of one little orphan girl. Of course, I realise that little orphan girl multiplied by thousands moves the issue from the individual to the social sphere. After I'd given my response to that social worker, I thought of you and the very different response I had just put into the mouth of the little African girl. I explained my different responses to the same situation in this way: I know you and I have formed an opinion of your values and attitudes, and this makes me tell that African child that she is better off where she is. It is not a knee-jerk reaction to trans-racial or trans-cultural adoptions in itself.

I know that you will find my attitude surprising and hurtful, for after all you are only trying to help. The way I see it, if one does not value and respect as full human beings the people who are the on the receiving end of one's good works, what is the use of all your good works? To be seen as an object, even to be an object of charity, is not a human state, and that is at the heart of my distrust of and discomfort with you and what you represent. If you sense a note of bitterness and anger in this letter, it is because there is bitterness and anger here. Not all of it is to do with you personally. I hope you can take what is yours and do what you like with it, and ignore the rest.

I think I've said enough.

Letter number four

Dear Sister,

I hope that by now you have begun to understand some of the reasons for my long silence. I do care about you, very much. I just could not take the pressure – I tried but I felt helpless – and you seemed intent on dragging me down too. I had no choice but to turn away from you. Just for a little while, I told myself, but a little while became a long while, and now it is so many years since we've been in touch.

Last summer I was passing through your area, and somehow found myself at your door. Your car was outside, so I knew you were at home; but I just sat in *my* car and thought about you and me. Then I drove away. Did you see me? Did I ring the bell? Are you all right now? Have you found someone else to dump on? Or perhaps you are all sorted and don't require anyone to dump on any more. I really hope that things have worked out and that you are once again the composed middle-class English housewife that you were when we first met. If I am right, then my only regret is that I am no longer a part of your life, and if I am wrong then I have no regrets.

I did try to tell you, even as a social worker, I was not much good with substance abusers. My inclination is that grown people should be able to have what they want by way of drink or drugs, but they must be prepared to cope with the consequences. The problem is that very few people are so prepared, and when things get out of control they want someone else to pick up the pieces. I guess that is when I ask to be excused.

You were my first real friend when I first came to live in England, my first "true, true" friend as we say in Barbados. You and I never went in for all this sentimental stuff, all this kissing and hugging so much on display these days. We talked a lot, argued, disagreed. I can remember laughing when I heard that you had described me to someone as your "intellectual friend". What about the time you cried and cried? I did hold you then. And you promised to kick the habit, and you did, for a little while. Later I grew to resent the fact that you never showed any care for me, and the effect of what was happening to you on me. It was very disturbing and worrying for me. But it was as if I had become your dumping ground, with no feelings of my own, or that is how it seemed to me. We got bogged down, you and I.

I can hope only that this letter will help you to understand the reason I could not go on being your friend. It was all too difficult, too painful, too overwhelming. I started to feel out of my depth, helpless, completely useless. So I left. That's it.

How shall I sign myself? Your former friend – will that do?

Letters to India

Letter number one

Dear Bengali Sister,

How is my ex-Naxalite sister doing these days? How do you manage to reconcile the doctrines of Ramakrishna with the teachings of Marx? Or have you abandoned the one for the other? From where I stand, all religious beliefs seem remarkably similar and equally bankrupt. To be honest I know that you have changed faiths, and I was not all that surprised to hear it. The only indication I saw of your previous allegiance was your protection of the servants from the police search. You put me on the spot when you said that if I allowed the servants to be searched then you and your husband would also have to be searched. But I knew that whatever happened, whoever was searched or not searched, I would never see my bag again. That's practical equality for you!

After all this time I thought you might like to know that I have completely recovered from the theft of my bag during my visit to your home. Peter said that I mourned the loss of my computer as though it were a person, but I eventually recovered most of the information and managed to do without the rest. I do not think that it was only the loss of the computer and the data it contained that I was mourning. I had lost a lot more than that. I felt totally exposed and betrayed. I had felt very relaxed and comfortable in your house, totally unprepared for the invasion of this apparently safe and well defended space. As I mentioned to another friend in a recent letter, being stolen from is not a new experience for me. So I would not normally be fazed by something like that. It was the manner of the theft and the way the whole thing was dealt with that threw me.

Why did the police want to know the secret code for the computer? How did the thief gain access to the room without the dog barking? When my youthful companion and I arrived at your apartment, the dog barked and barked. I think the reason why the dog did not bark was that he knew the thief; there is no other explanation. I don't know why I am going on about this, but it seems that I have not put this matter behind me as completely as I had thought. I will have to continue working on it.

I suppose you are wondering why I have not written for such a long time. It is nothing to do with the theft. It was your last letter. What I do find difficult is responding to your very simplistic classification of people as "Western" as being by definition more "relaxed" about morals, more materialistic and more accepting of, well, of anything really. Whereas you in the "East" are more spiritual, more demanding of high moral standards, less materialistic etc. When I turned up at your house in the company of a young man, you could not see that I was simply accepting his kindness in showing me the way to your house. You believed your cook when she told you that she had seen us holding hands! When I said that I don't go around holding young men's hands, you explained to me that "you in the West think nothing of holding hands". There was nothing more I could say. I knew perfectly well that the young man was innocent, that he could not have gained access to your house without alerting the dogs, and I could only speculate as to why your cook would make up such a story. But you repeated the story as if you believed it, and you clung to the idea that the young man was the thief. I mention this incident to show why I have such difficulty in understanding and relating to your view of what happened that day. I do have a problem with the way you see the world, and this problem goes far beyond the unfortunate theft of my bag in your house in Calcutta.

You are always going on about the materialistic West, and the spiritual East. Ignoring the fact poverty makes people more materialistic, in the sense that they are more willing to do very gross things for very little money. Take for example child beggars. It is alleged that some poor people in India deliberately mutilate their children in order to make them more effective beggars. I have no idea of the earnings of the mutilated as against non-mutilated beggar-child, but let us guess at 10p (£1 equals 100p). I do not believe that child mutilation would be justified even if it brought in the lakhs of rupees or thousands of pounds. But if it did, at least it would make economic sense, whereas the mindless cruelty of child mutilation achieves very little in monetary terms, and is morally reprehensible. I guess an equivalent comparison would be with parents in the West who prostitute their children, but as I am sure you know, there are parents in the East who do this too. There is no monopoly on badness.

The end result of all this is that materialism triumphs in the East as much as it does in the West. The amount and scale of corruption throughout the world clearly demonstrates this. Eastern societies are as prone to corruption as Western, and for me this exemplifies the supremacy of materialism in contemporary Eastern society. I hope you can see the point I am trying to make. All societies have their "holy people", their ascetics who reject materialism, and I know this to be the traditional way of the East. But it is not the way of the contemporary East. At the level of the market, materialism and capitalism unify both East and West. I hope you can bear with my preaching. I felt that it was time I gave you a taste of your own medicine!

As a practitioner of yoga I am on the debit side of Eastern spiritualism and philosophy. I am not arguing about or trying to deny historical truths, but what I find difficult is the way that some people, in this case you, behave as though those historical truths apply with equal force today. The last time I had this argument was in the English Lake District, when I went on a walking/yoga week. You should have heard these Western devotees go on about the superiority of the Eastern, in this case Indian way of life. I listened bemused and fascinated, until I could not keep quiet any longer, and asked why India had so many poor people, and why Calcutta is such a hellhole if India has the answer to life, the universe and everything. They thought me a bit of a maverick, so that was that. Interesting.

How do you now respond to the problem of poverty and corruption in India? Time was when your reaction was violent change, revolution no less. Now what is the current path to truth and enlightenment? Have you returned to the faith, and see it as the destiny of the beggar child to be mutilated and eventually die of her injures, to be reborn later, hopefully in slightly improved circumstances? I can't accept that these are our only real choices, metaphysics or murder, Naxalites or Ramakrishna, Ghandi and Martin Luther King, or the Rev Farakhan. You are not alone in your division of the world into such simple categories, then to associate everyone in these categories with the values and attitudes you think go with the geographical areas of the world in which they were born or live. To me this is so simplistic and superficial that it is meaningless.

I trust that I have made my point. Are we still friends! If the truth is known, I think that we are both at the stage of looking for fixed points of reference, something to hold on to. Your division of the world into East equates to good, West to bad, does give you a point of reference, and makes your world secure. And me? I have found no equivalent refuge, no certainties, only doubts and disappointments.

Well, I think I have covered all the outstanding matters. I await your reply with interest.

Letter number two

Dear Malayalam Sister,

I have often thought of you and wondered where you are and what you are doing. I remember when you came to the hostel from your village in Kerala, as innocent as a person could be, and trusting too, a terrible combination, which meant that you were sure to be exploited in the wicked city of Calcutta. And you were.

So many memories crowd my mind: lice, thousands, millions of lice, clinging to your skull, and you crying as you were shorn of your beautiful long black hair. Your demanding question: "When can I have a boyfriend?" As if a boyfriend was the latest brand of yoghurt. Then there was the matter of your "guardian", the man of moral and religious stature who was appointed by your parents to look after you. He certainly did. He told you that the Lord had sent you so that he could lie with a woman of his own people and his own race. And he did. He obviously saw it as part of his pastoral role to have sexual relations with you. And you? I know that you enjoyed the attention and the sex. That whole episode certainly started you on a more, shall we say, interesting lifestyle, and you very soon found out all there was to be known about "boyfriends".

It was all just a phase, and passed as such phases do; but if you sent your daughter to college in Calcutta, I hope you did not appoint a priest as her guardian. I still have your photo.

The trouble is it is not a very good one, being shiny because of the light Indian photographers use to dilute skin colour, and your look is quite severe. I still have not yet visited Kerala, but I hope to soon. A friend of mine is planning to buy or build a beach house there and when he does I will be among the first visitors. I will try to find you, always supposing you are there, though you may still be in Calcutta. I don't think I could find you in Calcutta. Maybe I should start my search at the hostel in Mission Row? I found it very difficult to remain in that area for very long when I visited Dalhousie Square in 1993. Maybe I should try to forget about ever finding you, and continue to live with my memories.

It was funny how you clung on to me. You sort of made me your very special friend right from the start. I suppose the American would call it being a "mentor". How awful! But you did seem to think that I was the font of all knowledge. Want to know something? Want a boyfriend? Just ask Maureen! I don't know why a girl from a village in Kerala, South India, should have related in this way to a young woman from a village in Barbados, but that is how it was, wasn't it?

With fond memories, and best wishes.

As ever, your friend.

Letter to Nagaland

Dear Sister,

It is so many years since I have thought of you and my other Naga sisters and friends. Two things have happened to bring you back into my thoughts and feelings. In 1992 I went back to India. I visited Calcutta and went to the Mission Row Christian girls' hostel. I was literally overwhelmed by memories, but the good thing was that the whole place had changed so much that I had great difficulty actually locating it. The experience took on a rather dream-like quality as I wandered around looking at buildings and trying to place them in my mind. I could not go there and revisit those memories without thinking of you.

The second thing, which happened more recently, was a documentary on the Discovery channel about the Nagas. I did not recognise you or any of the other Naga people I knew in Calcutta as the Nagas shown in this documentary. The film painted a picture of wild and fierce headhunters, who lived in the hills between Burma and Assam, and who engaged in constant battles, and when not fighting each other fought the Indian government. I found out during my visit to India in 1992 that your war with India is still going on. The film made no attempt to give the history or background to the struggle of the Naga people. Had I not been fortunate enough to know you I would have been left with a distorted, romanticised picture of a savage, fierce hill tribe.

As a black woman I am very aware of the role of anthropologists in portraying a distorted and patronising picture of so-called primitive people and culture – even to the point of direct lies. Some American journalist is supposed to have said: "The more I read what anthropologists write about New York the less I believe what they say about New Guinea." And that about sums it up, but it is only when they operate on home ground that their assumptions can be challenged and their frauds uncovered. I am sure that there are some good, i.e. honest anthropologists. I listen to radio a lot, and some time ago I heard a radio play about an anthropologist in Nagaland. Yes, after years of hearing nothing about you and your country, within a matter of months I've watched a TV film and listened to a radio play about the Nagas. The latter was about a woman who was known as "the queen of the Nagas". She was an English woman called Ursula Graham Bower, and she was an anthropologist who apparently led your people into battle against the Japanese, and won! Have you ever heard of her? I'd be interested to hear your views, though I suspect they will be very different from what the play would lead us to expect.

I was really sorry to learn that your war is still going on, and in fact it was a revelation to me how many small wars there are in India. Are you still actively involved, or have you moved on? Are you still so religious? You were always praying. My mother was of the same mind, for she too was always praying.

Apart from the TV documentary, there was another thing that brought you and the Naga problems to mind, a film called *At Play in the Fields of the Lord*. It was about the efforts of a group of white American missionaries to bring Christianity to Indians living in the jungle of South America. It was not really similar to the Naga situation, except that as I recall it was white American Baptists who brought Christianity to you. In spite of accepting their religion so completely, you seem to hate them and what they stood for. I really found your attitude hard to understand, and I still do. I can remember arguing with you about it, but we never got anywhere, did we? Anthropologists and such "experts" would never credit the Naga people with such complex personalities, as you must be made to fit the role of noble savage. All this made me quite nostalgic, plus I found some photos from our days at the Mission Row young women's Christian hostel. There are three of us in these photos, with myself in the middle and you and another Naga sister on either side. We have our arms around each other and we are laughing, or trying not to laugh! Happy days!

In fact, not so happy days. You had the shadow of the Naga-India war over you. And me? I had two more years in Calcutta. I did not last long at the hostel after you left. I was thrown out, asked to leave, and this in a way led eventually to my marriage to Peter. Peter took me. You can imagine the stir that caused among the British in Calcutta! We had to keep very quiet about it, and I soon found proper lodgings as a paying-guest with a Bengali family. At the time my friends at the hostel thought that I'd been thrown out for breaking the ten o'clock curfew. I felt unable to tell either my Indian or Anglo-Indian friends what had really happened.

The real truth is that I was asked to leave because I'd refused to condone the superintendent in her use of the word "niggers". It was the night of the earthquake. She and I were alone in her office, and she used the "n" word to refer to the Indian residents. We had both dismissed the quake as nothing, then she laughed and said, referring to the Indians: "The niggers will be scared out of their wits!" I was amazed and without thinking said something like: "I don't know whom you mean. I don't use that word to describe anyone." She looked daggers at me, and told me to leave her room at once. After that night she never spoke directly to me again. Within a matter of weeks, for no reason that I could fathom, I was told that I was no longer a suitable resident for the hostel. I wrote to the vicar or whatever he was, trying to explain what had happened and asking him to intervene. I did not want to leave the hostel, and I was afraid of – of what I don't know – but I'd become used to the hostel. Anyhow, the vicar or whatever was an Anglo-Indian himself, and almost certainly shared the same views as the superintendent, so no hope there. Out I went.

Writing to you about it now, it seems incredible that I, a black Caribbean woman, could be victimised in India by an Anglo-Indian woman for refusing to be associated with a racial slur, against Indians. And that this racial slur should be expressed by use of the word "nigger", a word that was invented by white Americans, to insult and dehumanise the black race. The irony is that, as you know, during this time and indeed throughout all my three years in India, I was subjected to the most blatant, crude racial prejudice and hostility that I have ever experienced. Indian society is not kind to blackness. I did not think about any of this when I responded to the superintendent that night, my response was purely automatic. And to this day I still feel that if I had to be expelled from that hostel, it couldn't have been for a better reason.

Thanks for returning the money I lent you. I know I'm a bit late (thirty-two years, almost) but it is always worth saying thanks. I bet you had no idea that the 250 rupees I lent you was the sum total of all my savings at the time. Well it was, and do you know I was asked – I won't say by whom – whether I'd got a receipt from you. I simply replied that such formalities were unnecessary between sisters. If you could pay you would, and if you couldn't that would be the end of the story. I couldn't see how a receipt was relevant to our situation. It was the general opinion at the hostel that I had seen the last of that money. There was all sorts of speculation: You would either be killed before you reached home, or once you got home you would forget about the money. You had more important things to do (like winning a war). It was also said that even if you managed to get the money yourself, you would not be able to get it to me in Calcutta. Any messenger entrusted with 250 rupees would almost certainly take the money and run! In 1963 that was worth about £20, but by the talk given to the matter it might easily have been £250! So, when your brother turned up at the hostel with a packet of crumpled, dirty rupee notes and a message from you, I was delighted that we had proved them wrong!

I have waited all these years to tell you this, and I can hope only that the reading of it gives you as much pleasure as the writing of it has given me. I do hope that you have found peace and contentment. If not, then I hope that at least you are convinced that the path you took and the journey you made have been worthwhile.

Please remember me to all my Naga friends and sisters.

Letter to Africa

Dear Sister,

I will have to discipline myself in writing this letter; otherwise it will become a mini-book in itself, or at least the written equivalent of one of our all-night talking sessions.

There are so many things I want to talk to you about that I don't know where to begin. Have you been down south recently? Remember the time we bussed and hitch-hiked to South Africa to see your husband? I had to go to Africa in order to learn how to hitch-hike. I don't think your husband quite approved of me. I always felt a bit uncomfortable around him somehow, and kept getting negative vibes. I think that it started after you told him that I wanted to interview him about his experience of polygamy. The truth was that it was you who really wanted to know which of his wives he preferred. We looked in vain through the house for any sign of another woman, let alone another wife. He seemed to be meticulous in arranging it to reflect the marriage of the wife visiting. Remember how we both laughed as we speculated about his lives with the others! You seemed to approach the whole matter with a pragmatism that I admired then. But now I wonder how real your pragmatism really was.

I don't know how I got started on that topic, except that whenever we got together we always ended on these or similar subjects. Has our other sister found a husband yet? It seems strange to me that you should have chosen to become a second wife, even though you knew that your sister had left her marriage when she found out that a second wife had no legal status in your country. I have recently written to another English sister about the way some women cannot live without a man; in Africa it seems to me that life can become almost intolerable for a woman without a husband. And it is not always a question of choice: a sister from the Caribbean married an African man and went to live in his country, but unfortunately he died quite early on in the marriage. Within a few days his brother turned up at the matrimonial home to claim both the home and the wife. She had other ideas and she barricaded herself inside the house and stayed there till he left. A long struggle followed, and in the end she sold up and escaped to the USA, or somewhere where she felt she was safe from the requirement to accept her brother-in-law as a replacement husband.

I have been reading a book called *Divided Sisters*, all about the problems that black and white American women face in trying to maintain their friendships. I didn't relate much to it in those terms, but thinking of you and of our friendship, and of my friendship with many African sisters, I find this description more relevant. We are close, you and I, but at the same time we are far apart. We are sisters divided by history and culture, but we are together in friendship. We, you and I, laughed and joked at your husband's expense about his other wives, but when all is said and done you are one of these wives. I saw both the laughter and the pain come together in you, in your face and in your eyes. At that time it seemed to me that we, you and I, were truly the "divided sisters", separated by language and culture.

I mention this not as a complaint about the limitations of our friendship, which all relationships have (I could almost say need). The important thing is to know and accept the limits, whatever they are. When one of my African sisters greeted my return to her country with the words "welcome home" I felt a very warm glow. I have since come to accept that she had her own reasons for welcoming me in this way, and she must have known how much such a greeting would mean to me. She got what she wanted, and depending on my mood I think "good luck to her, and more fool me", or with less bitterness "it was a fair exchange". I can see now that right from the beginning she had certain expectations to do with the friendship, whereas I liked her and was simply interested in her. I think you know what I am talking about, and if you do not know I am sure you can guess.

Let me tell you about something completely different – about one of my African walks. This was the time I walked to the well with another sister in another African country. We had been at a conference together, and afterwards she invited me to visit her village. When we got there she changed completely from the sophisticated urban professional into the African daughter of the soil, even volunteering to go to the well to fetch water. I was told to sit and wait in the house while she went, but I said that I would enjoy the walk, and so I was allowed to go with her. It was hot, and it was hard work getting the hand-pump to work, but we managed to fill the bucket. Although she was much younger than I, the sister was not very strong, for as you know I go to the gym and keep reasonably fit. Of the two of us I was better placed to carry the water, but she would have none of it. So she struggled back, lugging the water and walking slowly and painfully in the extreme heat. The next day as we were driving back to town I mentioned in passing that I was no stranger to the art of water-carrying, and that it had been one of my jobs as a child growing up in Barbados to fetch water from the standpipe. I don't think she believed me.

This reminds me of another African sister who, just to impress me, I suppose, invented a rich background for herself. What she had not anticipated was that another colleague would, during a visit to a housing project, point out the house in which she grew up and that went with her father's job – policeman, not ambassador. I have no idea why she felt the need to create this fiction, and I could not see that there was anything to gain from telling her that I knew the truth. I would have liked to tell her that my father was also a policeman, and I am not ashamed of it – also that unlike her father, my father's job didn't bring a house, or even a shack with it.

You can see, can't you, that there is a whole range of tensions between my African sisters and me. Tensions that I sometimes find challenging and exciting, and at other times very confusing and therefore very stressful. I think it has to do with how we see each other and the preconceived ideas and notions we have of each other. I think that you are one, probably the only one, that I have not experienced this with. We have always been able to communicate without misunderstandings and without these tensions, at least as far as I am aware. I met an African sister in Australia, in Canberra at the national library café. We just happened to sit close by and started talking. I think I asked her if she was a student. We spent the rest of the day together, and found out that we shared quite a few acquaintances from her days as a student in London. The tension came about as a result of the story I told her of our visit to her country.

To cut a long story short I had to pay a bribe to the health official because Peter did not have a cholera vaccination certificate. She became really angry and tore a strip off me, telling me that things will never improve if people like me went around encouraging corruption by paying bribes. I explained the difficulties we were facing, the trouble we had experienced getting to the border, hitching lifts off virtually anything that moved, and that we could not face the prospect of a return journey. She would not accept this and insisted that we should have called his bluff. In her view there was "no way" he could have sent us back. I defended my actions and explained that we had not been in a position to know that we couldn't have been sent back. I did not want to upset the sister any more by telling her that everyone, including the local guys we were travelling with on the oil tanker, all paid bribes. Local people paid a lot less than foreigners. That sister and I ended up spending the rest of the afternoon together, and we still keep in touch, but the matter of the bribes was never really settled.

I want to tell you one last thing before I close this letter, as I know you will enjoy this and have a laugh. This sister and I were talking "waiting to exhale" style about her traumatic divorce, and associated matters. She said she didn't miss the sex part at all, and then told me of this friend of hers who had been divorced after twenty-eight years of marriage. She, my friend, asked this other sister how she was getting along without a man. The other woman replied that she was just fine, and all not having a husband meant was "no more semen running down my leg!", her years of marriage summed up as sexual slavery. I still don't know why my friend and I both found this statement so very funny, but whenever we were alone we would think of these words and without saying anything would laugh and laugh! We also wondered what the poor man would do if he knew how his ex-wife had described those years of marriage. I know that if you'd been there you would have found it funny too, funny and sad both at the same time.

Have you been to any pre-wedding parties lately? Are things under control now or are the husbands and prospective husbands still worried about the happenings at these parties? I was told that some husbands were stopping their wives going to these parties for fear that they would turn into permanent lesbians. Did you hear anything about that? It seems that your African men, in spite of their traditional power and control of their women, are just as insecure as all the other men in the world are.

I said from the start that I would have to be very disciplined about this letter, and I have failed. Look at how it has gone on and on: things just kept coming up. Anyhow, although I could continue, I feel I must leave it at that.

Until the next time, then.

Letter to South America

Querida hermana,

I thought I would make a little effort to address you in Spanish, but for the time being, that is my limit. One day I hope to be able to write a letter completely in Spanish, but that is still some way off.

I am really very insecure about my Spanish, but I am hanging on in there, as the Americans say, hoping that one day it will all come together. Thanks for the help and encouragement you gave me, it really helped, especially as we had so many interests in common, literature, politics, minority rights and women's issues. I am now into Latin American literature, even managing to read some of it in the original Spanish. *El Beso de la Mujer Araña* by Manuel Puig was the most unusual book I have read for a long time. The reader more or less joins these two men in their prison cell in Argentina, listens to their conversations and observes their lives as the story unfolds. The play of the book was on in San José when I was there in December 1996, but I was in Quepos and by the time I returned to San José it had ended. I am right now struggling with *Uno se Vuelve Loco* by Daniel Múgica. The story couldn't be more different from the Puig one. It revolves round this man called Max, who is trying to find the reason for the death of his girlfriend Gloria. He is really searching for the meaning of life, or at least the meaning of contemporary Spanish low-life. I say that I am "struggling" with it, but I am quite enjoying reading it, even though it is hard work at times, and very slow.

You may wonder why, if I am into Latin American literature, I am reading Múgica, who is a Spaniard. Well, I was attracted by the title, that's all. I am interested in Latin American writers for the simple reason that there is a great big gap in my knowledge of that place. My head is full of stuff about Europe, sometimes more so than I realise. Let me tell you a story. It was September 1995. I was in Aachen, in Northern Germany. I found myself with some spare time and my German colleague suggested that I visit the cathedral. My response was to ask the way to the spa. I was given directions and a map and headed off to for a relaxing afternoon in the spa. But somehow I found myself at the cathedral. Some people might say it was the Lord's will, but I know that I am not very good at map-reading.

As I was at the cathedral I decided that I might as well have a look around. It was indeed spectacular, a truly magnificent building. I wandered around looking at this and that, soaking up the atmosphere, along with all the other visitors. Then, as I read the inscriptions, I slowly began to realise that I already knew quite a bit about Aachen cathedral. There followed much rewinding of mental tapes. The experience took on an almost dreamlike quality, until the memories surfaced: Charlemagne – Loreto College, 1963 – medieval European history – lecturer Mother Joseph Michael. We even did little drawings in a brave effort to understand the architecture. Later on in the spa, which was quite near the cathedral, I reflected on my earlier experience in these terms: there I was a Bajan woman, standing in a German cathedral, recalling my studies in European history undertaken in Calcutta, India. And I knew that I could never have such an experience in Africa or Latin America. You see what I mean about big gaps?

Religion! If only it was limited to beautiful buildings. I have tried to get hold of *At Play in the Fields of the Lord*, but no luck; it seems to be out of print. I will keep chasing it. I have read *La Cultura Guajira se Extingue*, and I keep dipping into it. I also keep returning to what I still think of as *The Anancy Stories*, but what in Latin America you call *Cuentos Picarescos*. Thank you so much for these two books, one a sociology text on the imminent extinction of the Indian culture in South America, and the other a collection of children's stories – a perfect choice. There is another book I want to tell you about, *Brazil* by John Updike. It is about this poor little rich girl who defies her family and goes off with a boy from the slums. Unlike your own story, this one does not have a happy ending.

I've just (November 1996) returned from Spain, Pamplona to be exact. Now that I am a bit more educated about Latin America, and the history of Spanish colonialism, I am having big problems associating the Spain of today with the Spain of the conquistadors. Even more problems than I have in associating the Britain of today with the British empire of yesterday. Let me try to show you what I mean, with this extract from one of my Spanish courses. I do not know the origin, but I am sure such ideas will be very familiar to you.

> Y del descubrimiento y conquista de América hay un hecho que ha sumido en la perplejidad a cuantos lo han estudiado: el arrojo y la temeridad de los conquistadores. Debemos tener en cuenta a que Cortés acabo con el imperio de Moctezuma con un ejército de seiscientos soldados y que Pizarro, para someter a los Incas, conto solo con ciento ochenta hombres... .

> University of Bournemouth: Department of International Communications (1995), *Spanish Self-Learning Course Stage Four*, Bournemouth, UK

I will try to overcome timidity, and lack of confidence about Spanish, and give a rough translation of the above. Please feel free to correct it for me when you reply. Here goes:

> The discovery and conquest of America is something that has perplexed everyone who has studied it: the pride and courage of the conquistadors. We have to tell about how Cortés finished off the Moctezuma empire with an army of 700 soldiers and how Pizarro subdued the Incas with only 800 men... .

How did he do it? Just think of it, Cortés finishing off the Moctezuma empire with only 600 soldiers, and Pizarro the Inca empire with just 800! And the most we have to worry about Spain these days is whether we'll be robbed in Barcelona or mugged in Madrid. When I listen to Latin American radio or read the newspapers I am amazed to find how topical these historical issues are. There is one article that I clipped out and have read and re-read several times. It is from a Gautemalan newspaper and is a feature article by a woman journalist, Carolina Vásquez Araya. In it she discusses a film by Werner Herzog, *Aguirre, la Ira de Dios,* which tells the story of the exploits of Pizarro in his search for El Dorado. I will try to improve my Spanish even more with a quotation from the opening paragraph of Araya's piece:

> En su pelicula 'Aguirre, la ira de Dios', el productor alemán Werner Herzog ensan con aguda ironia los extremos del vicio

y crueldad a los que condujo la ambicion a los primeros conquistadores del continte americano.

Shall I try another translation? Why not! Here I go again:

In his film *Aguirre, la Ira de Dios*, the German producer Werner Herzog shows with rich irony the extremes of vice and cruelty that directed the ambitions of the first conquistadors of the continent of America.

Herzog's film did not paint an heroic picture of Pizarro. Nor did Carolina Araya in her article contest the accuracy of the film. She argued instead that the conquistadors were no different from other men of that time. Interestingly she attributes many of the social problems in present-day Guatemala to the way in which the country was originally conquered by the Spaniards, and the way the Indian people were deprived of their land and of their religions, and were forced into Catholicism and slavery. Travelling through Central America and Mexico, I was surprised at how raw such matters are, and how open and festering are the wounds they caused. I am learning fast. The big gap in my knowledge is slowly becoming less so.

Back to the literature. I've recently been reading about Genaro Estrada, and having visited Mexico, I can see why he wanted to expose and satirise the Mexican obsession for everything colonial. Genaro poked fun at the colonial Mexican's eagerness to copy Spanish ways in everything: art, architecture, literature and life itself. What about Estrada's work: are you familiar with any of it? I am thinking in particular of *Pero Galín*. Do let me know what you think of it. I had a very bad experience in Mexico. I do not have a very high opinion of the place, or of the descendants of the conquistadors – especially the ones who pretend to be "mestizos" but spend their time imitating everything Spanish. The true mestizo, like Gabriel Márquez, whose values identify them as such – those are my brothers, even as you are my sister, ¿verdad?

I will sign off here, and I will continue working on my Spanish. I am even trying to do the grammar, would you believe! As promised, one day you will have the doubtful pleasure of receiving from me a letter written in Spanish. And I hope that you will take some pride in knowing that you contributed towards improving my Spanish and lessening the gap in my knowledge of the history and culture of our region. Nice.

In the meantime, this will have to do, so "hasta la vista, y que la vaya bien!"

Letter to Australia

Dear Sister,

How are things down under? I saw the scenes from the Threbor disaster on the TV; it looked very different from when I was there. At that time it did not look like landslide country to me. Ignorance is bliss. So, you see, when it comes down to it nowhere is really safe. Did I ever tell you about my other Ozzie friend, who was too scared to travel on the bus to Bhutan? I've had quite a collection of odd Ozzie friends or acquaintances over the years, real characters all of them. I must tell you about them some time.

My reason for writing at this time is to tell you that I have checked on the commission report on Aboriginal children, which is called "Bringing them home", and costs £59. It is enormous, so I will wait and consult the library as soon as one becomes available. Do you think that Australia should declare a "day of shame", and that the government should apologise to the Aboriginals for the genocide that was attempted on them? Personally I can't see what good it would do, when the values and attitudes of white Australia towards the Aboriginals remain unchanged. So many of your fellow white Australians seem to think that it is perfectly reasonable to make the most crude racist remarks about Aboriginals. In Canberra I inquired of my host, who at the time was reading the newspaper: "Any interesting news today?" He replied: "Nothing much. Except that they are giving the whole damn country to the blacks." He obviously saw nothing wrong in talking like this to me.

I do try to keep up with the news. From time to time I even succeed in getting Radio Australia on my short-wave radio. I see that racism and anti-Asian feelings are taking a hold both in your country and in New Zealand. Well, you can be sure of one thing, clocks cannot be turned back. Australia was never "one nation". Ask the Aboriginals; ask Peter Carey. What do you think of Mrs Pauline Hanson? What is new about Mrs Hanson that's what I want to know? I know that she wants to keep Asians out of Australia, but has she any other plans – for example another go at the "assimilation" of the Aboriginal?

What about if the Aboriginals in Australia, and the Maori in New Zealand, send all the descendants of the settlers back to Europe? On the organised hikes, which I did in Australia, the guide would always point out foreign species and tell us of the harm these imported plants and animals were doing, attacking and killing off the native species. I know they are trying get rid of the feral horses and feral cats, and to eradicate certain species of imported plants. Interestingly these wardens never said a word about the imported human population and the harm they have done to the original human, animal and plant life. I wonder why?

This was meant to be a short note, but there is just one thing I must mention before signing off. I see your High Court has ruled that Aboriginal children, taken from their parents by past Australian governments under assimilation law, cannot sue for compensation, because the Australian government and the Northern Territory had acted "in accordance with laws in place at the time". I can't quite see the point of a "day of shame" or of apologies, if those sinned against have no right under law to seek redress for such appalling crimes. So I'm afraid that even if I had £59 to waste I would not buy that report. I hope I have not bored you too much, I know you are not really much of a political animal but I keep hoping that you may yet opt to be part of the solution, rather than remaining part of the problem.

No worries, mate!

Letter to Mexico

Dear Sister,

I am working on my Spanish but it is still not up to letter-writing standard. In fact I am not sure that my English is good enough to meet the demands of this letter, but I will try. I think you will understand what I mean by that when you read what else I have to say.

Of all the places I have visited, Mexico left me the most confused and angry. Next to Barbados, Mexico seems to me to be the most pretentious and hypocritical society on earth, and it is also extremely corrupt, which Barbados is not – not "extremely". Maybe just a bit here and there. You appeared to welcome me into your home – "mi casa es su casa", you said – then you charged us more than we had paid in the four-star hotel that we'd left in order to go local! I tried, in a rather feeble way, to query the amount. But it was very difficult; for after all I was still a guest in your home. And before my very eyes you changed into one of those street traders who are always trying to sell something.

109

With your "Maureeen, I give you good price, Maureeen". Like hell you did! You shouldn't leave notes by the telephone – my spoken Spanish may not be up to much, but I can read it very well indeed, especially when I see my name written down. I still have one of those pathetic, almost illiterate notes I wrote to you in Spanish, trying to find out exactly how much you were charging us. All I got from you was, "Don't worry, Maureeeen... don't worry."

It was the same with everything about you, saying one thing and meaning another. You said, quoting Márquez, though I didn't know this at the time, "I am a mestizo." But there was nothing to suggest anything but the most tentative connection between you and your Indian "ancestry". What makes you a mestizo? When a man like Márquez makes a statement like that he is simply underlining the essence of his life, and the values that have informed them. When you say it, you are simply mouthing empty words.

You have become for me the symbol of Mexico. In the matter of racism, for example, no Mexican will admit that racism exists in Mexico. It is only the USA, that giant to the north, that is racist and discriminates against poor Mexicans, people just trying to walk across the border to earn a living. Yes, the USA *is* a racist society, so, in my experience, is Mexico. Would you be an Indian in Mexico today, or at any time in the past 400 years? Mexico is full of pretentious nonsense, including Mexican society providing a living example of how all the races on earth can live together. Did you hear about the incident concerning Microsoft and some computer software, which they produced for the Mexican market? The software shows a Mexican wearing broad-brimmed hat and cowboy shoes. These caricatures of the Mexican people caused great offence. Bill Gates himself apologised, and at great expense agreed to have the whole thing redone. Well, sister, I have news for you. I have in my possession a children's book that bought in Mexico. This book was written, printed and published in Mexico. In the section "People of the World" the picture of a Mexican is of a person wearing a broad-brimmed hat and cowboy boots. So what has Bill Gates got to apologise for? You tell me.

When the story broke I thought of faxing this page to Bill Gates, but I really couldn't be bothered. But you can pass it on to him if you wish. When I first saw these pictures I thought nothing of the way the Mexican was shown, because it was the picture of the black person that I found offensive. I even thought of complaining to the publishers, but we were still on the road and I put it to the back of my mind. Then I heard the report of the Microsoft incident on the BBC World Service.

My own direct experience of racism in Mexico was the incident that occurred at your house, which you never apologised for. I was refused entry by a young woman who barred my way, and would not accept that I was staying with you. I pushed her aside and walked in – and that was before I knew how much over the odds we were paying. Your son did apologise and said that the woman, who worked in his office, had been trained to act in this way for security reasons. I wondered how many black women there were in Mexico City breaking into people's houses. It was clear to me that this woman could not accept that someone like me, a black woman, could be a guest in your house.

Although it was annoying at the time, and still is when I think of it, I know that my experience of racism in Mexico is nothing as compared with what the indigenous people suffer and endure on a daily basis. I am ashamed to speak of the two things in the same breath. To me it is an outrage that Indians can be treated as sub-human in their own land.

What's happening about the Zapatistas? Did you know that after the 1917 revolution the Mexican constitution actually guaranteed land to the peasants? Mexico didn't just promise, like say Zimbabwe. The Mexican government actually guaranteed the peasants a share of the land. And as in Zimbabwe the peasants are still waiting, except that in Mexico they have been waiting nearly seventy years. This is Mexico, other governments make promises and don't fulfil them, while Mexico gives useless guarantees. Just like your useless assurances to me not to worry, and that there was "no problem". All the while you were planning to take me to the cleaners. As things turned out there was every reason for me to worry and there were many problems, mostly to do with money.

I hope you understand now why I did not return your kiss and resisted your hug, as we were leaving. I thought your attempt to blame Peter for what you called our "misunderstanding" over the money was particularly despicable, especially as there was no misunderstanding, only greed. It seems to me that we were very much at odds in our hopes and expectations, and you saw us as a chance to make a few quick bucks. We saw *you* as a chance to improve our Spanish and to get to know a bit about Mexico. Looking back now I can see that both sets of expectations were fulfilled: you got the money you wanted, and we got to know a lot more about Mexico than I had dared to hope or expect. For that, much thanks.

Before I leave you I must take you back to some of those discussions we had about the state of Mexico today. Since that time I have been reading around the subject, and right now I find that I agree completely with Jorge Castaneda's analysis of Mexican society. In case you are not familiar with his views let me try to summarise them. Castaneda argues that Mexico today is composed of three nations: criollos, the elite (such as yourself), or mestizo (the huge majority), and finally the "Republic of Indians", known today as "el Mexico profundo": deep Mexico. Deep Mexico really means the real Mexico. Its day will come. I hope that it will be some time soon. What will become of you then? Will you be able to save your paintings?

I will not say "hasta la vista", because I do not think either of us would benefit from a second meeting, so I will say: "Adios, mi hermana; it could have been so different."

Letter to New Zealand

Dear Sister,

How are you? I do hope that you have successfully completed the course and have found a new job.

I have tried to keep in touch with what is happening in New Zealand. I read about the recent settlement of the Maori claim in the South Island. Will that affect you at all? I don't fully understand the technicalities, but New Zealand seems to be handling these matters much better than Australia. I am told that the difference is that the Maori made a treaty with the settlers, whereas as we all know Australia was an empty land when the settlers arrived. That is odd, when the latest research on the Aboriginal rock paintings suggests that there have been people living in Australia for more than 60,000 years.

When I was trying to get an idea of how you felt about the Maori question, you told me that you are not political and that you just want a quiet life. Don't we all! So I will not go on about politics. Can you tell me anything of what happened with the court case in which a religious leader (of some small sect) was charged with sexually abusing child-members of the church?

I actually met a mother and daughter who had been members of the sect, the daughter now a mother herself, who had been abused by this man, and was involved in court. I was amazed that normal people like them could become involved in such horrors. The mother said that she had been "totally blind" to what was going on, and had rejected her daughter when she first made the allegations and left the church. It was only as the evidence began to accumulate and others began speaking out that she changed her mind, becoming reconciled with her daughter and leaving the sect. She put it down to having been "brainwashed".

The New Zealand children were not alone in their experience of sexual abuse in a religious setting. Do you know that the year we spent travelling the one item you could be sure would be covered in the newspapers, on TV, on radio or all three, was child abuse! It seems that every country has its own version of it. At about the time that I was in New Zealand, listening to this mother and daughter story, I was aware that in Australia, Canada, and Ireland there were similar cases against the Catholic church, brought by young people who as children had been abused by paedophile priests. It was also around the same time that allegations concerning Michael Jackson became public. Wherever you turn there was child abuse, TV and radio talk shows, documentaries, dramas – it must have come pretty close to saturation coverage.

In Ireland an incident involving a paedophile priest led to the resignation of a prime minister. And the population of Belgium has become unified in their anger at a system that has protected paedophile murderers and kidnappers, at the expense of innocent children. The papers reported that more than 250 people demonstrated in a "white protest march". "White" to signify the innocence of the betrayed children. Do you know if there were any demonstrations in support of the New Zealand children? I wonder if saturation coverage is helpful at all, or whether it blunts people's feelings; and also by giving the impression to those that are tempted that since it is so widespread, there is no need for restraint. What do you think?

Did I tell you that after I left you I visited a women's refuge? It took me back to the time I worked in the very first women's refuge anywhere in the world, which was in Chiswick, West London. It was started by a woman called Erin Pizzey. The refuge I visited in New Zealand was pretty much like Chiswick Woman's Aid – a big house, lots of women, lots of children – and lots of problems. All the result of male violence against women. It seems that some things never change.

As I travelled around the world there were things that kept coming up all the time: child abuse, the gender war, and people trying to re-possess lost lands. In New Zealand my afternoon with that mother and daughter saw child sexual abuse as the topic. Then I visited the refuge and saw the effects of the gender war New Zealand style. All this took place against a background of the continued efforts of the Maori to settle their outstanding land claims. These were very demanding experiences, very challenging. I begin to wonder whether these things are more related than we think, whether societies founded on theft, murder and dispossession can ever hope to be healthy? I begin to speculate as to whether this explains why child abuse and wife-beating are equally prevalent among rich and poor people and rich and poor societies. Never mind the statistics. And don't forget that the statistician is almost certainly male and middle-class. In the so-called developed world, welfare agencies are set up to target, identify, and control poor people, and that is what in the main they do. If they had a wider brief, we would soon see the true scale of child abuse.

Maybe my next letter will be more personal. In the meantime this will have to do.

Goodbye until then.

4

WALKING AND TALKING WITH MY BROTHERS

Stories from around the world

My brother and I

> Men have played a comparatively small part in my life. And yet paradoxically the expectations and terrors that dominated my childhood and adolescence were shaped by the legend left behind by a shadowy man... .

> Naipaul, S (1992), *Unfinished Journey*, Penguin, London

> And it came to pass, when they were in the field, that Cain rose up against his brother Abel and slew him.

> Genesis 4: 8

I WAS very interested to read an article in the *Guardian* on 16th October 1996, where the writer argued that rebels are "created by big brothers and sisters". The report, by Ian Katz, summarised the findings of research by Dr Frank Sulloway of the Massachusetts Institute of Science and Technology in the USA. The researcher studied the background of 6,500 historical figures over twenty-five years, and concluded that: "birth order is more likely to determine whether someone displays nonconformist traits than gender, race, or economic background." This was due to the fact that from the very start "later borns", as he called them, had to be more inventive and charming to get what they wanted. As adults they were more likely to back liberal/left-wing causes, and to be more receptive to new ideas. As the sixth child in a family of seven I am hardly likely to argue with such a positive, even flattering description of "later borns".

Unlike Shiva Naipaul, who grew up in the shadow of his famous brother, but was brought up by women, men played a very significant part in my life. I grew up sandwiched between three older and one younger brother. My sister was the second and I was the second last of the seven children in our family. There was a big age gap between my sister and me. For the first ten or so years of my life I actually behaved as though I was a boy, wearing my brothers' clothes, playing cricket and pitching marbles with them whenever I got the chance. For me the boy's world was more interesting than the girl's, though I also had plenty of girl friends. I moved between these two worlds, adapting and improvising as I went along, much the same as I do now in the several different worlds that I live and work in. As a child there were times when I was rejected by and excluded from the boys' society, and this usually happened when I was winning at marbles or bowling someone out at cricket. Then I would be dismissed as "only a girl" and shooed away. I would find refuge with the other girls, or in books. On reflection, I think I have to agree with Dr Sulloway's research findings, because in my case that birth order certainly helped in shaping my character.

My father was away in Grenada when I was born, so my brothers were the first men in my life. My mother was born in Grenada and my parents had lived there for a time during the war. My mother had returned to Barbados, without my father, while pregnant with me, and I was almost three before my father saw me. Unlike the fathers of many of my friends, my father did come home. He was not very impressed with the latest addition to his family. From all accounts I was a poor specimen. At two and a half I was unable to walk, and I have written elsewhere of how I was eventually forced to walk, and of my very first walks with one of my brothers to "strengthen my legs and to get fresh air". It was from my five brothers that I learnt to stand up for myself, to fight my corner and to hold my own. I owe a lot to them, and being their sister was a very character-forming experience. But the Bible was also a major influence in my life, for our family started each day with Bible reading and prayers. I knew my Bible very well. I knew that Cain killed his brother Abel. I knew that brothers could and did kill each other, and we children had a saying among ourselves, that Cain killed Abel underneath the breadfruit tree! The stem of the breadfruit has a mark like a "C" in it, and we explained this as being due to the fact that the murder of Abel had occurred underneath such a tree. Abel's blood caused the mark of Cain, the "C", to appear.

My brothers were one of the major influences on my early life, forcing me to defend myself, and also inadvertently teaching me how not to be a victim, a lesson I learnt very early on, and one that has remained with me all my life. I will try to show how this worked and what my brothers' lessons actually meant in practice. I will tell this story by way of a conversation that took place between my son and me when he was about thirteen, the same age as I was when the incident occurred. My son and I were on a plane to Canada. I was deep in thought, when suddenly my son broke the silence and asked, "So what is this uncle like, the one we are visiting in Toronto?" This question, coming so directly and completely out of the blue, threw me and I replied that I had not seen him for many years. But he persisted, "What was he like when you were growing up? Did you like him? Did you get on?" It was obvious that I would not be able to avoid his questions and that he would not be satisfied with bland replies.

So I told it like it was. I explained that this brother had never been very nice to me and that he had actually bullied me quite a lot. I told my son how during the last of these bullying sessions I had more or less bitten off one of his fingers. My son's reaction was quite dramatic; he was horrified. "Does my father know about this?" he demanded to know. I was able to confirm that Peter did indeed know about it, and that I had made a point of telling him before we got married, just in case he ever had any ideas of hitting me. "Not that he ever would," I continued, "but," trying desperately to lighten things up, "you can't be too careful, can you?" Silence.

My son was now lost in his own thoughts. After a while he spoke again: "So what happened after that, after you... ?" He could not bring himself to say after you almost bit your brother's finger off. I told him that my brother had gone to the hospital, where the finger had been stitched back on, as it had been only partly detached. I heard from someone else that he had been too embarrassed to say how it had happened, and had said that it had been caught in a door or something. After this incident this brother had completely ignored me, and had refused to speak to me even up to the day he left for Canada. After some time, maybe three or four years, he had written to me from Canada, a normal letter telling me about his life and his work and that he liked playing tennis. There was no reference to the finger.

This had been one of the most formative experiences of my life, as I had experienced both the negative and the positive sides of standing up for myself, and of fighting back. The positive side was the immediate and absolute cessation of further bullying; the negative side was the possibility of being seen as a violent person. It was a price I'd had to pay. I had no choice.

Now back to the conversation on the plane, between my son and myself. After a very long pause he asked me if I felt ashamed about what I had done, and of talking to him about it. I had to admit that at the time I felt no shame at all, mainly because of the beneficial results: to be ignored was bliss compared with being bullied! As to my feelings in telling him about it? I was not proud of it, as it was not something one could be proud of. But by the same token there was no cause for shame, and I felt none. I had taken a lot of bullying from my brothers and especially from that one: numerous slaps, hair-pulling, being shouted at and being ordered to do this or that. On this occasion the worm turned, and as the next slap came, aimed at my face, I'd opened and closed my mouth. No other person's hand should have been in that position, and as it was it got what was coming to it. So I tried to explain to my son that without victims there can be no bullies, and on that occasion, I had decided to stop being a victim.

But all my efforts to explain that I had acted only in self-defence in a situation not of my making fell on stony ground. I could see that he could neither understand nor accept my reasoning. He had never experienced me as a violent person, he had never once been smacked, and I think he found it difficult to reconcile this new picture of me that was emerging as we crossed the Atlantic. I think that there were other things that may have limited his understanding of my life experience. He was growing up in middle-class suburban England in a two-child family, whereas I had grown up in poor working-class Barbados, in a family of seven. There was a huge cultural gap between these two experiences of growing up. And now this picture of his mother almost certainly clashed with whatever view of womanhood was beginning to take shape in my son's mind.

After a month or so in Calgary and a train ride across the prairies, we arrived in Toronto. We are staying with my brother and his wife. My brother and I are sitting at his dining-room table chatting, and I am trying to get a glimpse of the finger. This is something I had not thought of in years and now because of that conversation on the plane, I am very aware of it. My brother turns towards me and opens the palm of his hand, and I see the finger very clearly. There is an unnatural silence, and I point at the finger and at the stitches which are clearly visible. I ask my brother: "Do you remember how you got that?" He nods. I nod. Nothing more is said.

Two other brothers joined us for our weekend in Toronto, and before long these three were emotionally back in Carrington's Village, fighting old battles and reliving old hurts. As voices became raised and emotions heightened, I slipped down to the basement to listen to music. When I was growing up I watched many fights between my brothers, from just rough horseplay to what seemed to me like a fight to the death. I had always been frightened that one of these fights would leave someone badly hurt. Ironic then that it was I who had actually left someone hurt and scarred for life. And now here we were after all these years, adults in another country, with children of our own, careers, lives separated by years of never seeing each other. It seemed to me that in some ways we had never left Barbados, never left off being children. I felt the same old fears and anxieties coming back, so I quietly escaped into the basement to listen to the music. The first song was Kenny Roger singing "The Gambler", with the words of the song apparently meant for me: "You've got to know when to walk away, know when to run." I felt very glad that I'd known when to walk away, and had!

This incident stirred other long lost and almost forgotten memories of the past; and it began a process of reflection and self-analysis that eventually led to my isolation from all of my brothers. I had always known that I'd been something of a scapegoat and an outsider in the family. This knowledge had been a part of my life, something I had grown up to accept, but still I had tried to be as much of a sister as I could be. Then major changes in my life forced me to re-evaluate everything. I started with my family of origin and I began to question everything, including my role in that family. That visit to Toronto was the start of it. To begin with, I was cautious, as I tasted the freedom of virtually being without any family. Then I began to welcome it. I did not know that I was carrying a load, until the load was lifted from me: the load of being somebody's sister, the load of being the family scapegoat. The lifting of this load freed me from the bondage of family, and enabled me to focus more of my energy on myself. Most of this happened at an emotional level: there were no "showdowns", no confrontations. I simply drifted away and took every opportunity I could to increase the distance between my brothers and myself.

We had never been a close family; and each of us had grown up and moved away, leaving not just home-the-house, but home-the-island – Barbados itself. When I reflected on this as an adult, it seemed to me that any chance for closeness had gone as each of us had moved away. This seemed to me the price we Caribbean people pay for our perpetual search for work in other people's countries. Many of my school friends had grown up with fathers, uncles and older brothers whom they had never seen. In some ways I had envied them and thought of them as lucky, especially when they received lots of presents from absent male relatives. I grew up in a community in which the shape of family life varied tremendously, from the traditionally wedded like my parents, to families with only mothers and or grandmothers. As a consequence my ideas of family have always been very fluid. I had not grown up in the expectation that "closeness" was a necessary or inevitable part of family life.

So with the passing years my thoughts about my brothers would have been along the lines that time had changed them for the better. If I'd been asked I would have said that we had moved away from our childish concerns and jealousies and that as adults we now had better relationships. That is how I saw it, until that visit to Canada showed me how wrong I was. I soon discovered that nothing had changed; the parameters of our relationship had been set a long time ago, and remained firmly in place. Except that now, I for one was no longer willing to perform on cue. As I observed the growing gulf between me and my brothers, I became more and more convinced of the limitations of biology. I realised that biology in itself, without the reinforcement of affection, common interests, respect, feelings of goodwill and friendship, was not enough for me. When I was very small the brother whose finger I almost bit off used to tell me that I was not really his sister. He said that I was too black to be his sister, that I was really "Gladys' child". Gladys was the lady who helped my mother with child care and everything else in the home. I often wished that he was right, as I did not enjoy being his sister, and I fantasised about what my real brothers and sisters must be like. The only drawback was the thought of having a different mother, something I could not bear to think of. Now that my mother is dead I am free to choose who is to be my brother. My brothers now come in all shapes, sizes and colours. Some are nice and some are nasty. They are just men.

So in these stories that I am about to tell I use the term "brothers" inclusively to refer to all the men I have walked and talked with, and who have been a part of my life. These accounts include the negative as well as positive: brothers who helped and those who hindered me, those who nurtured and those who have tried to destroy me. I make no effort to distinguish between brothers who are related to me by blood and those I have acquired. This is not important to my case. In fact I make no real effort to distinguish these men in any terms at all. I simply try to tell their stories, and hope that they are worth the telling. And always I approach the matter of brothers in an open manner: if I am walking and talking with a male person, and enjoying his company and his conversation, then for that little while he is my brother. During such encounters I may have shared and exchanged views and have experienced a closeness that I have seldom felt with any of my biological brothers. At other times the experience may have been all too familiar – being put down or picked on because I'm too black, too bright, too stupid or "just a woman".

These stories then are not so much about me, and my relationship with men as friends and brothers; as about the men themselves, and how they reveal themselves, either in the way they treat me or in what they choose to talk to me about. The personalities that unfold, the words they use, the views they express, the issues they touch on. I still have very strong emotional reactions to some of these occurrences, and even after many years the telling of some of these incidents makes me feel weak and vulnerable. It just happened that I was in a certain place at a certain time; and so I became the recipient of confidences; the sounding-board for ideas; the object of attack; or, however briefly, just a sister to these diverse "brothers". And yes, I will still call them all my brothers.

These stories have not been chosen to be representative of anything. They cover the period from 1962–96, beginning in India and ending in Trinidad, passing through Africa, Europe, and North and South America. All the stories are based on fact, they all happened, with nothing added. There is no order to them, they are told more or less as they came to me. Although many of these stories are associated with a walk or hike, call it what you will; the walk itself is not central to the story, so there is no map provided and no descriptive account or route-plan to follow.

A Walk in Digha

Digha is a small seaside town in West Bengal, India. I met my husband
Peter in Calcutta while I was a student at Loreto College, Calcutta
University. Peter's idea of how to spend a weekend was to fly with this
Australian friend of his to Digha, and spend the weekend walking and
swimming, etc. I loved it. This friend of Peter's had a little four-seater
plane, which he used to land on the beach, and part of the fun of the
exercise was for us guess whether the tide would be out or whether we
would have to fly back to Calcutta. The tide was always out.

An occasion arose for us to spend a whole week in Digha, with Peter
doing one of his British Council visits to a university nearby. This meant
I would be alone for a few days. India, rural India, West Bengal, a young
black woman left alone for a week – we discussed it at length. I felt fine
about being left; I felt quite safe and could see no problem. Even so
Peter was quite anxious and insisted that I should not go out walking
while he was away. Of course I agreed.

On my first day alone I went for a stroll along the beach. I had no
problems at all. No one seemed to notice me, and there was not even a
single person gaping and staring at me! This was very unusual for India,
and made me feel relaxed in a way I seldom felt then. So on the second
day, feeling more confident, I walked a bit farther and saw on my right
a forest. I am irresistibly drawn to forests, but remembering my promise
to Peter, this time I resisted the temptation, turned round and went
back. On the third day, and by that time I was sick of the beach, the
trees seemed to beckon me on, and I somehow found myself walking
in the forest. I was wearing shorts and a T-shirt, which was quite
acceptable beachwear for a "Western" i.e. non-Indian woman. I walked
along a path enjoying the peace and beauty of the forest. Then I saw a
man coming towards me wearing wellington boots and carrying a scythe,
or cutting blade of some kind. I thought nothing of it. I felt no fear or
anxiety as I saw him approach me, and I was all prepared to do my
salaams to him and continue my walk. Then warning bells sounded!

I have never been able to explain exactly what happened, but from
one moment walking happily in the forest, I somehow found myself
being chased by the man with the axe. I ran as I've never run in my life;
I felt that I was running for my life! All my efforts seemed doomed to
failure and I came to a junction and took the path that ended in a
thicket. I turned and could see the young man catching up with me. I
took the next path, and this time it was the right one; in a few minutes

I was back on the beach. I fell down on the sand, breathless, but very relieved, and I waited to see the man come out from the forest. I don't know whether I intended to confront him in my non-existent Bengali, my few words of Hindi or in English. But I waited, and waited. After waiting fifteen or twenty minutes he still had not come out. So I went back to the cottage and waited for Peter.

When I told Peter what had happened his only reaction was relief. In the week following our return to Calcutta, as we were walking along Park Street, I told one of my Caribbean brothers what had happened to me in Digha. His reaction completely threw me. In his view I needn't have bothered running away from the man in the forest, as Indian men do not find African women attractive. I was completely dumbfounded by these comments, and also deeply hurt. For all my black brother's comments did was to add insult to the injury my brown brother had caused me. In effect my black brother had told me that I had completely misread the situation and had caused myself needless worry. I knew full well that men did not have to find women "attractive" in order to rape and murder them. And it was more than thirty years before I felt able to tell anyone else about what had happened in the forest that day in Digha. I told the story to two Indian sisters, and they had no problem understanding my fear, and the danger I escaped from. They knew that the matter of "attraction" was not relevant to this experience. These sisters knew that attraction is not an issue in the rape/murder of women by men who are strangers to them. Needless to say I did not tell them of the comfort of my African brother's words, and again needless to say, I never walked alone in India again. To this day I still have dreams, or nightmares where I am running away from a man who is chasing me, and I always end up in a cul-de-sac. At that point I wake up, sweating.

"Ma'sa come back"
Indian and Caribbean brothers weep for a lost empire

When I was a child growing up in Barbados we celebrated something called Empire Day. The main significance this had for me was that we had a day off school; something I did not enjoy at all, as I liked school very much. Although I did not really understand what Empire Day was about, I did enjoy the cakes and sweet drinks which all school children were given as part of the celebrations.

Over the years the term "empire" took on several different meanings as I studied history and began to understand the true significance of such events as Empire Day. At Loreto College I had experienced the tyranny of mind control, when most of the teachers were Irish nuns who taught us from books written mostly by Englishmen, the British empire in India. I had come to India in the belief that I would escape such brain-washing. I couldn't have been more mistaken. India became independent in 1948, and I arrived there in 1962. Meanwhile the Caribbean islands were emerging from under the blanket of the empire and becoming nation states of various kinds and sizes, including my own little Barbados, all 144 square miles of it.

In 1963, when I was a student in India, I went with an American student on a trip from Calcutta to Northern India and Kashmir. Like the Mahatma we travelled by train, going third class because that was all I could afford (whereas my companion was from a rich, East coast white American family and could easily have bought the train itself). There we were. My friend carried the weight of all the insufferable Americans in India on her shoulders. She felt that she made up for their terrible behaviour towards Indians by accepting and eating every offer of food or sweets that came our way. And there was a constant stream of such offerings throughout our travels. Since the food was peppery hot and none too clean, she became more ill and more pale the farther north we travelled. As I was travelling light, at least as far as colonial and/or imperial baggage was concerned, I was able to refuse the gifts of food and sweets and to remain more or less well during the whole two months.

The American became quite weak from her continued illness, and when we arrived in Kashmir and did the more or less compulsory trip to Pahlgam she felt unable to walk the last few miles. So she stayed behind with the ponies and her guide, while I hiked the final few miles with *my* guide. It was lovely, truly unforgettable. Kashmir remains the only place in the world that I do not want to return to, just in case that would spoil my memory of perfect beauty. It was spring in the Kashmir valley, but there was still some snow in the hills, and it was to the snow that we were headed, and it was there where I had my very first sight, taste, smell and feel of snow. All this would have been enough to make the experience memorable, but the real lasting memory for me was in the conversation I had with my guide.

On the way up we were both quiet. He walked ahead and I followed. On the way down he began to talk, and asked the usual questions. Where was I from? What was I doing in India? What job did my father do?

When I told him that my father had been a policeman, he told me that he had been an officer in the British army. His chest visibly expanded, as he puffed himself up and said that he had been among the first "natives" (yes, he did use that word) to be promoted to officer rank. He then became quite, how shall I say, wistful, sorrowful even, as he spoke about those days. I don't recall saying much, or asking any questions, or prompting him in any way. I listened as he spoke. He spoke very quietly, and could have been talking to himself. Then he returned to the present day, and ended his speech with these words: "The British should never have left." At this point I felt compelled to speak. I could not let such sentiments pass unchallenged. So I said something along the lines of you don't really mean that. He insisted that he did mean it, that Indians did not know how to govern and that the country needed the British to rule it. I kept quiet after that, as he explained all the reasons why the British empire was the best thing that ever happened to India. I'd already decided that it had to do with the British making him an officer and a gentleman. That meant that for him at least they could do no wrong.

That encounter in Kashmir took place in 1963. Then in 1996, during a visit to Trinidad, I had a conversation with a brother that bore an uncanny resemblance to that previous exchange all those years before. I had come to Trinidad in the company of an Australian friend with whom I'd become acquainted through the Staines ramblers in Surrey, and since our first meeting we had we had walked together in other parts of the UK, in India, Bhutan and in Australia. So when my friend visited me in Barbados I was keen to introduce her to some really nice Caribbean walks. Because in my view the best walks are to be had in Trinidad, we headed for the Asa Wright Centre, which in itself is a haven of peace and tranquillity. As it turned out my friend did not want to walk in the rain forest, as she was afraid that it might rain and that she would get wet. So on that Sunday morning in June I turned up alone to do a walk that had been especially organised for a visitor from the other side of the world. Had my guest been present this walk would almost certainly have been a very different experience for me. As it was I was able to spend a lot of time talking with my Trinidadian brothers and sisters, most of whom I'd never met before. In fact the only person known to me was my Trini-sister and long-standing walking companion who had arranged the walk for me.

It was a most enjoyable walk, crossing streams, swimming in rivers, relaxing. The Australian foresight had been correct and on the way back it began to rain. We continued walking along in the pouring rain, enjoying the forest and talking about this and that. Then as happens on walks, we somehow ended up in pairs, probably due to the nature of the path. My companion was a very interesting man who, when he heard that I worked as a researcher, told me that he'd been doing some research of his own, "right here in Trinidad". His area of special interest had to do with the way women in Trinidad chose their mates. He told me that from his research he could now say that in Trinidad the brighter and more intellectual a woman was the more likely she was to choose "a foolish man, a loser". He could not explain why this was so, but he was working on it and hoped to develop more insight as time went by and his research progressed.

The two of us stayed with this topic for quite a long time, and inevitably it led to a more general discussion of social problems in Trinidad: drugs, crime, domestic violence, murder. Then came what for me was the big surprise of the day. My companion explained the economic and social failures of the country as being due to the absence of colonial rulers. His actual words were: "We should never have kicked out the British."

I did not try to hide my amazement and consternation at the views he had expressed, and I challenged him to justify them. He replied with studied tolerance as he told me that he fully understood my reactions of amazement and disbelief, and he said that there was a time when he would never have believed himself capable of the views he had just voiced. But times change and he had come to realise that Trinidadian people needed the "hate figure" of the British colonial presence: "We need an enemy, we need someone to hate, it's the only thing that unites us. And besides, the empire was not all bad." By this time, thoroughly soaked and rapidly losing body heat, I had also lost the taste for argument. We finished the walk in silence, as I tried to keep the rain out and also to make some sense of the views I'd just listened to. This brother had come to me highly recommended, not just as a person who loved walking and the outdoors, and had an extensive knowledge of the flora and fauna, but as a fellow-spirit, someone I would like and get along with. I did not know what to think, so I put it aside.

Later that night, lying in bed in the lovely surroundings at the Asa Wright Centre, I brought it back to mind. As I recalled that conversation with the Trini-brother, I became convinced that I'd heard a very similar view some time in the dim and distant past. Who was it? Where was it?

Then it flashed into my mind, and I knew immediately, as every detail came back, recalling my visit to Kashmir and my conversation with the Sheikh guide. I recalled in detail that earlier conversation, and was at once struck by the similarity of the views of the two men I had walked and talked with in India and Trinidad. The first one, the ex-soldier, was now almost certainly dead. At the time of our encounter in 1963, he appeared to be well into his sixties. That two men, different in almost every respect, should be united in a wish for times past, for a return of the British empire, for a return to colonialism. For the Sheikh soldier "empire" meant something to love, to admire, to look up to; whereas to the Trinidadian it meant something to hate, to unite and fight and struggle against. I suppose that a Freudian would say that they were both looking for a father figure. As for me? All I can say is that the whole experience left me with a feeling of complete weariness, and of utter disillusionment.

Canada – walking and spitting on Young Street

Al Capone is supposed to have asked when someone spoke about Canada, which Street is Canada on? If the someone had wanted to continue the joke, they could have replied Young Street. I know that I would have done, because for me Young Street seemed to sum up Canada. I have walked along Young Street often, different parts at different times, and I am told that it goes straight to the border with the USA.

One of those times was with a young man, a brother of course. This young man was going through a hard time, working and studying, while he and his wife were going through a divorce. He could talk of little else, and wherever the conversation started you could be sure it would end up with his wife and her many and varied shortcomings. I made what I hoped sounded like sympathetic noises, at the same time trying hard to change the subject. Every now and then I thought we had done so as he paused and pointed to something of interest. But it was *only* a pause, and he soon returned to his favourite topic.

At some point he must have begun to notice my lack of enthusiasm for his wife's failures, because he turned to me and said: "Listen, see what you think of this. This will show you what kind of person she is." Then he told me that once when they had been walking along Young Street, his wife had spat! He was almost shouting as he said, "Can you imagine that? She spat on Young Street!" I did not want to appear too ignorant of what constituted civilised behaviour in Canadian society, but I could not help asking him: "Was that very bad then?" He looked at me as though I had taken leave of my senses. He instructed me to look around me, see the place, the people, for was it the kind of place a young lady would spit? "Would you spit here?" he demanded of me. I did not know what to say, so by way of reply I asked him if he wanted me to spit right there and then? He took a deep breath, sighed, and said nothing more on the subject, either of spitting or of his wife. In fact during the rest of my time with him he never once returned to the topic of his author and their impending divorce.

From what I knew of her, I thought that that his ex-wife had spat because she needed to, and not to offend him. This particular story, although it did not have a violent or dramatic end, remains for me an example of the type of behaviour by women that can assume a significance out of all proportion, and for some men may be a trigger for violence.

Am I my brother's counsellor?

I met the brother in this story during one of my escapes to the Asa Wright Nature Centre in Trinidad. It turned out that he also was running away. But unlike me, he had brought his troubles with him. When he walked in I was sitting on the veranda, reading, the only black person apart from the servants. The brother came straight up to me, pulled up a chair, sat down and introduced himself. He assumed that like him I was local. As we talked it became clear that I was not quite as "local" as I looked.

"What brings you here?"

"Escape, what brings you here?"

"Well, I wanted some time to myself, time to think."

I heard the warning bell and saw the signal: problems, keep away! But I was wrong. Our conversation took off in the direction of political rather than personal problems, as we talked until just before dinner about the situation in Trinidad and the Caribbean in general. I really enjoyed it and readily agreed to meet again after dinner. In this way we passed a very pleasant few hours and, as we parted, we agreed to take a walk together the following day. I was very glad about this arrangement, as without his company I would have had to get a guide or walk with a group, and at that time neither option appealed to me.

We didn't walk very far. The Asa Wright Centre has many beautifully named paths, and we walked very slowly along the Blue Bell, and soon came to a bench and sat down. We stayed seated there for the best part of the morning while he told me his story. During the short walk it had become clear to me that I had been sent there to listen to this brother, and there was no way that I would be allowed to escape. I accepted that I was going to be drawn into his world, and whether I liked it or not; and for better or worse, on that day at least I would be my brother's counsellor.

So what was his story? He was a man of thirty-eight years, married with three children. His father, or the man he had until recently regarded as his father, had recently died. After this death his brothers and sisters had started to act "strange" towards him, especially over the matter of the division of his father's estate. Hints were dropped suggesting that he should not expect the same as the others. Eventually he worked out for himself what the hints were about. It had to do with his parentage: there was a question about whether his father was his "real" father. No one actually told him this in so many words, but over the period since the father's death he had been forced to this conclusion.

I said: "What does your mother say?"

He said: "Well, this was the problem. I ca'n talk to my mother about it, I do'n want to upset her."

I: "What does your wife say?"

He: "She says I must either talk to my mother and clear it up once an' for all, or ignore the rumours and get on with my life as before."

That was the dilemma he faced, the problem he was running away from, for he could neither confront his mother nor ignore the hints and rumours. On top of that his wife was finding it increasingly difficult to live with him, with his moods, his depression and his self-absorption.

Having told me his story he now wanted to know my views. I said that I agreed with the wife, and why not follow plan A and ignore the whole thing: did it matter anyhow? Legally he was the man's son and he could not be disinherited without a lot of trouble. That was not the point, he was not worried about the inheritance, he did not care about the farm, all he wanted was to know who his father was. Worrying over this had changed him, making him depressed and weepy. His wife was fed up, and it was affecting the children. He had to do something. The something he had done was to retreat to the hills to walk and to think (and to find me, I thought). So what was it to be, acceptance or confrontation? He replied that he had known the answer all along; that he would have to talk to his mother, get the whole thing out in the open, and try to accept whatever she had to say and get on with his own life. It had been good talking to me as it had really helped him see things clearly.

Shall we go for a swim now? Or would I like to continue our walk? I opted for the walk and we went on to the Oily Bat's caves. During the rest of the morning, neither of us talked very much, and I was not very surprised when, as we walked towards the house at lunch time, he told me that he would be leaving after lunch. It was clear that this brother had done his "thinking", and that he was ready to move on.

London – a walk on the wild side

This is a very difficult story for me to tell, the reasons for which will become clear in the telling. I have already mentioned that I once worked at a refuge for battered women, where part of my role was as a support worker to the women in the refuge. In this role I often listened to their stories. Some of the accounts were truly horrific, and although I could understand to some extent how men could lose their tempers and beat women up, the thing I found totally incomprehensible was the repeated stories women told of having being urinated and defecated on by their men. It never ever occurred to me that among my own friends and acquaintances, among my brothers, there was a man who had actually done this, and had felt quite justified in doing it. To quote his own words: "I would do it again. The bitch deserved it!"

How did I come to be the recipient of such confidences? Quite unexpectedly, as it happens. For that is one walk I would have avoided had I the slightest clue of what was going to happen during it. This was in the streets of West London, though I cannot now recall the details. It was a fairly aimless walk and the conversation was also pretty uninspiring. Then, our journey took us quite close to Chiswick High Road and I mentioned that I had once worked at a women's refuge nearby. My companion responded by saying that he had no time for women who ran away from their homes to live in places like that. I tried to explain some of the reasons why women often had no choice, having to escape domestic violence and find a refuge wherever they could. I said something like, "Can you imagine what it must be like to be beaten up, and peed on, shat on?" I did not know that I was talking to an expert in these matters, until he said, with something like glee: "I have done that."

We were at a pedestrian crossing waiting for the lights to change. The lights did change, the green man flickered, but I stood still, stupefied. Then, as the lights changed back again and the green man disappeared, I collected my thoughts and got ready to move. My companion did not appear to notice the effect of his words on me. I felt complete revulsion and wanted to quit his company pronto and forever. I was speechless, and in my silent confusion we continued on our way.

Once we had cleared the crowds and the traffic lights the brother began talking again. He started by explaining to me in great detail exactly what he had done, why it had been deserved, and why he would do it again. Several times he repeated that he had "shat on her, the bitch". I had heard these things many times before, but always from the victim, never from the aggressor. It was a new and terrible experience. I continued walking, not saying much, and only just managing to contain my feelings of revulsion. We had a drink, then he went on his way, and I went mine. I cannot explain or justify my silence, except on the basis of utter confusion and at some level, fear. I had to remain silent; and my silence hid my horror. I knew that I could never really feel the same about this man.

At least ten years passed before we finally parted company, ostensibly over an entirely different matter. In fact the parting of our ways had already begun on that day on the streets of West London.

A walk up Mt Teide

I could not help noticing the young man who was dressed in hiking gear, reading a guidebook. Peter and I were sitting in a bar in a village in Tenerife, away from the hustle and bustle of the tourist resorts. It was less than a year since Peter's heart by-pass operation and we were taking things easy, short strolls instead of the long walks that we were accustomed to. This meant that we could not even think of walking up Mt Teide, though ever since arriving in Tenerife I had been looking wishfully at that mountain. The winter of 1991 was very cold, and a lot of snow from the Pyrenees had been dumped on Mt Teide, Spain's tallest mountain. From the beach, from every bar and restaurant on the Costa del Sol, we could see the snow-capped mountain. I very much wanted to walk up it, but it seemed that I would have to content myself with just looking.

That was before we got talking with the young man sitting at the table next to us in that beach-bar. Soon we'd invited him to join us for lunch, an invitation he readily accepted. He wasted no time in telling us about himself, including the fact that he hated spending money and would never turn down the chance of a free lunch! He was an Englishman, a hiker and also something of mountaineer. He spent a month walking and skiing in the Alps every winter, and in a couple of days he was going up Mt Teide. On hearing this last piece of information, Peter and I looked at each other, and before he could say anything I'd arranged to join our new friend on his walk up the mountain. The following day Peter and I went shopping for a pair of suitable boots, as I had not come equipped for hiking. The day after that I set out with my newly acquired friend and brother for Mt Teide.

I don't really know where to start. To say it was a lovely sunny day sounds so trite, and I've said that so many times already! But that was the kind of day it was. There were quite a few cars in the car park, which we took as a sign that it was a good day for the walk. We started off with enthusiasm, walking briskly in the cool morning air. I always enjoy the approach to the tree line, and I revelled in it more that day, thinking of people sun-bathing on the beach and swimming in the sea a few miles below us. Then the conditions changed, the walking became much harder, the slopes steeper. It soon became evident that my new boots were not up to the demands, as they were soaked through. My companion was better knitted out, his boots were ideal, and he also had ropes and an ice pick, crampons and other bits of essential equipment. That was just as well, because within half an hour or so of reaching the snow line I was unable to walk. I kept slipping back and falling down. In the end we tied ourselves together with the rope and I was more or less dragged along by my companion. I looked longingly up at the electric wires of the tram that I could have taken if only I had waited until the summer! I tried not to think of all those people lying about in the sun on the beach.

Somehow we reached the lodge, which was deep in snow, with entry through a small window in the roof. I decided against going in, as I did not think I would want to leave the warmth and comfort of the indoors, therefore it was better to remain in the cold outdoors for the duration of my visit. We rested and had something to eat. Then we had to decide whether or not to continue to the top of the mountain. We were within about three kilometres of the top, and people returning from there said that the snow was deeper and harder, and that they did not advise going any farther without skis. We did not have skis. And I had already decided that I had come far enough and I was not the least bit tempted to go any farther. However, my companion would not hear of turning back. He would go on, and I would wait for him at the lodge. I waited for a while, then I hitched a lift with a group of German students. They had skis, and I was carried down the mountain in style. All I had to do was relax and enjoy the ride.

I sat in a comparatively warm car waiting and hoping that my companion would arrive back safely. I must have waited for an hour or more when I saw him in the distance. He was smiling, because he had made it to the top. It had been so important to him to complete the climb, to reach the summit, and he was very elated and pleased with himself. I for my part was very pleased with my decision to turn back, as I felt sure that I might have been a hindrance to him, and also might well have endangered my life, or at least my limbs.

In the days that followed the Mt Teide expedition, Peter and I saw a lot of our new friend, and of his female travelling companion. When he spoke of our adventure he was always most flattering about my walking ability and my bravery. But I said that I'd had enough of hiking up cold mountains and that next time I'd be taking the aerial tram. The next year both Peter and I went hiking in the foothills of the Himalayas! The memory of bitter cold and of being dragged up the mountainside, tied to a rope, had faded, and all that was left was the challenge and the feeling of excitement that went with it. In the long run my walk up Mt Teide had left me wanting more of the same, which, come to think of it, is exactly what happened!

A walk in Wordsworth country

In common with other Caribbean children educated under British colonial rule I have been familiar with the poetry and imagery of the English Lake District since childhood. I grew up on Wordsworth's poems, even though I had no idea what mountains or daffodils looked like. Peter knows the Lake District very well, having worked as a scientist at Windscale, and so this was one of the first places he took me walking when we came to live in England in 1965. At that time I found the Lake District quite ordinary, because I think I must have been comparing it with Kashmir! When I go there now I am completely enthralled and I can't think why I failed to be impressed the first time.

The walk I am going to write about here took place during a very difficult and stressful time of my life, when I was quite literally overwhelmed by problems of one kind or another. I am a great believer in self-help so I developed my own coping strategy: walking plus yoga plus learning Spanish. Walking had always been a part of my life, yoga I had dabbled in from time to time, though without any real commitment, and Spanish likewise. My self-help programme offered me the right combination of physical and intellectual challenge, and was sufficient to stop me going completely off the rails. So I went for it. I found yoga especially helpful and I was encouraged from reading the research literature, using it as an alternative to drug therapy. So when I saw an advertisement in the *Guardian* for a course that combined walking and yoga in the Lake District, I was tempted. At the same time I felt rather cautious, held back by my picture of the type of person who might well be drawn to such a course: very serious, very intense, not at all my type. But I really wanted to improve my yoga: all my yoga practice had been based on books, and I needed practical lessons. The fact that only half the day would be given over to yoga, while the other half would be spent hiking, helped me to decide in favour of going. I felt that the walks would offer relief from the intensity, if any, and would add balance and variety to the programme. After much thought I signed up.

The yoga was fine. The group was not intense at all, though it soon became clear that most knew each other and were yoga teachers of varying levels of skill. As luck would have it there was another woman who had come alone. We found ourselves laughing at the same things and both a bit sceptical about quite a lot, and we very soon teamed up for the duration of the course, excepting the walks. This sister was not a hiker, and was extremely scared of heights. The only walk she went on was around the small lakeside town at the end of the week, on our way to the station. The circular route around the town included a short stretch through some gardens, and over a little bridge. This little wooden bridge caused us a major crisis, because, when the sister was half-way across, she became totally unable to move. She was terrified. She grabbed me and held on to me as though her very life depended on it. We completed the crossing clutching each other. But well before this event I'd already had my own experience of fear and terror in the Lake District.

It was a spectacularly beautiful spring day. In March of that same year I had visited Norway for the first time, a trip that I had really enjoyed, especially as I learnt to ski cross-country. I found the Norwegian countryside in winter very beautiful, but with the Lake District in April Norway paled by comparison. There was still snow on the peaks, the lakes glistened, the grass was green and the contrasts of colours gave the countryside a unique, almost fragile quality. I had been looking forward to a walk to the top of Coniston Old Man. We stopped by a stream for our picnic lunch, and just when I thought we were ready to re-start, the leader took out the yoga equivalent of Mao's *Little Red Book*. First he read a bit, then he began to give us what he considered an uplifting talk. I began to get very impatient. This was yoga creeping into walking, and it upset the balance of my programme. Added to that, qualifications as a walk-leader do not necessarily equip one to be a philosopher. I thought that the ideas being dispensed by the leader were extremely half-baked and very questionable.

For example, he seemed to be arguing that, in yoga, Indian philosophy had found the answer to life, the universe and everything. When I could stand it no longer, I asked him whether he had ever been in Calcutta. No, he had never visited India. "Well," I countered, "I was in Calcutta last year, it's a hell-hole – if India has all the answers, you would think they would try them out in Calcutta first, wouldn't you?" Not surprisingly he completely ignored my question. This was okay by me, since I really did not want to get embroiled in a "discussion" with him about the merits or otherwise of Indian philosophy, and I could see that he had not expected me to challenge him, not being like himself a white Western convert to Indian philosophy. He did not expect a black woman to have the knowledge or the confidence to challenge him. Later on in the walk I took the opportunity of telling him that I had been to university in India, and that I had recently spent three months in the sub-continent travelling. I must also have told him that we'd been in Bhutan and that I had done a bit of walking in the foothills of the Himalayas. It would not be very long before I would bitterly regret this conversation.

This man, as well as being ill-educated in matters about which he purported to be an authority, was also an awful leader. He actually boasted that on a walk he had led in the Swedish Alps, he had so terrified a Swedish woman that she had cried all the way back to base camp. Well, I wasn't reduced to that extremity, but it came quite close. The problem came at the top of the Old Man. It was extremely windy with gale-force winds, and lots of snow. The wind-chill factor must have been very high. I hate winds because they scare me. High winds always make me think of hurricanes. I will not normally go walking when it is windy, though rain and snow I don't mind. We came to the pass and the leader decided that we had to slide down on the snow. I watched while the ones in front slid down laughing and screaming with pleasure. When it came to my turn, I just stood stock still, terrified.

The walk-leader saw his chance to get even with this cheeky black woman. He stood at the bottom laughing at me, then he taunted me about having been in the Himalayas. After that I had to do something: there were others behind me waiting to slide down, so *I* slid down, and somehow made it to safety. Then I walked silently back to the hotel. If his aim had been to even up the score, he had certainly succeeded. He had certainly put this black woman in her place. From then on I kept my distance. When the course came to an end I overheard him asking around, trying to scrounge accommodation in Leicester, where he was going to visit his Indian guru. I managed to restrain myself, and I didn't express any surprise that he did not have a huge following among the Indian community in Leicester, and a choice of accommodation!

This man, the walk-leader from hell, was very interesting: macho, racist and sexist in his views. I'd been aware of this even before the events recounted above. On an earlier walk the topic of divorce had come up and he had expressed very hostile and prejudicial views towards women. So much so that some of the other walkers had wondered why a person with such views would want to be part of a yoga course. Underlying this question was an assumption that yoga and/or hiking would attract only people with certain values, values that all the members of the group would share. What this man typified for me was the belief by some people that some part of a culture or a religion, in this case yoga, can be extracted, packaged and used in isolation from everything else. In this way the cultural or religious extract has no influence on the practitioner's own values and attitudes. So this man, who was able to glorify yoga teachings and make the wildest claims for them, had the greatest difficulty in relating to his fellow-human beings. Clearly yoga practice does not bestow wisdom or tolerance or love of one's fellow-creature. If it did, would India not be showing the way to the rest of the world, instead of suffering like the rest of us?

To be fair, this man, this brother (I will call him brother) was at least trying. He spent a lot of time reading and studying the Vedic scriptures, practising yoga, and walking many miles, striving for self-improvement (and falling well short of his aspirations). All the women agreed that we should at least give him credit for making an attempt. We agreed on that, even acknowledging the difficulty in trying to imagine what he would have been like without the benefit of his self-improvement regime. As for me, I now practise yoga at the gym or at home alone, and this was my first and last involvement in that kind of experiential learning.

Talking turtles – a moonlight walk in Barbados

Turtles are an endangered species. Once, while we were staying in Charlotteville, a small fishing village in Tobago, a fishing boat brought in one of the largest turtles I have ever seen. It was approaching the size of a small car! The turtle had become entangled in the fishing net and had been dragged in by the boat. I pleaded for its release and it *was* released. It was no use to anyone, nobody wanted it, but no one was in a hurry to do anything about releasing it. We used to eat turtle eggs when I was growing up, when there was no talk of turtles being an endangered species then. Now I am not fond of eggs of any kind, but I love to watch the turtles come ashore to lay theirs. For me there is something almost magical about turtles, creatures that seem to connect me to the long lost fairy-tale land of my childhood.

So, when this brother I met on the beach one day told me that he would be going to look for turtles later that night, because it was the turtle laying season, and it was also full moon, I immediately invited myself along. He was happy for me to join him, so I agreed to return at around 8.30 in the evening. As I got ready to leave the house I thought that I was not being very sensible, meeting a man I did not know on a lonely beach at night. What if he read something different into the occasion? It was a bank holiday weekend, and there were lots of people in the park where we met, but I knew that where the turtles were it would be quiet and deserted. I went but when we met I explained to the brother that I did not want any misunderstanding between us: I had come only because of the turtles, nothing else. He told me that he was not that sort of man and that I was safe with him. Anyhow, he continued, after I left in the morning, a white woman, a tourist, had come along the beach and chatted him up, and they had arranged to meet later in the evening. So once we'd checked out the turtles, he would be on his way. So far so good!

At about ten o'clock we set off for the beach where he said we would find the turtles. On the way we stopped and he retrieved a large plastic bag from behind a rock. He explained that he'd hidden it there earlier in the day, and that it was for the eggs. It was only then that I realised that we didn't have the same agenda: I was there to watch the turtles lay their eggs, while he was there to steal them. I judged that this was neither the time nor the place for a talk on turtle conservation, so instead I decided to be an interested observer. I wanted to know what the eggs were for. To sell them, of course. They fetched a good price at the hotels. I mentioned that I had never seen turtle eggs on a menu anywhere in Barbados. More explanations followed. The eggs would not be listed on any menu as turtle eggs, but as "chef's choice" or something like that, and when customers asked what the chef's choice was tonight, they would be told, he said, and "in a very soft voice, almost a whisper".

I am glad to say that the turtles did not turn up that night. The next day, Sunday, during the Barbados National Trust walk, I mentioned this incident to one of the walkers who had knowledge of and an interest in Caribbean conservation. He told me that although the turtles are supposed to be protected, there was a problem with people stealing their eggs, and yes, he was sure that what the man on the beach had told me about "chef's choice" was true. The restaurants and hotels made their own rules. He commented that if people keep taking the turtle eggs there would come a time when there wouldn't be any turtles left. I could see the argument, but I could also see the situation of my egg-stealing friend, who was a really nice brother. All he wanted was to make some money to supplement his earnings. Just like my almost speechless Mexican-Indian guide (see below), all these local working-class men want is a small piece of the tourist trade. I understood and sympathised with this, but even so I was glad that our moonlight walk and our search for the turtles ended in failure. I never saw the brother again, but I hope that he had better luck with the white woman.

Mexico: a walk in the Copper Canyon – always Coca-Cola!

Sometimes it seems to me that the world is becoming rapidly homogenised. Like so many things this put me in a double bind. On the one hand I rejoice in cultural diversity, and on the other I am always glad to hear a familiar tune on the radio wherever I am. Arriving in San Jóse Costa Rica by bus from Panama and checking into a hotel at two o'clock in the morning, to the strains of Bob Marley singing "Don't worry 'bout a ting" was very comforting. In China, a Beatles song bridged the language and cultural gap between a Chinese sister and me. On a long hike in Bhutan I had become separated from my companions and ended up cutting across a rice field. A teenage boy was working in the field, and when I asked him the way he pointed and came out of the field and accompanied me to the path. As we walked across the rice field he asked me if I knew Michael Jackson. I said not personally. In Canberra, Australia, I pressed "play" on my friend's son's tape recorder and heard one of the most violent and anti-woman songs deceitfully packaged as rap music. While I do appreciate popular music, both local and international, I am bored with every city in the world looking more or less the same, and one hotel room being pretty much like another. But I now understand that this globalisation is only skin-deep, and that there is a balancing act going on, and that alongside the thrust towards sameness goes an opposing force towards diversity.

I can see this happening in Barbados, where many local children seem to me to be almost monolingual in the Bajan dialect. Through television, children growing up in Barbados are exposed to a standard American and standard (British) English from early on in their lives. Yet the actual use of standard English seems to me to be declining, in favour of Bajan dialect. Our parents considered it rude if as children we spoke rough, i.e. in dialect to an adult. In conversation with adults we were expected to try to speak "proper English". My father in particular was a great one for his dictionary, and would be forever correcting our "bad" English. We now know that what we were speaking was not bad English at all, but a dialect of English and of other long forgotten languages that our ancestors brought with them from Africa. It would have been quite useless for my father to know that dialect was another language. For him, and for quite a lot like him, dialect would always be bad English.

Another expression of the opposing force between local and global is nationalism. As people are able to move more easily around the world, so more fences have to be built to keep them out. But only if they are wearing the wrong tag. If the tag says "tourist" then the message is "Bienvenido, Benvenuti, Welkom, Velkommen, Welcome, etc. Can we relieve you of your money!" If the traveller bears a label that identifies her as "refugee" or "immigrant", the response is "KEEP OUT!" The irony is that the people who are being kept out are usually suffering a double dispossession. For these people have often already been deprived by colonialism and imperialism of their land and their birthright. Thereafter they may suffer further dispossession in the wars and corruption that seem to ride on the back of independence. So people travel away from home, trying to do what so-called "settlers" did in their own countries: to find somewhere to live and to work. The difference is that the settlers were not refugees, and that these new settlers lack the confidence that comes with guns, and with feelings of racial, moral and religious superiority.

These were the kind of thoughts I mulled over on a walk in Mexico, in the Barrancas del Cobre. From the time I arrived at the hotel, and looked down into what seemed a massive crater with a path across it, I knew I had to explore, that I simply had to go there. I lost no time in fixing it up, the choice being between a pony trek or hike. I had no difficulty deciding on a hike. I was told that the guide would call for me the next morning after breakfast, and when he came, I was ready and waiting. We set off in silence and remained so for the best part of eight or so kilometres; I was beginning to regret my choice of man over horse. The guide appeared to be dumb. He made no effort whatsoever to communicate, to point out features of interest or to impart any information. He walked ahead and I followed. After about an hour and a half of this we came across a group of German tourists and their guide. They were resting and we joined them for a while. During this time my guide engaged in a heated exchange with the other guide, it was only then that I knew for sure that he could actually speak. We walked on, as I am not one for resting, and the walk itself was not really very strenuous, though the Germans did seem to think it was.

After another eight kilometres or so as we descended into a valley, the guide pointing to a little hut nestling in the valley below. As we arrived, the owner, an old man, came out to greet us, and my guide had no difficulty in talking to him either. I decided that I too needed some human contact and began a conversation with the old man. The place was very dry, and there were no streams and no evidence of a water-source, and as my guide provided no information, I decided that I would have to find out for myself. I asked the old man how they managed for water. He told me that when it rained, he and his wife collected and stored it. And what happened when there was no rain, when there was no more water? He replied, "Well, then we drink Coke." And indeed there were Coca-Cola bottles lying around. Is there any place on earth that is free of discarded Coca-Cola bottles and cans, and lots of plastic bags, of globalisation?

We stayed there for a while and it emerged that my guide was waiting for the other party to catch us up and for us all to return together. When they joined us I complained to the other guide about the lack of information and the complete silence I had had to endure. He told me in English that my guide was a local Indian who knew no English and very little Spanish, and was known locally as the "quiet one", having very little to say, in any language. I like quiet, but there is quiet and there is quiet, and my guide had been way over the top in that league. Whatever the other guide said to him, mine began to speak to me and asked whether I wanted to go back the way we had come or by the long hard route. Since I hate backtracking, it had to be the latter. The Germans expressed their admiration at this, then we all bought horrible tatty souvenirs from the lady of the house, before setting off along opposite paths. The German group went in one direction, the silent one and I in the other.

The walk back was very different; on several occasions the guide actually spoke to me. Little bits of information were passed on in a Spanish that was even more tentative and halting than my own. I shared my fruit and drink with him, something I would not have done earlier in the day. In the morning, at the start of our trek, it had been quite chilly, cold even, but by this time it was very hot, and the guide had brought nothing to drink. Yet he was happy enough to share mine. To be fair I do not think he expected me to choose that route back, so he was not prepared for such a long walk. For me this rescued the day, and without it I would have been left feeling resentful and cheated.

Back at the Pasada Mirador hotel I tried to identify the walk in the brochure. It was certainly not the trek to the Cerocahui waterfall. Was it perhaps the one to Tarahumara Rancho of Wakajipare? That was meant to be an eight-kilometre round trip, and we had easily walked sixteen or more. I gave up, and looked instead at some of the other offerings. My eyes fell on the tour of a private Tarahumara Indian girls' boarding school, where girls would sing in Tarahumara for groups, and visitors were most welcome. I cannot understand why local people are used in this way, and what on earth could be especially interesting about a girls' boarding school.

But this advert brought to mind a tour I once made of a girls' boarding school in an African country. My tour guide was the deputy headmistress, and the tour turned out to be a very interesting experience in a way that was not intended. I am never keen to gape at people's living arrangements, but I am interested in educational facilities and equipment. After we had looked round the school I tried to be excused from an inspection of the girls' dorms. I felt that dorms were more or less the same the world over, but she wouldn't have it – we must complete the tour. When we approached she entered, I noticed, without knocking. Inside we were greeted by girls washing, ironing, plaiting each other's hair, reading, writing, and just off in the corner of the room were two making love. These latter were totally absorbed, and unaware of our presence, at which we turned and walked out, with nothing said. My first thought was that she should at least have knocked. My second was how normal everything had been, everyone going about their activities, including the two lovers. I wondered whether things like that went on at the Tarahumara girls' boarding school, when they were not singing for the tourists.

Some days later I tried to untangle my feelings about that Mexican walk and the almost silent guide. Until he had pointed to the cottage in the valley, I had felt the walk to be pointless. I had no idea where we were going, and although I felt I should be pleased to have a Tarahumara Indian guide, this brought me no advantage. He couldn't or wouldn't share his knowledge of the place, and although paid to be a guide, he had been so only in the most minimal sense of the word. The hotel had told me that guides were chosen for their local knowledge – but where was it? I was willing to make an effort to speak and understand Spanish, but he spoke no English and hardly any Spanish, so how could he be my "guide"? This was the kind of double bind that someone like me was sure to fall into. We wanted to preserve indigenous languages, as long as indigenous people would speak to us in a common tongue. So should I apologise for expecting value for money, for expecting the same from the Tarahumara Indian guide as I would from anyone else? I don't think so.

The global and the local: what has this walk to do with these issues? Everything! My local guide was one of the dispossessed, for his people are now beggars in their own countries, and their language had no currency beyond the narrow confines of their own small communities. Without the Spanish language, the language of the conquistadors, Indians were unable to function and be a part of the Mexican economy. Indians were totally marginalised in the Mexican tourist trade, and even their crafts were generally marketed and sold by Spanish-speaking people. For myself, I want to do anything I can to end discrimination against and marginalisation of indigenous peoples. I do really want indigenous languages to survive, though if I am on an escorted walk in a strange country I would prefer a guide I can communicate with. Apart from the overpowering majesty and splendour of the natural world, my visit to the Antigens del Cobra left me with some very powerful images. The first was of the old man and his wife, who at times of water scarcity drink Coca-Cola, and the second was of the Coca-Cola bottles, cans and assorted plastic bags littering this isolated and almost desolate place. And of course I was also left to puzzle over the dilemma posed by my (almost) silent Tarahumara guide.

Bhutan – all the king's pheasants and all the king's men

Bhutan retains a unique place in my memory. The country has a distinct identity, which it is striving to preserve. Unfortunately the cost is high, such as quite severe punishment for failing to wear the traditional dress. This means that in Thimpu at least young people end up wearing the most bizarre combination of the old and the new: jeans and T-shirts with Bhutanese traditional clothes. One evening, two Bhutanese invited me for drinks, ladies of much wealth and high social standing. They turned up wearing slacks or something equally unsuitable by Bhutanese standards. One of the others present took great exception to this breaking of the law, and observed that they got away with it only because they were able to travel by car!

In the countryside, where we spent a lot of time travelling by bus and going on hikes, the Bhutanese women worked in the fields with their babies on their backs, and seemed untroubled by the latest designer wear. I wore the Bhutanese costume once, and was quite glad to get out of it at the end of the evening – but then I have the same feeling about most formal clothes. It seems a shame that Bhutan should require the force of law and the threat of fines and imprisonment in order to preserve its cultural heritage and distinct identity. Both language and clothing have evolved, and will continue to do so, even in Bhutan. The Bhutanese people have also preserved their architectural heritage, and Thimpu, the capital, is a uniquely beautiful and interesting place. To think that Thimpu and Bangkok are both capitals of Buddhist countries! Thimpu nestling in the foothills of the Himalayas, with Dzongs, monks and prayer flags everywhere, and Bangkok a hell on earth, with noise, pollution, jam-packed with people and streams of never-ending traffic!

Obviously I loved Bhutan, and even the contradictions in its society had a new and different flavour. We did some lovely walks, visited many Dzongs, and met many interesting people. This particular episode concerns a weekend spent hiking up to about 4,000 metres. Peter and I set off from Thimpu in a jeep, which dropped us at the start of a path, which we were told led up to the tourist cottage, where we could stay for the weekend. We had already been to the tourist office, discussed our weekend plans and had their agreement to use the cottage – free of charge. That should have warned us. Instead we were just delighted and excited by the prospect of going for a weekend hike in the foothills of the Himalayas. Never mind what Peter's doctor had said about the risk to a man who two years before had undergone a triple bypass operation! As we got out of the jeep to start our hike to the cottage, we saw a group of what appeared to be soldiers, with pack ponies and boxes containing something live.

We introduced ourselves. They seemed very pleased to hear that we were going their way and invited us to join their party. We gladly accepted. They were wardens, not soldiers, and the "something live" in the crates were pheasants, which they were going up into the hills to release. The king of Bhutan had chosen this weekend to start the re-introduction of pheasants into this part of his kingdom. What luck! The two leaders quite literally took us under their wing, as it were, putting our heavy backpacks on the ponies and leading the way up the mountains. The walk was extremely difficult, very strenuous and demanding, even without the backpacks, and Peter was walking extremely slowly, while I more or less kept pace with the leader. From time to time monks or young acolytes would pass us, going to or from the monastery, which was not very far from the cottage. I fell into conversation with a monk and we walked together for a little while. He was wearing light shoes without socks and was totally at ease. He explained to me that the best way to walk in the mountains was to be slightly bent, and not to walk upright. He showed me. I tried it, and it felt good, so after that I tried to walk in his footsteps, and to bend as he did. When he returned to his normal speed I could not keep up, and he soon disappeared in the distance.

As we ascended we began to walk through snow, which was quite deep, but even then the monks and nuns were still in light shoes with no socks. Dressed up as I was, and walking hard, I still felt the cold, while they were running around almost barefoot. We arrived at the cottage just as darkness was beginning to fall, and found out why the lodge was free. It was a very solid building, but minus windows, doors, water, a toilet or any other facility associated with overnight accommodation. One of the two young men, who by now we referred to as our minders, went off to find firewood, while the other used what little wood there was available to get a fire going and to make some tea. Things were looking up.

We spent a cold but glorious weekend in that cottage, looked after by our two newly acquired friends. On the Sunday I went for a walk in the snow, and soon after leaving the house I was joined by one of our friends. He felt that it was not safe for me to wander around alone. We talked. He was happy to share his knowledge about Bhutanese society with me, and having been in the tourism business he was quite well informed and knowledgeable. I told him that I was interested in marriage and in the relationship between men and women, and I asked for his views. He seemed to think that jealousy was the cause of divorce in the West, and he explained that this was not so prevalent in Bhutan because sex in itself was not considered of great importance. He said that in Bhutan married people were free to have other sexual partners, without creating problems for the marriage. I wondered whether many Bhutanese women would agree with him. He said that in this matter there was equality, and that Bhutanese women were generally in a better position than the men, because upon marriage it was the men who left their homes and moved to live in their wives' homes. He gave me his version of the Bhutanese courting customs, which as I remember it had to do with a young man visiting a young girl over a period of time. It began with the young man knocking on the girl's bedroom window. If she liked him she opened the window, and he went in and stayed the night. That became the pattern until at some point he decided to stay for good. From that time on the couple were regarded as husband and wife, and they were married. My informant told me that he himself had been married for twelve years and had two sons.

We also talked about the wildlife, the problem of poachers, and the king's wish to re-introduce pheasants into the Himalayas. Wild dogs had already killed many of them, and others had flown away and could not be found to be given the food that had been brought for them. These would almost certainly die of hunger. To ensure the survival of the remainder the wardens thought that they might have to kill the wild dogs. I said that I thought that Buddhists were not supposed to kill. Well, they said, if the birds were to live the dogs must die. By this time we had more or less covered sex, religion, philosophy, and were now back at the cottage. Somehow Peter and I got through the second night of even more bitter cold, and in the morning we left. But before leaving we had to go to the monastery to pay our respect to the monks. One of them was the uncle to one of our guides. Bhutan is the kind of place where everyone seems to be related in one way or another, and there seemed to be a limited supply of surnames. We had spent two memorable nights in the tourist cottage, and had coped (with a lot of help from our friends). As we left the mountain the conditions could not have been more different from when we had arrived two days earlier. The snow had melted, and it was a warm and sunny day in the foothills of the Himalayas

When I had first arrived in Bhutan, out of the blue one of the numerous European aid workers informed me I was not the first Barbadian to visit the country. I told him that this was the story of my life, but that one day I hoped to do something original. I had not realised that I'd come to Bhutan to set a record. I thought I'd come to visit my friend and to see something of this unusual country, to live and learn. During our time in Bhutan, I talked to many people, went to meetings of various kinds, attended at least one conference and lots of social engagements, and of course I also read books and academic papers. As guests at India House Peter and I were allowed to travel freely around the country, which we did, almost always by local bus. We did not travel on tourist buses and we never had a guide with us. After two months I felt I knew a little bit about Bhutan. My walk/talk with my Bhutanese brother in the snow that Sunday was for me the country's quintessence. How accurate was that version of Bhutanese marriage customs was not really important. What mattered was that I had been allowed to share in a vision of his society, and that for a few brief moments I felt myself to be part of that world.

In the days that followed, Peter and I met with our two warden friends many times. The first occasion was soon after our weekend adventure, when they joined us for dinner. Here we planned another hiking expedition to the mountains, though the plan came to nothing. I also had a chance to find out more about Bhutanese marriage and family life when I attend an international woman's day conference, and also visited a number of projects connected with family support and intervention. I am not going to dwell on any of this here, except to say that the woman's day conference seemed to me to be a very male-dominated affair with only one woman on the platform. The men were generally agreed that Bhutanese women were exceptionally lucky compared with women elsewhere. Bhutanese women had always been financially sound, and the development of tourism had made them more so, as they were able to earn good money from sales of their blankets and other woven goods to tourists. The lone woman speaker, while taking great care to agree with everything the men said, nevertheless added to the discussion. She drew attention to the high levels of alcohol consumption among both men and women in Bhutan, and suggested that this was leading to domestic violence and the break-up of families. This was for me an all too familiar story. And so, the walk/talk with my Bhutanese brother took its place alongside many other experiences and added to the richness and variety of my knowledge of his society.

Me and my white brothers talking

It has been my unfortunate experience, on at least three occasions, to have met a certain type of white, middle-aged American male person, who always starts the conversation by telling me which political party he votes for, being the Democrats, and which civil rights marches he has been on. It is not as if I ever ask, or am interested. This information is delivered almost ritualistically, and more or less follows this pattern:

He: "I always vote Democratic, have never been tempted to do otherwise."

I: "Oh really."

He: "Yes. I've always been committed to equal opportunities. I was there throughout the sixties, I heard Martin Luther King speak at... ."

On and on.

That rendition usually takes a few minutes, but it always seems like hours to me and after that the white brother behaves more or less normally. I have puzzled over this for some time and wondered whether other black sisters suffer in the same way, or whether there is something about me that brings this on. All replies to this question will be gratefully received and treated in the strictest confidence, or not as the informant prefers.

It was after a conversation in Costa Rica with another person fitting the above description that I began to make the connection, and to wonder about it. Why this desire to establish a political identity, and to answer a question that I had not posed, i.e. "What did you do during the civil rights movement?" I can't quite understand why these men think it should matter to me what they did or did not do during that time. I listen to these brothers as I have listened to so many others, and I just hope they feel better for voting Democrat and for marching with Martin Luther King. Always supposing they did in fact do these things, and were not instead members of the Ku Klux Klan.

In November 1996 I entered a period during which I seemed to be the target of harassment by my white American brothers. My next encounter with the species came at the American embassy in Barbados, where I went to get a visitor's visa. It was a very interesting experience, as I sat for three hours waiting in line. I did wonder how would they treat this Third World person carrying a First World passport in a Third World country applying for a visa to visit heaven. The answer was "with suspicion and hostility". The first thing was an order to "remove your dark glasses!" I sweetly explained as I took them off that they were actually prescription glasses. "Well then you can put them on again." How kind.

This man had enormous difficulty in accepting that the person standing before him was what she said she was. Nothing in his life had prepared him for the sight of a black woman saying that she worked in an English university. "What do you do? How many degrees have you got?" The questions went on, and on. Then he settled on money. How could he know if I was able to support myself on a visit to the USA? Did I have any savings? Did I have a bank statement with me? No, I did not. But he had two passports of mine in his hands, one expired, one current. These spanned a period of more than twelve years and provided ample proof that I had made repeated visits to the USA, and had left presumably without troubling the welfare services too much. More questions. This time about my relatives, my sister and my brother, both residents or citizens of the USA. I said that I had no knowledge of them, that I was not in touch with them and I could not help with any information about them. He eyed me suspiciously, and was clearly unconvinced about the truth of this reply.

So he asked again: "They are your family, are they not?"

I: "So what?"

In spite of my resolve to be calm, my irritation was beginning to show. The man glared at me: "Why should I treat you any different from those others sitting there?" he asked. I didn't recall having asked to be treated differently. But I took the opportunity of reminding him that there was a visa waiver agreement between the UK and the USA. He agreed that this was indeed the case. So I asked him point blank whether he was refusing my request for a visa. He said that he was not refusing me a visa, but was requiring me to provide proof of income. After a week I returned with two bank statements, and a few days later I collected my passport with the visa stamped in it. Peter's USA visa had expired at the same time as mine, but he had managed to get a new one without the kind of questioning, I may even say harassment, I had been subjected to and without producing any proof of income. I guess that US embassy staff in Third World countries are entitled to their bit of fun. It must increase their job satisfaction.

Of men and madness – pictures from some walks

I don't know when I first became aware of a state of mind called "madness", but it must have been quite early on in my life, because I seemed to have grown up with the idea that one of my Grenadian cousins was "mad" and lived in a mental institution. I never knew his story, and still don't. That cousin was on my mother's side, her nephew. On my father's side I later had the experience of at least two more mad cousins, and at some point my youngest brother also joined the ranks of the insane. Then a few years ago the final addition was my own son. I think that it is safe to say that as a family we have had more than our share of male madness – and those are the ones who have been formally diagnosed.

Professionally I have also been involved with madness. As a social worker I have worked with the mentally ill, and as a social work lecturer I have marked and commented on many, many essays and theses dealing with the subject. There is a view among so-called radicals that there is no such thing as "madness", because all behaviour, including madness, is manufactured by society to serve society's purpose. Following my son's illness, well-intentioned, and not so well-intentioned people, black and white, have tried to comfort me by telling me that it was down to his experience of "racism". It was the familiar explanation adjusted for a different scenario – black male madness is manufactured by a white society, which is especially oppressive towards black males. For me this is too simple an explanation for complex human behaviour, we human beings are the totality of our social experience plus whatever our ancestors bequeath us through our genes. So it would be just as easy for me to blame my grandparents, as it would to blame society. And what is the point of blaming anybody or anything? For most black people in Britain racism is an inevitable and inescapable part of everyday experience. This simple fact can sometimes get in the way of our understanding and acceptance of the problems of existence, which may not be directly related to racism. We may well be tempted to explain all life's problems as due to racism – and some of our problems may well be exacerbated by racism – but that is not the same as saying that racism is the cause of them. I have to say that I am generally very suspicious of the motives of white people who explain to black people the evils of racism. I think that racism must be the one thing we black people do not need lessons in from white people. And racism is not a white monopoly. Just look at Guyana, and at Trinidad and Tobago. The most extreme form of racism I myself have ever experienced was in India.

And now I want to present some of the many images I carry around in my head connected to the notion of men and madness.

The first has to do with the American invasion of Grenada in 1983. I listened to the radio and heard that one of the US bombs had fallen on the psychiatric hospital in St Georges. I thought about my cousin, and wondered how he fared. The news report said that the patients were wandering around the town, but it did not mention any deaths. I thought of my aunt, her first born inadvertently freed by the US army, her last born imprisoned by it. My sympathies were with the psychiatric patients, as I imagined them wandering around St Georges dazed and confused, even as I was dazed and confused, by what was happening in their country. If it was not long before things were set to rights, with the hospital repaired and all the patients safely back inside, then my mad cousin's confusion may well have ended with a return to the familiar surroundings of the hospital – however my confusion and inability to understand these events remains and deepens with the years.

We change scenes, from the Caribbean to Australia, for my second picture. We were based in Canberra, but this weekend we were heading north, Sydney being our first stop. A weekend hike through Sydney National Park had been planned, but turned into a day-hike instead, which was just as well as I was feeling extremely unwell. I put it down to a reaction to the hepatitis injection I had just received. I don't know what it was but by the time we emerged from the park I was walking in robot-mode. As soon as Peter and I reached our hotel I showered, turned the TV on and I collapsed on the bed. It was national schizophrenic week in Australia, and I watched a documentary about a family in which a man (himself a doctor), and his son and daughter were all suffering from this illness. The father and daughter either were not severe cases or had periods of remission, because they both worked. But the son lived in a caravan at the bottom of the garden in a completely paranoid state, isolated from the rest of the family and, it seemed, from all humanity. The sight of him, and the sound of his mother's voice talking about his condition, triggered in me a very deep sadness. I thought of my own son, while the woman's words of confusion and loss echoed my own feelings. These threatened to overwhelm me and I began to feel adrift. Then the telephone rang and I turned the TV off, but the images and the feelings remain.

Images of madness sometimes come upon me in the most unexpected of places, when I am least prepared and most vulnerable. My next such experience occurred in Botswana in Southern Africa. My Zimbabwe sister and I more or less hitch-hiked from Bulawayo to Gabarone, the capital of Botswana. When we failed to get a lift we got the bus and made it to Gabarone in about twelve hours. Before leaving Bulawayo I had failed to consult an atlas, and all the time we had been travelling I was convinced that we were headed for the Okavanga. I was therefore quite disappointed to find myself in Gabarone, which is virtual desert and nothing at all like the lush delta of the Okavanga. It served me right for not checking, but even had I known the correct destination I would have gone anyhow. In Gabarone, when a paving stone is dislodged, desert sands emerge. It is a modern town, quite small and compact, and with lots of air-conditioned shops. Botswana is rich in minerals, diamonds and such.

One day my friend and I were walking around the town, window shopping, browsing among the crafts, souvenirs, the usual, when, as we came out of the air-conditioning and down some steps into the car park, I saw a young man, rolling in the dust. He was clearly in another world, totally absorbed in what he was doing and oblivious to everything and everyone. I stopped and stood beside him, wanting to say something, to reach out to him in some way, but I did not know his language, and I knew that there were no words in any language that could bridge the gap between us. My friend beckoned me on impatiently, and I walked slowly towards her and away from the young man. I did not want to catch up with her too quickly. For some reason I felt that I needed to be near the young man, but at the same time I did not want to draw attention to myself or to do anything that might require an explanation. Reality prevailed and I soon quickened my pace and caught up with my friend, who either did not notice or wasn't interested, as she made no comment at all about my strange behaviour.

The next image is from the Surrey countryside in autumn, a time of year I love to hike. On this particular occasion I was with the local ramblers. We were walking in what for Surrey is considered hilly country. There were about eight of us regulars, plus a young man who had come along for the first time. Although tennis shoes would do for many walks, they were not ideal for crossing muddy fields or walking along rough, rocky, country paths. On a walk like this it was not really necessary to spend a fortune on Basher boots, as any strong shoes would do, but this young man was wearing soft shoes, and very light clothing. Then it started to rain, at first just lightly, but then with increasing force. Out came raincoats and other gear. I had come equipped with an umbrella, which the others had at first found quite amusing. The young man had neither raincoat nor umbrella, and was totally unprepared for a hike in the English countryside in autumn. In order to stop him becoming completely soaked through I lent him my umbrella. "Lucky you brought that, after all," the group leader said as we trudged along. I nodded my agreement. She took this opportunity of telling me that a social worker rang her during the week and asked whether the walk would be suitable for her client, a young man suffering with mental health problems. She had encouraged the social worker to let the young man come walking with the group, "but I told her to make sure he wore suitable shoes and brought rain gear". She sighed as she said this last bit. During the rest of the walk each person took it in turns to say something about the young man's condition, in pity, or in anger and frustration. I kept my silence and was glad that I had not persuaded my son to join us. There are times when it would be nice to forget that my only son is mentally ill. I must admit that I have sometimes seen walking as a form of escape, a way of clearing my mind, so as to return renewed to face the inevitable problems. From time to time the escape route closes off, and I am reminded that we are never far from human suffering and that we take our own pain and our vulnerability with us wherever we go.

So it was in Hungary in 1996. After many years in the academic wilderness I found myself once more in the corridors of knowledge, or in the ivory towers or whatever universities are these days. During an academic visit to Hungary I was invited, more or less, to inspect a psychiatric hospital. I was with a group and all my colleagues were occupied on similar missions, so I was alone. Alone, in a foreign country, I suddenly I found myself back on the other side of the desk that divides the helped from the helper. Panic! In learning the role of carer I had unlearnt my other roles: social worker, academic, professional welfare person. Could I cope? Would I cope? When on a very long or difficult hike, and I have become totally exhausted, I always go into robot-mode. And now robot-mode came to my rescue, for in it I listened as the superintendent told me about the very high suicide rate among Hungarian men, among the highest in the world. The psychiatrist speculated about whether there may be a genetic component at work in the Hungarian male population. See? In the absence of racism, try genetics.

The Hungarians practise racism against Gypsies and other minorities, and are not themselves the object of racism.

Meanwhile my robot program had failed and I was wondering whether this information would be of help to my grandson in his efforts to understand his father's death by suicide. His grandfather on his father's side was Hungarian. Why did I ever think I was strong enough to venture back into that world? Somehow or other I got through the visit, even talking and joking with a young male patient who spoke a bit of English. As my visit came to an end I was left with the overwhelming impression that psychiatric hospitals are exactly the same the world over. I've seen it all before, and I am now part of this world. In spite of my panic and foreboding I can cope, and I can manage to combine these different roles, and I know that I can function if I have to. So, at least for the time the time being, I can remain on both sides of the desk.

A question of identity

I have sometimes found myself drawn into other people's lives almost against my will. I find myself being given a starring role or a small part, without knowing or understanding the plot. It was a bit like that with the two homosexual brothers who drew me, somewhat unwillingly, into their world.

The place is Port Arthur, Queensland, Australia, the year is 1993, and Peter and I had been out walking and ended up at a yacht club, which had been recommended for both its views and its beer. We were sitting quietly in the grounds enjoying both these aspects when a party of four joined us – three men and a woman. No sooner were they seated than it became evident that they were two couples, the younger pair being guys, a rather plump man in his forties and his slim, handsome young lover, while the other, older pair were the parents of the younger man. The dynamics of this encounter I find difficult to explain, but here goes. There were six people, but the conversation involved only three, the older man of the homosexual pair deciding that this was a perfect occasion to test his lover to the limit, and that I was the perfect fall person. He began by telling me that he knew London very well, that he had met his partner in London, and that he himself was Australian. His lover and his family were English.

The man addressed me in a very familiar manner, as though he knew me, and started talking in Jamaican, and telling me that he was sure that he knew black London better than I did. To prove this he started name-dropping. It was as though he felt that his access to black London gave him a special status with any black Caribbean person. He even called me "sister". Meanwhile Peter and his friend's mum and dad were chatting and exchanging the usual pleasantries and bit of travel information. This was not part of his script, for they were not allowed to talk among themselves, and as soon as he noticed them doing so he started to abuse his lover. He stated in a loud voice, "This man is homosexual, but he cannot accept it!" This announcement put an end to the pleasantries. We all fell silent as the young man visibly shrank into himself: no pity was shown as his lover continued to harangue him and to recount all the details of their highly fraught relationship. At one point his partner's mother ventured an observation along the lines of "it wouldn't do if we were all the same," but she was simply ignored. I remained the centre of attention, as the older man continued sharing his confidences with me, while the younger man looked helplessly on. His obvious embarrassment and discomfort seemed to challenge and provoke the older man.

The older man then taunted him with this: "Why are you so embarrassed? Is it because they now know you are a queer? Will you be leaving me again?" He then explained to all of us that the young man was always trying to walk out of their relationship (I thought to myself – no wonder!). Then my turn came as he brought me directly into his argument with this very profound statement: "She is not embarrassed about being black, why should you be embarrassed about being queer?" I have always regarded the homosexuality with colour comparison as rather spurious. Why did he expect me to be embarrassed about being black? What if I'd been a black lesbian? I decided that the older man was simply a bully, that he had seen in my black presence the opportunity to make some statements about white male homosexual identity, and in particular about his young lover. His lover's parents had come from England to visit their son, and it had all been done for their benefit, the aim being to tell them the truth about his sexual orientation. These parents were going to be made to see their son as he really was, not just a queer, but a queer who could not even accept himself. Coming upon me, a black person in his almost pure-white world, the aggressor had seen my situation as parallel to theirs: homosexuals in an almost straight world. So he had seized on the chance to assert his homosexual identity, and to score points against his partner.

Several times the aggressor invited me to join in his little game, either by asking my opinion or suggesting that his partner ask me something. "Ask her what she thinks" – about this or that, whatever he was going on about at the time. But I was not playing ball, even though I felt that my refusal to play the part he had assigned me might well be interpreted by him as an indication that I was after all insecure about my blackness. Still I did not join in, and before things could take another turn, we left. As Peter and I walked back to our hotel I said out loud, to no one in particular, "It's the parents I feel sorry for." And I meant it.

Talking about heaven

The walk/talk with one of my brothers that I like best is set in the Hampshire countryside, and probably tells more about me than it does about him, but still, here goes. This brother was on a visit to England from the Caribbean, and I was keen to show him something of the English countryside.

Unfortunately, like so many of my black brothers and sisters, he "had the Lord", so before our walk we had to go to church. Any church in Hampshire is sure to be filled with English people, who are, generally speaking, white.

I am positive that if there is a heaven it must be racially segregated, that it couldn't function otherwise. My visitor was not at all comfortable in this all-white environment. Even so he was satisfied that he had done the right thing in going to church. The Lord had got his due, and after church, we went for a walk. During the walk I took the opportunity of mentioning that he had more in common with all those white people in church than he had with me. He was taken aback: "How so?" I explained that, as I saw it, he and the church members as Christians shared a common belief system and worshipped the same God, hoping and expecting to arrive at the same place eventually, whereas as a committed non-believer I was outside this belief system. I continued to analyse the limitations of our relationship, by saying that as friends all we shared was social contact – nothing in comparison with what he shared with his fellow-Christians. "So you see you are closer to all those strangers than you are to me. You should not feel threatened or isolated in a white church, since you will be sharing eternity with those people." We walked in silence for a while, and then he spoke. But it was only to say that although he understood my reasoning, he could not accept my conclusion.

I was relieved that the conversation ended at this point. I have had some very strange exchanges with my black Christian brothers over the years, almost always focusing on their refusal to accept me as a non-believer. On one occasion in London a black Baptist minister flatly refused to accept that I was a non-believer, as he described all such talk as "white people's rubbish", stating categorically that there was no such thing as a black atheist. (Just as there were no black people who can't sing and dance!) It is not only black brothers who have difficulty. Once on a Barbados National Trust walk I had to endure an Easter sermon given by the walk-leader, an Englishman. After what I considered a suitable interval I explained to him that as a non-believer I did not really come on a walk to be preached at. He is a scientist but dismissed my objections with the words, "There's no such thing as a non-believer." I remembered these exchanges as my black Christian friend and I walked the Hampshire countryside that Sunday morning. Another thing I recalled was my mother's deep disappointment over my failure to accept the Lord when during my adolescence, and in spite of much pressure, it became clear that I was not going to follow the Christian path.

My mother took this very hard and said to me that of all her seven children, I was the one with the best reason for accepting the Lord. She reminded me that I had been snatched from the jaws of death, God had saved my life, and she felt that I should spend the rest of that life thanking and praising him for this miracle. I was a teenager, and I thought I was being very clever and sophisticated when I replied that the way I had turned out must also be part of God's plan, so why not accept it? Views like that were very hurtful and upsetting to my deeply religious mother.

My views on religion and my lack of faith came long before my travels and my contact with what the London brother had called "white people's rubbish". That brother had been way out of line in saying that I was glad that the walk in Hampshire did not degenerate into this kind of posturing, or into an attempt to convert me, and that we two black people could enjoy an autumn walk in England, having (at least in his case) worshipped in a white English church. I thought of his discomfort in the church, and his problem with the colour of the people, but his total unawareness of the colour of their God. I wanted to quote to him a few lines from a poem, which seemed to me very apt for the occasion, but caution forbade then, so I quote them now. I came across it in one of the first books on philosophy I ever read, and it has stayed with me ever since (I have no idea of the source):

The Afric God has dark skin
Black eyes and woolly hair.
The Grecian God is like the Greek
As green eyed, bold and fair!

In the Barbados of my childhood and adolescence, there were no "Afric Gods". Things have changed now, in the meantime I have found that I can get along quite well without gods of any kind: I manage just fine with my walks.

Soldier, will you walk with me with your knapsack, pipe and drum?

I suppose that on the whole I would prefer a world without soldiers, armies and such, but as to my feelings about any particular soldier – this would depend on the individual. The soldier brother I spent the day walking with one Sunday in the late spring of 1995 was very rewarding company. My walk with him was, as far as I know, the only time that I have ever walked with the military, so to speak.

As I said, it was a Sunday morning and I'd set out in good time to meet the Staines ramblers, but I went to the wrong car park and missed them. I made my way back home, until, just outside Haslemere, I saw a group of hikers in a car park on the other side of the road. Why not join them? Why not indeed. I turned around and went back, got out of the car and approached them ready to tell my story about the wrong car park. They were most welcoming, and very happy to have me join them, whatever the reasons that had brought me there. We set off and it soon became clear that this was a slow group, and I really wanted to stretch myself. I wanted a fast walk.

There was a young man in the group who was in the same predicament, and we fell into step and moved away from the group. The two of us walked fast, and it was good. I began to relax and enjoy the walk, and to forget about having missed my own group. We did not talk much, but at one point we missed the path and ended up in some thick undergrowth. Laughing and joking about being lost forever we pushed our way out. Should we go on or wait for the others? We decided to go on. I felt quite happy in his company, even though I did not know him: we had been lost in the undergrowth and come through, so now there was a bond between us. We began to talk and it turned out that he was a soldier, a captain in the British army, serving in Northern

Ireland. We talked about that, and he spoke very frankly and sensitively about what was going on there. Silently I wondered how such a nice young man could bear to be a soldier… . Out loud I expressed my amazement that a soldier would want to spend his spare time walking, for didn't they do lots of walking in the army?

He laughed and said that this type of walk was rather different from what they did in the army. Anyhow, he had not come from Ireland to walk, he had come to spend the weekend with his girlfriend, the woman who he expected would soon be his wife, though he had walked into a "Dear John" situation. Just the night before his girlfriend had ended their relationship, telling him she didn't want to marry a soldier. This news had spoilt his life and his plans for the weekend, leaving him on this Sunday morning with nothing to do. When he had seen the walk advertised in the local paper he decided that being out with a civilian group might be fun, and would certainly kill some time. Like me he had been disappointed to find that the group walked at such a leisurely pace. We were lucky to have found each other. We waited for the group at the pub-stop, and after lunch we were more inclined to stroll and so rejoined them. We had been stretched. I was surprised at how much I had enjoyed the company of a military man and how much we had found to talk and laugh and be sad about.

Black man's burden – a question of size

I think that I have done only two or three sponsored walks, as I do not feel comfortable with the idea of asking people for money, and I do not like to add that kind of pressure to my walks. This means that I can very easily recall the few among this type of walk I been on. The one I can recall in most detail I do so not for the walk itself, though it was pleasant enough. I can't remember exactly where we started off but I know that the route took us through Richmond Park, by the Thames, and ended at Ham House. Although this was a sponsored walk, in support of some charity or other, I came without sponsorship, and I had no form to hand in to the organisers. I explained my feelings about sponsorship to the lady in charge, but she was not impressed. Where would they be if everyone felt like me? Luckily for her not many people appeared to share my feelings, and everyone else had been sponsored. Anyway, she could hardly stop me from joining the walk, so off I went. No one could tell by looking at me walking that I had not been sponsored, so I was just the same as everyone else. I know this because somewhere along the road a black brother walked beside me and his first words to me had to do with the setting of records. Was I trying to set one? I laughed this off and replied that I was simply walking in my usual brisk style. We continued chatting, then discovered that we had once worked in the same social services department in London. "What caused you to leave?" he asked me. I explained that I had been there only on a temporary assignment and had left at the end of it. The way he'd framed his question prompted me to put the same question to him: "What caused you to leave?" He sighed deeply, and said that it was a long story. My curiosity was stirred and I decided to press on: "Well, are you going to tell me about it, or am I to be left in suspense?" It worked.

He began by saying that he had been forced to leave that office where at different times we had both worked because of "racism". I said that I'd not noticed any worse racism there than anywhere else. To that he replied, "Ah, but you are not a black man, are you?" No argument there, but how was that relevant, I wanted to know. The story contained the explanation. His boss had become drunk during the office Christmas party, and had asked him to sleep with his wife. The wife herself was present and her drunken husband had pointed to her and explained that in more than twenty-five years of marriage he had not been able to satisfy her. He had invited this black man, my walking companion, to fuck his wife and see if with his big black prick he could satisfy her.

The brother did not look at me as he was speaking, he avoided all eye contact, and he kept his gaze firmly fixed on the road ahead. I could see that he did not find the conversation an easy one, and he also mentioned that as a Christian he did not normally use four-letter words. After he'd completed his account we walked in silence for a while. In the end I broke it with another question: "What happened after that?" After the Christmas break a very chastened boss had apologised to him, saying that he did not know what had come over him, that there were no problems in his marriage, and he could offer no explanation for his behaviour. "So how did you deal with it?" He told his boss not to worry, that he understood it had been the drink talking. But he had already decided to leave his job as soon as possible. I said he'd been constructively dismissed, because his boss's behaviour had made it impossible for him to go on working there and that he should have sought legal advice. He said he couldn't be bothered with all that stuff, he simply wanted to be out of there.

The end of his story coincided with an end to another stage of the walk, and, as we joined the other walkers at the watering station, we just drifted apart. I did not see him again that day, nor have I had any further contact with him, but his story is now linked in my mind with another. There is a painting of a group of businessmen in a lift. I think that I may have seen this but it is possible I have read about it only. Whether I have seen it or not, the image is very clear in my mind. It is linked to an article about Fred and Rose West, the multiple sex murderers, of Gloucester. The painting is by an English artist, but it is set in America and is of a group of businessmen together in a lift, with one among them who is different, but dressed the same, in a business suit and carrying a briefcase. Two things set him apart. He is black and his erect penis is sticking out of his trousers, or pants, as the Americans say. I did not say a word about this painting to the brother on that walk, but what he told me made me think of this painting. Like the black man in the picture his boss, in his drunken state, had reduced him to a penis. The black man in the picture perhaps thought of himself as just another businessman, but to the white brothers he was nothing more than an erect black penis – at least that is what this painting means to me. So where do Fred and Rose West come in?

> To mark the new balance in their marriage, Rose at last agreed to go the extra mile for him… She would go with some of his black male friends, who, he had been assuring her, were massive.

> Burns, G (1998), *Happy Like Murderers – The West Case,* Faber and Faber, London

Fred West shared the same fantasies with the social work manager, that they were brothers under the skin. The liberalism of the manager was skin deep, whereas the pain and humiliation that he inflicted on his black brother and colleague scarred the latter very deeply.

Should I end this chapter with such an unpleasant tale, or should I search my memory for another walk/talk with another brother? Perhaps a more positive and uplifting story? No, I don't think so. I had just completed that last paragraph when I saw Elizabeth Young's review of that very book *Happy like Murderers.* Among the heinous crimes of which Fred West was guilty Elizabeth Young lists something she called interracial sex. I will quote in full the relevant section so that the context is clear and its meaning unambiguous. Ms Wilson describes Fred and Rosemary West's background and the challenge facing the author:

> Burns' task has been to do something different and individual with the now familiar facts: priapic cheeky chappie and jobbing builder Fred, and his sullen schoolgirl wife Rose, who came straight from an incestuous home to be groomed by Fred into enthusiastic prostitution, bisexuality, interracial sex and terminal sado-masochism.

> Elizabeth Young (1998), review of *Happy Like Murderers* in
> *The New Statesman* "Books" (October)

Ms Young, in placing what she called "interracial sex" with bisexuality, prostitution and sado-masochism, identifies the nature of her world view. Anyone indulging in "interracial sex" must by definition be deviant.

161

5

PART ONE – WALKING IN EUROPE AND TALKING ABOUT AFRICA

Over the last few decades of colonialism the colonial possessions served capitalism as a safety-valve in times of crisis… the first occasion was during the great economic depression of 1929–34… Africans had nothing to do with the shortcomings of capitalism, but when Europeans were in a mess they had no scruples about intensifying the exploitation of Africa.

Rodney, Walter (1972), *How Europe Underdeveloped Africa*,
Bogle L'Ouverture Publication, London

THIS BOOK began with images of women walking in Africa, and specifically the image of one white European woman and several black African women. In my experience it is very unusual to see local white women walking for pleasure in Africa. The only exception to this general rule is in the leisure industry, where one does come across a few local white women leading walks as part of the job.

Walter Rodney's analysis of the historical relationship between Europe and Africa helps us to explain the differences in the status and experiences of these two sets of women. Europe did indeed "underdevelop" Africa, and, to this day, Africa is still struggling to recover from the dual impact of slavery and colonialism. No other part of the world has had comparable experiences: millions of its people sold into slavery and shipped across the world, followed by the conquest and subjugation of most of the continent, the imposition of foreign rule and a system of government based on racism. As of July 1997, Africa is indebted to the World Bank by more than its entire annual output. However hard Africans work, however far they walk -- they do not move forward. They are chained to the same spot, weighed down by debt. The underdevelopment of Africa continues to this day.

I want to examine issues and ideas concerning Europe and Africa in a somewhat unconventional way. I do not have either the wish or the competence to attempt a sociological or historical analysis of the relationship between the two continents. I take it as read that the economic and social plight of Africa today is directly and inevitably linked to the recent colonial past and to the experience of slavery. Colonialism and slavery represent the dual legacy of Africa: to reverse the impact of these two experiences on the continent remains an ongoing and perhaps insurmountable challenge. Colonialism and slavery are the historical forces that have shaped and fashioned the relationship between Europe and Africa. I do not intend to deal with the political, social and economic relationship between Europe and Africa, instead I will use my own knowledge and experience to discuss and examine the prejudices and perceptions that each has of the other.

I start with Europe, where I have lived, worked and walked for most of my adult life. During my years of travelling and walking in Europe, on occasions I met people who have lived and worked in Africa, or visited an African country as tourists. European people with experiences of Africa are always very keen to engage me in conversation. They assume that I must be interested in what they have to say about Africa, and they are right, I am, though it can get a bit wearing at times. I sigh inwardly and think to myself "not another instant expert on Africa!", and I prepare for another onslaught. I have to say that I have not yet been exposed to a European view of Africa that is – how can I put it – more humanistic? multi-dimensional? balanced? complete? In my experience, Europe either glorifies or demonises Africa.

Educating an African academic

They've (Africans) moved out of animism into a superstitious kind of Christianity. They've yet to face the intellectual revolution of Copernicus and Einstein...

Spong, Bishop (1998), at the Lambeth Conference of Bishops, Lambeth, London

"African spirituality" is based on the notion of The Supreme God and a world of spirits between which and the spiritual world there is active continuity... . Bodies of water, trees, mountains may be given sacred designations... to attest to the presence and power of the unseen. This is no more "animism" than the placing of candles and offerings before clay statutes... . It is not the physical attributes of the object which are venerated, but the divine spirit it is intended to represent.

Gibbons, R (1995), "Syncretism and Secretism in the Manifestation of African Spirituality" in *At the Crossroads: African Caribbean Religions and Christianity*, Caribbean Council of Churches, Jamaica

Bishop Spong was commenting on the negative attitude of the African bishops towards homosexuality, and the bishop was obviously a very angry man. The bishop's quotation is from an article "Gay? We Don't Have That Here" in the *New Statesman* (7th August 1998), on Africa's war against the white man's perversion, homosexuality. I am very grateful to Bishop Spong for supplying me with such an apt quotation, but I am not going to get embroiled in the particular issue that caused his outburst. I quote Bishop Spong's words because, spoken in anger, they reflect the true feelings of a leading Western churchman towards the African church, and also because I think that these words form a very good lead into the story I am about to tell, and also in contrast to Rawle Gibbons' words.

An English woman academic returned from her first visit to Africa outraged at what she called the African's lack of feelings towards animals in general, and dogs in particular. Of all that she had seen in Africa, this matter seemed to have made the most impact on her, and it was certainly what she spoke about most. As a result, when the time came for one of her African colleagues to return the visit, she set out on a personal mission to educate him in the correct attitude towards animals. This man, this visiting African scholar, became for her the symbol of African indifference and lack of feelings towards animals. She did not use the word "uncivilised", but that would have just about summed up her views. She set about the task of educating him with vigour, and in typical academic style even besieged the man with bits of literature on the topic of animal care and so on. The visitor listened respectfully, nodding, accepting, and never questioning.

Towards the end of his stay in England I invited the brother to lunch. At that time we lived near the Thames, and before lunch I took him for a short walk along the towpath at Walton-on-Thames. Naturally, we talked about his visit and I learnt about, well, the harassment he had been suffering from his English colleague. He described in great detail, prompted by my questioning, all that had occurred during the four weeks. Then, with the first show of annoyance and a slight raising of the voice, he said, "Not once did she ever ask me if I have a dog!" After that I felt I could do no less than ask, "Do you have a dog?" He smiled and quietly replied, "Yes, I have an Alsatian," and went on to add that the dog was treated "just like one of the family". He had no difficulty in telling me this, but for weeks he had endured the misguided attentions of a fellow dog lover without once letting on that he too had a pet dog. I am not myself a dog lover, so I was not really impressed to hear that his dog was part of his family. Personally, I respect animals as fellow creatures with whom we share this planet, but I don't like animals being humanised, and paraded around like man-made objects.

When I was growing up in Barbados one of the few things I was told about Africa was that the people were backward, and that they were heathens who worshipped animals. I also learnt that many Africans had been saved from animal worship by European missionaries and converted to Christianity. However, there were many Africans still living in ignorance of Christ, and there were churches that made special collections to fund missionary work to try and stop those people worshipping animals and trees and nature in general. I could not understand just what was wrong with worshipping animals and nature, and I could not see why the Christian God was any advance on lightning or fire or any other form of nature, though I was sensible enough to keep such ideas to myself. Now all these years later I am hearing that the descendants of those Africans who were saved from animal worship, by the white missionaries, now require instruction from the descendants of those missionaries on how to treat animals! I think of my African brother's experience every time I hear, in connection with the Sudan civil war, that Northern Sudan is Arab and Islamic, whereas the south of the country is Christian and Animist. In Zimbabwe I made a friend for life in one of the British Council representatives when I asked him, in response to his proud announcement that he was planning to bring to Zimbabwe British experts in family therapy, shouldn't it be the other way round? He looked very puzzled, so I went on to add that I understood that the idea of family therapy had originated in Africa, based on the traditional way of problem solving, by involving the whole family. After this he looked even more puzzled. I could see that he did not know what to make of me, but at the same time he did not know enough to argue the point. So we left it at that.

The African boy and his radio

I was walking with my friend along the Grand Union canal in West London on a Saturday afternoon in the summer of 1994. I ended up telling her the story of my involvement with the African boy in response to her question about how I managed my correspondence when travelling. I told her that I'd not really experienced many problems, and that the longest delay was a letter that had been posted in Africa and arrived in Bhutan, where it just missed me. It had been re-directed to India and Bangkok, where the same thing happened, and eventually it had caught up with me in Hong Kong.

My friend then wanted to know whether the letter had been very "important". I replied to the effect that it depended from whose point of view you looked at it. For me the letter had not been very important, but for the African boy who had written to me it had almost certainly been very important. Then, in order to satisfy her curiosity, I ended up telling her the story of the African boy, the letter and the radio. The letter had been a short one, no more than five or six lines. The boy had written in order to keep his part of our agreement and now wanted me to keep my part by sending him a radio, as I had promised. Hong Kong was a good place to get this letter, as there were lots of radios on sale, so soon after receiving it I bought one and sent it to him, hoping against hope that he would actually receive it.

Why did I have to send him a radio? As he said, it was my part of our agreement. I had to take it on trust that he had kept his part of the agreement and so had no option but to keep to my promise. His mother, a friend of mine, came to me for advice, seeking help for her son. It was a very personal and distressing problem, as the boy was almost sixteen and still bed-wetting. My friend was desperate. She had tried everything, but nothing worked. Falling back on my previous experience of a very similar situation with one of my American relatives, I offered him a contract. If he went for six weeks without incident I would send him a gift (reward/bribe) of his choice. He opted for a radio. Some months later I received his letter, after it had followed me around.

Later that same year, when I was in Australia, I received another letter. This one was from the boy's mother, who was writing to let me know that her son had not been very pleased with the radio. He thought it was a cheap radio, and batteries for it were very expensive. She did not mention anything about the problem, and whether or not it had been solved or improved on. I did not know what to make of any of it, so I just put it all away and forgot about it. Later on I learnt from another member of the family that the bed-wetting problem had never been solved, but that the boy had more or less bullied his mother into agreeing that he could write to me and say that it had, so that he could get his radio. When I heard this account of what had transpired I was very glad that I had not bought him a more expensive radio, thinking at the time that the radio would probably get lost or stolen en route. I'd bought a fairly cheap one intending to take him a better one on my next visit, but now realised I had more than met any obligations to him.

I don't know if he still wets the bed, and I don't really care.

The letter had no doubt been important to him, and he probably felt himself to be very clever in fooling me and getting away with it. But as things turned out I got the last laugh when all he got for his lies was a cheap radio. I have to admit that I had simply forgotten about the high cost and short life of the batteries. The agreement had not specified any particular kind of radio, and I'd simply overlooked these details – something that was very easily done in Hong Kong. But it is a sad story, this tale of me and the African boy, and one that left my friend and me quiet and reflective as we continued our walk along the Grand Union that summer afternoon. My friend could not understand the importance of the radio to the boy. "If he wanted a radio so much, why didn't his mum simply buy him one?"

How does one explain the significance of the radio for that boy? The English sister could not understand the problem that the African sister would face in buying a radio for her son. How could she buy just one radio for one child? There were several children, not just her own to be considered, and each child would have to be given an equivalent gift. It was not just the *buying* of the radio either, for there was also the upkeep and the matter of batteries. I inquired of the sister whether she'd heard of the Baylis radio, a wind-up device that used no batteries or electricity, and that was developed by Trevor Baylis with Africa in mind. My friend had no idea what I was talking about, so I tried to explain some of the problems of technology in Africa, and why something like a radio, which people take for granted in England, would

167

be a prize to the African boy. Ownership of a radio would set him apart and would have made him the envy of family and friends.

This story came up again on another walk in another part of London. This time, both the context and the conversation were completely different. It was a sunny Sunday afternoon and another friend and I had gone to Southall to shop and lunch at Rita's. I remarked that since moving to Dorset my visits to Southall were extremely rare. I knew that my friend had grown up in the area and knew it very well. We chatted about this and that, then she pointed out the street where she'd grown up and where her mother had lived until her death. I asked how her mother had taken to the changes in her home town. My friend replied that there was no point saying other than that her mother had not much liked them. She went on to say that, although her mum had got on well with her Asian neighbours, she had wanted Southall to remain the same as she'd always known it. As my friend spoke, Tony Harrison's poem "V" came into my mind, and I mentioned it to her.

This sister had never heard of Harrison's poem, so I briefly summarised its content, especially the bit where Harrison talks about his father's feelings as Leeds changed from a familiar English town to something more like a suburb of Delhi or Bombay. I think I ended by muttering something about colonialism in reverse. My friend replied that her and her class, the English working-class, had not really benefited from colonialism, and that her mother had lived and died in a council house. She commented that the British working-class was not the class from which the imperialist and colonialist had come. By this time we were in another part of Southall, and my friend mentioned that Trevor Baylis, the man who had invented the wind-up radio, still lived nearby. She went on to say that the two of them had grown up in the same street, and that from time to time their paths still crossed. I'd stayed the night at her home and used her wind-up radio, and we'd been talking about it earlier. I'd complained that twenty minutes listening time wasn't very much for the hard work of winding up the radio! We both knew that it had been invented primarily for use in "the developing world", and that its use in Europe was something of a fad. Inevitably, this conversation led to my once again telling the story of the African boy and the radio.

On this occasion I did not have to explain to my socialist sister the importance of it to the African boy. The sister and her husband sponsor an African child, and were comparatively well informed on such matters. So as we continued our walk around Southall we wondered whether the boy might have been happier with a gift of the clockwork one, had it been available at the time. We thought that he might have been. But as I write this, I begin to think that he might have been just as disappointed with such a low-tech device. He had probably expected me to send him one of the most technologically advanced radios in the world. And then, like so much of the machinery I saw rusting and gathering dust in farms and co-ops in Africa, as soon as something went wrong with it, it too would have been cast aside. There would be no one who knew how to mend it, and, almost certainly, there would be no spare parts available.

Non-stop African wars

African wars are always in the news, always. It is not surprising that the topic comes up time and again wherever two or three are gathered and one is black. I recall, in particular a Sunday canal walk, when it was spring and it was lovely. On this occasion I happened to be the only woman in our group of regular walkers, but also present were a couple of guys from another local group. One of the visitors was a man who had lived and worked in Africa for most of his adult life.

That day we walked about twenty-five kilometres, a type of walk that can last the best part of a day, with four hours in the morning, starting off around 9.30, with a break for lunch. I generally dislike the lunch break, as I'd much rather complete the walk, then eat. After lunch we walked a further three or so hours, returning to base at about five o'clock in the afternoon. On that Sunday we had kept up a steady pace and had completed our hike in record time, arriving at the finishing point at 2.30.

I found myself walking next to one of the visiting hikers, a continental, Belgian or French, who had lived and worked in Africa for half a century or so. We were talking about different types of walks, and agreed that canal walks were among the easiest. He said that he found canal walks very boring, and I said that I don't find any walk boring, because I simply liked walking. Somehow this led us to discuss various types of walks and walking conditions in different countries. This is where my companion told me he had spent most of his adult life in Africa, but had never walked or hiked there, never having had the time. Indeed, it was only since retiring, and returning to Europe, that he had become an avid hiker. I already knew that only visiting whites walk in Africa, so I was not surprised to hear that he had kept this hobby for his return to Europe.

He talked a lot about Africa the place, but I did not get the impression that he knew much about the African people. His comments remained at a very general, macro level, and were invariably negative. South Africa was much in the news then, and my fellow walker reliably informed me that a war in South Africa was unavoidable, stating categorically that it "would take a miracle to save South Africa from war". He despaired for Africa, wondering whether independence had been a good idea. I suggested that this must be for the African people to decide and, if they preferred the wars and chaos of independence to the order and subjugation of colonialism, that was up to them. I also put forward my own view that many of the problems of Africa today, the poverty, wars, ethnic strife and so on, were at least in part the result of slavery and colonialism.

My companion took the opposite view: the view that colonial rule had been a blessing for Africa. This was based solely on his own personal experience of Africa. I asked him whether he had ever tried to deepen his knowledge and understanding of the historical background to the events that he had lived through in Africa. His reply was the same as before, and that he'd had no time for studies and had work to do. "And now," I said, "you can observe and comment on African wars and chaos from the safety of Europe." Things began to heat up a bit after that, and I realised that the time had come to change tack, and anyway we were just approaching the pub and our lunch stop. After lunch we continued our walking partnership, but we did not return to the topic of Africa. We talked about walking and hiking in other parts of the world, and we thought that one of these days we might even plan an expedition together!

Meat-eating – the abuse of power

The question of corruption and abuse of power is another one that seems inevitably linked to African peoples and politics. It is my experience that whenever it comes up it is dealt with as though the problem were unique to Africa, whereas it is really quite widespread in all societies. It is the shape and form that corruption takes, and the way that power is abused, that for the large part is culturally determined. In Africa meat is scarce and very expensive, yet I once sat in a meeting with the principal of an educational establishment while he ate what seemed an awful lot of meat! Half-way through our discussion he offered me a helping. I explained I don't eat meat. I also knew that from one

170

month to the next the young people at this institution never saw a scrap of meat. But here he was literally stuffing himself full of it, and that was not long after we'd had lunch! Meat is too plentiful in the developed world for it to be worth stealing, but even in residential institutions in England, it is well known and accepted that the staff and managers always eat better than the residents do.

Such were my thoughts as I listened to an English teacher recount his experiences, disappointment and outrage at the behaviour of his African colleagues towards their pupils. His comments were focused on the misuse/misappropriation of essentials, like food, clothes, gifts of money and other donations. This took place as I was walking round the grounds of an English country mansion where I was attending a conference. I had to escape from the conference hall for a walk in the gardens, to be alone for a few moments, to clear my mind. No such luck, as soon another escapee joined me. This was a man who had recently returned from a teacher-exchange visit in Africa, so instead of a walk to clear my mind, I found myself trapped into another conversation about Africa. Why try to avoid it? Who knows where this one may lead? I soon found out that it was not going to lead very far, for my colleague was not prepared to open his mind and to question his assumptions and prejudices. He simply wanted to offload his anger and disappointment with the African education system, and to complain about the shortcomings of his African colleagues. But this time I came back fighting, or at least I tried.

I suggested to him, much as I have written here, that corruption and abuse of power characterise all human societies, and that it is more a question of degree than of kind. He would not have it. He would bring up yet another example of the type of abuse that he said was common in Africa, but impossible in Europe. Before giving up completely, I changed gear and turned to the growing number of sexual and physical abuse cases linked to schools and residential establishments in England – what was that if not abuse of power? He thought that was very different. I said "different, but equivalent", because no teacher in a boarding school in England would want or be able to consume the total meat ration allocated to a whole school. In Africa, where the meat ration amounted to only a few pounds, teachers not only could, but actually did eat the total meat ration. In doing this he would be depriving the children in his care of much needed protein – and in these circumstances that was an abuse of his power.

The abuse of power that his English counterpart engaged in was equally reprehensible and equally, if not more damaging, to the long term interest of the children and young people in their care. I did not think that English teachers had any cause for moral superiority. Well, *he* did, and as we walked back to the conference room he was still trying to convince me of the correctness of his view and the misguided nature of mine. We were never going to see eye to eye, that much was certain, and I was glad it had been a very short walk. Years later I heard that this man was forced to quit his job as a teacher, amid allegations of sexual abuse of boys in his care, going back many years. Just another one of life's little ironies.

In September 1997 an English Catholic priest was sentenced to jail for the sexual abuse of boys at a top boarding school. During the trial it emerged that he had been suspected of similar behaviour towards boys at a boarding school in Zimbabwe. The church had fulfilled its duty to children by removing him to England. As I listened to the news report about this case, I began to wonder whether this was the man my social work colleague had been referring to, when she'd remarked in response to something I'd said about paedophile priests, "We have them here too." I could only hope that there were not several paedophile priests commuting between boarding schools in Zimbabwe and England. But since the Catholic church is a global institution, this is entirely possible.

Having mentioned that the sexual abuse of children in care institutions happens regularly in her country, my colleague went on to give me some examples including one at a Catholic boarding school where, over the years, several boys had alleged sexual abuse. The boys' allegations had been ignored, and nothing had been done. I was left with the impression that the racial politics of ex-colonial Africa played a large part in the matter not being dealt with properly and professionally. The allegations were against a white man, the boys were all white, and it was a white matter left to be dealt with by whites, or not.

In Africa as elsewhere in the world sexual abuse is not restricted to any one section of the community. In Zimbabwe sodomy is a criminal offence, but this does not stop the abuse of boys. I was told of an African boarding school where boys who were caught returning from illegal outings, paid for the silence of the guards by submitting to sexual acts. The abuse of girls, especially teenage girls, by teachers and other men in authority is such an everyday occurrence that it might just as well be considered normal.

Who are "my people"?

> Thank God my nameless ancestors, brought across the ocean in chains and leg irons made it out alive. Thank God I am an American.
>
> Richburg, K (1998), *Out of America – A Black Man Confronts Africa*, Harper Collins, New York

> The question of mapping the roots of our African Exodus is not actually the most important when considering modern mankind's origin. We know we came from Africa.
>
> Stringer, C and McKie, R (1997), *African Exodus: The Origins of Modern Humanity*, Pimlico, London

In the first quotation Keith Richburg, a black American male, thanks God for having brought his people out of Africa to the USA, and thus saving him from being an African. Richburg finds very little in Africa with which to identify, and this leads him to reject the notion of an "African-American" identity. In the second quotation two white British males, one (Stringer) a scientist, and the other (McKie) a journalist, explain that modern humanity has its origins in Africa. If Stringer and McKie are right, it seems that in one way or another we all "came out of Africa", and so we are all Africans of one kind or another. Thousands of years separate the timescale that the two sets of writers are concerned with, with Stringer and McKie's thesis being based on the belief that modern humanity developed in Africa some 400,000 or so years ago.

According to these two writers modern humanity began in Africa, then spread out across the globe as an exodus of people from Africa, hence the title of their book, *African Exodus*. Stringer and McKie present a lot of scholarly evidence, including that based on genetic and linguistic data, in support of their exodus theory. Not surprisingly it is a theory that has, as the authors put it, "entered the maelstrom of American racial issues" (p230). My own purpose in referring to this work is simply to note that Mr Richburg's ancestors were not alone in coming "out of Africa". Richburg's people, the black American people, came out of Africa many thousands of years after those original people of Stringer and McKie had departed the continent. Black Americans left Africa by a different route and by different means. His ancestors, like mine, were

173

sold into slavery and carried in chains across the Middle Passage to the New World of America and the Caribbean.

I must say that when I am out walking I generally try to avoid conversations that touch on such weighty matters, but I am not always successful. On more than one occasion I have been asked the question: "Do you see yourself as 'African'? Are you accepted as an African in Africa?" I explain that I am a black Caribbean woman, and that I do not feel the need to question whether Africans really are "my people". It seems to me that we are what we are and that it is not a matter of choice. I have felt and continue to feel an affinity with the suffering people in Africa. I know that I am not seen as "one of them" by African people: I do not speak any African languages, nor do I belong to any of Africa's many ethnic groups.

I am not culturally "African", yet as a black person I have always seen myself as "African". I have felt myself to be an African long before it was acceptable to be so, and when, in the Caribbean and North America, the word "African" was almost a term of abuse. I do worry about the contradictions in my own situation: being African but not "belonging" to Africa, I simply and happily accept the reality that is my life and myself. I do have to admit that sometimes this rational approach fails and one is left with raw emotions. I can remember feeling very angry and upset when, during my very first visit to Zimbabwe, a student on one of my courses objected to my not speaking Shona, her language: Who did I think I was? As a black person I should speak to her in her African language, though she did not expect the same from my two white colleagues. This woman obviously believed that all black people are born speaking Shona.

Towards the end of this first visit to Africa, I was sitting on my friend's bed and she and I were deep in woman talk. I decided to broach a subject that had been on my mind for some time. I began somewhat hesitantly, tentatively explaining to her that as a youngster, through my study of history, I had discovered about slavery and about my African ancestry. I had thought then that one day I would go to Africa to answer one question for myself, being: "In my own case had I been lucky or not in being Bajan rather than African?" My friend laughed and told me that I need not worry about that question any more: taking her life as the unit of comparison she concluded that I was more fortunate than she in every way, and that she would exchange places with me at once if she could. There was no doubt in her mind that I was fortunate to have been born in Barbados rather than in Africa. The African woman's lot is not a happy one. I did not much like the way things were going, so I put forward this challenge: "Does that mean that I should be happy about slavery, regard it as a blessing or something?" The sister said that we could never be happy about slavery, but one could be happy with oneself.

Who is my countryman?

This question of culture, language and identity leads me into my next story, and brings together Africa, the Caribbean and Europe. The first person I ever told this story to was one of my Caribbean sisters. We were walking along the coastal path in Dorset and talking about how small the world was becoming. This sister had just come from Paris, or Amsterdam, or somewhere, and while there had bumped into someone she had known in London during her student days. This led me into telling her that I once almost met another Bajan in a hotel in Africa. After that I had to tell her all.

I had been staying at the Manica Hotel, in the Mutare in Zimbabwe. It was a Sunday afternoon and I was having tea with one of my Zimbabwean African sisters, before setting off on another stage of my journey to Harare. I went off to the loo, and on my return to the lounge my friend pointed to a rather short black man, engaged in conversation with two elderly white women. My friend said excitedly, "He is your countryman! I heard him tell those people that he is from Barbados!" I was interested, for fancy meeting a fellow Bajan in this out-of-the-way place! Even so, I did not go up to him and greet him warmly.

I decided to wait until an opportunity presented itself, and my guest and I continued our tea and our chat. In the meantime the three people, the Bajan man and his two companions, came and sat in the seats backing onto ours. They were sitting very close to us and they were all three speaking quite loudly, so we could not help overhearing their conversation. I was deeply mortified by what I heard, and I was so ashamed! I wanted to crawl under the table and hide myself. My countryman, this Bajan man, was speaking in a very negative and condescending way about Africans. He referred to the local people as "natives", as in for example "the natives don't seem to know this" and "the natives are not aware of that… " and so on. The three of them seemed in full agreement over the reasons why things were not working out in Africa. His conversation demonstrated that his every effort was concentrated on allying himself with Europe and distancing himself from the African. Africans were quite definitely not "his people". I was thankful for my caution, and kept my distance. My African sister seemed upset and disappointed with what we had overheard, and there was nothing I could say in defence of my Bajan brother.

This was the story I told to my Caribbean sister as we walked together in Dorset. Her response was to say that the Bajan brother was mentally enslaved, and as such we had to pity him. But I was not so sure. It was too easy to label people whose views we don't share. Perhaps this man was simply an Afro-Caribbean version of Keith Richburg, and like Richburg he had made his choices and decided that Africans "are not his people". And who is to say that their choice is any less valid than any other choice? I know a Caribbean brother who has always identified himself as African, and who could not be more free of the kind of slave mentality that causes black people of the Diaspora to reject Africa. But this man did not like Africa at all, and when he visited Nigeria he hated it and couldn't leave soon enough. He hated the poverty, the dirt, the fact that nothing worked, the corruption, everything. He said he never wanted to visit "that place", i.e. Africa, ever again. Africa has not affected me in this way, and it may well be that I have my Calcutta years to thank for that. I have a positive and humanistic attitude towards Africa, in all its richness and poverty, its diversity and complexity, and with all its problems. In common with the rest of humanity I came out of Africa, and Africans are very definitely "my people".

Africa – a suitable case for discussion?

When I am out walking and I get into a conversation about Africa, I'd I'd much rather talk about fun and adventure than about war and politics: much rather talk about the fun and fear of white-water rafting on the Zambezi, of camping in the Masai Mara, of hitch-hiking to Botswana, hiking in the eastern highlands of Zimbabwe, of travelling by bus, lorry, boat, oil tanker, train and plane through Southern to East Africa, or of setting off by bus in Zimbabwe, through Zambia, Malawi, Tanzania and Zanzibar and on to Mombassa and Nairobi, Kenya. In Europe Africa is so completely associated with war, poverty, famine, misery and social dislocation of all kinds, so I welcome the opportunity to present another side of the African scene.

I tell of the friendships we made. For example, of the taxi driver and his friend the government officer, who befriended us in Malawi as we waited all day for the boat to take us down Lake Malawi. When the boat came the lake was too low for it to berth and we had to wade out to it knee-deep in water, then climb up a rope ladder to get on board. People were pushing, shoving and scrambling up the ladder and at one point I almost lost my grip, though not quite. Luckily our Malawian friend had arranged for two boys to carry our luggage. That is how the two of us, our luggage and my precious laptop computer and printer actually managed to board the boat. It was a night of African splendour, the moon was so bright it was like daylight, and the scene was almost surreal, as in a movie or a waking dream.

After three nights on Lake Malawi we travelled on the back of a lorry to the border where we stayed in the one available room in a newly built hotel. The hotel owner, out of concern for our safety, or just kindness, arranged a lift for us with one of his relatives, or employees, who regularly drove his oil tanker across the border to Tanzania. The driver and his brother, also called Peter, looked after us as though we were family. We spent the night with them in a truckers' hostel, and when we arrived at Mbeya early the next day they stayed with us until we were safely aboard the train to Dar es Salaam, at about four in the afternoon.

Africa, like the rest of the world, has had its down side. One can be robbed anywhere, but I was robbed of almost all my cash (US$2,000) in Zimbabwe. When, where, how or by whom I have no idea. Was it a friend or foe, a brother or sister? Did the theft occur in my hotel or in the safety of a friend's home? Whoever it was had been clever enough to conceal the theft, and by the time I discovered it, in that hotel on the shores of Lake Malawi, there was no one to ask. The young German student who travelled with us from the lake had all his money, passport and papers stolen during the night as he slept in his tent. He had to travel back the way we had just come, boat and all, to the nearest German embassy in Zambia. He had been very excited about the trip, as we had bumped about in the back of the lorry, with the African night rapidly closing in, and me wishing myself safely at home in Surrey. He had extolled the virtues of being in the "real Africa". He was telling us how much he was looking forward to sailing a dhow in Zanzibar, then boasting about it at his sailing club back home. We really felt for him, and as we said our goodbyes he set off, looking weary and depressed beyond his years.

At the Tanzanian border I was faced with the choice of paying a bribe or being sent back along the same route as our German friend, and I reached for my purse. The bribe had to be paid to the health

177

inspector at the Tanzanian border, because Peter did not have a cholera certificate. As we were coming from an infected area – outbreaks of cholera had been reported both in Zimbabwe and Malawi – Peter could be refused entry for failing to be vaccinated against it. So I paid. It took a while to figure out exactly what was required, but the penny dropped eventually and US$30 changed hands. We were allowed to proceed. Back on the oil-tanker we found that a bribe had also been paid for the driver's brother, and on the train to Dar es Salaam we found out that all the foreign travellers had paid bribes, ranging from US$30 to US$50. I had to assume that, like Peter, they must all have been missing a valid cholera certificate!

It was not cholera, but the e-coli bacteria that laid *me* low, and almost finished me off in Africa. It all started in Malawi, one morning when we came back from a walk and straight into the restaurant for breakfast. I was very thirsty and forgetting that I was supposed to drink only filtered stuff I picked up a glass of ice-cold water from the table and drank it all in one go. Three days on a boat on Lake Malawi did not help and I arrived in Mombassa, already very weak from prolonged diarrhoea. I had been looking forward to Mombassa and staying with a friend from my Calcutta days. I remembered how when I'd had chicken pox, this friend had looked after me, visiting me in hospital and bringing me fruit. In my imagination I developed an almost childlike attitude towards her ability to put things right. I wished for nothing more than to be in Mombassa, for I was sure I would be all right once there, and my friend would know what to do to help me.

And so it was that after many weeks of travel I arrived in Mombassa, to what was for me a deadly meal of seafood, which my friend had prepared especially. I felt unable to refuse it, even though I suspected it would do me no good. Within hours of the meal my condition worsened, and by the next day I was in a very, very bad state. I'd been right about one thing though, because my friend, a biology teacher, had taught many of the young doctors in Mombassa, so I received quick, reliable and effective medical care. Even so my recovery was quite slow. My illness kept us in Mombassa and by the coast for longer than planned, and when we resumed our travels we were unable to go by rail to Nairobi, because the train had crashed, killing almost everyone in the first-class compartments.

From Guildford to Harare – understanding modern colonialism

My experiences in and feelings towards Africa would take a book in itself, but there are three subjects that are central so far as I am concerned: slavery, religion, and colonialism. I will always write about these three whenever they come up in the course of writing this book, therefore I will not be labelling a section "Colonialism" and dealing with it under that heading. As colonialism has just come up quite in the course of things, I will write about it now. Here goes.

As a student of history, and as one who grew up under colonialism, I have long been puzzled and fascinated by the character of the coloniser. My very first experience of Africa allowed me to get a glimpse of the process whereby European people, who in their own countries are quite unremarkable, become giants as soon as they step on foreign soil, particularly if that foreign soil belongs to black or other non-white people. Out of such encounters colonialism or imperialism took shape and developed.

My first visit to Africa was in company with two colleagues from the Department of Educational Studies at the University of Surrey. We were running a three-week course for the Ministry of Youth, Sports and Culture, for the government of Zimbabwe. The course participants were youth workers and project managers from all over Zimbabwe. The enterprise was funded by the British Overseas Development Administration, with involvement from the British Council. I'd been invited to take part because of my experience in training and particularly in communication skills training for youth and related professionals. I had been very happy with the planning meetings and delighted to have been invited to go to Africa as something of an "expert". My contract with the department rested on a verbal agreement, which had worked well, and I saw no reason to change this.

On arrival in Africa, two things struck me: the first was the overwhelming beauty of Harare in bloom. It was October, the time of year when the jacaranda trees flowered, and the city was covered in their beautiful mauve blossoms. My second impression was the major change our arrival brought about on the personality of the team leader, Dr Karen Evans. It seemed to me that the same feet that walked normally in Guildford now bestrode Africa like a colossus.

We arrived in Harare, but our base was to be in the eastern highlands, about 200 kilometres away. After two days in Harare we set off for our destination, at about five in the morning. At about ten it was time for refreshments. Our leader, the suburban academic now turned English imperialist, explained that as funds were limited she would accompany the whole party to the supermarket, where each could choose one drink. She would supervise the whole operation and settle the bill at the end. That is what happened: these senior government officers lined up behind our leader and they all trekked to the supermarket, where she picked up a basket and they all followed her, each choosing one warm soft drink. At the checkout desk she paid, then they all came back to the car, and leaning against it drank their drinks. Then we all got into the very hot car and resumed our travels. Unfortunately this experience set the scene for all that followed.

In spite of being both hot and very thirsty, I'd refused the drink. Although our African colleagues accepted what had occurred without question and with a good grace, I felt very angry on their behalf. It seemed to me that our African colleagues had been treated in a way no European academics would have been. My feelings were deeply complicated because, as a black person I was also very ashamed for them, for acquiescing so readily in this treatment. The bill for the supermarket fiasco was the equivalent of £1.20, while just down the road from the supermarket was a little tea shop where we could have sat in comfort with tea or coffee or cold soft-drinks, for about £2. The shop was clearly visible from where we had stopped. The value of the Zimbabwe dollar against the pound sterling was well known to all of us – in fact Z$10 to the pound. I could hope only that our leader felt pleased with the success of her economy and her treatment of her African colleagues.

I must, in the jargon, "share with you" the introductory session of the course programme. It was a Sunday and we were all seated in the obligatory circle in what used to be the school hall. Our leader started off by giving her name, and her job description, and then went on to say that she was a vicar's daughter, "a committed Christian", and that she went to church every Sunday. Her statement set the pattern for all subsequent introductions, as every single person followed her formula to the letter. First the name, then the occupation, then the statement that she or he was a committed Christian who went to church every Sunday. Then it was my turn. I can remember my own words exactly. After the standard introduction I said: "I must be the only one here who is not a committed Christian. I am not a Christian, and I do not go to church on Sundays. Most Sundays I go walking. That is my form of worship." Silence. Then the leader gave a chuckle, the signal for everyone else to relax and smile indulgently and tolerantly at me. I suppose I had asked for it but I had not come to Africa of all places to apologise for not being a Christian.

I was very disturbed and deeply puzzled by the change in our leader, and I began to think that this was how the British had conquered Africa. Once on African soil they had changed into supermen and superwomen. So I began to treat the leader's behaviour as my opportunity to understand something of the colonial mindset. Having lived and worked in Britain for more than thirty years, and having had the opportunity of observing and participating in many facets of that society, I knew that British people were no different from the rest of humankind. How then did they inherit the earth, and control almost half of the globe? It was exactly the same thing, whatever it was, that enabled my colleague to lead those African civil servants into a shop to buy warm drinks, as if this was the most natural thing in the world. Behaviour, which in Europe would be unthinkable, in Africa would be become natural. Is that not at least part of the story of colonialism? That, and the compliance of my African colleagues, their willingness to be led and to accept what was offered. Perhaps my African colleagues had been conditioned by what has been called the "begging bowl" mentality, which meant that their role was to accept what was given. This was but one and not by any means the most significant example of European arrogance and African submissiveness that I experienced over the coming three weeks. Never once did I feel torn between the two cultures. I was just really glad to be an outsider to both.

The three-week programme was based at the Eagle Youth Training Centre. In the days before independence the Eagle had been a whites-only boarding school run by nuns. During the war of independence three of the nuns at the school had been killed by the Rhodesian army, who then placed the blame on the African freedom fighters. Knowledge of these events, and the fact that so many of our students were ex-combatants of that war, gave the Eagle a special feel. I was very aware of the background against which we were training the participants in communication, presentation and inter-personal skills. For me it was a very difficult situation, for as I've said I was constantly aware of the background of war, and sometimes imagined I could see the nuns lying dead, covered in blood, in the entrance to the school. I had been told that this was the place where they had been shot down. I was very conscious of the conflict and of the present reality of our own rapidly deteriorating inter-personal situation. So I suggested to my colleague that we should present what was happening among the three of us as a case study. This would at least be an attempt to acknowledge the problems and to learn from them. But he said that it was more than his job was worth.

The three of us from the UK, the leader and the two of us workers (I almost said "slaves"), were given a house to ourselves. However, I did not stay there very long, and after a day or two moved into the house of one of the participants, who lived on campus. If anyone asked me why I'd left I said that I wanted to be near the main building. The truth was that I could not stand the tension of living in such close proximity to the leader. The participants were not happy either. They were dissatisfied with the standard of accommodation and of the food. This led into heated discussion over the funding of the project and the availability of money. There were problems about everything including transport. Transport was a major problem, for there was no public provision and the single car that had been made available was totally inadequate, and was more or less co-opted by the leader anyway. I either did not travel at all or went in the school van or mini-bus with the girls. On one occasion the van's brakes failed as we hurtled down through the mist of the central highlands, and how we ever arrived safely I do not know. At our planning meeting in Surrey the three of us had agreed to forego our personal expenses, pool them and contribute them towards a better standard of catering for all. In Mutare, all this was soon forgotten, as keeping within budget became the guiding principle. I was soon informed that there were no expenses to be pooled, and without a written contract I had no proof of our agreement. Silly me. I should have known better.

All in all, my first visit to Africa was a very traumatic experience, though this had nothing to do with Africa itself, and everything to do with Europe. I emerged from that experience knowing myself a bit better, and I think that I was also better able to understand the personal nature of colonialism, and how it is that quite ordinary people can behave in quite extraordinary ways. But there remained many puzzling elements: many of our students were ex-combatants of the Zimbabwean war of independence, people who had fought to free their country from white rule. These men seemed very docile and unquestioning in face of white experts. We were supposed to be involved in a co-operative, learning experience, but generally speaking the participants brought very little to the course, and much preferred to be "taught" by us. I did not have any experience of working with ex-combatants, but I had expected a bit more spirit.

Throughout that very difficult and trying period, I walked. The Eagle is situated in a beautiful, hilly part of the eastern highlands. There was a five- or six-kilometre walk from the centre to the main road. I began each day with that walk. Then one day, as I returned from it, one of the security guards approached, and in somewhat hostile manner told me that I should not be out alone, because, she told me, "It is very dangerous." I had never seen any danger, and I was not aware of any, so I couldn't understand what she was talking about. Then she explained. We were but a few kilometres from the Mozambican border, and there was a war going on there, which sometimes spilled over the border. Soldiers with guns had been found wandering in these parts. She repeated that it was very dangerous for me to go walking alone, and that I must take a security guard with me or stay in the compound. No prizes for guessing what happened. I needed to walk, and I did not need a guard. Anyway, I felt more threatened by what was happening at the centre than from the Mozambican soldiers. So I continued with my solitary morning walks. Later I learnt that the local people referred to me as the mad black woman who walked when she didn't have to. It is only now, as I write this, that I realise that I have shared, with Ffyona Campbell, the common experience of having being ridiculed by our African sisters for walking when we did not have to (see Chapter One).

After the course ended I stayed on, to travel and see something of Zimbabwe. In the course of these travels I met up with some of the course participants and visited the projects they were working in. That visit developed in me a taste for Africa and I have been back many times, and visited other African countries. So in spite of the trauma, in my first visit to Africa I gained quite a lot. But I also lost something. I had no further contact with Dr Karen Evans or the Department of Educational Studies at Surrey University, though I did receive some token expenses! Such is life.

That was my introduction to Africa, and when some years later I needed a refuge for my son, it was to Africa that I looked. And this development brought me closer and deepened my interest and involvement in Africa.

Lead, kindly light

My next contribution to the Europe/Africa dimension takes me back to religion. I think it must be very clear by now that I am not a religious person. However, I am fortunate to include among my friends, my brothers and sisters, many who follow religions of various kinds. I respect their beliefs and ask no more than that they respect my lack of belief. Ironically it is with almost religious zeal that I am always eager to inform new friends and acquaintances that I am not a religious person. Even so, misunderstandings can still arise. In July of 1993, when we were in Banff National Park in Canada, we received an urgent message concerning our son. As a result we abandoned the rest of our tour, and returned to England, where I immediately set out for Harare. I was going to try to persuade my son to return to England to receive medical attention for his deteriorating mental condition. Unfortunately, he flatly refused to accompany me back to the UK.

I was staying with a Caribbean sister who had rescued me from the impersonal sterility of a hotel room. She was a dedicated Christian. She knew that I was not. Indeed, she had attracted a certain amount of criticism for taking an "ungodly" person into her house. On this particular day I returned from one more futile attempt at persuading my son to come back home with me. My mind was in turmoil. I was afraid to leave my son, and if he would not come willingly I felt unable to force him. I lay on the bed deep in thought – should I reschedule my flight or leave in a week's time as per my reservation? There was a knock on the door and the sister entered: "How are things? Is he still refusing to go with you?" I grunted, hoping she would take this to mean that just then I did not feel like talking. It seemed to work, and she left the room. Within a few minutes she returned, to inform me that she was so worried and concerned for me that she had – wait for it – asked her vicar to come and see me! Inside my head I screamed, "How dare you! How dare you!" Out loud I said, "Oh." To that she responded by saying that the vicar knew I was not a Christian, but it made no difference, he was still willing to see me and help me in any way he could. How I longed for the impersonality and sterility of a hotel room, as out of courtesy to my hostess I agreed to see her vicar.

Soon afterwards the vicar arrived, a young white South African, in his flowing black cassock. We shook hands and smiled as I counselled myself to try and ignore his accent. We sat and chatted for an hour or so, and he started with an account of *his* problems. As he already knew mine I was saved the trouble of going over what to me was a difficult and painful matter. The vicar himself was suffering the loss of his young daughter, due to divorce or similar circumstances. He approached my problem by telling me that as a parent he could understand my dilemma, at which point I realised that I no longer had a dilemma, as I had made up my mind to leave Harare as planned, with or without my son. I told him that I had made the decision to leave and return to England. His response was to ask me if I would join him in prayer. I said I did not mind his praying. So he prayed. I thanked him for his time and interest, and he left. After what she considered a suitable interval the sister came to find out how things had gone. I said that he seemed a very nice young man, then I mentioned that I would be leaving Harare the next week, with or without my son.

However desperate my plight, I certainly had not come to Africa to be saved by embracing the teachings of a white racist church. This same black sister was routinely subjected to petty and not so petty humiliation in this same Christian church by the likes of that same vicar. When she became one of the church elders, several white members who were part of her district, and should have been in her group, declined to join. A couple of them even telephoned and told her that it was "nothing personal", but they would be changing elders. She belonged to a group that met once a week to do their bible reading, and sometimes they met at her house and sat around her dining-room table, but the next day they passed her without speaking. They would all be equal in heaven, but she would have to wait until then.

Had my Caribbean sister invited an African traditional healer, previously called a witch doctor, the sociologist, would-be novelist and Africanist in me might well have been interested. White South African vicars, however well meaning, were well outside my pale. Unfortunately for me, this sister was not interested in African religion, and the absorption of some of the African cultural forms into Christianity was a matter of deep regret for her. She felt that Africans could not be true Christians while they adhered to the belief of their ancestors, and among other things retained their traditional marriage customs. For these and other similar reasons she strongly objected to the intended marriage of her son to a local girl. She did not agree with the African custom of paying a "bride price", as she felt that this lessened the significance of Christian marriage. In general it was her view that cultural differences between Africa and the Caribbean were too great to be bridged by these two young people. She was not happy, and I could offer her little comfort, except to tell her that I wished I had her problem!

I really did not find it funny that my Caribbean sister seemed unable to accept and value cultural differences, and that she also seemed totally unwilling to distinguish between culture and religion. Her version of Christianity was completely Eurocentric, with just a flavour of Caribbean. I once had another very interesting experience as a guest in an African home. It was Sunday, and my hostess told her teenage daughter that she could skip church as they would be taking me out for the day. I was then asked whether I minded missing church. I replied that I never went to church. The young girl then turned to me, and looking at me in wide-eyed wonderment asked whether I was one of those people who did not believe in God. What could I say? I had to admit that I was among the non-believers. The girl, still looking awed and disbelieving, said that she had never met a non-believer before, and after that she treated me as someone belonging to a different species. So total is the conversion of Africa that there is no room for the range of views and opinions that Europe takes for granted.

Wherever I travel in Africa, I always look for some sign of an Afric god, with "thick lips and woolly hair", but so far my search has been in vain. The Afric god had straightened his hair, lightened his skin and had plastic surgery on his nose and lips, and was indistinguishable from the Grecian, Arab, and all the other gods. The major faiths in Africa – Christianity and Islam – have been imported. I had to wait for my return to the Caribbean, to Trinidad, to encounter my African god for the first time. For it was in Trinidad and not in Africa that I was introduced to African religion, and to the Orisha movement. This happened after I told my sister of my futile search, and that the nearest I'd come to an African religion in Africa was the young Rastafarian men I'd met in the streets of various Africa capitals. I found this odd, since the Rastafarian religion was born in the Caribbean and out of a wish to return to Africa.

Then my sister explained to me that we, the African people of the Caribbean and North America, were the true inheritors and preservers of African religions. So I went with her to worship her African gods, and the experience was an interesting one. Not least because my visit coincided with that of a group of mostly white Americans, students of anthropology, I think. Most of them seemed distinctly uncomfortable, and one young woman, a Methodist, made it clear that she regarded these ideas and practices as evidence of paganism, and that for her this was an unfortunate and "backward" thing. I don't know what preparation she'd been given for the visit, but it seemed to me that she came away with views very similar to Bishop Spong.

But I continue to wonder about the significance of the loss of African religion for African society. I wonder about whether and in what way such a loss may have contributed to the disintegration of African society and such events as the Rwanda genocide and the ethnic and other conflicts that threaten to engulf the continent. Africa is unique in suffering two major losses: massive population loss through slavery, and the loss or absorption into Christianity and Islam of its traditional religions.

One could view the history of the African continent as, in some ways, a story of "replacement". African religions have been replaced by Christianity and Islam, and the millions of people lost through slavery have been replaced by settlers and their descendants. The people who conquered and colonised the continent were different in every respect from those sold into slavery. In the process of conquest and settlement traditional religions were replaced by the religion of the conquerors and colonisers. In time the majority of Africans would, like my Afro-Caribbean sister, regard the traditional religion with the same disdain as the settlers and colonisers.

I am not a black romantic, yearning for a glorious African past. Neither am I into denial of my African ancestry, unlike Keith Richburg. I am sure the African past like the African present was a complex mixture of good and bad. The selling of fellow Africans into slavery itself attests to that. In order to make sense of the present we have to understand and accept the past, and this is a painful and demanding process that, in my view, has very little to do with apportioning blame.

Africa in Europe

In the summer of 1997 I visited Southern Spain for the first time. The talk in Southern Spain is all about "los inmigrantes", African immigrants who are entering Spain through Cueda and Melilla. In the 7th September issue of *El Pais* was an article by a man called Jaime Garcìa Añoveros in which he argued that all borders are inhumane, racist and inherently unworkable. On the same page appeared a report that the civil guard or Spanish national police had detained twelve immigrants in Valencia. The article reported the Spanish authorities as saying that there was a network operating in the trafficking of immigrants into Spain, and as a result they had intensified controls in Algeciras and

Alicante. So whatever the writer in *El País* may have said, the free movement of people was a long way off. Capital and goods can move freely around the world, but not people – certainly not black and brown people. So the free market is a lie, because there can never be a free market without the free movement of people. This is not an original idea.

Walking along a street in one of the small towns of the Almeria province in Southern Spain, I met an African sister. We nodded and smiled at each other, and she asked me: "Are you new here?" She seemed a bit surprised when I replied that I was just a visitor, on holiday for a couple of weeks. We talked for a while and then she invited me to her church. I asked what kind of church it was and was told that it was a "kind of Pentecostal church". That was enough for me, and I accepted. The following Sunday morning Peter and I turned up at her place. The service wasn't until six, and we were hoping she would spend the day giving us an insider's view of Almeria, before subjecting us to the rigours of the Pentecostal ministry. In the event we were saved from the church service by a domestic crisis that developed in my new friend's family.

The facts very briefly were as follows. My new friend, a single parent, had sponsored and paid for her sister to come from Africa to live with her, to look after the home and children, so that she would be free to work. But within a matter of weeks of arriving the sister had left to live with her new lover.

Soon after our arrival we were joined by a delegation of people acting on behalf of my friend's errant sister and her lover. These representatives had come to tell her that her sister would not be returning to live with her, and that neither her sister nor her lover had the means to repay the money that she had spent bringing her sister to Spain from Africa. The discussions were conducted in their own African language, but it was not difficult for me to follow the general trend: the body language was quite expressive, and their tone of voice spoke volumes. Occasionally English words were use, notably "money", "dollars" and "police": something was badly wrong. We had arrived around 10 in the morning, at around 12.30 in the afternoon a white American pastor and his wife arrived to take part in the negotiations.

The spoken language switched to English. Against my natural inclination I was quite impressed by the role of the religious people and the way they handled the situation. But it made no difference. Lines were drawn and there seemed to be no possibility of compromise:

my friend wanted her sister back, her sister refused. If her sister would not come back, my friend wanted a refund of the money she had spent bringing her from Africa to Europe, but again she drew a blank. Then Peter and I decided to go off and do some walking and sightseeing. It was quite clear that my friend could not join us, and we promised to return to partake of the lunch that our kind hostess had already prepared.

Peter and I returned at about four, having been for a lovely walk in the hills around Almeria, where I saw an oasis for the first time. When we got back the discussions were still in progress, but the stalemate had not altered. At about five we took our final departure, having not been able to taste my friend's cooking (I had been so much looking forward to eating some ochres!). The next day I learnt that it was almost midnight before the meeting finally ended. Nothing had been achieved. The errant sister had eventually turned up at the house, but only to state in person what she had already said through her messengers: she was not coming back and she could not repay the money.

Through my African friend I experienced a different Spain from the one I had first visited in 1965. I never got to church, but the next day I spent the whole time with the kind of people whose situation had been analysed so sympathetically by J G Añoveros in *El Pais* (jueves 4 de seotiembre de 1977) in an article entitled simply "Inmigrantes". I spent the day with my African sister and some of her friends as they all made the rounds of the Spanish immigration and social security system, renewing their "papers". I saw Spanish bureaucracy at close range, and learnt that, as my friends put it, "everything is harder for black people where there are lots of us". This means that in Andulusia things are generally more difficult for Africans than in Northern Spain. Africans are employed only as agricultural labourers, including one of the men I met, who was a highly intelligent and articulate person, and a qualified teacher fluent in French, as well as Spanish and English. In Spain he had no hope of being anything but an unskilled farm labourer. Another African woman I met told me that she was trying to make arrangements to send her teenage daughter to be educated in England, because, as she put it, "there is no point in being an educated black Spanish girl". Spanish tourist literature speaks blithely of Spain's Moorish past, and is happy to capitalise on its African legacy.

The African (and Arab) presence in Spain today is a difficult and painful one – a highly marginalised minority. Spain's non-white population is represented on the football field, but if you want to see a non-white TV presenter you will have to tune to BBC World or CNN. The Spanish newspapers always seem to report the race of offenders if they are African or Arab. In 1965, when I first visited Spain, Franco was still in power, and my awareness of Spain centred on that fact. But today I am aware of Spain as the point of entry into Europe for many desperate to flee the poverty, wars and oppression of Africa. I think of what this will mean for this African child, who as a teenage girl will again be torn from home and sent on yet another journey: this time to be educated in England. Her journey is necessary if she is to develop into an educated and independent woman, something that her mother believes will not be possible in Spain, but may well be possible in England. For me the life of this African girlchild and her mother reflect and dramatise the continuing story of the relationship between Europe and Africa.

5

PART TWO – WALKING AFRICA AND TALKING ABOUT EUROPE

First they came to tame us, to satisfy their yearning for heroism. Then they came to see us as producers to be exploited. Then one trading company after another surrendered its charter to its own government and the colonial administrative machinery seemed set to go. Then we were considered their burden.

Mphahlele, E (1974), *The African Image*, Faber and Faber, London

There are as many misconceptions about Europe in Africa as there are about Africa in Europe. Africans think that Europeans generally have little family feelings or loyalty, with the practice of putting parents in residential homes often cited as an example. It makes no sense to say that the percentage of elderly people in homes is a fraction of the total aged population and that most old people live at home or with relatives. The irony of this lies in the fact that it is African families in England, for example, who foster (some say abandon) their children with English private foster-mothers, sometimes not having any contact for many years. This practice has at times resulted in child abuse tragedies and at other times in the opposite: the child becoming such a part of the foster family that the English parents apply for adoption. Some people may well regard this result as equally tragic.

My experiences in Africa left me with the distinct impression that the African family is under greater pressure than the European family.

It comes from both inside and outside society. From within there is the way that traditional practices such as payment of the "bride price" have been distorted by the values of the market, and there are wars, poverty, ethnic and other problems. From outside there are the European values that African society ostensibly deplores, but still continue to make inroads through radio, television and other forms of mass communication. I saw many, many examples of the stresses placed on the contemporary African family, and in particular on women, by these changes. Two examples come to mind: the first is the practice of dumping a woman's body on her family's doorstep if she has the temerity to die before the bride price had been paid in full. The second is the dumping of unwanted children by mothers who cannot look after them. Baby dumping and body dumping, both affecting women, are practices that suggest a breakdown in values and a losing sight of people's true worth.

The following extract from the *Daily Gazette* refers to the situation in Zimbabwe, but could equally refer to any African country. The national news section carried this headline: URBANISATION, HARDSHIPS, AIDS SHATTER EXTENDED FAMILIES.

The report continues with an account of an old man being thrown out of his nephew's home, as the nephew shouts at him, "Get out of my house. This is my house!" It carries on:

> To Zimbabweans who hold sacred the concept of the extended
> family and respect for their elders, they would automatically
> assume that this happened in a European family. Wrong. This
> is just one of the true-life changes taking place in Zimbabwean
> society's attitude towards the elderly.

The *Daily Gazette*, 9th November 1993, Harare, Zimbabwe

Conversations in Africa about Europe are of an altogether different character. In the first place, hardly anyone in Europe wants to go and live in Africa, whereas at times it seems to me there are an awful lot of young people in Africa wanting to go to Europe. As foreigners, we were often accosted in the street and asked about ways of studying or working in England (Peter), or America (me) – I was taken as an African-American. People in Africa are interested in Europe, in the wars going on in Europe, and there is an almost quiet satisfaction in learning that Europe is also divided along ethnic and religious lines, and that mutual suspicion, hatred and hostility erupting into war have roots deep in European history. The TV reporters now told of European women who were systematically raped, and showed harrowing pictures of white child victims of war. African wars could be compared and contrasted with their European counterparts. The wars in Europe suggested balance, and meant that perhaps Africa had not been singled out after all.

When I was asked about the wars raging in Europe, I tried to use my knowledge of European history to explain what was going on. I tried to explain that the borders of Europe were as artificial as those of Africa, and that ethnic divisions were as deep-seated and enduring. I said to my African brothers and sisters, "No one familiar with European history would be surprised by what is happening in Europe now." I was glad of my colonial education, which seemed in many ways superior to the education of my British contemporaries. I told the story of how very early on in the war in the former Yugoslavia, a BBC reporter in Sarajevo had shouted into his microphone in a mixture of amazement and terror, "It is as though people in Surbiton started to kill each other." I explained that that was a typical English middle-class suburb. The reporter would have done better to have compared what was happening in Sarajevo with an equivalent district in Northern Ireland.

Leaving aside Northern Ireland, there are historic tensions among the countries that make up the United Kingdom. Although these tensions may not correspond in kind or degree to the situation in Eastern Europe, they help to explain how, in certain circumstances, such tensions can develop and degenerate into war. Since that early stumble the quality of reporting on the European wars has vastly improved. Many countries in Africa are now part of the global communications network, where people watch CNN, BBC World, and of course continue to listen to the BBC World Service on the radio. The first event I am about to describe took place in a TV station in Africa, and some of what occurred was triggered by a news report of the war in Eastern Europe.

My next story has to do with war, but only indirectly. The place was the capital city of an African country where I had been invited to a TV station to watch the recording of the finalists in a competition sponsored by the very, very rich, almost black American pop star, Michael Jackson. The competition had been launched under the banner "Heal the World" and was open to children across the world. The competitors had been required to identify and write about the problems of the world, and to suggest ways of dealing with them. The six finalists in the TV studio had come to record their wining entries. The first prize was a trip to America and a meeting with Michael Jackson himself. The finalists ranged in age from twelve to sixteen. There were four girls, and one of the two boys was white. In order to have reached this stage of the competition, each one of them must have written convincingly about the problems of the world in general, and of their own continent in particular. As usual with TV recordings, there was an awful lot of hanging about, so I used the time to read the submissions. I noted that "child abuse" and "the environment" were the two most popular topics, for almost every child had referred to one or both of them.

I remembered this when, not long after my visit to the TV station, and while the competition was still going on, Michael Jackson himself was accused of the sexual abuse of a young boy. The matter did not reach the courts and neither did it affect the competition.

But back to the story. I finished reading and started looking around, and noticed that the lone white boy still had his mother with him. All the other parents brought the youngsters, stayed for a while, and went off to return later. Later on I was introduced to the mother and we started talking. With my usual tact I asked her why she had stayed behind. "Wouldn't your son be put off by having his mother around? Most boys of sixteen would be." She told me that far from being embarrassed by her presence her son wanted her with him. If she didn't stay he would leave. He was there only on condition that she stayed as well, so really his participation in the event depended on her presence. I wondered whether that was a good thing, almost forcing him to take part. Then she told me the story: at first it was his own idea to take part in the competition, and he was very highly motivated. Then his school friends found out and everything changed. As the only white in the competition, he had been mocked and laughed at for taking part in it, mostly, she said, by the black boys at his school. So when it came to appearing on TV he decided to withdraw, because he was afraid of the reaction of his classmates. By then his mother and the rest of his family felt that having got thus far he could not at this point withdraw and so pressure had been brought to bear.

So there we were, five quite happy-looking black finalists, and one quite miserable-looking white one, plus assorted hangers-on, including myself. We had arrived at the TV station at around ten in the morning. At some point in the afternoon, it may have been midday or one o'clock, the news came on one of the many TV monitors around the place. As it happened I was standing next to the white mother. The first item on the news was a report on the war in former Yugoslavia, accompanied by the usual complement of harrowing pictures and war scenes. Then there was a follow-up item on how the war was affecting children and of the many who were left as orphans, with no one to care for them.

The woman turned to me, and I could swear there were tears in her eyes, as she asked: "Do you know, Dr Stone [that is how I'd been introduced, to explain my presence, I think], do you know how one can go about adopting one of these children?" I had to admit that I did not know anything about that, and asked why she wanted to know. "Well, I have a friend who has just lost her baby and can't have any more. She would dearly love to adopt one of those children. Is there anything you could do to help?" She thought I was going back to England and could make some inquiries, and so could let her know. I had to disappoint her, because I could not help. She or her friend would have to find another way of adopting a white European war baby.

The irony of the situation was completely lost on her, or maybe for her there was no irony in the situation. For me, though, the situation was completely ironic. Here was I, a black African-Caribbean woman being asked in Africa, by a white African woman, how to go about adopting a white European child! And it was all done as if the most natural thing in the world. The response in Africa to the wars in Europe was something I could never have anticipated, never in a million years. My contact with white Africans has been quite limited, and mostly occurs in leisure-related activities, where people attend either in a group or as pairs. There is not much mixing as people come together and stay together. I know of an English woman who took her black children to visit an expatriate friend who was working in Kenya. She wanted her children to experience African culture, and to see a cross-section of black people in different social and professional roles. But in the white expatriate world of Kenya, the only black people they came into regular contact with were the servants.

I had exactly the same kind of experience as the guest of Kenyan Asians, for again the only Africans I met were servants. Peter and I attended an Indian wedding, at which there were hundreds of people, but only one African couple. When I visited Mauritius in 1978 my Indian hostess made a point of arranging for me to visit African projects, schools and so on, but all our social contacts were exclusively Asian. It was also in Mauritius that I had the unforgettable experience of singing, or rather croaking, the Indian national anthem to a huge Indian family gathering.

Our family had been invited to lunch, and somehow or other the conversation turned to languages, and I was asked whether I knew any Hindi. I said that I knew only a few basic words, but my daughter informed everybody that I knew the Indian national anthem by heart. After that there was no escape, and I was deeply embarrassed both by my Hindi and my singing.

In my experience urban African society is very racially segregated, and it is very unusual to find social mixing between people of different racial groups. In Zanzibar my local contact person was an Indian, a friend of a friend. When I asked the hotel receptionist to look up his telephone number for me, she seemed really puzzled by my request. Then she asked me whether I knew that he was an Indian. In Guyana I had the unusual experience of being entertained in the home of an Afro-Indian Guyanese couple, and of watching the three-hour video of their wedding. Some of the singing was almost as bad as my rendition of the Indian national anthem! Our hostess in Mauritius was an Indian woman who had been married to an African. At the time I met her they were still in the process of a protracted and apparently very bitter divorce. But the lady took obvious pleasure in telling me of the great social upheaval that her marriage had caused among the Indian community in Mauritius, and how her choice of partner had marked her out as an independent and strong-minded woman.

Mauritius is in the Indian Ocean and has a population consisting mainly of Indians, Africans, a small number of Europeans (French) and others who are classified as belonging to the "general population". Like mainland Africa Mauritius appeared to me to be quite highly stratified along racial lines, with little social contact between the main groups. I have been fortunate that I have been able to move between the African and the Indian world with relative ease, though it has not always been a comfortable experience. On a few occasions I have been a somewhat reluctant participant in the white African world, but these have always been quite interesting experiences.

On a Sunday-morning walk in Mukuvisi woodland at Hillside, just outside Harare, we met an ex-Rhodesian couple who invited us to tea at their house. We accepted their invitation and duly went along to take tea with them. This was fine, and the conversation was fine too, as long as we stuck to gardening and natural history topics. But somehow the Zimbabwean war of independence came up. We had to listen to the ex-soldier's analysis of the stupid mistakes that "we whites" had made and that lost them the war. Among these he counted as critical the "betrayal" of the British government. I asked him how he saw things now, and how he felt about being a Zimbabwean. His reply was amazing: "I do not understand the African mind." He continued, "I wish I could somehow get into their minds. Just when I think I know them I find I do not know them at all. They will always be a puzzle to me." He never answered my question.

I was once a visitor staying in the only black house in a leafy suburb of Harare. One night I returned to find the door locked and my friend apparently fast asleep. All my efforts to wake her failed. I went to the house next door and pressed the remote-control device, and a young white man came to the gate. I explained my problem and asked him if he would mind telephoning my friend and telling her that I had arrived. He said he would. I returned to the house and my friend was at the door. Apart from being apologetic about having fallen asleep, her main reaction was amazement that I had gone next door for help and that they had responded. She had lived in the street for more than twenty years and this was the first normal contact with her neighbours. Something as ordinary as what I had done seemed to be the equivalent of going into the lion's den.

From Chertsey to Mavingo – social responsibility and all that

My most interesting experience of white Africa came one afternoon in Masvingo Province in Zimbabwe. I had travelled with a group of friends by bus there. I wanted to visit Great Zimbabwe and to do some walking and exploring in that area. My guide was one of the participants on the course that my colleagues and I had been running in the eastern highlands. As it happened I visited Great Zimbabwe the day before some important dignitary, so everything was set up to receive this person, including educated people who knew the history and could talk very knowingly about the site. My colleague and I also went on an early morning horseback safari – needless to say we were the only two black people taking part. The safari was a completely new experience for this brother who was seeing tourist Zimbabwe for the first time. It was on it that I saw my first black rhino dead, its tusks hacked out, its body left to rot in the sun.

My colleague had put a lot of time and energy into making my stay interesting, so when he asked me if I would speak to a group of businessmen at a lunch meeting, I could hardly refuse, could I? He went on to say that he had been trying to get local businessmen to become involved in the youth training schemes by taking on and supervising trainees. He had failed. Coming fresh from the course he wanted to try again, and thought it would help if I set the scene by talking to the Rotary Club about similar schemes in Britain and how these worked. I was not keen, but accepted on one condition: that he would be there to introduce me and would stay throughout the presentation. Thinking about it now, I cannot explain why I set this condition, but I had a feeling that I might be abandoned and left to the mercy of the Rotarians. I was given all the assurance I needed, for of course he would be there – was I not his guest, and how could he just leave me like that? Having agreed I had to decide on a topic. I decided on social responsibility in business, and began my preparation.

I was staying at a local hotel, where the manager was a Rotarian himself and would be hosting the lunch. My colleague introduced us, and wonder of wonders – I found out he came originally from Chertsey in Surrey! We were living at the time in Surrey, just minutes away from Chertsey, so we chatted as people do who know places in common. We talked about how the area had changed with the building of the motorway – news of the M25 had reached him there. I was able to answer a question, which had long bothered him: would he still be able to fish near Chertsey Bridge? No problem – people were fishing near there every day, for the motorway had not disrupted the fishing, whatever else it may have done. I am sure that never in his wildest dreams had he considered being updated about his English homeland by someone answering to my description. Having dealt with Chertsey, we went on to discuss the title of my presentation and the rest of the arrangements for the afternoon.

Thursday, the day of the luncheon, and there was no sign of my African brother. Most days he had called in at the hotel first thing, but today? No sign of him! Maybe he would show up nearer the time, I thought hopefully. Wrong again. On that day the brother was invisible, so I would have to be introduced by the man from Chertsey. I was not bothered, as I knew my stuff. It was a good time for that talk on social responsibility, when Margaret Thatcher had not yet decided that there was no such thing as "society", so there was still the idea that business had an important role to play in the social life of the country. To be honest talking to Rotarians is not really my thing. But once I understood the situation facing the local youth service, and saw how it tied in with what the course had been about, I was ready to give it my best shot.

I arrived for pre-lunch drinks and met some of the people I would later be talking to. One man, a white farmer, was ready with advice for me: "Listen, this is not the UK, the problems here are very different." Coded messages: "Who are you, little black girl, coming here to tell us how to manage our affairs! We know this country, you don't." I understood where he was coming from, but I had a job to do. Then I got involved in a conversation with the regional manager for Coca-Cola, the one and only black member of the group. His sole topic of conversation was the African market for Coca-Cola, and he could see nothing but growth. I could see nothing but boredom, so rather rashly I asked him if he could ever see himself doing anything else. I do not have to make the slightest effort to recall his reply. "No," he said, almost visibly swelling up, "I am a Coca-Cola man, and will be for the rest of my life." It was Coca-Cola that had brought him this far, membership of the all-white Rotary – why should he want anything more? Ask a silly question.

Time for business. The completely male and almost completely (except for the Coca-Cola man) white Zimbabweans listened politely to my presentation. The first question concerned the youth training scheme. What was it? There was much muttering, suggesting that no one in the audience knew anything about it and had never been asked to participate in it. Where was the representative of the Ministry of Youth and Culture who had invited me to speak to them, and who knew the answers to their questions? I concentrated on the here and now, and gave such information as had been made available to me, and the chairman, otherwise hotel manager and ex-Chertsey resident, came forward as the contact person who would take the matter forward. But someone wasn't going to let the matter drop that easily, and protested that Rotarians knew about social responsibility and were willing to play their part, "But how could we play our part if no one tells us what is going on?" This was my cue to finish off. I had done what I had agreed to do, and anything else was beyond my remit.

The next day I heard from my colleague that he had been unexpectedly called away on urgent business, and so had been unable to turn up for the Rotary lunch. My own feeling was that he had never intended being there. I had sensed this right from the start, hence my stipulation that he should be present, and his assurances that he would be. Just as I knew intuitively that he would not be there at my presentation (undertaken at his urging and to help him), I also knew with equal certainty that had it been either of my two white Surrey University colleagues, the brother would have been there. No question.

Such are the racial politics of Southern Africa. That much I understood, and yes, I have to admit that I did feel a degree of resentment. But I soon got over it.

I think it helped my understanding and acceptance of what happened to know that to my African brother/colleague there was no particular kudos attached to my presence in Masvingo Province. Had it been one of my white colleagues instead of me, he could have presented such an academic with pride to the Rotarians. The visitor would be seen as his own "white person", someone like them, but not one of them, someone white who was there to speak in support of Africans. Whereas I, a black person, was not, and could not be in that league. So if the session went well he would benefit from having set it up, but if it went badly, by not being there, he would hopefully escape some of the blame. Outside his own traditional African community, power, authority and expert knowledge are located within the white power structure, be it local or foreign. So I did understand his difficulty, and these problems that I am all too familiar with are, after all, part of our common colonial baggage.

Africa and Europe came together in the most unexpected ways, in ways that perplexed and disconcerted me, such as being asked to help a white African adopt a European child when there were countless African children on her doorstep, suffering the same plight. In another part of Africa I was told of the generosity of the English Christian youth leader/teacher who came often and brought many gifts for the children, especially the boys. Over the years he became a trusted friend and guest in the homes of his African friends. It was he who arranged for their young men to go to England or other European countries to study, and his home became their home. Such generosity! Such kindness! Until many years later they heard that this man had been arrested by the police in England, and charged with sexual abuse of boys and young men going back over many, many years. All that generosity! All that kindness!

I am writing this in Barbados in the spring of 1997. It is four years since I was last in Africa, and I wonder, as I watch the TV reports on the Dutrox affair in Belgium, whether my African friends are aware of it. This matter concerns the kidnapping, sexual abuse and murder of young girls by a gang of paedophiles led by a man called Paul Dutrox. It is alleged that the gang received police protection and that membership of the paedophile ring extended across Belgian society. I wonder how my African friends feel about this. If they know about it, I wonder what they make of the incompetence of the police and the corruption of the politicians. Whether they are just happy to know that Europe has its own corruption and levels of incompetence as in Africa, or whether like me they wonder how people who cannot manage their own affairs ever thought themselves fit to rule the world? Was it a very different world, or was it the people who were different?

Just think – even as Europe was conquering and civilising Africa, English children were choking to death down the coals mines and Charles Dickens was writing his tales of poverty in Victorian England. It is always much easier to sort out other people's problems: ask any psychiatrist. So even as the Belgian state teeters on the brink of collapse, riddled with scandal and incompetence, Belgian soldiers will take off for Africa to sort out Zaire. The more things change the more they remain the same!

We know from all the anthropological and genetic evidence that Africa gave birth to humankind, that the first human beings came out of Africa, and spread across the world, changing and adapting as they went. Time passed and after many thousands of years one of the tribes of Africa, now changed beyond recognition, came back to Mother Africa – conquering, enslaving, asserting their natural right to rule their black brothers and sisters. Today European settlement is worldwide, but Europe wants to close its borders to people from other lands, and especially people from the African continent and their descendants living in other parts of the globe. European, and specifically British development and industrialisation were achieved on the backs of slaves and by the robbery of countries that they were pleased to regard as their own.

History has its own momentum, and as globalisation now shrinks the world, it will not be possible to hold back the tide of history or the flow of humanity. From Africa, Europe looks a most desirable residence, just as one hundred years ago, from Europe, Africa looked ripe for the picking. I can't see why it should be accepted as natural and right for Europeans to spread across the globe and live in other people's countries, but at the same time expecting their lands to be a fortress against others. These immigrants are seen by the French nationalist, Le Penn, as "invaders" of Europe. They may not have come in Armadas and pirate ships, and they may not be today's version of Captain Cook or Christopher Columbus, but just as Cook and Columbus were part of the march of history, so too are today's immigrants. The movement of people across the globe will continue, together with the movement of trade and money. It is an unstoppable process. The young people in the streets of Africa will not stop asking every foreigner they meet about how to get to Europe, and one day they will meet a man who knows a man. They will find a way or perish in the effort.

I do understand and sympathise with the cynicism of my African and other non-European brothers and sisters in their view that things often become off-limits as soon as they are within the reach of the non-white populations of the world. Fridges were fine until they came within reach of people in the hot, humid south where they are a necessity. Ditto travel. Now we are hearing about all the deadly diseases that are carried by travellers. Tell that to the indigenous people of the world, who were almost wiped out by the diseases brought to them by the European conquerors and settlers. So what's new?

A white Bajan man explained the problem of water shortage in Barbados to a visitor:

"It's got nothing to do with the golf club using up de water. If de blacks would stop building wall houses and having showers all de time dey won't be any water problem."

An interesting idea, which could pay dividends in other parts of the world, especially India and China!

Telling my African sister how I came to live in Europe

The footpaths of Africa are used for everyday walking, whereas the footpaths of Europe are used mainly for recreation. Travelling across Africa, especially by bus, one can see the footpaths criss-crossing the landscape, wriggling, people-size, going somewhere, going everywhere. I always want to find out where. In Europe I would be tempted to stop and explore, but I won't think of doing this in Africa: it is too vast, too unknown. This reminds me of another difference between walking in Africa and walking in Europe: in the African countryside cow dung is still recognisably cow dung, but not any more in England. Whether it has to do with the disease bovine spongiform encephalitis (BSE, or mad cow disease) or something else, I don't know, but over the years I have noticed a marked change in the composition and smell of cow dung in the English countryside. This is just one of the many differences between walking in the European and walking in the African countryside.

Walking in the city is much the same wherever in the world you are. Lots of shops, lots of people, hustle and bustle, feeling hot and bothered whatever the actual temperature. That is unless you have the good sense to walk in the city early in the morning or at weekends, but even this is changing, as city shops open around the clock. Walking around Nairobi with one of my Kenyan friends I thought how much like walking around any big city the experience was. An overwhelming feeling of tiredness swept over me, and I suggested we stop for rest and a cup of tea or something. We soon found somewhere, it may well have even been McDonald's. There seems to be a McDonald's in every city in the world, just further evidence of globalisation. My friend and I sat with our drinks and she began questioning me about my past. She had obviously been waiting for an opportunity like this. She started off with: "How long have you been living in England? Did you meet Peter there?" I didn't feel like going into all that so I said something like, "It's a long story." She replied that she couldn't wait to hear it. So I got on with it.

Sitting in a café in Nairobi in 1993 I told my Kenyan friend about my arrival in England and what immediately followed. I explained that I had met Peter in Calcutta in 1962, and that I left India in 1965. I vaguely intended going back to Barbados, but my ticket carried me only as far as London. I arrived in London to a not very welcoming reception from Her Majesty's Immigration Service, and as I did not have an onward ticket I faced deportation back to India. Something made me show an invitation I had received to visit one of my English friends in London to the immigration officer. By this time I was locked in a little room, more or less under arrest. The officer telephoned my friend's mother at her Hampstead home, and as a result of that conversation I was allowed into England.

As I recounted this story to my friend in that café in Nairobi, I realised that I had never thanked Elizabeth Luythen properly for her help and kindness. I don't think that at the time I realised the real significance of what she had done. It was only after I went to work as a community relations officer in London, and had to try to help people in a similar situation, that I fully understood my own predicament. I told my friend that I'd stayed in Hampstead until the son of the home had arrived from India, then I went to stay with my brother in Leytonstone, in east London. Then Peter arrived from India and the two of us went off on a tour of the UK. We spent a lot of time in the north of England and in Scotland, and we ended up getting married in a small town called Montrose. After we got married we set off for Spain to visit one of my friends from Calcutta, who was then living in Madrid. We returned from Spain expecting our first child and I settled down to family life and to begin studying for the career I was certain I was going to have. "So that's about it." End of story. It was time to leave the café and to make our way back to the house.

I will add here a little bit of information that I did not choose to mention to my African sister on that day in Nairobi. The truth is that when I left India my preferred destination was Africa, but Africa did not want me, and that is how I ended up living and working in Europe. For the full account of this story please see "Leaving India: Dreaming of Africa" in Chapter Seven.

Africa and Europe – two sides of the same coin?

After all I have seen and done, the walks, the talks, the teaching and the learning, I am left with the view that the problems of Africa are the problems of humanity – writ large. Africa always seems to get the worst of everything – the worst famines, wars and diseases. Europe takes the best of everything, including the best of Africa. As Walter Rodney so eloquently argued, Africa was "underdeveloped" by Europe in order to achieve European development. Long before the idea of development or underdevelopment Africa gave birth to humanity.

I have to admit, somewhat reluctantly, that nothing I have observed or experienced has left me with the feeling African society is more spiritual than European. I accept that there is a fundamental difference in values between European and African societies, and that, generally, European social values are more materialistic than African. For me, the significant thing about Africa will always be the slave trade, for in taking part in it Africa betrayed itself, and we are all of us still paying the price of that betrayal. In the past Africa was unable to withstand the violence and inducements of the slave traders, just as today Africa is unable to withstand the onslaught of capitalism. That is why so many Africans have forsaken their traditional gods and religions in favour of Christianity – as the way to salvation and materialism.

6

HOME GROUND – THE
CARIBBEAN AND LATIN
AMERICA

IF THE Caribbean is "home", then Latin America must be my neglected, taken-for-granted backyard. I had visited all the other continents before I set foot in Central and South America. I have written quite a lot about the Caribbean and Latin America in other parts of this book. Those pieces were in a particular context, for a specific purpose, but in this chapter I plan to write more generally about the Caribbean and Latin America, and of my travels and experiences in my own part of the world.

Whenever I am in the Caribbean I want to go to Trinidad, I must see my "Trini-sisters", and I must walk in Trinidad. Walking in Trinidad is tremendously exciting, not only because of the flora and fauna, the mountains and waterfalls, the abundance and variety of bird life, and the risk of snake bites, but also on account of the man-made dangers. You can be robbed, or worse, and there is always the possibility of returning from a walk to find that your car has either been completely stolen, or that so much of it has been removed, for example the wheels, that it can't be driven. Walking with my friend in the hills just outside San Juan we were stopped and told off by a short black man with a cutlass, who told us it was too dangerous for two women to be out walking alone. We looked suitably chastened, so he added that he supposed we would be all right, but that we should take care and watch out for (wait for it!) "a short black man with a cutlass!" We could not figure out whether he was warning us about himself, or whether the hills were full of short black men with cutlasses. So we continued our walk, and hoped for the best. Back in the city, people would listen with amazement when we said where we had been, and always remarked on the risks we were taking. My walking companion is a good Christian, and we walked in the certain knowledge that the Lord would protect us. Trinidad can be a very violent and dangerous place.

Even so, I am drawn back to Trinidad time and again, to hike and to be exposed to Trinidadian culture, which is like nothing else on earth. The sheer vibrancy of the people and the beauty and variety of the landscape draws me back. Just to be an onlooker at the never-ending theatre that is life in Trinidad is worth the risk of being there. The on-going dramas reflect the everyday life of the people, and racial politics plays an increasingly important part in it.

The population of Trinidad and Tobago consists of two major groups of people: Africans who were brought as slaves in the eighteenth century, and Indians who came from the Indian sub-continent as indentured labourers at the end of the nineteenth and the start of the twentieth century. The two groups do not live happily together, and there are major tensions. Sometimes it seems that these have been there forever, and it is difficult to know just how much they are a normal part of the life in Trinidad and Tobago, and how much they carry the potential for deeper conflict. Stories abound of training camps where East Indians (so called to distinguish them from Amerindians) are being prepared for the inevitable war with the Africans. The East Indian population now outnumbers the African, and in Baseo Pandy, Trinidad has its first East Indian prime minister, a reversal of post-independence history in which Africans were the natural leaders.

In 1996 I attended the 150th anniversary celebrations of Indian arrival day. Indians came to Trinidad 150 years before as labour to replace the freed Africans who no longer wanted to work on the land. Imagine the scene: all the great and the good were there, presided over by the president of Trinidad and Tobago, and the president of India. And there I was with my African-Trinidadian sister, her daughters, and my English husband, an African woman belting out the Indian national anthem. Even though there was a swell of Indian nationalism, masquerading as a "cultural revival" in Trinidad, I was one of the few Caribbean people at that function who were able to join in singing the Indian national anthem, which was in Hindi, of course. My performance met with puzzled looks, which only made me sing even more loudly and to be glad of all those Hindi movies I'd been to in my Calcutta days.

I keenly awaited the speech of the president of India, as I had anticipated something really stirring and original. But, for me, when the speech came it was a big disappointment. The president seemed mainly concerned with extolling the virtues of India, and its successes and accomplishments – which are indeed considerable. I have no quarrel with that. But what I did find surprising was his failure to acknowledge the problems that had forced so many people to flee from India in difficult conditions, for unknown lands. Many of these problems persist to this day, but the avenues of escape are considerably less than 150 years ago. I suppose it was too much to expect anything more than platitudes, but one continues to hope. In the context of Trinidadian politics India is a "great power", and great powers cannot admit to being less than perfect.

In Trinidad as in Guyana I am always conscious of the racial divide, and of the fact that racial politics invades all aspects of life. You are never allowed to forget or ignore the race group of the person you have just met or have just taken leave of. It is taken for granted that I, as an African, share the views and attitudes of the black people towards the Indian. This can lead to some awkward and embarrassing situations that I am not generally very good at dealing with. It can be very wearing always challenging the consensus and being in a minority of one. In Guyana I actually asked a taxi driver to stop referring to Indians as "coolies" while I was paying to ride in his car. He explained to me that this was the "Guyanese way" and that it meant nothing, and the Indians didn't mind. Later I discussed this with a group of Afro-Guyanese friends, who took the taxi-man's view. This time I could challenge, and I did: "So you don't mind being called 'nigger'?" At first they denied that this was the same thing, but eventually they had to agree that "coolie" and "nigger" are both terms of racial abuse.

In the Caribbean we are never far from prejudice and racism, of one form or another. Yet my black brothers and sisters often ask me whether I have "any trouble" when I am travelling. It is very well known that women travellers, including businesswomen, often encounter subtle and not so subtle discrimination and harassment. When dining alone, you can be given the least desirable seating near the kitchen exit, or you can have hotel rooms not equipped for female use, but with a suit-press, shavers and so on. As a black woman who is a professional, who also travels extensively, I have been questioned specifically about my experiences with racism and discrimination in hotels, and other types of accommodation.

I will try to respond to this type of query with accounts of two incidents, the first in England, and the second in Trinidad, a space of three or four years separating them. My life has not followed any fixed plan, so my travels, walks and related experiences reflect this fact. My stories, like my life experiences, criss-cross, and only much later, if at all, do similarities between different events emerge. The two events I am about to relate were both occasioned by our impulsiveness, when on both occasions we had set out as a family for a day trip to the seaside, and each time we decided to extend our stay. Once we had decided to stay we had to find accommodation for the night. And therein lies a tale or two.

It was the summer of 1970, and Peter and I with our daughter set out for the English south coast. We did not have a plan, we were simply heading for a day at the seaside, and as it happened we ended up in Selsey, in Sussex. It was a hot, sunny day and when the time came to think of heading home, nobody wanted to, so we decided to stay. There was only one problem: lunch was at home slow-cooking in the oven (no microwaves then). I telephoned my next-door neighbour in Shepperton, and explained the situation to her, and she was happy to pop into our house and turn the oven off. One problem solved. Next problem – somewhere to stay. Off we went in search of a B&B. There were many, but as it was a bank holiday weekend there might well be no vacancies. We were in luck, for the very first boarding house we called at had vacancies, and we were soon installed. Accommodation problem solved.

Next problem – toothbrushes. In the Sussex of 1969, there was no all-day Sunday shopping. Somehow it fell to me to explain our problem to the landlady: impulsive nature, sea lovely, not to be resisted, no toothbrush. The landlady smiled indulgently, went off and returned with a set of brand-new toothbrushes. We were very grateful, but she said to think nothing of it. I wondered if perhaps we not so unique after all, and maybe she had a constant run of families impulsively staying the night, minus toothbrush. The next day was also a bank holiday and we spent the morning on the beach and set off for home very early in the afternoon. For some reason, we have never been back to Selsey Bill, and have gone past it, always saying, usually simultaneously, "Remember the time when… " and laugh at ourselves. We have good memories of Selsey and that weekend.

In 1973, or thereabouts, we found ourselves in more or less the same situation in Trinidad, but this time we had no choice, because the way back was more or less cut off. Let me start at the beginning. We were exploring the Trinidad countryside from our base in Port-of-Spain. On this particular occasion we had set off very early in the morning, heading for the seaside by way of the coconut groves in the south of the country. We came to a small seaside village where all the people were engaged in the coconut harvest. The sea was not for swimming in, as you could walk endlessly and the water would still be at ankle height. So we just lazed about on the beach. Our children began playing with the village kids and somehow or other we all ended up joining in the coconut harvest. This involved just picking them up and putting them in heaps, not anything exciting, such as actually climbing the trees and picking them.

Children and adults alike, we all enjoyed being included in village life, and the time passed very quickly. Before we realised it, darkness was beginning to fall. We had been told when we left Port-of-Spain that we had to set off early because it was dangerous to drive through the dark forest at night. The danger came from two directions: firstly from the coconuts, which as they fell could shatter the car's windscreen, and secondly from the robbers who were lying in wait for naïve people like us. The villagers confirmed what we had been told, and we realised that we would have to stay the night. I asked if there were any hotels nearby. One of the villagers, an elderly man, shifted from foot to foot, hemmed and hawed and eventually told us that there was a hotel not very far away, "just down there", and he pointed straight ahead. My concern now was for the children and I wanted to get to the hotel as soon as possible, so straightaway we set off in search of it.

Just as the man said, the hotel was quite close by. As soon as we got there, Peter rushed out of the car and went ahead to book a room, leaving me to gather up the children and to follow on. The scene as I followed him onto the hotel veranda was straight out of a Somerset Maugham novel, or short story. There were ceiling fans slowly rotating, and around the bar were seated six or seven white men. Behind the bar was a black man, the waiter. As Peter walked in a white woman came up to him with arms outstretched and a warm, welcoming smile on her face. Then she caught sight of me and the children, and the smile froze, and her arms dropped to her side, and she said, or rather hissed, "We are completely full up, we have no room." I turned to leave. I wanted to be out of there pronto. Then a young woman came out of somewhere, and said more or less that she was in charge, and yes, they did have room, and would we care to have a look? Peter followed her, and, reluctantly, I followed him.

Out of earshot of the bar, she explained that the other woman was her mother and that she "had a problem". She went on to say to us that under her management things would have to change as she would not tolerate "anything like that". No doubt a reference to her mother's very obvious racist attitude. We looked at the room and I thanked her for her trouble and said that we would find somewhere else, that "it wasn't quite what we were looking for". Clutching my children I proudly walked out. We all knew that there was not another hotel for miles, probably not until Port-of-Spain, but I consoled myself with the thought that there was always the car. If homeless families in England could live in a car for weeks at a time, surely we would be all right for just one night. Luckily we did not have to find out. As our car turned out of the hotel drive, I spotted the old man with the shifting feet, standing by the gate, waving for us to stop.

We stopped. I got out, and, without going into details, simply said that we were not going to stay in that place. He was obviously familiar with it and the views of the landlady, and had been so concerned that he had followed to make sure that we were all right. Now seeing our plight, he invited us to stay the night with him. It was very humble accommodation, but for me it was as good as a palace, and the children enjoyed sleeping on the floor, thinking it all part of the day's adventure.

I wish that I could say that after that we never again stayed over on impulse. In fact we have, off and on, in other parts of the world, and fortunately we have never had a repeat of the Trinidad incident. How can these very different experiences be explained? Most people would have expected that problems would arise in England, not in Trinidad. But our experience that night in Trinidad was part of the legacy of colonialism and the plantocracy. Things like that can happen to people like us anywhere in the former British empire. For me the worst thing is that in spite of my knowledge and social awareness, such experiences invariably come as a most unexpected and unpleasant surprise.

In the Caribbean my defences are down, and that is when I am most vulnerable. It is a fact that most of the unpleasant experiences I have had when travelling, either on my own or with Peter, have been in the Caribbean. The worst experience of all happened in Barbados, when the two of us were turned away from the Glitter Bay hotel. The guard very rudely told us that it was management policy to refuse admission to "mixed couples", because of problems with drugs. So we went to see the manager, a young Englishman, who completely denied there was any such policy, but all the same advised us that in order to avoid such problems in the future we should telephone the hotel in advance. We have never done so. Without meaning to, I have now introduced Barbados, the gem of the Caribbean. So let us move on.

Beautiful, Beautiful Barbados

This poem is about porous limestone, my mother, Barbados

Most English of the West Indian islands, but at the same time nearest, as the slave fly, to Africa.

Braithwaite, E K, *Mother Poem* (preface) OUP, Oxford

My birthplace, Barbados, is one of the most racially divided societies in the world. An article based on a compilation of reports from three 1997 travel guides – *Fordor's, Berlitz* and *Cadogan* – appeared in the *Nation* newspaper (19th April 1997) under the headline, THE TWO SIDES TO BARBADOS:

It may be a cosmopolitan and sophisticated country whose people enjoy one of the Caribbean's highest standards of living… but underneath it all is a racial divide.

The reporter, the paper's North America correspondent, Tony Best, went on to quote from the travel guides, all saying more or less the same thing: that there are two distinct sides to Barbados, one black, the other white. *Cadogan's Guide*:

If the island has a problem, it is the residue of a rigid system of colour prejudice.

Tony Best then quoted an unnamed travel guide as blaming

both blacks and whites for the history of deep racial division which exists in 1997… . Although there is a substantial black middle-class and the social situation has changed radically since the 1940s and '50s, there is still more racial intolerance on all sides than is apparent at first glance.

Interesting. Especially in view of the quotation from the *Berlitz* guide, which stated that:

> More than the beaches, more than the scenery, more than
> anything else, the Bajans... are what you remember most. Very
> simply they're 'people's people'.

Make no mistake, it is the black Bajan people they are talking about.
The *Berlitz* readers and correspondents who eulogise these Bajan people
are almost certainly one hundred per cent white. So how can black
Bajans be "equally to blame for the continuing racial divide in the
country"? Answers on a post-card, please.

There are stereotypes associated with the Caribbean, just as there
are with other countries. The Caribbean stereotype is of a tourist
paradise. A "paradise", for everyone except the poor, whose country it
is. I have travelled fairly extensively throughout the English-speaking
Caribbean, and the longest time I have been away from the region is
the three years I spent in India and my first year in England. To be in
Barbados was a natural part of my life, which did not need any
explanation or justification. I have never had to re-discover my roots,
because I never lost them.

It seems that the Caribbean travel and tourism industry is now
encouraging something called "ethnic tourism" to the Caribbean. By
this they mean African-Americans, and other black people in the USA
and Canada. The choice of the word "ethnic" in this context strikes me
as very odd, given that ninety-eight per cent of the region's population
is more or less black. It seemed that special training would be needed
so that hotel staff treated these "ethnic tourists" in the same way as
non-ethnic tourists. I am not making this up, but I wish I were. Black
workers in the Caribbean tourism industry are unaccustomed to non-
white tourists or visitors, and do not behave appropriately towards them.
My own recent experience of travel in the Caribbean bears this out.
When I first visited the Asa Wright Nature Centre in Trinidad, had I
been of a more sensitive disposition it could have been a very
uncomfortable experience. As it was, I try to ignore the irritations and
annoyances which go with being a "local visitor" to such places; and I
must say that over the years since my first visit things have definitely
improved and there is a better local atmosphere at the Asa Wright
Centre. More local people, including children, now visit the centre,
and there are plans to develop educational links and projects with
schools. Outside Trinidad I have not met one single Caribbean person
who has visited the Asa Wright Nature Centre.

In the mid-1960s, when Peter and I first started travelling in the

Caribbean, we were often given "friendly" advice about where it was safe or not safe for us to go. In the 1970s we were strongly advised not to go to Dominica, as we were told that we would be a target for the "Black Power" movement, and we might be attacked, and certainly made to feel unwelcome. When we boarded the MV *Stella*, none of my family or friends in Barbados had ever heard of it, let alone travelled on it. We sailed away to Dominica, stopping off at St Vincent and St Lucia on the way. We stayed two or three weeks in Dominica and loved the place. Dominica was where I had wanted to visit ever since I was a child of eight or nine, when a woman from Dominica came to live in our village. She told me that there were 365 rivers in her country, one for every day of the year. In Barbados, where the few rivers we have are mostly underground, this sounded truly fantastic, and I promised myself that one day I would go there and visit her river-paradise.

In truth Dominica was a wonderful place, very mountainous and with many, many rivers and streams (there must have been five or six near our tent in the rain forest). It was our first experience of the rain forest, and we went to sleep and woke up to the sound of gurgling streams. Our host and hostess were a local black Dominican and his white American wife. This must have been one of the first attempts at eco-tourism in the Caribbean, or perhaps even in the world. We explored the island by bus, where buses where available, and walked or "took transport" whenever we could. In those days most people depended on "transport", that is to say lifts, as the main means of getting around.

I even managed to arrange a visit to Carib Territory, but this was very disappointing for me. Why? The children and I were put in a side room and were left for hours on end while Peter was taken to meet the head man and the Carib council: they spent the rest of the morning drinking white rum with coconut water as a chaser. The men were asking Peter lots of questions about community development, project funding, and so on – things that he knew nothing about – whereas I was lecturing to and supervising students on community development placements, and had a lot of relevant knowledge. This was one of the reasons I had arranged the visit in the first place. Things have moved on and looking at the 1996 Caribbean Council of Indigenous People's (COIP) conference report, I see women taking quite a leading role in its affairs and local councils.

In spite of my experience with the Carib Council, I was very glad that we had ignored advice and gone to Dominica. It was the same with our visit to Venezuela, when I left the UK to join Peter in Barbados for our first visit to South America: the BBC Ceefax information service said that the British government was advising against going to Venezuela at that time. I forgot to tell Peter about this until our return to Barbados, though I don't think it would have made any difference to our plans. We went walking in Venezuela as we do everywhere we go, and we even managed to misdirect ourselves and almost missed the boat to Trinidad. We took an internal flight from Caracas airport and a taxi to the port, where we arrived with time to spare. As though that was not excitement enough, Peter lost his wallet at the airport, and as he frantically searched his pockets and everything else trying to locate it, a young lady rushed up to us, wallet in hand. He had left it on the check-in desk. Nothing we had heard or been told about Venezuela had led us to expect such honesty.

To return for a moment to the matter of "ethnic tourism". We were travelling in Costa Rica, going by boat to Tortuguero, a journey of about five hours. The black boatman and I fell into conversation. He wanted to know where I was from, and when I told him he remarked that he had never before taken anyone from "the [Caribbean] islands" to Tortuguero. I expressed surprise at this, as we were on the Caribbean coast originally settled by immigrants from Jamaica, who came there in at the end of the nineteenth century to build the railway. "Don't you have any visitors from the islands then?" I asked. He said that there were visitors from the islands, but that they came for the music and bars, and stayed in the town with relatives or friends. The tourist industry would not be interested in such visitors. Tourism tended to distort prices, and to put the country's natural heritage and cultural resources out of reach of ordinary citizens. In Costa Rica this is currently a hot topic of debate, as families find it harder and harder to afford the entry fees to national parks and other places of interest.

I became an "ethnic tourist" when, after our round-the-world trip, I decided that my next priority would be South and Central America. In January 1995 Peter and I set off by plane for Puerto Rica, and from Puerto Rica again by plane to Panama. From Panama we went by bus through Central America, to Mexico, and in Mexico we travelled by bus and train, and then by bus again to Miami, Florida, from where we flew back to Barbados. The trip took about five months. In 1997 we returned to Costa Rica and stayed for two months, attending a Spanish language school, and exploring the country.

It is impossible to be in this region for any length of time without being aware that you are living in the shadow of the Big Brother in the north. There is a Mexican saying lamenting the fate of Mexico for being "too far from heaven and too close to America". My impression is that the USA is to South and Central America exactly what the USSR was to the satellite states of Eastern Europe and central Asia. The USA seeks to manage and control these countries by whatever means, while at the same time piously talking about "democracy". I will not go into the shameful role the USA played in Central America's many wars, as this has been well documented, not least by the US government itself.

There are two major excuses for US interference and control – the so-called Monroe doctrine (otherwise known as not in my backyard) and the "war against drugs". The US economic blockade of Cuba comes under the Monroe doctrine. In this region the fight between David and Goliath takes many forms. Currently it is little Grenada doing its own thing in relation to Cuba. The prime minister of Grenada has not only gone to Cuba and signed a treaty with Fidel Castro, but he also has invited Castro to visit Grenada. The 1983 US invasion of Grenada was partly justified on the grounds of stopping Cuban expansion into the Eastern Caribbean. Can we now expect another US invasion? After the political control of the region, illustrated by the US blockade of Cuba, comes the war against drugs, which the USA is fighting (and losing), not only in this region, but also across the world.

Apart from living in the shadow of the almighty USA, and drugs, the region has many other problems, some historical in origin, others truly contemporary and modern. The condition of the indigenous peoples of the region is terrible, and they are marginalised and discriminated against in all areas of life. It is rare to see pictures or reports in the papers about the normal daily life of the original people of these lands. Most of the indigenous people of the region are located in Central and South America, and there are only small pockets in the islands of the Caribbean. In Central America especially extreme poverty is another problem affecting the region, or that and extreme crime. Every now and again there is an armed rebellion, such as the Tutakamaras in Chile and the Zapatistas in Mexico, who try to challenge the existing order. They are killed as in Peru or marginalised as in Mexico, and either way they fail.

To Peter and me, coming from England and Barbados, Mexico and most of the other Central American countries seemed like armed camps. As we travelled across Mexico by bus, our journey was repeatedly delayed by stops for army and security checks. On one occasion the bus was stopped in the middle of the night and heavily armed soldiers boarded and removed one of the women passengers. Everywhere in Central America there are armed soldiers and security guards, guns at the ready, and even so they can't stop the rising tide of crime, for people have to live. I tried to adopt the same attitude as people on the street, going about their work, kids going to school and women shopping. Peter found it very disturbing and unsettling, and could not really relax in any of the cities, except possibly San José. In Mexico City the new fad of holding up restaurants was in vogue. Except in Costa Rica, many years of civil war and other disturbances have created a climate of fear and a high level of anxiety in the population. Costa Rica seems to be following suit, with more guns in 1997 than in 1996, and two explosions near the president's residence in San José.

"Wo'man smarta dan man!" – the battle of the sexes Caribbean style

In the Plymouth Brethren we were not allowed to listen to music of any kind, for all music was regarded as "ungodly". But I loved calypso, and I never missed the chance to listen to it, so I would go next door to listen at my friend's house, or simply lean out of our front window, and listen. I knew a lot of the calypso songs coming out of Trinidad. I made no effort to learn them, the words just stuck in my memory. The calypso songs of those days are now called "old time calypso", to distinguish them from the current variety. There is one old time calypso song that deals with the relationship between men and women, not only in the Caribbean, but everywhere else in the world. The song as I recall it goes something like this:

> From de time de worl begin
> Woo'man was always ruining men.
> An' dat is why,
> Up to dis day
> Woo'man smarter dan man in every way.
> Dat's right! Dat's right!
> De woo'man too smar't again!

I have relied on my memory, and I may not have got all the words exactly right, but there can be little doubt about the feelings behind the words: women ruin men, women are smarter than men, this has been so "from de time de worl begin". I did not realise it at the time, but now I can see that the words of this song express men's deep fears and anxieties about women: the fear of being ruined by women, and of women's "smartness". As the song says, women are "too smart". Too smart for our own good, and sometimes we women are too smart to be allowed to go on living. However, when compared with the anti-woman songs of some rap and slackness artists, songs like "Woman Smarta dan Man" are sweetness itself. Yet in some senses all these songs arise from the same deep-seated male fears and anxieties, and express male insecurity. I think that generally male violence against women has its roots in these feelings of helplessness and insecurity, and that every society adds its own, cultural, religious and economic flavours, but the basic ingredients are the same.

Ever since my stint at Chiswick woman's aid, under the wing of Erin Pizzey, I have maintained an interest in domestic violence. Through my research work and my travels I have been able to get a general impression of the state of affairs between men and women worldwide. As in the rest of the world, in this region it is dire. Domestic violence and child abuse is as much a part of the daily life here as elsewhere in the world. Then there are some dubious claims to fame, such as the exceptionally high rate of murder/suicide among East Indian men in Trinidad – one of the highest in the world. I know that women in general and "women's lib" in particular have been blamed for just about everything that is wrong with modern society, and I am not proposing to join in this debate.

I will try, with reference to the situation in the Caribbean, to draw on three pieces of literature that I hope will be of interest in themselves, and helpful to those who are trying to understand this problem. The first two extracts are from the Women and Development (WAND) occasional papers series. The third is a poem from *Shades of I-She*, a theatrical presentation of "everywoman's story", produced by a Caribbean women's collective. Beckles' piece approaches the problems from an historical viewpoint, and Nesta Haniff from the point of view of a feminist sociologist, while Eintou Springer is from that of a creative artist.

Elsewhere I have touched on the violence that characterised the creation of the Hispanic world, and that continues to be an everyday feature of Latin American life. Slavery is also a part of Hispanic history, and I believe that these excerpts apply with little modification and with equal force to the countries of Central and South America.

First to the historian. Beckles' 1996 paper, "Black masculinity in Caribbean slavery", is where Dr Beckles seeks to explain today's black male personality. Beckles argues that under slavery black men were subjected to unspeakable violence, but at the same time they "shared certain patriarchal values with white men and were allowed to exercise dominance over black women... but only with the sanction of the white male". Beckles concludes his paper with these words:

> Implosive community violence remains an expression of subordinate black masculinities. The seemingly rudderless quest for inversion of the dominant agenda has left the streets of communities, the language of discourse, sexual relations, political dialogue, and lyrics of popular music, shot through with violence, virtual and real.

> Beckles, H (1996), "Black masculinity in Caribbean slavery", WAND (Women and Development Unit) Occasional Paper 2/96, UWI, Barbados

Next to the sociologist and Nesha Haniff's paper, "The stereotyping of East Indian women in the Caribbean". The author tries to explain the reasons for the stereotyping of East Indian women (those whose ancestors came from the Indian sub-continent) in Trinidad and Guyana. When the submissive East Indian woman leaves her husband, the resulting loss of face that the man suffers can result in the murder of the woman who has failed to conform to the stereotype. According to Haniff, this is the image to which the East Indian woman in the Caribbean is expected to conform:

> The East Indian woman speaks pigin English, she cooks roti, dal, talcari and eats pepper... . Invariably pretty and sexy, she will always be willing, but is afraid... . It is the creation of the East Indian woman as a victim of the patriarchy that the stereotype has taken hold.

> Haniff, N, (1996), "The stereotyping of East Indian women in the Caribbean", WAND Occasional Paper 1/96, UWI, Barbados

This extract is from the beginning of Haniff's essay (p1), and towards the end (p10) the author deals directly with the issue of wife-murder:

218

Constructions of masculinity in the East Indian community are tied to controlling the female... . It is the violation of a man's self in the eyes of the community that makes a wife's departure intolerable... he has lost face... . In many cultures losing face is the worst possible thing that could happen to a man, but this is not a justification for killing a woman... . This is something that East Indian men who are sensitive to gender issues should take on.

Haniff, N, "The stereotyping of East Indian women"

Last but not least to the artist. *Shades of I-SHE*, by Pearl Eintou, Springer (1997) from her poem, "Bois".

There are no men!
The cult of warrior hood has died
almost.
Are there really no men!
I want there to be some one
just for me!
Who will not look at me
and strip me
with his eyes
imagine how it is
between my thighs
There are no men.

Are there really no men
who are more strong
than I,
with whom I can share—
everything.
give respect
without bondage?
No – there are no men.

Are there really no men
responsible and caring
gentle but strong
as rocks unmoving.
There are no men.

there are no men
to whom I can
with joy
entrust myself
for guidance
share thoughts
and words—
even silence

And so
the ache of want
becomes a high of celibacy
transcended to creativity
because
there are no men
worthy even
to climb
on my belly
Are there really no men.

Springer, P (1977), "There are no Men" in *Shades of I-She –
Every Woman's Story in Poetry*, The Collective, Diego Martin,
Trinidad

Eintou's cries of anguish and despair that there are "No men" gentle,
yet strong, who will share silence with us and also talk to us when we
need conversation: men who match up to her hopes and expectations
of manhood. Why are there no such men, and what is the role of women
in explaining this deficit? There is another side to this equation, which
I will try to illustrate with a quotation from *Demonic Males Apes And the
Origins of Human Violence* by Richard Wrangham and Dale Peterson
(1997). In Chapter Twelve, "Taming the Demon", the authors consider
how things may be changed and state that:

Women don't like many specific acts of demonic males. But paradoxically, many women do regularly find attractive the cluster of qualities and behaviours – successful aggression, dominance and displays of dominance – associated with male demonic behaviour. Both men and women are active participants in the very system that nurtures the continued success of demonic males; and the knot of human evolution with the demonic male at the centre requires an untying of both strands.

Wrangham, R and Dale, P (1996), *Demonic Males – Apes and the Origins of Human Violence*, Bloomsbury, London

People and places: Latin America and the Caribbean

I am now going tell a few stories about some of the people I have met, the places I have visited and the experiences I have had while travelling around the Caribbean and Latin America.

Jamaica farewell

I began working at the University of Surrey in 1975, and in 1976 I was sent on a visit to the three campuses of the UWI: at Mona, in Kingston, Jamaica, at St Augustine, Trinidad, and at Cave Hill, Barbados. It was not a successful visit, either personally or professionally. For one reason or another I was totally unable to relax, and it did not help that I was forbidden to walk or to go anywhere on my own, even on campus. There was then, and still is now, a lot of violence in Kingston, and on my arrival I was taken to my lodgings and instructed not to open my bedroom door, except in response to an agreed code. This made me feel so uncomfortable that after a few days I accepted Bernard and Phylis Coard's invitation to stay with them. Once I'd moved off campus I felt slightly more relaxed, and after making a visit in downtown Kingston, instead of getting a taxi and heading straight back as I'd been instructed, I decided on a little walk around.

I didn't get very far. I had just come out of the welfare office and was trying to decide which way to turn, when a very tall Rasta man approached me: "Hi, sister!" I am nothing if not "cool", so I returned his greeting in kind. We began to talk. He could tell that I was new in Kingston, he "just knew". He informed me that the place was "dread", and that it was not at all safe for a sister like me to be on her own. He told me that there were some bad guys around who would think nothing of robbing and shooting me. Oh dear, but stay "cool". I stayed cool and ask innocently: "Do people here carry guns, then?" He laughed, pulled up his shirt and showed me his. Then he advised me to get a taxi and go straight home. I did. And that was the end of my Kingston adventure. I was not surprised to learn that Jamaica invented the idea of "all inclusive holidays", whereby visitors are more or less segregated from the local population in a tourist ghetto.

That encounter with the Rasta man was not the only time I was in danger during that visit to Jamaica. As I started off by saying, the visit was not a success, and because the staff of the sociology department at the university were suspicious of me, I did not feel very welcome there. Gradually the atmosphere thawed, and towards the end of my stay I was invited to dinner by one of the senior staff members. Before I go on to tell what happened during that evening, let me take time out to mention the events associated with the visit of another overseas academic, who was visiting the department at the same time as I.

She was a white American social work professor. I attended a staff seminar given by her, and the burden of her message was that Freud was the answer to life, the universe and everything. When I asked how her message applied to the social conditions in downtown Kingston, she replied that Freudian insights apply to all societies. I was a social work lecturer at Surrey University, where we were trying to educate and train people for social work in the real world. I was amazed to find in Kingston, Jamaica, a home for such outdated, and, in the context of Caribbean society, socially irrelevant theories. The messenger also had no conception of what it was to be poor and black in the Caribbean, and was the type of person I am sure would not have ventured into the streets of Kingston.

Yet, the message that the American Freudian had brought to Jamaica was welcomed. For me the contrast between the approach to social work in poverty-stricken, downtown Kingston, and what we were trying to do in well-heeled Surrey could not have been greater. In Surrey we were trying to take issue with structural problems, of poverty, unemployment, racism. We were exploring ways of working with people in groups and communities, while not ignoring personal and family problems, or the "internal world" that is part of human existence. I was very disappointed with what I'd heard at the seminar, and with what I heard and saw of social-work training at Mona. That was my reaction then. Now, I think I am a little wiser, and can understand why in the face of the extreme poverty and social distress in Jamaica, Freudian theory, focusing as it does on the internal world, should have had such appeal. Freudian theory requires little more than complete acceptance of a revealed truth, much the same as with any religion. In Jamaica, a community approach might be dangerous work, where arguments are likely to be settled by a knife or a gun. With that kind of option it is much safer to be a follower of Freud. Having said that, I must now add that one of the most impressive community projects I have ever seen was in fact in Kingston. It was a community health project, run by a nurse-tutor. Most of the members were women, and the project leader had succeeded in getting a very high degree of participation from them.

Now we can return to my evening out. It went better than expected, and I began to understand some of the reasons why I'd found things difficult. There were several. Some were nothing to do with me, but my not eating meat had been taken as a sign of a "difficult person" and hadn't helped. The moon was full, it was a beautiful night, and after dinner I persuaded my companion to walk back to walked back to Bernard Coard's house where I was staying. It was a very short distance and the night was so beautiful, and so peaceful, that we were lulled into a false sense of security. We soon reached the house, but as we had taken a short cut we actually arrived at the rear, rather than at the front entrance. There we were, chatting and laughing as we walked across the back lawn, when all of a sudden came a military-style, "Who goes there? Don't move!" The two of us stood stock-still and waited. The question came again, and this time I ventured to speak. "It's only me, Bernard," I shouted back. "It's only Maureen." Safely inside the house Bernard reminded me that I'd been warned never to use the back entrance to the house. I said that I'd forgotten all about that. He remarked that to forget such a warning might have cost me my life. I never found out what that incident was all about, and why using the back entrance to the house had constituted such a grave risk.

I must now give a brief summary of the rest of my visit to the University of the West Indies (UWI). The UWI has three campuses, Mona in Kingston Jamaica, St Augustine in Trinidad and Cave Hill in Barbados. The Mona Campus at Kingston was my first stop and in Jamaica I had a Visiting Lecturer Programme which involved student contact. I also gave a couple of lectures and participated in other academic and professional activities in the Department of Sociology/Social Work. But In Trinidad and Barbados no programme had been arranged for me, there was nothing, nothing at all. During the time I spent at these two campuses all I did was to socialise with people I already knew at the university. I wondered why I was there, and I still don't really know. At the time I simply accepted that I was a pawn in somebody else's chess game, and that I should just live through the experience and get back to my family and my job, more or less sane.

The UWI has been associated with the some of the most bizarre and traumatic experiences of my academic career, beginning with that visit in 1976. I can still remember how puzzled and amused my Bajan friends were when I told them that I'd been taken on an "Island Tour" to be shown "places of interest" by an English expatriate Sociology Lecturer at Cave Hill Campus. I was known to this man from the time when he'd been a postgraduate student in the Department of Sociology at Surrey University and he knew full well that I am Barbadian – so I have no idea why he thought I needed to be shown places of interest in my own little island. But I simply endured that island tour as I'd endured so much else on that "homecoming visit" to UWI.

Some years later, in 1988, I visited the Social Work Programme at the Cave Hill Campus and attended a seminar on the subject of Child Protection. The Head of the Social Work Programme had invited me to the seminar but she did not introduce me or acknowledge my presence in any way. In the course of the discussion which followed the presentation on Child Protection issues, when the students needed comparative information about approaches in other countries, particularly the UK, no attempt was made to involve me or to draw on my knowledge. I'd recently completed and published research in this field, a copy of which I'd just given to Dr Jones, Head of Social Work and the Chair of that Seminar. Once the seminar ended I took the earliest opportunity to leave the room and have never had any desire to go anywhere near a UWI campus again.

The international mother

Costa Rica is my favourite Central American destination. You meet all sorts of people there, and the climate varies, from very hot to quite mild. I have mentioned elsewhere that Costa Rica attracts a lot of North Americans who are running away from the cold northern winters. These people live a life more or less apart from the locals ("Ticans"), and go to extreme lengths to defend themselves from intruders. For one whole month we lived in Casita in the hills outside Escazu in conditions akin to these. The couple we were renting from were so pathologically afraid of being robbed that they lived like virtual prisoners in their own home.

They could not both come to the bottom of their garden, where our mountain cabin was, without having a guard to watch the house. The security systems and armed guards around the houses in Escazu and San José tell their own story of these fears, or sometimes unhealthy paranoia. It was a thrill for me to visit a Costa Rican open-planned home with a veranda and windows without bars.

The international mother lived in a traditional cottage and her home did not need bars. She was thirty-eight years old and she told me very proudly that she already had nine, or was it ten children. The fathers were representative of the male population of Costa Rica, both visitor and resident. It was this variety that led her to describe herself as an "international mother". As I recall, so far the breakdown of the paternity of her children was: Costa Rican, three, German, one, American, two, Swedish, one. She was now seeking to extend her range to include a "Jamaican" man. She was very firm about not wanting a local Jamaican from Límon. Oh no – she wanted "the real thing", a Jamaica man from Jamaica. She told me how much she loved reggae, as though this explained everything. She became quite wishful, as though she thought that her child with a Jamaican man would be sure to be born singing reggae. I asked her how she was going to find the father of her next child. She was quite confident that this would not be difficult: "No problema," she said, again and again. "No problema." If past performance is any guide to the future, the next time I visit Costa Rica I expect to see a reggae-singing Jamaican baby among her assortment of children. I am sure that the woman who calls herself the international mother will not rest until she has completed her target range of children.

A fisherman's tale

Walking on a beach on a Caribbean island, I fell into conversation with a man, and we walked along together for a while. He asked me what I did for a living. I told him, and asked about him. It turned out that he had been a fisherman, but was now unemployed. But at one time, he *had* been a fisherman. I sensed a story, but I was not going to ask any questions. He would tell me if he wanted to. He did want to, he did tell me his story. I can't write dialect, but I will try to capture something of his mood.

He had been a fisherman working with the owner of a small boat. One day the owner said to him that there was a way to increase his money, and that it was safe and there was hardly any possibility of being caught. It involved picking up two or three men off a boat at sea and dropping them on the beach. In a matter of weeks he could get more than he earned from fishing in a year. The word "drugs" was not mentioned, but he said that he was sure: "Yuh know wa I talkin' bout." I did. He had refused the offer, which had not been difficult, for he thought of his old mother and how it would "brek she heart if I was to end up in prison or somting so". It was not long after this that the boat-owner told him that he had found someone else and he was fired.

Now he walked the beach instead of fishing the sea, but he was hopeful that something would turn up before long. Could he not find work on another boat? He no longer had any confidence in fishing, and he feared that even if he did find another fishing job, eventually the same problem would come up again. He felt that it would be better to change jobs completely, so he was looking around for something, and in between looking he sometimes relaxed by walking along the beach. He was living off the savings he had "put by". I could not help wondering how long it would be before his savings and his resolution both ran out. If, and when that happened, would he still be able to refuse the offer? Your guess is as good as mine!

Of pope and poet

It was always my misfortune while travelling around Central America in 1998 to arrive in places just before or just after a visit of "El Papa", or the pope to you and me. I don't find this pope a very sympathetic person: his priorities seem strangely at odds with the times we live in. I feel very strongly and very negatively about the role of the Catholic church in Africa. In Latin America the church has had a slightly more positive role, with some priests actually siding with poor people and putting their comfort and their lives on the line. Even so I did not feel any pleasure or interest when on two occasions, in Venezuela and in Central America, our visit overlapped with El Papa's. The streets where his car would pass were cleaned up, buildings and railings got a lick of paint, and everything was done to make the place look nice for the occasion. Never mind the people living in grinding poverty, and the shanty towns with rubbish piled high and rats the only form of life developing normally.

Never mind the scandals rocking the Catholic church worldwide. The paedophile priests exposed in Australia, New Zealand, North America, and in Ireland. The Catholic church has been putting aside massive amounts of money to compensate victims of abuse. Apart from paedophile priests, there are homosexual priests, and priests whose only crime is to take their role of "father" literally. But this El Papa, this present pope, concentrates on real sin, such as taking the contraceptive pill, and using condoms in safe sex, to lower the risk of contracting and spreading AIDS. It must be good to know that however stupid, you can still be infallible. On the whole I prefer poets to priests. In Nicaragua El Papa had come and gone by the time we got there, but we were lucky to arrive for the celebration of one of Latin America's famous poets – Rubén Darío. Nicaragua is truly a literary nation. I have never attended such an occasion in any other part of the world, and indeed, I very much doubt whether there are such occasions anywhere else: the celebration of a poet's life, with military displays, music, numerous bands, floats, poetry readings and competitions.

This was another side to Latin America, a beautiful and romantic side, a country unashamedly revelling in verse! You could almost forget about the civil war, except that around every corner there was something to remind us. I was glad to have missed El Papa's day, but I was very happy that I did not miss the poet's day. I was really pleased that quite by accident I'd been there in Darío's country, to celebrate the day of the poet.

My picture of a Latin American lady

On a long, long bus ride one dozes off, reads, sleeps, watches TV, anything to pass the time. The bus becomes a world in itself, as it moves along, crossing borders, passing houses, people, animals, forests, villages, towns, cities. From the bus window the outside world flows past in a constant moving procession. From time to time something catches the eye and stirs the imagination – a cottage or farmhouse of interesting or unusual architecture, a man or woman riding a donkey, a boy herding cattle. For a moment you enter their world, you admire the design of the house, and wonder about the people who live in it, then as the bus moves on so do your thoughts, and your attention turns to something else. This is how it was with me as the bus sped across Nicaragua heading for Guatemala. I was aimlessly looking out of the window, when *she* came into my view. She was running away from the houses on the hill, her long black hair still wet from the shower she must have just had, glistening in the gentle glow of the late afternoon sun. Although I said she was running, running is not quite the right word for what she was doing. She was almost skipping, and the look on her face was – ? It was a wishful, expectant look of anticipation.

She was in my view only for a few brief moments. That was enough, for I really needed this picture of Latin American womanhood to balance all the others. Those desperate, depressed women in the battered women refuge, women begging with babies in their arms, the young ones advertising their sexual services in the newspapers. The Indian women small and apparently encrusted in dirt, appearing to shrink even smaller when they approached the tourists. You, woman in a red, or was it a pink dress, with your long black hair tied in a pigtail skipping down the path at sunset – was it to meet someone? Your image came to balance the picture of my Latin American sisters, and your picture will never change. For me you will always be young, running, almost skipping, with an expectant half-smile on your face. You will never join your sisters at the well, carrying water on your head, while burdened down with children. Nor will you ever need to recover from a drunken beating or seek refuge in a home for battered women. You will never be among those who offer their sexual services in newspapers, special interest magazines, or anywhere else, because you are forever young and free, skipping downhill at sunset, my Nicaraguan sister.

Christmas in the Bahamas

The year we spent Christmas in the Bahamas, 1984, we camped on the beach at Abaco over the Christmas weekend. We were a motley crowd, fourteen of us, originating from about five or six different countries, including the USA, the Philippines, and of course the Bahamas. There was a Ba'hai family, a family of non-believers (us), a Roman Catholic man, possibly lapsed, and others somewhere in-between. There were seven children and an equal number of adults, the children ranging in age from four to thirteen. We arrived at the beach on the Saturday afternoon and left on Monday at about midday. It was the most unusual and delightful Christmas I have ever spent.

I had agreed to prepare Saturday night's dinner. I baked coconut bread, without which no Bajan Christmas is complete, at least not for me. Amazingly it turned out perfectly, because sometimes it's as hard as rock, even though the recipe and the cooking method are exactly the same. My spare-ribs and roasted chicken were also quite good, they told me, and the meat dishes were complemented with rice and side salad. Having made my contribution, I could relax. I had done my share of the cooking. The menu for the rest of the time was taken over by the Filipino who, as well as being a doctor, turned out to be a very good cook. Our Christmas-day beach barbecue was really special, unforgettable because of the place, the food and the company. It was a uniquely different and uniquely enjoyable way to spend Christmas.

As I always say, every silver lining has a cloud, and so it was with our Bahamian Christmas. There was the usual amount of alcohol, and since some of us hardly drank, others could over-indulge with impunity. One of the locals did just that, with the result that she ended up taking me for a walk on the beach, where she showed me, in much the same way people show each other operation scars, the needle punctures on her arms, from the injection of heroin. It was then that I understood why she wore long sleeves, in such a hot climate. She was engaged in a custody battle for her child, and was desperately trying to kick the habit. It was very difficult, as drugs were both readily available and cheap, but she wanted her child so she had no choice. On our arrival in the Bahamas, when the local people heard that we liked to walk and hike, they warned us against picking up or even looking at any parcels we might find lying around, either on the beach or in country areas. We were told that during chases by the American Drug Enforcement Agency (DEA), the drug planes would often dump their cargo, and return later to pick it up when it was safe to do so.

From talking to local people I learnt that until a year or two previously, the Bahamas had been mainly a trans-shipment point for drugs. There had been virtually no local use. Then things began to change. Why? Nobody knew, but more and more local people were using drugs, people like the young mother at our Christmas picnic. I have lost touch with every one of the people with whom we spent our almost idyllic Bahamian Christmas, so I have no idea just how that young mother's story ended, and whether or not the ending was a happy one. But I rather suspect it was not.

The drugs industry also touched the lives of many other Bahamians. At the time of our visit there was a commission of inquiry into the alleged involvement of members of the government, including I think the prime minister, in the drugs industry. The islands of the Bahamas can be strange and very mysterious places. Some appear frozen in history, fossilised like the dinosaurs. At least that is how it seemed to me as we went with our doctor friend on home visits to outlying islands, tiny places with minute populations of mostly white people. On one of these islands there was a notice saying something about the war of independence. I commented that I didn't know that there was an independence movement in the Bahamas, only to be told that the notice was referring to the American war of independence! I heard that these people were the descendants of people who had fled the USA at that time and escaped to the Bahamas to live under the Crown, or something.

There are several memories and impressions that have stayed with me from the Bahamas. One is of that wonderful Christmas weekend. Another is of the prevalence of "drug-talk", and the way all conversations seemed to begin or end with a reference to the subject of drugs. Yet another was those island communities where people seemed frozen in time. Finally there was the very high cost of living. Abaco has the record for the most expensive place I have ever visited.

A bus ride in Barbados

In Barbados tourists ride the buses. This is not a big deal. I was on the bypass once when some Danish people got on it. This bus route is from the north of the island, from Speightstown, to Oistins on the south coast. One of the Danish tourists placed a large bag in the front next to the driver and went happily to the back where there were empty seats. I thought to myself that the last time I'd seen anyone do that was in Norway, where, on entering the train people take off their expensive coats, hang them up and take whichever seat is empty. They did not keep glancing over their shoulders to see if their coats were still there! I have never seen this anywhere else. It made me feel good to see this happening in Barbados, and to see the confidence with which that woman placed her bag at the bus entrance and went to the back. She was saying something about her experience and expectations of bus travel in Barbados. When the bus reached her stop she got up and with the same assurance took her bag and departed. Ever since my bag was stolen, from right under my nose in Calcutta, I have always held it very, very close to me.

I was thinking about all this when an elderly Bajan lady got on the bus and sat in the seat next to me. She was reading the newspaper and muttering to herself, and after a while she turned to me and explained why she was muttering. She had just read a report that a rape conviction had been quashed on a technicality. She was disgusted and felt that this was "all wrong". We got talking, and she told me that she now lived in St James, but she was really from St Michael. We got onto the topic of change and how Barbados had altered. The bus was now in Belleville, an avenue lined with palm trees and full of plantation-style houses. This was her cue to tell me that she could remember a time when servants were the only black people allowed in this area.

As I listened my memory also began to work, and I recalled how as a small child of about ten years old I had been sent by my mother to deliver a parcel to a house in Tenth Avenue, Belleville. I went to the front door and rang the bell. A white woman came and looked out of one of the side windows, and as soon as she saw me started shouting and beckoning me to come round to the back. I stood my ground. Eventually she came to the front door, and before she could say anything more I handed her the parcel and said, "Mrs Rawlins sent you this." She took the parcel, and asked, changing her voice to normal pitch, "Are you Mrs Rawlins' little girl?" I said yes, then ran off as fast as I could. Some days, or perhaps weeks later, my mother asked me what had happened when I went to Belleville that day. I felt that it was best to be cautious, so I said nothing had happened. It seemed that the woman had spoken to my mother about the incident and said that she had not realised that I was her child. My mother asked me again what had happened. Fearfully I told the story – fearfully because for me all this was new territory, and even in old territory I was always getting into trouble. This time it was okay, my mother told me that I was right not to go round to the back. "After all," she said, "you are not a servant – are you?"

As a small child I could neither understand nor accept that woman's excuse for behaving towards me as she did. She told my mother that had she known that I was her daughter, she would not have treated me in that way. One little black child would be treated differently because she was Mrs Rawlins' little girl. But, I wondered, what about the other little black girls – why was it okay for them to be shouted at and shown the back door? Even at that age I knew that I could not accept that. Change of country, twenty years on, and I face the same problem, but this time I have the benefit of my Barbados upbringing and experience. While I was working in community relations in the London borough of Wandsworth, I went to a meeting with a police inspector at the local station. Together with the other, mostly black people, I was treated very discourteously and made to wait for a very long time. On my arrival at the station I had tried to identify myself to the officer at the desk, and tell him that I had an appointment with the inspector. Before I could get the words out, he shouted at me to "sit there", and pointed at a bench. So I did.

I welcomed this unexpected opportunity of seeing what went on in that police station. At the community relations office we received daily reports and complaints of discourteous treatment, and worse. So in fact I was quite happy, in my anonymity, to sit and observe what was going on and how people were received as they came in. Eventually the inspector came out of his office. There was a whispered conversation between him and the desk officer, after which he came out to me, apologised that I'd been kept waiting, and led me into his office. Among the first things he said was that I should get a business card, suggesting this would protect me from embarrassing situations like the one I'd just experienced. Back at the office, when I told my story, they ordered a whole bunch of business cards.

There was no mention of what was to happen to all the black people *without* business cards. Not long after this I left that job. Just like the woman in Belleville all those years ago, the police inspector wanted me to have special treatment – and not as just another black person. Whereas I wanted to be treated as an ordinary black, because that is what I am. I don't see why one should need to be somebody's daughter or hold a business card in order to be treated with courtesy. And incidentally I still don't have a business card.

Back to Belleville. By the time I left Barbados for India, about thirteen years after that incident, my family were actually living in Belleville. So much had changed in those thirteen years! From being ordered by a Bajan white woman to use the back door, I could now enter our very own Belleville front door (though not quite, as it was a rented house, but near enough). That old lady on the bypass bus was not the only one with memories of Belleville and of Barbados, in the days when there were hardly any tourists, and no by-pass bus, and the only black people who could walk freely in Belleville were servants.

El Tucuche – a walk in search of the little golden frog

It was four o'clock in the morning and very dark when my friend and I set out for our walk. We aimed to drive for about an hour and to start walking at about five. We would walk for three or four hours, then drive to the beach for a swim and breakfast, before driving back to town. We were driving along a deserted road, when just ahead we saw some activity, lots of cars, people with rucksacks, a man with a stick. My first thoughts were that the man with the stick must be a guide and this must be a party of walkers. If that was correct I wanted to join them. So I asked my friend to stop so that we could check out the action. The party was a group of about twenty students from the UWI, with their two lecturers and a guide, on a field trip to El Tucuche.

I have always wanted to hike up El Tucuche, so please may I join you? Warnings from them were "at your own risk", and assurances from me were as an experienced hiker who could cope with a walk of this type. I hoped that my walking boots attested to my claims, and as well as the boots I was wearing shorts, a swimsuit, and I was carrying a large beach towel. The next concern was something for me to eat. My friend asked in a worried voice, "What about food? What will you do for something to eat?" My friend, who had sensibly declined to go, offered me our breakfast picnic. I refused, for even I could see the folly of trying to hike up a mountain carrying a beach towel and a picnic basket. Offers of food and drink come from all round: "Don't worry, there is plenty of food." There is always plenty of food at Caribbean picnics, enough to feed the proverbial army.

We set off, and the walking was good. The morning was fresh and the air cool, and I thought to myself, I am going to enjoy this! Very soon we began to ascend, the terrain changed, becoming muddy and very slippery, and it was also much cooler. I advised myself to walk faster – advice it wasn't easy to follow. How could I walk faster, slipping uphill in a group of twenty or more people? I did the best I could. It soon became clear that many of the students, though very young, were not very fit and were unused to hiking. The walk was tough, but I had done tougher. What I found difficult to cope with was the totally unexpected cold, and the very heavy mist. We could have been in England, except that in England I would not go for a walk up a mountain, wearing only a swimsuit and wrapped in a beach towel. In spite of the conditions I was able to enjoy the flora and fauna, with the wild orchids growing in great profusion a special delight.

The guide led us on, giving advice on how to keep upright, and information about the trees and plants. I was very impressed with him, because he was not only very good, he clearly knew the forest and the mountain very well. I stuck close to him and tried to follow his advice. After about two hours we reached the summit, and the reason for our being there – the search for the little golden frogs. I was amazed at the way the students and the lecturers went about their search, as it was never like that on the nature programmes I watched on TV. The bromeliads didn't stand a chance as they were torn apart and peered into in the effort to locate these frogs. No frogs were located. We had lunch. There was "plenty, plenty food", but no one really enjoyed the meal, as we concentrated on trying to stop rainwater dripping into it. The two lecturers were the only ones with flasks and hot drinks, and the rest of us looked on enviously as they drank their cups of hot coffee.

The students were disappointed that there were no little golden frogs to be found. We were hoping that after lunch conditions would improve, but if anything conditions got worse, the mist was even thicker, the cold colder, and the rain was falling heavily. I hung on to my towel, which was wrapped around me, and tried to stop my teeth from chattering. I noticed that apart from the two lecturers and the guide no one was properly dressed or equipped for this kind of field trip. Granted, I was the only one wearing a swimsuit, but all the students were dressed in shorts and T-shirts and were shivering with cold. Their lecturers seemed to think this was very funny, and they joked about how many of their students would be absent from classes due to pneumonia. I put all my effort into stopping my teeth from chattering, but I was impressed by their lecturers' indifference to the welfare of their students. I wondered whether the students had disregarded advice regarding what to wear or whether no such advice had been given. I knew better than to ask any questions, and anyway I didn't want to draw attention to myself. I didn't want anyone to notice my barely successful efforts to stop by teeth from chattering.

Decision time. A meeting was held and the choice was this: to return directly without having seen a frog, or to continue the search and explore other regions of the mountain. It was very cold, the mist was even thicker and heavier, and the rain continued to fall. My beach towel was soaking wet. I silently indicated my willingness to go along with the majority decision. Fortunately, the majority was as cold and wet as I, so they voted to accept defeat and return to base. The lecturers decided otherwise. We were told to stay put while they went to explore another part of the mountain, where they were confident of finding the frogs. They were taking the guide with them, and they instructed us to wait for their return. We waited.

And waited... and waited... and waited. After what seemed an age of waiting one of the male students decided that we should move, if only to keep warm. Consultation time. It seemed that there were at least two people in the group who had been up El Tucuche before and they thought they should be able to lead us safely down. The group decided to risk it, and I decided to go with them, as there seemed little choice.

As we set off I decided to go into automatic pilot and kept putting one foot in front of the other until we reached our destination. This worked okay for a while, until I slipped and almost literally fell off the mountainside! Somehow, I really don't know how, I managed to grab the roots of a tree and pull myself up. After that I realised that robot mode wasn't quite the thing for this occasion, and a more versatile approach was required. I varied my pace and adjusted the length of my steps to suit the conditions. By this time, what with the fall and the quick downhill pace, I was much warmer and feeling hopeful about coming out of the experience alive – hopeful enough to be amused when one of the female students announced to no one in particular that "one day we will be able to tell our grandchildren about this!" I thought to myself "some of us rather sooner than others", as she walked on down the hill ignorant of the fact that one of us was already a grandmother. Soon after this incident there was a discussion about a tree, our two student guides wanting to check that we were at the "right" tree, which marked the spot where we had to make a right turn. Since all the trees looked remarkably alike to me, I kept quiet. It must have been the right tree though, because soon after that the two lecturers and the guide caught up with us. Their search for the little golden frog had also ended in failure. Bad luck for them, but perhaps lucky for the frogs? We continued our descent. One of the lecturers was making a very quick pace, almost running, then he slipped and his head slammed into the trunk of a tree. His collision with it made such a bang that I was amazed to see tree and man were still standing, both apparently undamaged. Soon after this we heard the barking of dogs.

I have never ever in my life before or since welcomed the barking of dogs. That day as we came down El Tucuche the bark and snarl of the village dogs was music to my ears. Dogs meant people, people meant a village, a village meant a shop, a café, chairs and a telephone. Soon I was actually sitting in the café, my towel now discarded. Who needs a wrap at eighty degrees Farenheit? I was drinking a delicious cup of tea. It was probably just ordinary tea, but to me nothing was ordinary at that moment. An old man came in, sat at my table and asked me about the expedition, wanting to know what the conditions were like up there. Had it been cold, had it been raining? I assured him that it had been very cold, and yes, it had rained non-stop. He told me that the expedition should not have gone up on that day, as there had been warnings about the likely conditions, with advice for people to stay away from El Tucuche. After talking with him I understood why the students had not been dressed for the unusual conditions on El Tucuche.

Within an hour of coming off the mountain I was getting ready for an evening at the theatre in Port-of-Spain. Later that night, in the heat and humidity of the city, the cold swirling mist of El Tucuche, with its beautiful wild orchids and elusive little golden frogs, already seemed to belong to another world.

Notes

French and Bacon's 1992 *Nature Trails of Trinidad* describes the El Tucuche hike as "hard walking". Special features were as follow. Beautiful views from the summit of Trinidad's second highest mountain (937 metres). Interesting flora and fauna, especially above the 610 metres ridge. There was nothing, however, about checking on the weather conditions or carrying warm clothing.

Almost exactly seven years after my El Tucuche experience, in June 1997, I saw one of the little golden frogs in its home in the giant bromeliads that grow around the Kaieteur Falls in Guyana. It was sunning itself on one of the leaves. This frog lives all its life in its tree home.

Guyana – land of my father

For many years all I knew about Guyana, or British Guyana as it was then called, was that my father had been born there. For a long time this was one of only two facts I knew about that place – the other was that it was in South America. In Barbados both of my parents were foreigners, my mother being from Grenada. Very early on I worked out that there was a big difference in being from somewhere and in simply having been born somewhere. My mother was from Grenada, and we had a lot of contact with that place (two of her children were born there, my father was working there when I was born, and we had visits from family and friends). Grenada meant something more than just a distant land where someone happened to have been born. My family had no contact of any kind with Guyana, no visitors of any kind ever came to see us from there. From time to time I wondered about this, and puzzled over just how my father had come to have been born there. As a child I never had the courage to ask any questions, and as an adult I kept waiting for the "right time" to broach the subject with him, though that time never came.

After my father died, I decided to ask his brother, my uncle, about my father's background, and especially about how he came to be born in Guyana. My father had one brother and one sister, the sister dying before I was born, and his mother dying not long after he was born. He was raised by an aunt, a tall, stern, unsmiling woman who we always referred to as "Dear Aunt". Why the "dear" I do not know, as she was certainly not dear to me, or from what I could see to my father either. But as I was saying, after my father died I decided to talk to my uncle about the Guyana thing. Every time I saw him I had to listen to his moans, for as he got older nothing seemed to give him any pleasure. He even went off his wife of more than fifty years. So when I visited him I listened to his endless complaints, and waited for a suitable time to raise the matter of my father's background, but again, a suitable time never came. After my last visit I decided that next time, whatever happened, I would ask him straight out. But my uncle died before "the next time", and I still don't know anything of how my father came to born in Guyana. I still wonder whether my grandmother just happened to be passing through at the time of his birth, or whether she was there because her child's father was Guyanese. So, long before I went there, Guyana was a source of mystery and fascination for me, and continues to puzzle me even more so after having been there.

Guyana should be one of the richest countries in South America and the Caribbean, but it is in fact one of the poorest. I have tried to work out this equation in several ways. However I try, it does not add up, and I can't get it to make sense: Guyana has much land, gold, diamonds, bauxite, few people (i.e., under a million, in a country about the size of the UK). As a basis of comparison, the population of the UK is approximately 56,000,000. With all those natural resources and its low population, Guyana manages to be poor. I can't understand how the countries of Asia and the Pacific have been able to turn their economies around and to become "tigers", when Guyana, with so much going for it, is still stuck in poverty and under-development.

Guyana has most of the virgin forest of South America: one can fly over the country for hours and see nothing but trees. Yet wood for house-building is out of reach of all but the very rich. More than twenty-five per cent of households in Guyana are squats. The size of the problem is enormous. The government has initiated a *National Development Strategy*, subtitled *Shared Development Through Participation*. If all it took was lofty sentiments the problems would all be solved by now. What does "participation" mean in a country where many of the population cannot read? Who but the educated few will bother to look at the massive tomes of the national development policy? I had a very revealing insight into education in Guyana during a visit to a primary school, where I had gone more or less in loco parentis. I went by appointment to meet the class teacher of my friend's ten-year-old son, who was worried that in spite of her best efforts, including lessons after school and on Saturdays, her son was making little progress, and could hardly read. I went to the school during one of the after-school sessions, when those children whose parents can afford to pay receive extra lessons.

I explained my mission to the young woman teacher, and she in turn explained to me her difficulties. She said that many of the children were "hyperactive" (how did teachers ever manage before that condition was invented or discovered?). She also said that there was no formal teaching of reading at any stage in the school, so that when the children came to her class at age ten, very few were able to read adequately. But, all was not lost, for she had developed a "strategy", based on the use of flash cards. She had asked the parents to supply cardboard squares for the purpose of developing these flash cards, but in spite of repeated reminders she had not received a single contribution. She sighed at this as an example of parental indifference, but said that she intended to keep working on the parents through the children, because the success of her strategy depended on flash cards, which in turn depended on her obtaining a supply of cardboard.

While I was being told all this, fifty or so children of different ages were sitting quietly, with books open in front of them, in semi-darkness. If they made the smallest sound the teacher turned her attention on them – all it took was a look and a word, and quiet would at once be restored. It seemed to me that what went on in that classroom was much closer to child-minding than education. It seemed to me that the extra lessons were purely ritualistic, and that the children were given tasks and left to get on with them quietly. Provided they made no noise, they would be okay. At the end of each session they closed their books and went home, and there were no tests and no real homework. Homework was another ritual. I thought that, under this system, a few of the children might learn something, but that most would achieve very little, or perhaps nothing at all.

There are two further points to this story. The extra lessons brought in more than double the teacher's salary. Teachers in Guyana earn on average G$10,000 per month, and the lessons cost G$500 per child per month. In the class I visited there were about fifty children. When I learnt more about the flash cards and the cardboard, I realised that it was very unlikely that the teacher would ever get the chance to employ her "strategy". I learnt that she had specified laminated cardboard as being the only type suitable, and this cost G$200. The parents probably could not see the reason why they should buy "special" cardboard, and not simply use cardboard boxes. By stipulating material that she knew many parents could not or would not supply, the teacher ensured that she would not have to do anything about the children's reading – beyond talking about her "strategy".

That teacher with talk of her "strategy" was just part of the ritual, and another part was to set reading tasks to children who could not read. One can only hope that there is more substance to the *National Development Strategy* of the Co-operative Republic of Guyana. In the meantime I do feel deep pity for and anger on behalf of the children, who are so cruelly and cynically exploited. One day when they understand the terrible deception to which they have been subjected, they themselves will be very angry, and what will they do then? This is the way many societies create and perpetuate their unique social problems.

Another aspect of Guyanese life, in which I am very interested, is the lives and traditions of the original people of the country, the Amerindians. As a child growing up and going to school in Barbados, I had pencil and slate, nothing sophisticated like flash cards, and the word "hyperactive" either did not exist or was not in such common use as it is today. Everyone in my class could read. Among the things we read or were taught was that when Barbados was first "discovered" by the Portuguese, the island was empty, and covered with bearded fig trees. Now we know that this was all wrong. The Caribs and/or Amerindians had lived on the island for many years, for excavations have uncovered evidence of their occupation of the island and of their way of life. Guyana had quite a significant population of Amerindians and I was interested to see how well they fared as compared with the rest of the population. Volume III of the Guyanese *National Development Strategy* states:

Guyana has a race-based geography with the non-Amerindian majority concentrated on the narrow coastal plain which makes up about 5% of the total land area.

The "non-Amerindian majority" consists of East Indians (49.49 per cent), Africans (35.53 per cent), mixed (7.05 per cent) and these live on 5 per cent of the land. So the Amerindians

(6.81 per cent) should have the 95 per cent of the country! This would make them unique among the indigenous peoples of the world. In fact the Amerindian people of Guyana are facing the same problems that confront indigenous people all over the world. In 1996 the prime minister of Dominica gave the opening address at the COIP conference in Dominica.

The conference report reads thus:

He [Prime Minister Edison James] told delegates that Both The Indigenous Peoples and their Afro-Caribbean counterparts have similar historical experiences of struggle and achievement, and the time for them to work together to ensure that they protect their values, customs and cultural beliefs had arrived.

> COIP – Caribbean Organisation of Indigenous Peoples
> (1996), *Conference Report*, Carib Council of Dominica,
> Commonwealth of Dominica

In the racial geography and politics of Guyana, there is no sign of this "working together" of which the Dominican prime minister spoke. A big issue in Guyana in 1997 was the renaming of the international airport from Themiri to Jagan. The change was meant to honour Dr Cheddi Jagan, independence fighter and prime minister of Guyana, who died earlier in the year. But there is little in Guyana acknowledging, much less celebrating, the Amerindian heritage, and many Amerindians protested against this change, which would remove one of the few Amerindian words in everyday use from a key place in the country's public profile.

The Afro-Guyanese were not overjoyed with the change in the airport's name. In Guyana the biggest tensions are between the two main ethnic groups: Guyanese of African origin, and those of East Indian origin. Amerindian issues are ignored or marginalised by both the main groups. Perhaps in Dominica things are different, but in Guyana the impression is of an indigenous people who are mainly isolated from the mainstream, and in a land of plenty living in the extreme of poverty. Of course they share in common with other Guyanese the painful reality of poverty, but for them it is more extreme, the education poorer, access to health care etc. more difficult. At the removal of the airport's Amerindian name, one of their leading activists, a medical doctor, was called to account for his absence from duty, and to explain his presence at a demonstration against the change.

Visiting Guyana's interior I went to Madhia, a gold-mining area. In Madhia the talk was all about the gold itself, being robbed of gold, being badly injured or killed, and the dangers of malaria. In Georgetown I had been warned that Madhia was like the wild west, and that I had to be very careful as anything could happen there. The day I arrived, one of the miners had been attacked, beaten and robbed of his gold, and the next day he died from his injuries. I was under the protection of my friend's husband who had several claims and who had arranged my visit. At a meeting with a representative of the Amerindian community in Georgetown I had been told that in gold-mining areas such as Madhia, the indigenous people had been corrupted, their lives, environment and culture damaged, both by the gold-mining process itself and by the lifestyle associated with it. The received wisdom was that Amerindians did not make good miners, because they had no long-term interest in the gold itself. This was the way one Afro-Guyanese miner explained it to me: "They [the Amerindians] work for a while to get the money and go off and spend it until the next time, so they will never make real money." The way he told it there was clearly a big gulf between his world and theirs.

I am very glad that I visited my father's country. There was much to puzzle and disturb me about Guyana, and, in the weeks and months following my visit there, I read a lot, thought a lot and checked out my Guyanese contacts. One of the things that had puzzled me was the absence of any reference to the communal riots that occurred during the 1960s, in which Afro- and Indo-Guyanese killed each other. Was I thinking of somewhere else, or was there collective amnesia about this event? In all the columns of newsprint that celebrated the life and mourned the death of Dr Cheddi Jagan, I could not find a single reference to these events, or to Dr Jagan's role at the time. I looked in vain in the Guyanese edition of the Caribbean social studies reader for an analysis of the 1960s' riots: nothing. I asked my Guyanese friend about them. Her reply was very vague: she was only a child at the time, and she didn't want to talk about it. At least her response had reassured me that the riots had indeed happened.

I had to wait for my return to Barbados before I could find anyone willing to talk frankly about it. From my Afro-Guyanese friends now living in Barbados I heard stories of terror, killings, mayhem. I also met my friend's mother, an old lady approaching ninety, very frail but very clear-minded. She remembered the riots, particularly the one of 1964, confirming what her daughter and son-in-law had already told me. I asked her how she felt about it all now. She did not respond, and had not heard my question. Her daughter then repeated my question in a much louder voice – "She wants to know how you feel about it now?" The old lady lifted her shoulders off the bed, sighed and said simply, "It happened."

I think I am beginning to understand the Guyanese situation a bit better now. It seems to be very closely linked to racial divisions and the lack of trust that characterises the relationship between the two main racial groups, the Indo- and Afro-Guyanese. Having arrived at this opinion I was interested to find support for this idea in a book by a Japanese-American writer, Francis Fukuyama, *Trust: The Social Virtues and the Creation of Prosperity*. As I understand it, Fukuyama's argument is that economic success is based on social trust. This means that in order for a society to prosper, strangers have to trust each other. In Guyana it struck me that there was a total absence of trust between the two major ethnic groups, and so Fukuyama's argument would appear to be correct. Fukuyama also used this thesis to explain the poor economic performance of African-Americans. In the American context that smacks too much of blaming the victim, but it is a very different scenario in Guyana, and there I do think that a little trust might well go a long way.

Journey to Monserrat

Without trust people could not survive in Monserrat. There the people have no choice but to trust the scientist and other experts who have taken control over their island and their lives. Sometimes this trust has been misplaced, as when the people have been misrepresented, and depicted as self-indulgent and money-grubbing, expecting others to pay their bills. Monserrat had been on my list of places to visit for quite a long time, then in 1994 the volcano blew up and it looked as though that would be off-limits for the foreseeable future.

There was no thought of us visiting Monserrat when we set off for Antigua in February of 1998, but we could see the island very clearly from the house where we were staying in St Johns. We could see the wisps of smoke rising from the volcano, and my friend's lawn and backyard were covered with the volcanic ash that it was constantly spewing out. Peter and I arrived in Antigua from Barbados on a Friday, and the next morning we joined the environmental awareness group on a ramble and visit to a farm. During that walk we learnt that in order to reduce the isolation of Monserrat, a new ferry service had been organised between it and Antigua. The walk finished at midday and we spent the rest of Saturday finding out about the ferry. Eventually we located the correct office and were given the relevant details. We tried to book our passage but were told that this was not necessary: "Just turn up at five o'clock on Tuesday morning." We did just that, only to find that we had been wrongly advised and that, although the boat was almost empty, we would not be allowed on it because our names were not on the ship's manifest. Someone suggested that we try the helicopter. So we made a mad dash to the airport, and had a long wait in the queue, only to find that there was only one seat left. Tired and disappointed, we returned to our friend's house, hoping for better luck next time! And it was so.

Well, we did have better luck in actually getting on the boat, but when we arrived in Monserrat we could find no place to stay. We arrived on the Wednesday, and as a total eclipse was expected on the Friday people had come from afar. Before leaving Antigua I had tried emailing several people about accommodation, but had had no luck in getting through to them. I was told that the lines were probably down. So we arrived with a list of names and enticing pictures of B&B accommodation and studio apartments. Several of the people on my list came to meet the boat, and it did not take us long to find out that they were all fully booked. Then our taxi man took over. He knew everyone in Monserrat, and if anyone could find us somewhere to stay on the island, it was he. We felt quite hopeful as we set off, but after the third stop we were beginning to despair. I began to think that we would end up sleeping on the beach. Our next stop proved to be our last, and we were in luck, and what luck! We ended up in one of the most luxurious B&Bs we've ever stayed in. A builder's home, now virtually empty except for the bitter and very lonely builder, whose wife and daughter had moved to cold, cramped London. His daughter was at the exam stage and they could not afford to neglect her education, so sacrifices had to be made.

We listened as he railed against the British, their deceptive ways, their arrogance. He said the British could not believe the high standard of living of people in Monserrat, and he compared his people to the drunken British who spent all their money in the pub, content to live in council houses. "We are not like that," he said, "we work hard and we live well." We listened in silent sympathy. There was nothing we could say to assuage his grief and loneliness, and the painful uncertainty of living under the volcano. A new threat had just been identified, and it was possible that he might soon have to abandon his lovely home, as so many lovely homes had already been.

One night in Monserrat and I could hardly breathe, for the dust was choking me, and my head ached all the time. The next day as we drove around the habitable parts of the island, the dust masks hung unused in the taxi, the driver did not offer them to us, and we did not ask for them. The atmosphere was something he was used to, and he probably forgot that we were not. We went in search of stamps for our philatelist friend, and near the post office I met a lady who used to live in London, who had retired "back home" in 1994, the year before the volcano erupted. "Have you ever been tempted to go back to London?" I asked her. She laughed out loud at such an absurd idea, and she was still smiling when she gave me her reply: "I am staying put, this is my home and I am staying here." End of story.

The spirit of the people of Monserrat made a tremendous impression. I know that not everyone is equally impressed and that some people see those who have remained on the island as stupid and foolhardy for exposing themselves to the risk of injury or death. For me their decision to stay on is a heartening and encouraging one, and I wish I could be confident that in the same situation I would have their courage. In an age where people have been led to expect certainty and comfort as of right, at least some choose uncertainty and discomfort. The next morning I listened to the radio and heard the reports of the deaths, in England, of elderly Monserratans, those people who had been evacuated to the UK, and had died there. The English winter is death's harvest time for the elderly, and since many home-grown elderly die off at this time, old people from tropical Monserrat would die off in even greater numbers. Had it been a good idea to evacuate the elderly to the harsh conditions of an English winter? In their situation no decision that they made would have been risk-free, and if they and their families preferred to risk the cold of the UK to the warmth of the Caribbean and the heat of the volcano, who am I to question this? All the same these deaths in England meant that the nice new home for the elderly that was built at such expense would remain unused for some considerable time. If the volcano did not get it first!

I left Monserrat with a wealth of feelings, feelings and impressions that would take a long time to process, to reflect on and to learn from. It seemed to me that a struggle was going on between the volcano and the people, a wrestle for possession of the island, and after more than four years it was still not clear who would win. Odds are on the volcano, but in the meantime the people of Monserrat are holding on and fighting back.

Back in Antigua we got the most fleeting glimpse of the total eclipse, but I did not manage to win a prize in the eclipse raffle, nor did we get to the eclipse party that we'd come back specifically to attend. It all turned out to be very tame stuff, and quite disappointing really. As the sun went into total eclipse the clouds rolled over! Better luck next time. That Sunday, our last in Antigua, we were introduced to "hashing". A "hash" is a kind of walk, but the walk is not the main priority. It was a fun thing, and very much a family affair, ending in a lot of eating and drinking, which we did not partake of. I heard that hashing is an international activity, with groups everywhere, including Barbados and England. Very interesting, but I think I'll pass on that.

The French connection

My first visit to France was in September 1965, and since then I have been a regular visitor, but it has taken me until 1998 to visit the French West Indian islands of Martinique and Guadeloupe. It was another leg of our island-hopping tour, after Antigua and Monserrat. After that, also in the September of that year, came our visit to another French island – the Isle d'Oussent, just off the coast of Brittany. The three days that I was in Oussent I kept on comparing the three French islands – the one in Europe with the two in the Caribbean. There is no comparison, outside the tourist havens and international hotels, the major roads and the airport, as the French West Indian islands are most definitely Third World and third class, alongside their sister islands off the French mainland. The Isle d'Oussent is First World and first-class everywhere, as is the rest of France. The most notable difference is in the signs of poverty and in the heaps of rubbish lying on every street corner, which was especially true of Guadeloupe. Before I went there I'd been expecting that these islands, which are legally and administratively part of France, would be enjoying more or less the same standard of living as the rest of France. I found that this is not so.

In many respects these islands are in a similar position to Puerto Rico. They even have a small independence party, but unlike Puerto Rico there is to be no referendum, and France will continue to have two colonies pretending to be two departments of France. Even so I liked Martinique, and would visit again. I wonder what plans Mr Le Pen, the leader of the French National Front, has for the French West Indies? Mr Le Pen plans to rid France of immigrants and foreigners, and I wonder just what part these islands will play in his ethnic cleansing programme.

Love hotels, Santa Semana and the Andes – Venezuela revisited

Our first visit to Venezuela, in 1995, had been interesting and very exciting, if somewhat stressful. I've written about these experiences elsewhere, so if you haven't yet come across it, please wait. In the spring of 1998 we returned to Venezuela for the second time.

We arrived in Caracas on a Friday night. At the airport, a well-dressed English-speaking man approached us and said that he was a taxi driver, and we agreed a fare with him. But when we got to his car we both noticed that it did not have a taxi sign on it. Oh dear. Peter was sitting in the back seat, and I was in the front, so we couldn't exchange glances. The ride from the airport seemed very long, much longer than I remembered it, and my mind filled with fantasies – of abduction, robbery, and worse. Then we were in downtown Caracas, safe and sound. Peter clutched his list of hotels, gleaned from guide books and tourist literature. The taxi driver took us to the first hotel on the list. Peter went in and came back to report that he had been told that there were no rooms available. So on to hotel number two, just around the corner. Even as Peter was speaking came the reply, "No hay nada," there is nothing. He must have seen us coming, and we wondered whether the other hotel had warned him about us. We agreed to try the next on the list, and if we were unsuccessful then perhaps we would have to change our criteria and move a bit upmarket – away from the lovers' hotels and the bus station, and more into tourist land.

The taxi driver could have abandoned us at this point, but he decided to help us find a hotel room near the bus station. We wanted to be near there as we planned to leave Caracas early the next morning. At the next hotel he went into reception, and I heard him telling the receptionist that he wanted a room for two tourists. I heard him repeat the word "tourists" several times, and in the end he was successful, we got a room.

Later that night, when we discussed what had happened, I asked Peter about the conversation he'd had with the hotel receptionist, and he said that he'd asked for "una habitacion por dos personnas". I knew from previous experience that Spanish people often misunderstood our pronunciation of "dos" (two) and of "doce" (twelve). Later, when Peter recounted how the receptionist had looked at him in amazement, and denied having rooms for rent, I guessed at what had happened. On a Friday night in Caracas, a night popularly referred to as lovers' night, an Englishman had turned up at two hotels asking for a room for twelve people. Or so it must have seemed to the receptionists.

The next morning we were up at the crack of dawn and off to find the bus station, and a bus to where? We didn't really mind. We simply wanted to see more of Venezuela, so a bus to anywhere would be okay. In the end we decided to go to Maracaibo, mainly because there was a bus going there in half an hour. There are always many touts hanging around bus stations, beckoning and cajoling people to get on a particular bus. At Caracas bus station we landed up with a nice tout. As soon as he heard that we had to return to the hotel to collect our luggage, he agreed to accompany us and carry our bags for us. On the way to the hotel, after about five minutes (if that), he and I chatted away in Spanish – he even complimented me on that. Then he told me that the area we had chosen to stay in was "muy peligrosa, muy" (very dangerous, very). We had been very lucky to have avoided trouble, and pointing down a street we were passing he told me that the day before a man had been killed there, and muttered once more "muy peligrosa". We reached the hotel, collected our bags and returned to the bus station, without incident. It was time to pay our nice tout and to bid him farewell. I asked him how much? He replied, "You decide." So I decided, but he did not look happy with my decision, so I increased my offering. "Is that all right?" I asked, smiling nervously. For an answer he bent over and gave me a big kiss on the cheek, and said, "Hasta la vista." He stood and watched the bus until it moved off, smiling and waving until I was out of sight.

That night, in another hotel in Maracaibo, we watched a documentary about crime in Venezuela, where I learned that the city of Caracas had one of the highest murder rates in the world, and was indeed a very dangerous place, though it seemed peaceful enough. Our hotel overlooked a square on one side and a lake on the other. Maracaibo is full of oil and gas, and the oil industry is one Peter is very interested in. Once again we were lucky to have a well-informed guide, in the form of a taxi driver, who also doubled as a local businessman. We learnt that Venezuela got its name from Venice, because the Indian people living in houses on stilts in the estuary reminded the Spaniards of that Italian city. It looked a poor place to me. I could not see anything Venetian about it, and I remembered that the last documentary I'd seen about it told us that the water and the fish had been contaminated with cholera. The church was the most prepossessing building, but even that had holes in the roof. Where did all that oil money go, I wondered?

We left Maracaibo with its dirty streets, its extreme poverty and extreme wealth. We headed for the Andes, by way of the longest bridge in the world. But on that bridge was a strike, so we sat in our shared taxi and waited, and waited, and waited. Then the soldiers turned up and cleared the strikers in no time. They really know how to do these things in South America. A few soldiers, a few guns and just like that the strike is over, traffic begins to move, and we were off to the Andes. Was I happy? Did I approve of the soldiers breaking the strike? What can I say? I know that I was very glad to be moving after three hours sitting in a hot car, but I was sorry that it had taken soldiers with guns to do it. But that seemed to be the South American way. As I understood it, the strikers were public servants, teachers and the like, pressing for better pay, for a bit more of Venezuela's oil wealth.

We travelled to the Merída in another shared taxi, but this time we bought the whole back seat and so we travelled in style! We arrived in holy week, or as they say in Spanish "santa semana". Religion and violence, violence and religion – that about sums up my impression of Venezuela. Holy week is like a craze, and everywhere you turn the expression "santa semana" is on someone's lips. The TV spills over with programmes about it, and the shops have special offers. I wondered how many people were killed during santa semana, 1998. From Merída we set off on a hair-raising ride in a Range Rover for a village high in the Andes, where we would stay two nights and return by donkey and cable-car. We were sharing this excursion with a French family, with the man of that family working for a multinational, and based in Venezuela.

At dinner on the first night I sat next to the man of the family. We chatted and then I told him about something I'd overheard earlier in the evening. It concerned an American, a retired man who was doing voluntary work in education, who explained to a visitor – another American – why he would not own a car in Venezuela. In Maracaibo people, especially Americans (but also local people), were constantly being hijacked, robbed of their cars, and sometimes beaten up. That made it extremely dangerous to own a car there. I recounted all this to the Frenchman, thinking of it as just the usual table talk. But his reaction was totally unexpected. He went quite pale and his hands began to shake. Slowly he took a sip of his beer and only then did he speak. "That happened to us," he said. Then he told me the story. They had been newly arrived in the country, a matter of three or four weeks, when he was hijacked. He described it as a "terrifying" experience, from which they had not fully recovered. He spoke very quietly, and I guessed he did not want his wife and children to overhear what we were talking about. After this I made no further attempt at small talk.

I had to go to the Andes to be questioned by the police about a missing person. We were sitting on the veranda of the Posada, having a cup of tea and taking in the stunning scenery. I heard the sound of a motorbike in the square above, but thought nothing of it, sure it was nothing to do with us. The next thing I knew a policeman was standing beside me, holding a poster with the photograph of a young man. He showed it to Peter and me in turn, and asked us the same question: "Have you seen this man?" Of course, we both said that we'd only just arrived in the place, and had not seen the man in question. He explained that he had gone missing in the mountains, and was the son of a very rich American, and a reward was being offered for information about him. His name was John Hubbard, the son of the founder of scientology. One day he had gone for a walk in the mountains, and had simply disappeared. Our guide told us that it was very easily done, but we were not about to find out.

Black people in Latin America

I grew up knowing that there were black people like myself, living in Latin America, and at school other children had fathers, brothers and uncles working "away" in Panama, Brazil, Curaçao and even in Venezuela. During the time I was in Latin America, white or non-black people would tell me, without my asking or inviting an opinion, that there was no colour or race prejudice in Latin America. The evidence of one's eyes and one's own experience told a different story. Take the newspapers: it was very rare to see a black person other than in the sports pages. I have not so far visited Brazil, but Pele is for me a prime example of what I am trying to say – a black sportsman, footballer, and the only black Latin American person to be widely recognised outside the region. The impression I am left with is that the image Latin America wants to project on the world is of a completely Hispanic society. In the visual world there are few images to challenge this almost completely white mainstream, with black and indigenous people rarely featured. Generally we are the exotic, the ethnic, the savage, the stranger.

In Guatemala I made a comment to the manager of the hotel where we were staying, to the effect that on my next visit I wanted to see something of the Caribbean coast. Her reaction was very interesting. Adopting a low, almost secretive voice, she explained that she herself was of Caribbean origin, but had been adopted by a white family, and had lost contact with her original family. Whether she was being secretive about being black (she was quite light-skinned) or about having been adopted, I don't know, but I found the whole thing very strange indeed. She went on to tell me that black people "do not live in this part" (of Guatemala), and then to direct me as to where black people could be found. All this in the same hurried, low, whispered tones.

A Venezuelan woman, again quite uninvited, explained to me the absence of colour or race prejudice in her country, by telling me that the Spanish word for black is used as a term of endearment. For example a white mother will call her child with black hair "my little negrita", my little black one. In Costa Rica I was often called "negrita" by men in the street and at the bus stop. It was also in Costa Rica that I was informed by a white man that we black women "are made for love", and that we are, in his words, always ready and willing to be loved, always receptive, unlike white women, who are usually frigid, and always tired. Although he used the Spanish word for love, it was clear that he was really talking about sex. I was surprised and disappointed to find similar views expressed in a book written by two black Costa Rican brothers. The book, *El Negro en Costa Rica*, was written to fill a vacuum: the non-recognition of the African presence and the contribution made by Afro-costariccense to that country's development. What a context in which to see this negative view of black women!

> Uno de los rasgos salientes del negro es la poca cohesión familiar, que lleva con frecuencia a la inestabilidad del matrimonio. La familia matrifocal, a menudo es el resultado de la facilidad con que cae la mujer en concubinatos con otros hombres.
>
> Melédez and Duncan (1972), *El Negro en Costa Rica*, Editorial Costa Rica, San José, Costa Rica

My own very rough translation of this: "One of the characteristics of black people is the lack of cohesion of the family unit, which is associated with marital instability. The female-headed household is often the result of the ease with which women fall into relationships with other men." Black women are to be blamed for family instability and the high levels of illegitimacy in that community. In Latin America as elsewhere in the world it is the black woman who has been and still is the mainstay of the black family, both in the old world and the new.

Meléndez and Duncan's book had a serious purpose, and a necessary role, and it is a shame to find its message compromised in this way. Black people are part of Latin American life, culture and history. This must be acknowledged – it is not enough to talk about an absence of racism and prejudice if this is achieved only by making black people invisible. It was not so long ago that in Costa Rica, black people were restricted to certain parts of the country, and were forbidden to travel beyond certain restricted areas. I stay with Costa Rica for my next example, not because it is the worst area of Latin America for black people, but because it is probably the best. There is a very telling passage in Annacristina Rossi's (Rossi is a Costarican writer) *La loca de Gandoca*, where the "loca" (the woman) who wants to stop the demolition of Gandoca by so-called developers, tries to persuade a government minister to block the scheme. She tells the minister that if the land is sold to the developers, "Los negros van a paser de son prepietarios a ser mucamos" (the black people will stop being the owners of land and become cleaners). How does the minister reply to this? He says to the lady, "Mira, Daniella, aqui entre nos? en que vas a poner a trabajar a los negros si no es de macamos?" (Look, Daniella, between the two us, what else can we do with the blacks if not put them to work as cleaners?) Later on Daniella remarks that as the Costa Rican minister made this statement he had been walking towards a member of the US government, a black man.

In the supposedly "non-racial" Latin American societies, black people are almost always bottom of the economic and social scale, followed closely by the indigenous people. See Trevor Purcell (1993) for a more academic analysis of the black Latin American experience: *Banana Fallout – Class, Color and Culture Among West Indians in Costa Rica*. How can these societies, founded on theft, violence and slavery, and reflecting the highest degrees of social imbalance and injustice, make any claim to be free of racism and prejudice? In this connection it is important to remember that it was Latin American countries that gave safe haven to the

Nazis fleeing from Germany at the end of the Second World War. Apparently Mexico boasts that it has among its population members of every race on earth, and that out of this mixture will come a new race, "la raz de la cosmos", which will show the way to racial tolerance and harmony in the world. One can only speculate on the nature of the delusion that led anyone to entertain such hopes about Mexico – one of the most divided, unjust and violent societies in the world. I for one did not experience Latin American society as "non-racial", and I really don't think they have anything to boast about or any lessons to teach the rest of the world.

7

THE LOTUS AND THE DRAGON, MABO MYTHS AND OTHER THINGS: TRAVELS AND EXPERIENCES IN ASIA

To look to Asia for mystic enlightenment and spiritual guidance has become as much an anachronism as to think of America as the Wild West.

> Koestler, A (1960), *The Lotus and the Dragon*, Hutchinson, London

Eastern religion seems to have arrived by mystical contemplation and insight at an understanding of the deep structure of physical reality that Western Science has only recently been able to formulate in empirical mathematical terms.

> Reanney, D (1991), *The Death of Forever: A new Future for Human Consciousness*, Souvenir Press, London

IN 1962 I left Barbados, my little island home, for Calcutta in West Bengal in the huge Indian-subcontinent. I was twenty and had more or less given up hope of going to university, when I was offered a government of India scholarship to study at Calcutta University. At the time I did not know, and I still do not know, anything at all regarding the criteria for the award of scholarships. It was enough for me that I was offered one. I was very happy to be following an unusual and different route into higher education, and not the well-worn path to Europe or North America. I knew very little about India. I could find it on the atlas, and I knew that it was part of "the mysterious east". That was the extent of my knowledge.

Through my mother, who was a midwife, I had met one or two Indian ladies. They spoke no English, they had smiled at me, I had smiled at them, and that had been it. I also had an Indian classmate at high school, but I don't remember much about her except that her name was Jenny. After I left school and before I left for India I did have one "Indian" friend – except that in the Caribbean he would be referred to as an East Indian. He was a Trinidadian businessman who I first met at the guest house where he stayed during his business visits to Barbados, and where I had gone for a post-"A" level break. We kept in touch, and when I told him that I would be going to India, he did not think it a good idea. He did not give me any real reasons for that reaction to my plans. He just talked vaguely about the problems I would have with food, the language, and the people. He did not think that I would like it. Furthermore, he did not think that the education I would get would be particularly good.

Maybe my friend knew that Indian society would not be kind to an African woman, but he said nothing about that. I never thought to ask him whether he himself had ever been in India. Thinking about it now, I would guess that he had been there. Perhaps, like his fellow-countryman, the writer, V S Naipaul, he had found India to be *An Area of Darkness*, and not be to recommended to anybody. I will never know. Concerning the matter of me and India, all I can say is he was both right and wrong in his views. He was right that I did not like India, or rather India did not like me, and I responded in kind. He was wrong in that I gained immensely from my three years there, and that I had a more complete and lasting educational experience than I could possibly have got in the best universities in the world. India completed the job my brothers had started in Barbados: the job of toughening me up. When I left India in 1965 I was mentally and emotionally equipped to live anywhere in the world. It seemed to me then that whatever problems and challenges lay in store for me, nothing could be worse than what I had already experienced and survived in Calcutta.

> Calcutta... some taxis have two drivers because it is not safe for anyone, even a taxi driver to go it alone in Calcutta. We hop into a taxi... people are dying in the streets, human

corpses are strewn like flies, women are giving birth to still born babies. Dom says that we will have to live in the face of death in Calcutta... . We think of many, many ways of getting out of Calcutta.

Metha, V (1962), *Walking the Indian Streets*, Faber and Faber, London

My real education began the day I landed in India, for the streets of Calcutta were very instructive. I had grown up in Barbados thinking that our family were poor, but at my first glimpse of the streets here my understanding of poverty underwent rapid and complete change. I came to realise that, far from being poor, the people of Barbados were well off, and my own family life had been positively comfortable. This was how my education in India began, and without being aware of it I had been introduced to the concept of relative poverty. My formal education at Loreto College was the least challenging part of my life in Calcutta. The teaching was the least inspired of any I have been subjected to, with the possible exception of the social-work teaching at the London School of Economics.

At Loreto College the library was my refuge. I escaped there as often as I could and immersed myself in books about Indian philosophy. I was supposed to be studying Indian history but I found philosophy more interesting. As a result of this I got very interested in Buddhism, and flirted briefly, and very mildly, with the idea of becoming a Buddhist. It was in Calcutta that I met Peter, and through him was introduced to recreational walking and hiking. One of my Loreto College friends still says that we ended up married because I was the only woman in Calcutta who was prepared to go walking with him in temperatures of 120 degrees in the shade! Walking was certainly an important part of our courtship, and is still an important part of our relationship.

I had come to India to study, and on the first day of my attendance I found that I had been allocated to a Bengali-speaking Hindu college. On that same day I became ill and was away for a month or so. I dreaded returning to the Bengali college, and my new friends, some of whom were Roman Catholic, helped me to gain entry into Loreto College. Before I continue, let me backtrack a bit to my arrival in Calcutta. On coming in at Dum Dum airport from London, I had been met by a delegation of African students. They had come in place of the Bajan student with whom I had made contact and who had written to me in

London promising to meet me on my arrival. Unfortunately, when the telegram with my flight details arrived, my Bajan contact was away from Calcutta and so his flatmates came to meet me instead. They had also booked me into the Calcutta YWCA in Park Street, but my stay there was very brief, and within a few days of checking in I was admitted to hospital (of which more later).

On coming out of hospital I went to the Salvation Army hostel for young women, while I searched for a fixed abode. Eventually this was found and I moved to live at the Mission Row Christian hostel for young women, in Dalhousie Square. For most of the three years I was at Loreto College, I lived at this hostel. During the first few months in India, if a fairy godmother had offered me a return ticket to Barbados, I would have accepted with alacrity. But now I am glad that such things do not happen in real life. My Indian experiences were to shape the rest of my life, and without them I would not be the person I am today.

As time passed I made a life for myself in Calcutta, but I never lost the urge to leave, and I never really settled down. After I'd been at the hostel for more than two years I was thrown out (see Chapter Three, the "Letter to a Naga Sister", for more details). After hiding in Peter's flat for a few weeks, I found lodgings as a paying guest with a Bengali family, where I had my own room. Bliss! However, I knew that even when I was living in the hostel and sharing a dorm with six other women, from the point of view of personal space I was, in the Indian context, quite well off. But although I was well off in one way, in other ways there were things that made my life as a black woman very difficult. Indians reacted to my presence with stares and shouts of "Habshee!", pushing and crowding round me to get a better view. A Scottish friend and I went to Calcutta zoo: my friend was very pale, very blonde, and the two of us caused an unbelievable stir. People deserted the lions, elephants, monkeys and other animals to come and stare at us, and especially at me.

On the streets and on the trams in Calcutta, mothers also would point me out to their children, using me as "Kali" to frighten their children. Kali is one of the Hindu goddesses, very black and fierce with many heads. Very ugly. On the morning of the day following the Chinese invasion of India, as I came out of the hostel, I saw that Dalhousie Square was swarming with heavily armed soldiers. As soon as they saw me they started laughing, making monkey noises and pointing their guns at me, making as if to shoot me. They really enjoyed themselves.

I came of age in Calcutta. As my birthday approached a friend decided to have a party to celebrate my twenty-first. I was instructed to invite my friends, so I announced to the whole class that there was to be a birthday party for me and everyone was invited. The fact that the party was to be held in one of the residences of the British Council was almost certainly a big draw, and I was surprised to see how many people came, including a young man called Peter Stone. We never have any problem remembering when we first met! Although it was not until at least a year later that we met again, then we struck up a friendship. Back to that birthday party. I was twenty-one and this was my first party, ever. Apart from Peter it marked the start of other lasting friendships, so it really was a significant occasion. I was beginning to feel less unsettled, to accept my situation and to try to make the best of it. It was not easy.

For a start I had no idea that Indian society would be so unhealthily obsessed with skin colour. I was amazed by the practice of using very bright lights when taking photographs, so as to make a dark person appear lighter. Coming from the Caribbean I was painfully aware of our own brand of colour prejudice, which I had experienced often enough myself. But I was very disconcerted to find myself living in a society in which people quite unashamedly said things like, "In the East fairness is the mark of beauty." Within a few days of starting college, one of my fellow students explained to me why she was an only child. She told me in a very matter of fact way that when her parents saw how dark she was, they knew that they would have to pay a very high dowry to get her a suitable husband, and because of this they decided not to have any more children.

The Indian version of the colour problem and Indian racism, together with the inescapable signs of poverty and all forms of human distress, made it difficult for me to enjoy life in Calcutta. Other foreigners said things like, "You'll get used to it, we felt the same when we first got here." They were wrong. There are some things one should never "get used to". Anyway my life was different from that of the other foreigners, even that of the foreign students. I was the only African-Caribbean woman in Calcutta, probably in the whole of India. There were African women student nurses, who came to India in small groups, worked and lived together, spoke the same languages, and were a mutual support group. There were also a few Trinidadian-Indian women students, who with saris were indistinguishable from local Indian women. These Caribbean sisters and I did not seem to have any common bond, and we only ever met up at parties or functions for foreign students.

Being the only Afro-Caribbean woman in Calcutta was not in itself a problem. I had not gone to India hoping to join a little expatriate Caribbean community. I had expected to be pretty much on my own, but I had not expected to feel so totally adrift and isolated. My background, my lifestyle and my interests seemed to separate me from everyone else around, especially from the majority of Loreto College students. I lived in a hostel and every day I travelled to college in unbelievably over-crowded trams. My long-distance travel was done either like the Mahatma third-class on Indian trains, or by private plane. I just did not fit anywhere, and Indian society was built on people fitting into their allotted place.

With the passage of time my life changed. During those three years I lived in at least four different worlds: the spoilt little-rich girl world of Loreto Convent, the world of the hostel, with families sleeping outside on the pavement, the world of the "overseas students", with its constant baiting of the imperialist British, and finally Peter's British expatriate world. I could never complain that life in Calcutta lacked either variety or interest. India challenged my views and beliefs and forced me to examine my values and attitudes, and I see now that my moral and intellectual development were nurtured and strengthened by the dilemmas and challenges of daily life in Calcutta.

1962: from my island in the sun to the black hole of Calcutta

> You have developed the head, the heart did not keep pace. With us it was the opposite – it was the development of the heart that we have been concerned with in India.
>
> Vinoba Bhave in an interview with Arthur Koestler, 1960
>
> The setting of the British sun left us with contempt for English values but emotionally we were too far committed to withdraw…
>
> Metha, V, *Walking the Indian Streets*

I soon learnt that in India most people had fairly fixed perceptions of the West and of the East, and as everyone has to belong to one or the other I was assigned to the West. I found out that Eastern and Western were always at opposite ends of the spectrum and were always in contrast. The comments of Vinoba Bhave to Arthur Koestler summed this up very well: West equals brain, East equals heart. The comparisons could go on with – West equals bad, East equals good, West equals rich, East equals poor, and so on. I began to understand that such views were very limited and very much based on false premises. Returning to these issues in 1997, I also returned to my well-thumbed Indian history textbooks, where I was interested to read Vincent Smith's speculations on the future of India after British rule:

> Whatever form that future might take, it would certainly contain a large element of the West. It is at least arguable that in dying politically the West in India bade fare to triumph spiritually.

Smith, V (1958), *The Oxford History of India*, OUP, Oxford

The British Raj did come to an end, but the departing British would be leaving behind their railways, their ideas and their system of government. And as Metha observed, India was too "emotionally committed" to withdraw, East and West had met and merged. It did not take me very long to see that for myself. I was a student of Indian history and I could see that the modern state of India had emerged from this meeting of East and West. The democratic system of government and the Indian civil service were two of the most obvious results of this.

All this was still to come, and in May 1962 all I wanted was to leave India. As soon as I arrived in Calcutta I knew that I had make a terrible mistake. I was overwhelmed by the desperate poverty and misery all around me, and I myself became miserable and unhappy and wished myself miles away. Within a few days of arriving I went to college for the first time. When I returned, as I was going upstairs to my room at the hostel, I stumbled and almost fell down the stairs. I was unable to see because my eyes were blinded by tears and my head was throbbing with pain. I thought that my first session at the Bengali Women's College had reduced me to a quivering wreck. I had been mobbed by hundreds of screaming, pointing Bengali girls, and every class I'd attended had been disrupted by my mere presence. Also, I did not understand a word of Bengali, and Bengali was the medium of instruction. Somehow I got through that day.

After that fall, someone helped me up the remaining stairs and I collapsed on the bed. Before long one of the other residents knocked on my door, as she had come to see how I was and whether there was anything she could do to help. This was the same person I was to put such faith in when, more than thirty years later, I fell ill in Africa. The superintendent came to check on me, found that I had a temperature and called a doctor. The doctor diagnosed chicken pox.

The next morning the superintendent came to my room and told me that, as I was suffering from an infectious disease, I would have to be removed to the appropriate hospital. She was accompanied by a government representative, and they both felt that I should also have a friend with me. Did I know anyone who could go with me? The government representative and I set off for 77 Keraya Road, where the only other Barbadian student in Calcutta lived. He was at college, so one of his flatmates, who was also a medical student, came with me. When we arrived at the hospital, I was told to lie on a bed, with only a thin, very stained mattress and no sheets. I refused to lie down. I said that I would only lie on a bed that was made up with sheets. We waited, and, eventually, some sheets were found.

Before I go on with the account of my stay at the hospital for infectious diseases, let me jump forward a couple of years. The medical student who came with me had completed his studies and was ready to leave for home. His home was Ghana, and he wanted to return with a wife, and he decided that I should be that wife. He was a very attractive man, who, as far as I knew, had a long-standing relationship with an Anglo-Indian lady, so I was somewhat mystified by his proposal of marriage. I asked him, "Why me?" He told me that he had decided that he would like to marry me that day at the hospital when I'd refused to get into the bed until it was properly made up! His relationship with his Anglo-Indian girlfriend had ended, leaving him free to make his move. I was flabbergasted! I had not realised that I cut such a heroic, defiant, and obviously attractive figure. The marriage proposal came to nothing, mainly because he insisted that I would have to marry him in the few weeks before he left Calcutta. He should have known better than to insist that I do anything. We parted as friends – we'd never been anything else – and when I eventually went to Africa (see Chapter Five) it was as a British academic. I had missed my chance of becoming an African wife.

Now back to my first night in the hospital. I passed the night in a daze, barely conscious of what was going on around me. I had never been into hospital before, and now after just a few days in India here I was in one. I felt very sorry for myself, and I did not sleep very much. I just lay in bed listening to the noise of an Indian hospital, of which there was much: the continuous splashes from buckets and bedpans from the floors above fell on my bottom-floor window. The next day the hospital superintendent came to see me. Having seen my name on the admission list he knew that I was a foreigner, and when he heard that I was from Barbados he asked me if I knew a Dr R. As it happened I did, for my mother had often worked with this doctor. He and the superintendent had been students together in Edinburgh. So that was all right, he and I knew someone in common, and now I could be placed in an appropriate pigeonhole. Instructions were given: I may not have looked like a memsahib, but I was to be treated like one. An additional mattress was found (the single mattress was very thin), and I was told that "Western" food would be prepared for me.

I was in the hospital for ten days, and many times I was sure that I would leave it, feet first. No, I did not really think that I was going to die of chicken pox, which I had contracted in England during my stop-off there on my way to India. I was sharing a ward and the same nurses with patients who were suffering from cholera and smallpox. I felt sure I would be infected with something much worse than I already had. I first became aware of this possibility when I saw a small boy of eight or nine walking around the ward. I asked what was the matter with him, to be told he had cholera. The next day or maybe later that same day, I saw a woman with smallpox. It is not a sight one can easily forget. The cholera boy lived, but the smallpox lady died. In the meantime I had become very friendly with the Bengali nurse who was in charge of our ward, though she spoke very little English and I spoke no Bengali.

One morning, as she was about to push the thermometer into my mouth, she said, "*You* first... always *you* first." It was some time before the meaning of what she had said got through to me. There was only one thermometer and I got it first. This caused me to wonder about the needle for taking the blood samples, but I decided it was best not to think about it. Hindu fatalism had taken hold. When the time came for me to leave I tried to give the nurse some money as a gift for looking after me so well, but she refused. In her halting English she told me that I was her friend and her patient, and that she could not accept money from me. Indian nurses are paid a pittance, and I am sure she could have used that money. Her refusal was a statement about our relationship and her professionalism. So I accepted it and promised to keep our friendship going by returning to visit her – but I never did go back to see my Bengali nurse.

However, I have not quite finished with the hospital for infectious diseases . Before leaving Calcutta, in 1965, I went with one of my friends to see a Hindi film. Before the main feature there were the usual trailers and government information films, which my friend and I were as usual talking through. Then I saw a picture of Pandit Nehru, and heard something about "India's first Infectious Disease Hospital… ". I stopped talking, and focused all my attention on the screen, and it was incredible. There was Mr Nehru opening a hospital, brand new and beautifully clean, with state of the art equipment. This hospital we were told pointed up the way India would be dealing with infectious diseases in the future. But this one on the cinema screen did not look at all like the place I had been a patient in for ten long days.

That hospital, my hospital, had been a filthy, dirty place with urine and excrement running down the outside walls, where sick people were expected to lie on dirty blood-stained bare mattresses without sheets. How had this hospital changed so much? Why had it been allowed to? Where was the World Health Organisation (WHO), whose money had partly funded it and whose representative stood proudly at the opening? If only he too could be stricken down with chicken pox and be admitted there! Never mind – by then I had absorbed enough of Hindu thought to accept that it was "my fate". It was my fate that I should have taken chicken pox from England to India, so that I might have first-hand experience of Indian hospitals, and survive living in close proximity and sharing a nurse with patients who had smallpox and cholera. It is also my fate that I should now be writing about it, and, at long last, telling the story of what life was like for a young black woman in 1960s India.

Saying "goodnight" in the Western way

While I was living at the Mission Row hostel I saw quite a lot of a certain Bengali gentleman. I met him not long after moving in, and he showed me around Calcutta, introducing me to yoghurt – my first taste – and Indian char (tea). From time to time he would invite me out to dinner, and after dinner we would drive around Calcutta, perhaps go by the Maidan, then rush back to be at the hostel before the gates were locked at ten p.m. At the hostel I would shake hands with him as I thanked him for a lovely evening, before hastily passing through its iron gates.

This went on for quite a long time. Then one night as I stuck out my hand to do the handshaking bit, he held on to it and asked me: "When are we going to say goodbye in the Western way?" I guessed that he was referring to the passionate kissing that he had seen in the cinema: he had assumed that since I was from the "West" my behaviour would conform in every respect to what he saw on the screen. After that episode I always found a reason not to accept any more dinner invitations from him. I was not quite ready for the Western way, and anyhow, in such matters, I much preferred the Eastern way.

Peter once overheard me telling this story to a friend, and he started laughing and laughing. I could not understand why he was laughing so much, as I did not think that the story was that funny. Eventually he stopped and said that he never realised that I had "done that to other people"; he thought that my hand-shaking ritual had been a joke between us. I was on my own in Calcutta, and I had to look after myself; as it was even my hand-shaking didn't stop me developing something of a reputation.

The Mission Row hostel for young women: Calcutta in the 1960s

Thinking of the young women's Christian hostel, it is the people I can recall most vividly – the "young women" whose ages stretched from eighteen or nineteen to sixty or thereabouts. Time was when the hostel had been predominantly Anglo-Indian, but during my time the racial composition was beginning to shift, and the Anglo-Indians were moving on while the Indians were moving in. Much divided and separated these two groups of women: the Anglo-Indians associated themselves with the British and the British Raj, and were always, it seemed to me, trying to exploit their rather tenuous link with the British. Whereas the educated Indian women, who were also moving away from the village and the joint-family system, embraced an independent life in the city. This was something completely new in India. The hostel and Loreto College, the two institutions that dominated my life, were both all-female. I had never before been part of any single-sexed institution, and it took some getting used to. Loreto was a Roman Catholic institution, but I had only one Roman Catholic friend. All the rest of my college friends were Hindus.

In the hostel the differences between the Anglo-Indian and Indian residents were never acknowledged, and did not cause any obvious problems. Only Christians were accepted as residents, and the religion had the effect of masking and smoothing over the differences. It also seemed to me that being "Christian" was interpreted as being culturally Western European, and the Indians for the most part accepted this Anglo-Indian cultural dominance. All the Indian women expected to have arranged marriages, so there were areas of life where Christian/ Western values did not hold sway. There were always exceptions, and I recall there was one "love marriage" among the Indian residents. Once the families of the couple became involved all contact between the young people ceased, and the rituals began and proceeded as though it was in fact an arranged marriage. I myself never had a problem with the idea of arranged marriages – I could see that it had disadvantages, but it also had a lot to recommend it.

Among the Anglo-Indian women in the hostel there was A. She waiting to marry her Scotsman, a soldier she had met during the war. It was more than twenty years since she had seen him, but she was still waiting for him. In the meantime she chain-smoked and sang or rather bawled out lots of romantic ballads, about lovers returning to their deserted loves after many years of separation. What with the smoking and the singing, her lungs took a lot of punishment, and she started every day by hawking and spitting for what seemed like an eternity. In two years she did once receive a letter with a Scottish postmark. Then there was B, very vivacious and very attractive, who described herself as the "unlucky one" in her family. She was unlucky because all her brothers and sisters were fair enough to "pass as white", but she was not. Although she was desperate to leave India, she turned down the chance of emigrating to Australia, on the grounds that she did not want to live among the descendants of convicts!

B did eventually make it to England. I got on especially well with C, who took me under her wing and taught me to play cards and the few words of Hindi that she knew. She would have liked to pass as an Indian. But India did not want her. She eventually moved to Australia, not minding at all about the descendants of convicts. I was very fond of C, who had a very open-minded and generous personality. Then there was little V, who came to the hostel direct from her village. She spoke no English, but she learnt fast, and among the very first English words she acquired was "boyfriend" closely followed by "I want one," as when a child says such and points to an ice cream. In fact, she was to have several boyfriends, starting with the priest into whose guardianship her trusting parents had placed her welfare. At the Mission Row hostel, as well as the more or less permanent residents of Anglo-Indians and Indians, there were the Naga girls and women who came and went. The Nagas were tribal people from the hills, who had been converted to Christianity, and who were involved in an independence war with India. (For more details of my involvement with my Naga sisters, see the letter in Chapter Three.) As well as the Nagas, there were visitors from Europe and North America, including female students staying at the hostel from time to time. I teamed up with one of these visiting students, an American, in the summer of 1963, and we travelled north to Kashmir. This particular person stayed at the hostel for much longer than other visitors, and became almost another resident. The two of us were known as the "two lost souls", as we were the only ones who never went to church.

All the servants at the Christian hostel for young women were male, including the dhobi (laundry man), and they were mainly Muslim. They addressed the female residents as "Baba", as in "Maureen-Baba, telephone." I shared a dorm with six other women, and I rented a desk, which I placed in a corner of the room. For more than two years the totality of my personal space consisted of that around my bed, my wardrobe and that desk. Whenever I could I would escape to the spacious rooftop. This was my safe haven, and from there at night I could look down on the families sleeping on the pavement below, with their personal space the bit of ground currently occupied by their sleeping bodies. I was learning fast.

Singing for our supper – the undiplomatic dinner party

For reasons that I never fully understood, overseas students in Calcutta were always being invited to dinner or some function at various embassies. I mostly avoided these occasions, especially the American ones, but for some reason that I can't now recall I accepted an invitation to dinner at the American embassy. At the appointed hour some other overseas students picked me up and we set off. The dinner was okay, nothing special, though I am not a big eater at the best of times, so I certainly wasn't there for the food. Americans seem to think that people would kill for their cuisine. If there are such people, I am not one. After the meal we sat around talking, but the conversation was dull, in fact boring. Then we got onto the subject of songs and singers, which led our American hostess to ask if anyone could sing. With one voice we disclaimed any vocal ability whatsoever. The lady would not accept this and kept on and on. "Surely one of you must be able to, say, ah come on… just a little song," and so on.

Maybe he did it to shut her up, or maybe he had a more profound reason, but suddenly one of the Caribbean brothers said he would sing. We, the overseas students, all black, and our white American host and hostess, were seated on the floor of the spacious lounge, more or less in a circle. Once the offer to sing was made, we fell quiet, and we waited expectantly. I could never figure out whether he sang this song in protest at the badgering we'd been subjected to, or the history we brought with us, or whether it was the only song he knew all the words to. He was known as one of the most non-political overseas students around, very quiet and unassuming. For a person who couldn't sing his voice was rich and deep as he sang these words:

> Freedom! Freedom!
> No more laughing no more laughing,
> No more laughing over me
> And before I be a slave
> I'll be buried in my grave
> And go home to my Lord and be free
> Freedom! Freedom!

Whatever our hostess had been expecting, I am sure it wasn't this. A deep silence followed, then we slowly got up off the floor and took our leave. Not one of us spoke about the dinner or the song as we walked away from the embassy – not the singer or anyone. We had sung for our supper, and they had got more than they had bargained for. That was my last visit to the American embassy in Calcutta.

Shantinekaten – the abode of peace

After a few months living in Calcutta, capital of the Indian state of West Bengal, I knew about Rabindranath Tagore and the "abode of peace", which he had established in the Bengali countryside. So when, one Friday night at a party in Park Street, I was invited by an American woman to accompany her to Shantinekaten for a weekend visit, all expenses paid, I accepted without hesitation. We met at Howrath station at six o'clock in the morning the following day, my new friend bought our return tickets, and we set off.

The journey proved to be a demanding experience in a somewhat unexpected way, so that by the time we reached Shantinekaten I was desperately in *need* of some peace. My newly acquired friend had talked non-stop during the whole trip. What I remember very clearly was that this was the first time in my life that anyone had identified him- or herself to me as Jewish, and this information emerged in a most curious way. My companion wanted to tell me all the details of her life in the USA, and to impress me with her lifestyle and her money. Why she should want to do so, to a poor little black girl from Carrington's Village, Barbados, was beyond me.

Anyway, amid all the riches and glamour of her life there was one fly in the ointment: she had been refused membership of the local country club. I was at a loss to understand what she was talking about. I had no idea what a country club was, nor why she should have been refused membership of it. She continued on and on about it and their refusal to admit her. I decided to seek clarification, so I asked her: "What is the problem, why can't you join this club?" In reply to this she explained to me that the country club did not accept Jews as members. This information meant nothing to me. I understood black and white, but what was this Jewish thing?

So I asked how the country club people knew that she was Jewish, and she explained that they would know by her name. I obviously did not understand the gravity of her situation, or the complexity of upper-class social life in the USA. I asked a simple question: "Why not join another club, where it didn't matter what your name is?" No, that would never do, it had to be the country club. I tried to understand her problem by linking it to my own experience. Her club must be like the Barbados yacht club, which at that time accepted only white people as members. I mentioned this to her, and her response was that whereas a black person could not change colour, a name could easily be altered. I could see the logic of her argument, and that a name, Jewish or otherwise, could be manipulated in this way. But I was beginning to feel uncomfortable. I tried to change the subject. No luck – she would not let go of the topic – and after all *she* was paying for the weekend.

So finally I came right out and asked the question I'd been wanting to for a long time: "Why don't you just change your name then?" She must have been waiting for that, and she was ready: "That is just what I am planning to do." Then she told me that on her return from India she was to be married to an Irishman. It seemed that she had chosen her partner as much for his name as anything else. She mentioned with obvious pride that he had a very Irish name, O'Malley or O'Reilly.

She would show them at the country club, with her new Irish husband and name to boot. I could not help wondering why someone like her, with the values she had, would want to visit Shantinekaten. I was new to the world of travel, and did not realise that for some people it was all a matter of ticking place-names off, and having something to impress people with at the country club.

Only once did she depart from the subject of her Jewish identity and with it the country club, but when she did I wished she'd stuck with her original obsession. I can't now recall what exactly happened and how the conversation took the turn it did, but I can remember her pressing me to tell her about myself. She clearly expected me to have something interesting to say, but I explained that I was living in a Christian hostel where the gates were locked at ten o'clock every night, and we had to have a pass to stay out after that. Before this, I'd been living with my parents in Barbados, and hardly had any social life at all. After telling her that, I did not expect what followed. She questioned me about how many lovers I'd had, and invited me to pronounce on the question of size. "Was it true," she asked me, "that black men were so much bigger than white men?" I could not believe my ears! Fancy asking me a question like that! If she was so curious why didn't she find out in the usual way? These were my thoughts, but I managed to maintain my composure and replied that I lacked the necessary experience to be able to make these comparisons.

There we were, on a train in West Bengal, India, on our way to Shantinekaten – the "abode of peace". I was in the company of a white woman with a (soon to be dumped) Jewish name and soon to be acquired country club membership. I, a black woman, had been the recipient of strange confidences, and even stranger questions, more or less as a way of paying for the visit. Was it worth it? I can't answer, because I really don't know. Once we arrived at Shantinekaten, I spent a more or less solitary but very peaceful weekend, walking and reading. The journey back to Calcutta was very quiet, as there was nothing more to be added to what had been already said. At Howrath station we said our goodbyes, and I wished her luck with the marriage and said that I hoped that all would go as planned at the country club.

My education in the matter of Jewish identity was extended when I became quite friendly with another American, this time a male academic. He was a Sanskrit scholar from Harvard, or somewhere equally prestigious, and he was doing research in Calcutta. I had another friend, a Spanish woman who was married to a Bengali, and one day I had to leave her in order to meet the American. When she heard the reason for my departure she remarked that she hoped I wasn't getting too involved with him, and added: "You do know that he is Jewish, don't you?" I said something like, "What do I care? It doesn't matter to me." I deeply resented her question and the tone of voice that went with it, but I didn't want a quarrel so I held my peace.

Since my Shantinekaten weekend my knowledge and awareness had increased and I knew that the views of my Spanish friend reflected centuries of European/Christian hostility and hatred towards Jews. But as I was neither European nor Christian I could not see what it had to do with me. I decided to talk it over with my Jewish scholar, as he might have some ideas. We had a very long and thoughtful discussion, and I began to understand the meaning and the depth of European anti-Semitism. A year or so after this incident, at one of Peter's gatherings, I met another Jewish man, middle-aged and very sad-looking. He was working with the UN or one of its offshoots. During the party he got drunk and quite literally started crying on my shoulder. I heard that he had spent most of his childhood in a concentration camp and had lost all his family in the Holocaust. What with the lady on the train, my scholar friend, and the survivor from Hitler's "final solution", my education was progressing in leaps and bounds.

Footnote

In 1975, when I went to work at Surrey University, I learnt from Professor Asher Tropp that Barbados has one of the oldest synagogues in the western hemisphere – the Bridgetown synagogue, founded in 1627. In January 1977 I read in the Barbados newspapers that it had just been completely restored by the Jewish community in Barbados, and I visited it for the first time, ever. By 1997 I had also learnt that it was a Jew who was responsible for my being a Barbadian. In 1637, a Jew from Holland called Pieter Brower introduced the sugar plant to Barbados from Brazil, and showed the British how to make sugar. Without the sugar plant Barbados would not have needed slaves and my ancestors would not have been brought from Africa. In 1962, I was totally unaware of all this, and I can truly say that my education in these matters began on that journey to Shantinekaten, Tagore's "abode of peace".

A Kashmiri summer

As I've mentioned before, in the summer of 1963 I teamed up with a visiting American student and went on a journey to North India, which ended in Kashmir. We visited Chandigar, Delhi and other parts, including Simla. We had lots of adventures on the way, but my memory of that summer is dominated by my Kashmiri experiences. I have written elsewhere (Chapter Four) of my visit to Pahlgam and my walk/talk with my Sheikh guide. Let me start my Kashmiri reminiscences with one of my near-death experiences. In Salman Rushdie's book *Midnight's Children* there is a story of the death by drowning of a German woman visitor to Kashmir, which ends with the remark that there is a place on the Dal Lake where foreigners go to die.

When I read that piece in Rushdie I wondered whether I'd almost drowned at that place too, though of course I did not die. Two Bajan brothers dragged me out of the lake just as I was going down for the third, and presumably the last time. In 1963 there was an international students' camp in Srinager, and although my friend and I were not staying there (we were in a houseboat) we went along to all the social gatherings. On this occasion we were attending a picnic on Dal Lake. Before coming to Kashmir I had never even seen a lake, much less swum in one. Everybody was messing about in the water, so I jumped in. I assumed that it was no different from being in the sea. When I got tired I went to stand up. Nothingness! A deep void, emptiness, nowhere to stand. I shouted, but everyone else was shouting, as all part of the fun. Then my friends realised that I was really in trouble and two of them dived in and dragged me out in the nick of time. How can I ever forget Kashmir?

The houseboat we shared with a newly married couple whom we had met on the bus. We were all on tight budgets, and it would help us all to share. Our attempts to talk to the woman didn't get very far, so we asked the man whether his wife spoke any English. We almost burst out laughing at his reply. He said, "I do not know, I will ask her." He then explained that this was their first time alone together, as they had only just got married. We all very soon found out that his new wife did not speak any English.

Kashmir was so beautiful. I marvelled at the balance and perfection of nature, the snow-capped mountains, and the lake. I touched snow for the first time in India, and that was here in Kashmir. All this beauty, and all those new experiences, and I had no means of recording anything. I was too poor to own a camera, so the houseboat proprietor lent me his – my budget just about stretching to the purchase of film. One afternoon I went on an excursion into the hills, and at some point I wandered off for a little walk on my own. I crossed over a mountain stream and continued walking, deep in thought. Then I checked my watch and realised that I ought to be heading back to the group. I retraced my steps and soon came to the stream, but it was now a fast flowing river: the water seemed to be rushing by at several knots. I tried to find a safe place to cross, but everywhere seemed impassable. Time was passing by. I could not wait any longer. I would have to make a dash for it. I put the camera on my head, and felt sure that the water would come up only to my chest. I had no money to repair or replace the camera, so I had to return it undamaged. I will never know quite how I did it, but both the camera and I got to the other side safely. The irony was that I never actually took any photos, so the next time I was offered the loan of the camera I had the good sense to refuse. This means that pictures of Kashmir are all in my mind, and are always as fresh and as beautiful as in the summer of 1963.

Leaving India and dreaming of Africa

As I've mentioned several times, from the moment of my arrival in India I counted the days to departure. Sometimes urgently, at other times more leisurely, though leaving India was always on my mind. In spite of that I returned to Delhi in 1965 to say goodbye to one of my friends who had married and left college before completing her degree.

In India I had many "firsts". I first came into contact with Africa in India. In the few months I'd stayed in London en route in 1962 I'd seen many African people on the street, though I never personally met any. In England fellow West Indians had told me that African people look down on us as the descendants of slaves. From the day I touched down in Calcutta, when I was met at the airport by a delegation of African students, and for the rest of my time there, I had many African friends. I'd also received a few proposals of marriage, which I suppose would have been one route into Africa. I now believe that these proposals were related to two factors: one was that those African men wanted to return with an educated "African" wife, and the other was I was known to be very keen on Africa. Everyone knew that on leaving India it was my preferred destination, rather than a return to Barbados. So when I went to Delhi on my way out of India, one of my friends who worked in the diplomatic service arranged an interview for me at the Nigerian High Commission. I knew that Nigeria was recruiting teachers in India, and I wanted to see if I might be considered for one of these teaching posts.

I think I saw the high commissioner himself, but I can't be sure. He was an extremely tall, fat man, who seemed mostly concerned to know about my marital status, and whether I was looking for a husband. He did not question me about my studies or mention anything related to my reason for being there. It was very frustrating, for every time I tried to turn the conversation to teaching he would shift back to these personal questions. After about fifteen minutes of this I could see it was leading nowhere, so I said I would check it out later in London and left. In London I never bothered, because I felt that I could not face another interview like the one I'd had in Delhi. So, my dream of going to live and work in Africa rapidly faded, and I settled into a very different way of life from the one I had known in Barbados and India. It would be more than twenty years before I would have the opportunity of visiting Africa.

Some time in the late 1980s a delegation of African academics visited the university in England where I was working, and over lunch the man sitting next to me started quizzing me about my work. In particular he wanted to know why I was working in an English university: "You should be helping us in Africa... we in Africa need you... they [the English] don't need you as much as we do in Africa!" I felt myself under attack, and I instantly recalled that interview at the Nigerian High Commission in Delhi all those years before. I smiled and said nothing in my own defence. Before leaving to return to London our African visitor invited me to lunch and I accepted, thinking that I would hear more about how Africa "needed me", and also perhaps get some leads for my research consultancy. But no, it was the Delhi experience all over again, and all he wanted was to chat me up. There was no useful information, and no leads. I was presented not with an opportunity to network, but with an opportunity for an affair. It seemed that Africa did not really need me after all, or at least not in a way I could respond to. Shame.

In the summer of 1965, soon after arriving in England, I wrote a short piece about my experiences in India and sent it to the *New Statesman* magazine. Paul Johnson, who is now a right-wing journalist, was at that time a left-wing journalist, and he rejected my article. A few years after that – in 1969, I think – I was invited to be part of a panel discussion at the Cave Hill campus at the UWI, in Barbados. I do not now recall the topic under discussion, but somehow the subject of the Indian sub-continent came up, and I made a few off-the-cuff remarks, alluding to the prejudice and racism which I'd experienced in India. Jan Carew, a Guyanese writer who was also on the panel, threatened to walk out and denounced me as an unsuitable person to share a platform with. After that I decided to leave the subject of India alone, as it seemed that in both my adopted country, England, and in my native Barbados, I would have great difficulty in being allowed to tell my story.

1993 – return to Calcutta

In the years since 1965, I used occasionally to dream about Calcutta. The dream was always the same. I was on a tram that was full to overflowing. It was winter, and as the tram rounded a corner the Victoria memorial would appear out of the mist, looking very beautiful and quite enchanting. In the dream I relived the journey I had taken to college many, many times, with that image of the mist-enshrouded memorial one that had entranced me in real life. When I returned to Calcutta, in 1993, there was no winter mist, the Maidan was changed beyond recognition, and the memorial seemed different, smaller, and quite dirty.

After a period of almost thirty years I had returned to what in many ways was a different Calcutta, and in many ways I also was different – not the young woman who had left there in 1965. What were these differences, and what was the same? The city had more people, and that meant increased poverty, more sleeping on the pavements, more rubbish, more crowded buses and trams. There was a metro, and a new Howrath bridge, which was empty of traffic – something to do with the high tolls, but still very impressive. The Ganges was the same, and it seemed to me that the same people were bathing in the same ghats. A black African woman on the streets of 1993 Calcutta attracted very little interest, except from the more sophisticated beggars, wanting to talk cricket, "and by the way can you give me a few rupees!" Peter and I were lucky to meet up with some of our old Calcutta friends, who gave us a warm reception and many happy hours reminiscing.

I went to Mission Row, vastly changed, and looked at the hostel: the whole area seemed very run-down. I wondered about ringing the bell but decided to let sleeping girls lie. Loreto College also seemed very run-down, or was it that my perceptions had changed? I made my way to Lord Sinha Road via Theatre Road, and rang the doorbell at my friend's aunt's house, not really expecting a reply. She was in. We talked: yes, it *was* all very run-down now, a different class of people altogether, not as in the old days. But on the notice board outside the convent I'd seen that the notices were written in English, Hindi and Bengali. In my day this would have been unthinkable: girls were punished for speaking Bengali in the college.

Here on my second visit I found myself having a very different experience of trauma – that was, trying to cope with someone else's on arriving in Calcutta. I have to admit I did not do very well. In my eyes, the Calcutta of 1993 seemed a much better place, in human terms, than it had been in 1965. For this reason I felt my Australian friend's reactions were somewhat over the top. We had agreed to meet there, then make our way by bus to Bhutan, but her reaction to Calcutta was so profound that she went into shock, and for a while it seemed she'd abandon the plan of going on to Bhutan. When I considered my own first experience of Calcutta, and facing the prospect of living there for three years, I could not feel a lot of sympathy for someone passing through for a few days. Such sympathy as I had was targeted at the people who had to live their lives in these appalling conditions. I had instructed her to watch *City of Joy*, and to be sure to read the book as well.

In my previous incarnation as a student in Calcutta, I can recall only once having something stolen, and that was my diary. It was leather-bound and looked like a purse, and it went missing on the train journey from Calcutta to Delhi. On my return visit, as Peter and I left the aircraft in Bombay and approached the terminal building, a young Indian man with a North American accent advised, "Keep hold of your things." He went on to inform me that: "Here they will steal things from right under your nose." I had not visited Bombay before, and I thought how different this was from my first arrival in India thirty years earlier.

That young man at Bombay airport must have had the gift of foresight, because I did in fact have my belongings stolen from "right under my nose". These articles included a gold watch given as a wedding present by Peter, and my computer with all my addresses and other irreplaceable information. I had gone to visit a friend from college days, and as the afternoon got hotter and stickier I decided to take a shower. I left my bag lying on the sofa in the living room, and when I returned ten minutes later the bag was gone. What followed belonged in the realm of farce.

At first I could not believe it had gone, and I kept looking under chairs and behind the sofa, thinking that the dog may have been playing with it. Then I had to accept that it had really gone. We had to inform the police, who came to the scene of the crime. My friend refused to allow her servants to be interviewed by them, saying that she would not have them singled out – either everyone or no one would be interviewed. So no one was interviewed. My friends kept a very noisy dog, which had barked and howled when I first arrived (with a young man) at the apartment, though there had been no barking when I was in the shower. This suggested to me that someone known to the dog had taken my bag. My friend had another theory. She decided that the young man whom I had "picked up" on the streets of Calcutta was the guilty party. He had returned to the flat and stolen the bag while I was in the shower. Unfortunately this did not explain why the dog had failed to bark on this occasion.

If the young man in question had wanted to steal my bag he had ample opportunity during the time we were walking the streets of south Calcutta, and on the three flights of stairs to the top-floor apartment. I'd been about to give up the search for her street when I stopped for a drink of coconut water and fell into conversation with the young man, who was also at the stall having a drink. He'd heard me asking for directions and offered to show me the way. After the theft, my friend informed me that I had been "seen" walking with this young man. Of course I'd been seen with him – he had escorted me to the house, and up the stairs to the apartment. He had greeted my friend's husband and explained that he had come to see me safely to their home. Now I was informed that this behaviour was very "Western" and unwise and had almost certainly resulted in the theft. This I could not accept.

By the end of that day I began to see that I would never see my bag or any of its contents. I'd been told that in the unlikely event of the police recovering my property, they would keep it. The eagerness of the police officer to know the code for the computer's secret information made me think that there was something more to this. I felt the loss of my computer very much, as I had been storing lots of new information as we travelled, and I had no backup. But more than the loss of the computer, the circumstances of the theft completely threw me off balance, and left me feeling extremely vulnerable. Peter said that I went into mourning for the computer, but he was wrong. I was in mourning for something much more precious than that: the betrayal of trust.

Reflecting on India

What about me – how had I changed in the years since leaving Calcutta? Well, my first visit to India, and in particular my life in Calcutta, had been the equivalent of being born again, for nothing in my life was ever the same. I left Calcutta in 1965, and I returned in 1993, a mature woman, a mother, a grandmother, an academic. I was looking at India through different eyes. I am aware that many people in the West (Europe and North America) see the answer to their own spiritual bankruptcy in the teachings and philosophy of the East, and India in particular. Unlike my "First World" brothers and sisters I have no guilt about empire and all that. I have instead the confidence of having myself descended from slavery and emerged from colonialism.

This freedom and confidence enables me to be honest about India, and I consider that I have been very close to the real India in all its complexity and diversity, its lies and its truths. My experience as a black woman in India makes it impossible for me to buy into the fantasy of it, which is packaged and dispensed in yoga and meditation classes. In Western society Indian philosophy is detached from its roots, and we are presented with what is attractive and useful to people searching – for what? For something that they think the West has lost. But India has made other contributions to the world, not least the iniquitous caste system, and the swastika also has its origins in India.

I know that the Germans adapted the original Hindu swastika symbol, and I am not suggesting that this symbol has the same meaning in Hindu philosophy as it did in Hitler's Germany. But there are "Aryans" in India. Racial politics is part of the history of India, and Hitler's Germany did have its Indian sympathisers and active supporters. The light-skinned North Indians regard themselves as the descendants of the conquering Aryans, and look down on the darker skinned southerners. The southerners are regarded as the descendants of the Dravidians – the aboriginal people who were conquered by the Aryans. Whenever I wore a sari in public in India I would be referred to as a Tamil.

In India there are people who see themselves as Aryan in the same sense that people in Germany considered themselves so. These people sympathised with and supported Hitler in the Second World War. The roots of the Bharatiya Janata Party, the right-wing Hindu Party, rapidly gaining strength in today's India, lie deep in Indian history, religion and culture. Mehta's book about India was published in 1962, the year

I arrived in Calcutta. Metha had returned to India to rediscover his roots and to explore the country.

This is how Metha described the origins of the caste system:

> This is the caste system, whose origins lie in history and religion. The conquering Aryans made slaves of the Dravidians... . The Dravidians fled south and enslaved the aboriginals. Brown Aryans, black Dravidians, blacker aboriginals – this is the source of caste and class.... . This is the caste system. This is India.

Metha, V (1962), *Walking the Indian Streets*

The 15th August 1997 is the fiftieth anniversary of Indian independence, and India is feted as the world's largest democracy. In his book *The Idea of India* (1997), Sunil Khilnani argues that the fact that democracy has survived in India is in itself a cause for celebration – even though he admits it has made little difference to the suffering masses. After fifty years of independence India continues to struggle to remain intact: there are numerous freedom fighters wanting statehood or independence, and the problem of Kashmir remains unsolved. On the subject of democracy Khilnani remarks that "Few states created after the end of European Empire have been able to maintain democratic routines" and adds that "India's own past... prepared it very poorly for democracy". Khilnani's analysis continues with a description of contemporary India:

> Huge, improvised, crowded with cultural and religious distinctions, with a hierarchical social order almost deliberately designed to resist the idea of political equality, India had little prospective reason to expect it could operate a democracy. Yet fifty years later India continues to have parliaments and courts of law, political parties and a free press, and elections for which hundreds of millions of voters turn out, as a result of which governments fall and are formed.

Khilnani, S (1997), *The Idea of India*, Hamish Hamilton, London

Khilnani appears to be enamoured of the idea of democracy as much as of the idea of India. He admits that Indian democracy has had marginal impact on Indian poverty, which was at the heart of the Indian independence movement, and the reason for getting rid of the British in 1947. As usual, I prefer the creative writer to the social scientist. I can understand far better the India of Rushdie's *Midnight's Children* than the country Khilnani defends in his "idea of India". I can only guess that Khilnani has never himself experienced poverty, for only such a person would defend a system that delivers the vote but leaves the vast majority of the people in extreme poverty.

In Port-of-Spain in 1995, I attended the 150th anniversary celebration of the arrival of indentured workers from India, to replace the free African slaves in the cane fields of Trinidad. I heard the president of India give an address extolling Indian achievements in industry and technology. He was celebrating aspects of India often ignored in favour of the "Oxfam image" of poverty and the begging bowl. In August 1997, at our home in Dorset, I listened on the radio, and watched on the TV, programmes about India's Fiftieth Independence Anniversary celebrations. In their speeches the president and prime minister both lamented the fact that India was still such a long way from realising the dreams of Gandhi and Nehru.

I watched and listened, and I recall the views of the ex-soldier in Kashmir who said that the end of the British Raj was the worst thing that ever happened to India. The president was right to celebrate the country's achievements in Trinidad, and to boast of that country's advances in science and technology, just as in 1997 the president and prime minister of India were right to express regret for their country's failings and backwardness. India is indeed a technologically advanced society with a nuclear capability. The lifestyle of the Bangalore computer-class is closer to California than to the slums of Calcutta. But *all* India is a country where the vast majority of the population lives in abject poverty, and where the twin evils of the caste system and all kinds of corruption exert a powerful hold. Is this the price to be paid for democracy?

This seems a good time as any to turn from the world's largest democracy to the world's largest dictatorship. Or as I would rather have it, let us turn away from the seductions of the Indian lotus to the harsher world of the Chinese dragon. But before we do that I want to take time off to visit a country that lies at the foot of the Himalayan mountains, between India and China – i.e. the kingdom of Bhutan.

Journey to Bhutan

When it came to organising our transport to Bhutan, Peter and I had agreed long before leaving the UK that we would travel to Thimpu by bus. From that time, months ahead of our arrival in Bhutan, I had been really looking forward to that bus journey. I had imagined leaving the hustle and bustle of Calcutta, with its dirty crowded streets, as we headed for the hills of Bhutan. We would pass through the lush Bengali countryside, with sugar cane and mango trees, to the tea fields of Assam, then climb into the cool hills as we approached the border between India and Bhutan. Unfortunately fate decided otherwise, and I had to wait months before I could experience the reverse journey by bus back to Calcutta, from Thimpu, Bhutan. We were forced to change our plans because our Australian companion, as well as being traumatised by the horror of Calcutta, had also been frightened off the bus ride with tales of steep, narrow, treacherous mountain roads, careless drivers and bad accidents. My friend made it clear that she was not prepared to risk her Australian life in an Indian bus, and she would come with us only if we went by plane.

Getting the tickets was an adventure in itself. There were very few direct flights to Thimpu, and these were usually booked well in advance. One of Peter's friends from our Calcutta days was now a semi-retired travel agent. He made all the arrangements and somehow managed to get all three of us booked on the next direct flight. The cost was only a few million times more than the bus fare – but we tried not to think about that. We were the first to arrive at the airport – just in case, and felt happy only when we had our boarding cards safely in our possession. As I sat with the other two, surveying the almost empty waiting area, I heard an English woman instructing the baggage handler on how not to handle her cameras and other photographic gear. I looked across and saw a small white woman, quite agitated, directing the airport staff as though on a film set.

This was my first sighting of the journalist. I heard her refer to her occupation a number of times, in an obvious effort to intimidate staff members into treating her and her equipment with the required deference. This was despite the fact, as she reluctantly admitted, that she was not actually on a working visit, but simply taking a well-earned break in Bhutan. The drama played itself out, the equipment was safely packed, a boarding pass issued, and the little lady waited with us ordinary mortals for the departure process to begin.

The flight was uneventful, and I suppose I ought to say that the view as we approached Thimpu was worth the thousands of rupees we had paid to fly. But at the time I did not really think so. Entry into Bhutan is strictly controlled, but on that day it seemed there were quite a lot of visitors, and the incoming procedure seemed to take ages. After the heat of Calcutta, Bhutan seemed very cold, and that seemed to bite into my bones. We were going to be guests at India House and the embassy driver had come to meet us at the airport. We were escorted to a waiting jeep, where we found, yes – right first time – the journalist. We were fated to become better acquainted, as we were all to be guests at India House.

The journalist had a very interesting approach to people who were not her social equals, based on a combination of deference and bullying. Although she was small in stature her presence seemed to fill any room, however large. Such details were still unknown as we made our way from the airport to Thimpu, but on an exchange of names I recognised her name as that of someone our hostess had asked me to contact many months before we left for India. I now understood why my efforts had drawn a blank, as my calls had competed with world events. I had already seen her in action in the airport lounge, so I knew we were in for an interesting time.

Over the next few days she and I became great buddies, especially after we found some people we knew in common. It turned out that she'd once been engaged to a certain other famous journalist, who had been married previously to a person I'd worked with in the past. The circle closed neatly around us, as I became, however briefly, a person worthy of inclusion in it. I liked it. I was amused. The journalist and I were about the same age, but in contrast to my jeans or casual gear she wore very short skirts, make-up and the usual paraphernalia of European womanhood. Her current concern was her profile, as she had apparently been involved in an accident. Although there was no evidence of this, she was convinced that, especially as seen through the TV camera, her face would be less than perfect. Every day we went through the same charade, examining her profile to see if it had improved, and every day I swore that it had, slightly, hoping to bring this particular performance to a permanent end (a strategy that didn't work). I did like it when we compared our hysterectomy stitches, and mine were almost invisible, while hers covered the best part of her stomach. The poor thing! No more bikinis for her! Such stupid vanity brought out a bitchy streak in me, which I did not know I possessed.

There were several things that made the journalist memorable. The list included her open hostility towards the Australian, her meanness, her obsessive pursuit of an interview with the king of Bhutan, her interview with a young Bhutanese monk, and her love of dogs and children – on which and whom she lavished her kisses equally. She made no attempt to hide her dislike of the Australian, while at the same time I was her flavour of the month. The former was a non-person, the journalist either ignoring her (which was most of the time), or if not doing that then talking down to her. I have to say that the Australian was extremely patient and tolerant of all this.

The journalist was also totally against spending any money except on herself, and even managed to get out of the dinner we had all planned for our host and hostess, saying that she had a headache. The rest of us suspected that her absence had more to do with the purse than the head – as we had planned to split the cost between us. Worse than that, especially given her love of children, was the time she and I went to view the craftwork of local school children, which was on sale to raise money for the school. The journalist minutely examined every single piece, asked interminable questions, then shook her head and put everything back. She did not buy a single item. I squirmed in shame at being in her company and left as quickly as I could, also without buying anything. I'd decided to return to the school on my own at a later date, but I never did.

The first few weeks of our stay in Bhutan were dominated by the journalist's "quest". This was for an interview with the king of Bhutan. The king was married to four sisters, and the journalist, although technically on holiday, had promised her London paper to get an interview with His Majesty. She seemed to be the only person who thought this possible, for discreet inquiries soon revealed that His Majesty was not interested in supplying work for a journalist holidaying in his country. Nothing daunted, our intrepid reporter persisted, seeking help and support from all quarters. Even my views were solicited, and I agreed to say, should I be asked, that her newspaper was a very respectable rag, and that the weekly column in which she proposed to feature him was extremely innocuous.

I waited to be asked to testify before the king himself, but no such invitation was forthcoming. I was planning to employ my presentation skills, in explaining to him that a quality English newspaper would never feature him in lurid headlines such as KING BONKS FOUR SISTERS, but in something more tasteful, such as A NIGHT IN THE LIFE OF

THE KING WITH FOUR WIVES. I never got the chance. Just as I had completed my preparation and knew my lines to perfection, the journalist reluctantly accepted that there was not going to be any interview with the king. At that I was relieved, and we all gave thanks.

The journalist did in fact manage to interview a Bhutanese man on camera, but unfortunately for her not the king but a young monk. She was of course an expert on Bhutan and its neighbours, and I had already been presented with an autographed copy of her book on the region. It was a book I am told people had died for, when apparently, after its publication, many were killed or disappeared. But to hear her talk about it one would believe that nothing but good had come of it.

On the memorable occasion of her Bhutan interview, we had gone for a day in the hills, where we planned to have a picnic lunch, then to walk to the nearby monastery. There were just the four of us, Peter and I, the journalist and the Australian. After lunch we set off for the monastery, where we were well received. As we made our by now familiar tour, it was the journalist who asked all the intelligent questions, laced with sympathetic observations on the state of Buddhist learning and treasures.

Once during one of these tours, when we were shown a painting of Hanuman the monkey god sitting on Ganesh's back (the elephant god), masturbating, I took over from the monk who was our guide, commentating with, "This is a monkey having a good time!" The rich diet of religion and mysticism had got to me. My capacity for solemnity is strictly limited, and this spontaneous outburst was an indication that I had reached that limit. Luckily, the monk did not quite get the full import of my observations, but I think he suspected that something irreverent had been said.

As we left the monastery a number of the younger monks continued talking to us and came with us to the gate. Filming inside the monastery was not allowed, but in the courtyards and outside Peter's camcorder began to roll. I took over just in time to record an interview between the journalist and one of the young monks. Mindful of my awesome responsibility I tried very hard to avoid filming her in profile – or was it the other way round? She had obviously decided that in the absence of the king this poor monk would have to do, and she went after him with vigour. She chose to question him about his choice of career, and plied him with an equal mixture of flattery and pressure, wheedling answers out of him. It was a master-class in journalism, and I will always treasure this video, together with my copy of her book. This is tangible evidence that in the remote Himalayan kingdom of Bhutan, the journalist and I were, however briefly, part of the international sisterhood. Memories I will always treasure.

And now we can return to the question of democracy and dictatorship, as we depart from India, the world's largest democracy, and make our way to China, the world's largest dictatorship.

So what about the dragon?

The remainder of this chapter is based on the 1992–93 round-the-world trip that I made with Peter, and more or less follows our itinerary.

During my student days in Calcutta, I became aware of and very fascinated with China. At college there was another person who shared a similar interest and we often discussed and compared Chinese with Indian society. We were really taken in by China and use to speculate about what would happen in India "when the revolution comes!" We were sure that it was simply a matter of time. The college librarian, Mother Joseph Loreto, was also a China-watcher, and the way she saw it the present, or twentieth century belonged to the Americans, but the twenty-first would be dominated by the Chinese. In the mid-1960s the news coming out of China told us that their model was working, and in India we could see that the Indian approach certainly wasn't. There were no beggars in Beniji, whereas in India begging was more or less an industry in its own right. The US government hails India as the world's largest democracy, and vilifies China as a communist dictatorship. And was it not worth mentioning that the majority of Chinese were almost certainly better off than the majority of Indians? When comparisons are made, they can be most illuminating.

On 8th September 1993 I read an article by Nicholas Kristof of *The New York Times*, comparing the quality of life in India and China. The article appeared in the *Star-Bulletin* newspaper under the headline: "Oppressed Chinese never had it so good". Kristof wrote that, "With China's economy being the fastest growing in the world, moral judgements about the Communist Party's role become more complex." Another way of saying that it was difficult to criticise success. The writer went on to document the ills of the Chinese system, including corruption and state control in every detail of peasants' lives. The report was accompanied by a diagram, prepared by Kevin Hand of the *Star-Bulletin*, which compared the quality of life in China with that in India. If it were a boxing match, Indian democracy would have lost to Chinese dictatorship in the first round. The dragon would have beaten the lotus silly.

In the years since the 1960s the truth about the Chinese approach has come out, and we know that Mao liked jazz, Western movies, and that he had built up a personality cult. The worst excesses of the Cultural Revolution have also been documented in books, and in numerous radio and television programmes. After what happened in Grenada, nothing surprises me, so I can listen with interested detachment as the truth about Mao's China continues to unfold.

It is interesting to compare the Chinese attitude to birth control with the methods used in India. When Indira Ghandi and her son Sanjay developed a strategy to curb the growth of India's expanding population, they were accused of initiating a policy of forced sterilisation. Mrs Ghandi's family planing policy failed and its introduction also damaged her political reputation. India's population continues to grow.

The Chinese simply made a law prohibiting people from having more than one child, and imposing penalties on those who broke it. In this connection it is instructive to note that both China and India have the problem of female infanticide. Perhaps the dragon and lotus are not that far apart after all. Another twist in this debate has nothing to do with China or India – it seems in Spain they have achieved the one-child family without even trying! Spanish women have decided that "con uno basta!" – "one child is enough!" – and have proceeded to make that a reality. Perhaps the Chinese and Indians should study the Spanish situation and see what, if anything, they can learn about population control, and this from a Roman Catholic country with the lowest birth rate in Europe.

As I mentioned earlier, I have had a long-standing interest in Chinese politics and society. More recently I became interested in China from the perspective of a black woman traveller and as a researcher, with a professional interest in women and children. A friend and colleague in Hong Honk tried to dissuade me from visiting China: I was told that it would be an awful experience, and that I would come in for some very unpleasant attention, as the Chinese were not used to black people. Well, that would not be new to me, for my three years in Calcutta had prepared me for anything the Chinese could offer. Faced with the prospect of a visit there, I remembered my first contact with a Chinese person, a girl in my history class at Loreto College. Like all converts, she was fervently religious, and one day, when I made a remark that she regarded as anti-religious, she told me that being a sub-human I needed religion, as that was the only way I could become fully human. I just laughed and told her I was quite happy as a sub-human. Ever afterwards, when in her presence I would always refer to myself as that, I would preface replies to questions or comments with, "being a mere sub-human I think that... ". I made capital out of it, and I know that she came to regret her use of that term to describe me.

So I had a good idea of the Chinese view of African people, and since that time I have heard reports on the radio and read stories in the press about African students in China having a hard time due to their colour. My understanding of the Chinese view of humanity is that they are the only really civilised people, while black people are the least civilised of all. I think I was quite well prepared for my visit to the People's Republic of China.

In fact I experienced China as a very welcoming place, and I much preferred it to the frenzy of Hong Kong. Within hours of arriving on the mainland from Hong Kong I was being photographed with a smiling young man who came up to us in the restaurant and asked me for a picture in the way young men usually ask for a dance! Was I a star or something? I wondered, as we stood smiling together. This marked the start of a good experience of China, for we made friends, and I was invited into Chinese homes, despite being told that this never happened (my English colleague, after two years in Hong Kong, had never had such an invitation). I was photographed too with other friends, as this seemed to be the fashion. I think I got a glimpse of the "real China", and with that there were some funny moments, and also some scary moments, which was all part of the totality of the experience.

We travelled by bus, we walked about freely, we were robbed, and we had contact with the police, twice. We visited museums – we did the usual tourist things and a bit more. (For more details of the police and other contacts, see the letter to the Chinese sister in Chapter Two.) From my visit to the South China province of Guandoung, I took away two main images. There was a lot of building in progress – bridges, airports, apartment blocks – indeed the whole place seemed to be a building site – but perhaps more striking than that was the precious one child. Everywhere there were families consisting mainly of adults, and just the one child. I watched a TV programme that warned that the one-child policy was turning China into a nation of spoilt children, parents over-indulging their offspring. The fear was that these would grow up unfit for adult life. Interesting.

We spent three weeks in Hong Kong and one in China. I would have much preferred the longer time in the latter, where we went walking, travelled by bus, found ourselves robbed, went to the police, and got laughed at. My knowledge and experience of India are quite extensive, and I feel I know that country well, both through my studies and direct experience, while I can't quite say the same of my contact with China. Even so, on the whole I think I know which of these two countries I would prefer to live in. The most important thing for me was that I did not come across a single destitute person in China, no families sleeping on the pavements, no mutilated children, begging.

Buddhism, Mabo myths and Maori rights: travels in Asia

Our round-the-world journey included visits to Bhutan and Thailand – two Buddhist countries, where the lifestyle and cultures could not be more different. We spent two months in Bhutan and about three weeks in Thailand. I have written elsewhere about Bhutan and I don't propose to elaborate on that. About Thailand there is not much to say, except that it seemed a very schizophrenic society, supposedly adhering to Buddhist values and the eight-fold path, though one would look in vain for indications of any real adherence to that discipline. In 1993 a Buddhist monk was on trial for declaring that Thailand had lost its way and could no longer be described as a Buddhist country. His offence was to say what seemed patently obvious to anyone with eyes.

Thailand was now one of the Asian tiger economies, and having gained that status something had to go. How long will it last? Perhaps it's a fair exchange, perhaps not, but why try to deny that an exchange has taken place? The only Thai person I met was the young woman in the hotel in Bangkok who gave me a massage. I told her how my friends had joked and warned me against Bangkok massage parlours. Her English was quite good and this led us on to a discussion about prostitution etc. in her country. She said that many young women from the countryside ended up in prostitution because they had no choice, though she had been one of the lucky ones. She told me that rural poverty was "terrible", and young women were forced to come to the towns to survive. I knew that as well as young women, young children, of both sexes, were also part of Thailand's sex tourism industry. The benefits of the tiger economy did not yet extend to protecting Thailand's children from sexual exploitation.

On to Australia, and the question, are we in Europe, Asia, or the

USA? Has Australia an identity crisis? The Aborigine "problem" dominates the news, and the way the story is told it seems that in order to compensate them, all of white Australia will be disenfranchised. I soon learned that the racist hysteria that has gripped white Australia was the result of the decision made by the Australian High Court, now referred to as the Mabo decision – or in the Australian way simply as "Mabo". Eddie Mabo was a Torres Straight islander, living on the Dauar island, who in 1982 launched a legal battle challenging the concept of "terra nullius", asserting that as an original Australian ancestral rights to land were vested in him and could be passed to his children. In May 1992, the Australian High Court found in his favour, though by then Eddie Mabo was dead.

Mabo the man may be dead, but Mabo the myth was born. I had not expected such virulent and open racism in Australia. This forced me to recall an experience I had at Surrey University, which should have prepared me, at least in part. At the time I was the course leader of the social work diploma/MSc, and one day a man came into the department asking about part-time teaching. He was an out-of-work academic, who had virtually fled Australia, and had returned home to unemployment in England. His said that his main reason for leaving Australia was that he: "could not stand being part of the racism and hostility towards the Aboriginals". He had not expected the place to be so racist, and he had found himself unable to cope with the pressures this put him under. So he left and brought his family back to England. At the time I found all this very curious, to say the least, for how could a white man be forced out of his job by racism when that was not being directed at him? Was Australia another South Africa, or was there more to this story? At the time I was very puzzled, but now that I have visited Australia I can understand the man's situation much better. There was certainly a very unsubtle racism in Australia, with newspaper reports and discussions on Aboriginal issues often lacking in sensitivity and compassion, and in very offensive terms.

I am not suggesting that the white Australian is completely racist and totally hostile towards the indigenous and non-white people, but there is little doubt in my mind that there is a strong and pervasive strand of racism in Australian society. Myths have grown up around the Mabo decision that give legitimacy and a voice to the hatred and fear of Aboriginals.

Very few people would disagree with the statement that racial discrimination is an insidious cancer which eats away at the fabric of society... because of Australia's colonial history, our inadequate education systems, and insensitive media reporting Australians are tinged at least with racist attitudes themselves.

ACT Teacher (1993), *Rebutting Mabo Myths*, Canberra, Australia

The *ACT Teacher* is the trade union magazine of teachers in the Australian Commonwealth Territory (ACT), and the writer of the above article enjoins readers in these terms: "As unionists and educators, believers in egalitarian society, we must take a stance against racial discrimination." It is a call to arms, and the magazine responds to its own injunction by devoting most of the issue to "Rebutting Mabo Myths". In December 1993 the then prime minister of Australia, Paul Keating, described the decision of the Australia High Court recognition of native titles, commonly referred to as the "Mabo decision", in these words:

Mabo is an historic decision – we can make it an historic turning point, the basis of a new relationship between indigenous and non-Aboriginal Australians.

Of all the places I have been in my travels, and in all the public toilets I have used, I had never encountered racist graffiti until I went to Australia. It was so crude and offensive that I was almost put off the task in hand. When an Australian acquaintance asked me what I thought of the country, I replied that I was "still processing data". I was not really prepared to say. I was not yet ready to admit how deeply and negatively I'd been affected by what she thought of as her "wonderful country".

Just like the USA, Australia was constantly described to me as "wonderful", as "God's own country", and such like. However, I found that in order really to enjoy being in Australia, one must be willing to ignore both its history and the contemporary situation of its original inhabitants. It was the view in some places that the Labour government wanted to reach a settlement on native titles as a basis for greater integration of Australia in the Asian Pacific region. Yet, even as the government was taking such a bashing for "giving away the country to the blacks", and allowing increasing Asian immigration, Paul Keating (the then prime minister) was known to be culturally committed to Europe and not to Asia. Australia had developed its economy to exploit its geographical location as part of Asia, but culturally most white Australians, including Keating, regarded themselves as European, while at the same time looked and acted very much like Americans.

Since 1992 things have moved on in Australia as elsewhere: there is now a One Nation party, led by a woman, Mrs Pauline Hanson. It campaigns on an openly racist platform, calling for, among other things, a return to the white Australian immigration policy, and a reversal of policies that her party regards as "favouring" Aboriginal Australians. There is currently (I am writing in the summer 1998) a general election taking place, and it is speculated that Mrs Hanson's party may well emerge from it with the balance of power, between the Conservative and Labour parties. In spite of Mabo myths, the situation of the original Australians seems set to worsen, or at least remain unchanged. Just as, in spite of a royal commission inquiry report into Aboriginal deaths in police custody, these fatalities still continue. In 1997 the commission of inquiry into the stolen Aboriginal children, called "Bringing them Home", was published.

Under the assimilation policy of previous Australian governments, lighter-skinned Aboriginal children were removed from their own families and placed with white Australians. The report condemned the practice as equivalent to genocide, and called for an apology and a day of mourning. In August 1997 the Australian High Court refused leave for people affected by the assimilation policy to take legal action in their bid for compensation. The court ruled that since the policy was part of the law at the time there could be no grounds for action. The Australian Aboriginals have been dispossessed of both their land and their children, and in the five years since the Mabo decision there have been no major changes in this situation. The issue of dispossession and reparation/compensation are among those I hope to return to in the final chapter of this book.

I would now like to change gear, and topic. I did not spend all my time in Australia reading the newspapers and thinking about social problems. From our base in Canberra we explored New South Wales. We also went north to Cairns and across to Darwin on a ten-day coach trip, advertised for the eighteen to thirty-five age group. We hired a car and drove to the Northern Territories, and saw there cave paintings that looked very much like the ones I saw in Zimbabwe. Or perhaps I am a bit of a Philistine. In the Northern Territories it was good to see Aboriginal people living like the rest of us, not dead drunk as in the cities. In one of the small towns we stopped at, Peter and I were turned away from a bar, as we had not seen the Aboriginals Only notice. That night around the camp fire there were complaints and muttering, as it seemed that others had also been turned away from the bar, and did not like it.

After three months in Australia it was time to move on to New Zealand. I promise not to say a word about sheep. So far as "liking a country" I suppose I liked Australia less than I liked New Zealand. For starters, New Zealand is very much smaller, and for me small really is beautiful. There was also less overt racism or tensions around the Maori issue, and I personally did not come across any Maori lying about dead drunk and stinking of urine, a fairly common, and for me very distressing occurrence in Australia.

In New Zealand I visited a women's refuge, and could have been in Chiswick – even the building was of the same architectural style. I half-expected to see Erin Pizzey's bulk appear any moment. A young mother, a big woman with a very small baby only a few weeks old, was assigned to show me around and tell me about the work of the refuge. She did a good job, and inevitably I learned of her own experience of violence, which seemed to have so much in common with women's stories across the world. Our conversation took an interesting turn when my guide asked me why I was so concerned with domestic violence. Had I been a victim? I explained that in the early 1970s I had worked with Erin Pizzey, the founder of the first women's refuge, and had been interested ever since. My questioner still wanted a direct answer to the question about my own personal experience of marital violence. My reply was negative, and I added a rider, to the effect that if any man dared to hit me I would be the last person he would ever do that to. She smiled at me indulgently, as though she'd heard that kind of fighting talk lots of times. She was not to know, but the difference was that this time she was hearing it from a woman who really meant what she was saying.

In New Zealand, through a series of mishaps, I met and became friendly with a mother and daughter who ran a hotel on the South Island. What happened was this. I had become increasingly paranoid about being robbed, and losing my bag with my passport and everything of value in it. We arrived at the hotel and unpacked, and when I looked for my bag it was nowhere to be found, so I panicked. I got into a right state. I was sure that I had left it at the museum about 250 kilometres away. Off I went to see the hotel manager to explain my plight. She calmed me down with cups of tea, then rang the museum and spoke to the lost property people, who took the matter in hand. Peter, who had been out walking, arrived back on the scene, heard the story and went off to search the apartment. Bag found (it had fallen behind the sofa). Very relieved and feeling very foolish, I became my usual charming self, and I invited the manager and her daughter, who had also joined in the fun, to tea the following afternoon.

They came, and Peter went off on another walk, so there were just the three of us women. It was quite an out-of-the way spot, and at some point I must have expressed surprise at finding two such enterprising women in this kind of a place. The story was that the mother and daughter had been separated for some years, and had only recently been reconciled. From them I learnt that New Zealand also has its religious cults, whose practices included the sexual abuse of child members. The daughter had left one such cult some years before, but the mother could not accept her reasons for leaving and refused to join her. As a result they had not been in touch for many years, until recently. This came about through a court action taken on behalf of abused ex-members, which exposed the working of the cult to public gaze. The evidence was so conclusive that she could no longer remain in the cult, and realised she had been completely fooled by its leader. She told me that it was impossible to explain to anyone who had not experienced it the hold that membership of a such group has. "You stop thinking for yourself." It all sounded very much like the Plymouth Brethren to me.

I don't know if it was to do with this case, but an Oprah Winfrey show was screened on this subject, and also a TV film about the sexual abuse of boys by Catholic priests in Canada. Child sex abuse was very topical in New Zealand at this time. One could not turn on the radio or watch TV without some reference to it. There was a radio phone-in programme, where a woman caller gave a very articulate and derisory assessment of counselling. She seemed to blame all child abuse and especially sexual abuse on counsellors, not for themselves abusing children, but for going on about it all the time. I sense that she had a point, but I also felt that her point was lost in the venom of her attack on those trying to help, however misguided, rather than on the perpetrators. There have been times when I myself have felt the urge to attack the tyranny of counselling, times when it seemed that you had only to stump your big toe to be offered counselling. But my feelings are in a different league from that radio caller. I know that counselling has its place, but I also know that too much is claimed on its behalf.

Also on radio and TV was the continuing debate over the settlement of the outstanding claims and compensation for the Maori over the theft of their land. I mentioned elsewhere that I somehow thought these problems had been mainly resolved. It seemed that a complete settlement had still to be agreed, and in the meantime the dynamic of racial politics in New Zealand appeared to have changed. The tensions had shifted away from Maori concerns to the perceived threat from the newcomers – Indian, Chinese and other Asian immigrants. It was now the turn of the Maori to show that racism was not the exclusive domain of white people.

From New Zealand on to Hawaii. There I learnt about the theft of the Hawaiian islands by the USA, and how it would now be almost impossible to right that wrong. We went to a concert in celebration of the birthday of the last Hawaiian queen. We walked a lot, rode bicycles, and swam. At the B&B we met a couple from Europe, two academics. Naturally we got talking, and later the woman of the couple shared a drink with me, when we talked about the four of us spending an evening together. However, we had a limited time, and we already had plans for the next day, which was our wedding anniversary. The mention of it caused her to speculate about her own marriage, and to say rather sadly and pensively: "I wonder whether we will have another one?"

I asked no questions, made no comment, but she did want to talk, and talk she did. She was a battered wife, and this trip to Hawaii was an attempt to give their marriage one last chance. But she did not have any great hopes, and no longer believed that her husband would ever change. He might be better for a few weeks, or even a few months, but sooner or later he would return to his old ways and the beatings would start again. She said that she was quite sure that on their return to Europe she would leave him. It seemed to me that she had made the decision to do that some time before, and that the holiday was just a gesture. For lack of anything else to say I went on about how very civilised, cultured, educated and charming her husband seemed. She agreed that most of the time her husband was all those things, but there were times also when he became like a devil, and then she feared for her life. At this point the "devil" joined us, and that was the end of the conversation.

I do not go around the world looking for stories about child abuse and domestic violence. In fact on that occasion I went around the world partly to search out new areas of interest, and to get away from familiar territory. I was not to know that escape would be impossible. When I think of my meeting with that couple in Hawaii, I know that I would much rather have kept my picture of the young husband as "civilised, cultured, well educated, charming". I would not have minded not knowing that he could sometimes become like the "devil".

The lotus or the dragon?

My return to Calcutta had been less traumatic than I had anticipated, and I returned to friends and places I knew and was familiar with. Apart from being robbed, it had been a surprisingly pleasant experience. When I left in 1965 I had no intentions of ever returning to India, and it took me all of thirty years to change my mind. By then, I found that I could take India more or less in my stride. The shock of the new was no longer there, though Calcutta was in many ways a much worse place in 1993 than it had been in 1962. The city was more dilapidated, more crowded, and very much filthier, yet it seemed to me a less hostile, more familiar and a more humane place. I preferred it to Bangkok or Hong Kong. I loved Bhutan most of all, in spite of or maybe because of the obvious contradictions and tensions in that society.

But although I am attracted by the philosophy of the lotus, I find the approach of the dragon more practical, with more achievable goals and objectives. So if I had to make the choice between the two it would have to be the Chinese dragon. But as it is I am an African-Caribbean person and that will do me in this life.

8

DREAM OR NIGHTMARE?
CANADA AND THE USA

ACCORDING TO my librarian friend, Mother Joseph Loreto, of Loreto Convent, the twentieth century belonged to the USA, and the twenty-first will belong to the Chinese. She was certainly right about the former. She made these comments long before the collapse of the Soviet Union and the emergence of the USA as the undisputed great power of the world. Just as it was impossible to escape from the horrors of child abuse and domestic violence – wherever in the world one may be – so it was with the image and influence of the USA. Wherever one is in the world there will always be something American, be it Coca-Cola, Michael Jackson, Oprah Winfrey, CNN, or Walt Disney. The unfortunate fact was that unlike yours truly, most people can't get enough of the USA. It seems that everywhere in the world people can't wait to tuck into their Big Macs and Coke and to live out their version of the American dream. I prefer to boast that Barbados is the one place in the world where the McDonald's food chain was forced to close down and move on. Bajans may be just as America-crazy as the next person, but they do like to eat real food.

The American presence is so all-pervasive that it has really been a challenge to write about other countries without reference to it. In this section I want to home in on one or two specifically North American issues, then move on to relate some stories about my travels and experiences in Canada and the USA.

At one time I was quite keen live in Canada. I knew many people who had emigrated there, and it sounded a good place to live. My impression was that Canada had many of the advantages of the USA, minus many of the problems. But Peter was not interested: Canada was "too cold", and that was the end of that! It was many years before I would visit. Elsewhere (Chapter Four) I have given an account of that journey across the Atlantic with my son. This was in 1983, when the two of us (my son and I) spent the summer in Canada, in a combination of study tour and holiday.

My work took me first to Calgary and later to Toronto, and we travelled by train between these two. This was my first really long railway journey and I really enjoyed it, as did my son. When we reached Toronto we reluctantly got off the train. In 1993 I returned to Canada, this time with Peter, on the last leg of our round-the-world trip. We landed at Vancouver, spent some time being tourists, then drove to Calgary. We'd planned to drive across the country in stages, but due my son's illness this plan was abandoned and we got as far only as Calgary, before flying back to London. As I said, my first visit to Canada was, in the main, a working visit. I had just completed a piece of research on young offenders, and I was there to look at the Canadian juvenile justice system: through a legal system that was in the process of changing its approach to young offenders, from welfare- to justice-based. Those who opposed such changes might prefer to describe the change as moving from treatment to punishment, though it had to be said that in Canada as in the UK, the welfare approach had failed to protect the civil rights of juveniles, and had also failed to reduce juvenile crime.

In Canada and in Britain, social workers and probation officers used the term "welfare" to impose quite harsh punishment on young people. Under such provisions they could be "treated" rather than punished, and this meant that the accused person could undergo this without having had access to the due process of law. Thus a child or young person who was innocent of any crime could be deprived of his or her liberty and placed in the so-called "care-system" – often just another name for prison.

Ironically, that has resulted in a welfare system that could at times be more punitive than the criminal justice system: there was either a presumption of guilt or of the need for "treatment". Either way the young person was trapped. Added to that, the welfare system did not have the safeguards that are built into the criminal justice system, with most notably the absence of a right of appeal against decisions made on the basis of welfare.

My career in social work started in 1967 as a residential social worker in a senior girls' approved school, in Surrey. Ever since then I have maintained a professional and academic interest in juvenile justice.

My visit to Canada in 1983 confirmed my own growing scepticism about the role of welfare, so I personally welcomed the changes being initiated there, though soon found out that the Canadian social-work profession did not. Professional self-interest dictated that they opposed change that would result in a diminution of their role and status. On the face of it self-interest didn't come into it, as the "best interests of the child" sounded much better. This is why social workers will always have a reputation as "do-gooders", when in fact they are motivated by the same self-interest as any other professional group. In relation to young offenders, social workers have often used the language of welfare to impose punitive measures, under the label of "treatment". That is another example of words meaning what one wants them to, and this is why, in the matter of criminal justice, I will always opt for the due process of the law, rather than the "treatment" or welfare approach.

During that visit I also took the opportunity of visiting a number of residential establishments for children and young people. Many of these were of native Canadian background, who were now a "minority" group in their own country. In England many similar establishments were filled with black youngsters, who were a more recent minority group. Another big issue dominating the Canadian media at that time was the report of the Bagagley commission, which had been established to inquire into child abuse. The report documented a high rate and the long-standing nature of it, particularly sexual abuse. It caused great consternation and much soul-searching, but eventually the federal government accepted most of its recommendations.

Ten years later (in 1993) while visiting New Zealand I saw a TV docu-drama about the sexual abuse of boys by a priest in a Catholic children's home in Canada. A few weeks later, when I was in Canada, I learnt that this film had not yet been shown there because of continuing legal action. It seemed that the problem of child sexual abuse in the Canadian Catholic church was not an isolated one, and that several of its priests had been sexually abusing boys in care homes in Canada over more than twenty years. The role of the church was exposed as one shielding and protecting paedophile clerics in much the same way as had been done in Australia and Ireland. The role of the Canadian child welfare board was shown to be as ineffectual as elsewhere in the world, and ditto the police. As I became aware of the extent of these scandals, I could not help but remember the hype that surrounded the Bagagley report ten years earlier. I was convinced that many of the people – welfare professionals, research workers, teachers and so on – who had taken part in the commission's work must have been aware, or at least suspicious of what was going on in those children's homes. I began to wonder whether the whole inquiry, like so much else in child welfare, had been little more than a public relations exercise.

In 1996 I was asked to review a book about child care in Canada for the *British Journal of Social Work* (*BJSW*). The book was by Professor Swift and was called *Manufacturing "Bad Mothers" – A Critical Perspective on Child Neglect*. With permission of the *BJSW* I produce the review in full. The book raised many issues for me and also illustrated what I saw as the continuing dilemma of the white feminist academic confronted by the "challenging" behaviour of her sisters from the lower social classes and the "ethnic minorities" (in the case of Canada this meant, "native Americans"). As a mother herself, Professor Swift would never act in the way the women in her study did, neither would she expect from them the same standards of motherhood she expects from herself and her social equals.

Of *Manufacturing "Bad Mothers" – A Critical Perspective on Child Neglect*, Karen J Swift, Toronto, University of Toronto Press, 1995:

> Swift's critical perspective leads to the conclusion that the state through its social work agents manufactures "bad mothers". She argues that this manufacture of bad mothers is the end result of a social work process, which identifies, classifies and labels certain types of maternal behaviour as "child neglect". This procedural, administrative and professional process ignores and disregards the significance of the social context which gives rise to "neglect". To underpin her argument the author presents a critical review of the history of child protection and the development of social work in Canada, and explains how and why the practice of social work has taken the shape it has. Swift argues that when dealing with neglect the social worker is responding to legal and administrative directives, and following set procedures which allow little space for the exercise of discretion. The author draws on her own research to provide examples of social work practise which convincingly illustrates this process.
>
> It is encouraging to find Swift paying equal attention to the social context of the "clients" and to the professionals and organisations, which "manufacture" and process them. She

regards the Canadian child welfare system as a failure, and links this to the failure of the social work profession – both in the preparation and training of social workers, and in day-to-day practice, to confront issues of gender, race, class and poverty i.e. the social context, in which child abuse and neglect occurs. Swift says: "After a century of failure, it is clear that the kind of resources typically deployed through child welfare systems must be questioned" (p. 193). This is a very serious indictment of social work practice and of the Canadian child welfare system, all the more so since it comes from within the system itself. We in Britain can take little comfort from the fact that Swift is, in the main reviewing and commenting on the Canadian child welfare system, for many of her observations apply with equal force to our circumstances.

There are problems with Swift's use of such terms as "manufacture" which suggest a deliberate, rational process. But this is contradicted by the fact that, as Swift herself notes, the very concept of "neglect" has emerged, not through any specific legal, administrative or professional activity, but through "discourse", i.e. talk. This *ad hoc* process continues and even now, such terms as "emotional harm" and "emotional injury" are beginning to emerge and to be accepted as legitimate areas of concern. And so the state extends its control and supervision of "bad mothers" although there is no general agreement on what constitutes "neglect", or the balance between the family's right to privacy and autonomy in child-rearing practices and the child's right to protection from abuse and neglect.

Women are the predominant characters in this book. The author presents a scenario peopled with different types of women, most of whom, including the author herself, are mothers. We have to assume that these are "good mothers", since they are white, middle-class, professional women. On one occasion the author/researcher gives us a glimpse of what it means to be a mother/researcher researching child neglect. Swift describes how she and her social worker colleague, "as mothers ourselves" feel for children who have been abandoned and wish that their mother would come back. It is therefore somewhat disappointing that the author did not explore the significance of this women's world of social workers, home-workers, "bad mothers" and female researchers in more depth. Society's response towards those who are classified as "bad mothers" – the provision of "help" and the exercise of "authority" over these women by a mainly female workforce – deserved attention or at least a mention, in a book of this kind.

After gender, comes race. Take it as given that in any welfare system minority groups suffer from not just the inadequacies inherent in the system itself, but the additional prejudice, discrimination and oppression which is targeted at the specific group. Swift's chapter on the experience of Native Americans of the Canadian child care system "The Colour of Neglect", almost exactly reflects the history of Australian Aboriginal children, and will strike a chord with those familiar with the experience of black children in care in Britain. Swift brings a very thorough approach to these complex and difficult problems, she does not avoid confronting the problems and shortcomings, which she knows, are an inherent part of the history of social work.

So what is the answer? Swift's proposals for transforming social work practice seem unlikely to impact on professionals whom she describes as "anti-intellectual". The critical perspective is both intellectually and emotionally demanding, and requires a level of competence and confidence which is not too evident in a profession more or less always under attack or scrutiny – much like the "bad" mothers that Swift is writing about.

The major shortcoming of this book is the author's failure to identify personal responsibility as a relevant issue in child rearing and child neglect. Swift appears to deal with this issue by asserting that neglect is not a personal problem, but "the visible appearance of underlying social relations".

Stone, M (1996), book review in *British Journal of Social Work*, June

In the course of writing this book I have looked again at Professor Swift's idea of the manufacture of bad mothers. I am now able to agree with the notion of the state manufacturing parents. These "bad parents" *are* manufactured, and are put to work in the homes and institutions that supposedly "care" for children and young people whose legal parents are in fact the state itself. The abuse of power and the abuse of children that occur in these institutions are legendary. This is true wherever these institutions exist, in all countries and societies, be they "First World", Third World", advanced or developing. With rare exceptions, they seem to encourage the abuse and oppression of children and young people. In March 1996, the USA and the People's Republic of China were locked in a slanging match about the fate of mentally handicapped children in their respective countries. This followed the screening of a TV film about the terrible conditions in children's homes in China. China hit back with massive amounts of data gleaned mainly from US government and other publications, which showed the unhappy truth about some of the US child care institutions.

The institutional abuse of children legally under state care has a long history, with state policies showing total disregard for the legal and civil rights of children and young people. Cases of physical and sexual abuse from around the world have been well documented, but I will highlight just a few examples. In the UK the scandal of sexual abuse in children's homes continues to unfold with sickening regularity. In Australia the policy of assimilation resulted in the forcible removal of light-skinned Aboriginal children from their parents. In theory the state was supposed to be rescuing children from their "bad parents", usually the mother. The state often replaced the bad mother with much worse parents, parents "manufactured" and employed by the state itself. Unfortunately for the child or young person, institutional care is very often the end of the line.

I am a mother, who has also worked as a residential social worker, and I have undertaken research with young people leaving care – Stone, M (1991). I know that in the UK the picture is not an unremittingly bleak one, but I also know that it is pretty dire, and I have no reason to believe that the UK system is any worse than similar systems elsewhere in the world. I have come to the conclusion that the state is generally not better, and is often much worse than the bad mother/parents it purports to rescue children from. I now think that on the whole most children and young people are best off taking their chances living in ordinary homes, taking more or less ordinary risks.

In spite of what I have just written, I accept that institutions do have their uses, limited though these may be. For example, some of the young people I interviewed during my study "Young People Leaving Care" actually preferred life in an institution to living with a foster family. For such young people there should be few small children's homes and/or residential institutions provided. Nevertheless, it should be accepted that as inmates they might be exposed to as great if not greater risks than had they stayed with their inadequate natural parents. I say this because my knowledge and experience tell me that there is no way in which these institutions can ever be made safe for the people they are meant to benefit. There are things that *could* be done to reduce the risks. The most important would be to make use of research findings and the revelations resulting from court cases world-wide, in order to develop an education and information pack for children and young people whose legal parent is the state.

I am very grateful to Professor Swift's idea of the bad mother being manufactured. We live in an imperfect world, where fathers and mothers are good or bad by reason of a complex web of personal, social, cultural and economic factors. When the state assumes the parent role, one expects that at the very least children will not be worse off. The truth is often quite the opposite: states the world over do indeed "manufacture bad parents", and systems that are often more brutal, more abusive, more intrusive and more inhumane than the "bad mothers" (it's usually the mother) from whom the unfortunate children have been "rescued".

Enough said. Let me return to Canada and try to give an account of some of my travels and experiences in that country.

A Canadian journey

The train journey from Calgary to Toronto lasted two nights and three days. During the afternoon of the first day my son made a friend, a boy of his own age, who was also travelling with his mother to Toronto. Mother and son had been on a visit out west, to Vancouver, and were on their way home. We were invited to join them for tea in Winnipeg. We accepted, and found ourselves in a very Victorian hotel, which could have been in Windsor, Berkshire. At first sight it appeared that we mothers would not be very well suited as friends, one white Canadian, the other an Afro-Caribbean woman, one deeply religious, a regular church-goer and active in church affairs, the other a complete non-believer. One an academic, the other a practical housewife, with no interest in academic matters at all. During much of the journey through the Canadian prairies we talked, argued, or sat together reading and laughing.

The prairies rolled by, and time also rolled by, and eventually we arrived in Toronto. I half-expected, half-wanted it to end there, but the boys had other ideas. They wanted to meet again and spend some time together. This was arranged. Thirteen years on, and the friendship between the two boys lasted for just that moment, while for the two women it was the start of a friendship that seems set to last. From time to time, over the years, there have been long periods of silence. Sometimes, during one of these, I have thought to myself, "Ah well, that's that." Then as if on cue I will receive a card, a letter, or a telephone call from my friend. In the summer of 1983, on a train travelling across Canada, our paths crossed, and we have been friends ever since.

In the USA I had an encounter of a very different kind on a train, with another white woman. I was travelling from New York to Boston. I had planned to fly but all planes had been cancelled due to snow. The woman who sat next to me told me that she never travelled by train, and that she was on Amtrack on this occasion only because the airports were closed. She started the conversation with a remark about how crowded the train was, and about train travel being a new experience for her. I would really have preferred to continue reading my book, newspaper or whatever it was I had with me, but decided to be polite. Somehow it emerged that I was visiting Boston for the first time, so she started to educate me about the city. She talked almost non-stop, the time passed quickly and we were soon at our destination. Then there was all the business of gathering our stuff together, putting on coats and so on, and we went out separate ways. Then just as I'd got off the train, and was looking around to try and identify the person who was meeting me, I saw my travelling companion coming towards me. I was about to say something like "nice meeting you, bye!" But something told me, some sixth sense, that this would not be appropriate. I remained silent as the lady looked through me and passed me by as if she'd never seen me before. So not all encounters with strangers on trains have happy endings.

Upstairs and downstairs – and in the basement loo

My next story shows a different, and some might say a more typical side of white Canadian women's attitudes towards their black sisters. These two experiences provided me with a more "rounded" experience of Canada. As I mentioned earlier, I spent the summer of 1983 looking at changes in the Canadian juvenile justice system. During the course of my studies I met with some of the judges who sat on the court benches, and I also sat in on several court sessions. One afternoon I arrived for a meeting with the judges, and, as I was early, I decided to use the toilets, just in case the meeting went on, and on, as they were always inclined to do. I asked the receptionist where the nearest toilet was. She replied, "In the basement." We were way up high, on the twenty-third floor, if not higher, so somewhat surprised I asked whether there wasn't one any closer. Back came the snap response: "I told you, the toilets are in the basement!"

From a distance of thirty years I recognised the "Belleville phenomenon", and the child who had refused to use the servant's entrance in Barbados had not given way to a woman who was prepared to use basement toilets in Canada. I would sit this one out, so I sat in the reception area, and waited. I did not have to wait very long. After a few minutes the secretary came out at the appointed time to receive me. To my question "where is the loo?" she pointed to a door straight ahead of me. I had been sitting right in front of it all the time. As I entered, who should I see but the receptionist, busily doing her face, her back to the entrance. I decided that if she was still there when I came out I would say something, and if not, not. She was still there, so I had to say something.

I began with a rather tentative, "Excuse me, may I ask you a question, please?" Before she could say anything I went on to ask her why she had directed me to the basement toilets when there were toilets nearby. She simply shrugged her shoulders and looked stupid. So I took the initiative. I told her that it was quite clear to me that she had a problem, and that although I would not be making a formal complaint against her, I would suggest that she get some help. I remarked that the next person might not be so tolerant. She did not argue with me or contest my reading of the situation, so I assumed that she accepted my analysis. This was confirmed when she apologised to me. I accepted that and we left the toilet together, not hand-in-hand, but at least we had not shouted at each other or scratched each other's eyes out!

The next day I related this incident to a black Canadian brother in great detail, including the apology. When I had finished telling my story his first question to me was, "Are you accusing her of racism, do you think that she was racist?" I had begun my story with this opening line: "I'd had

303

a very interesting experience yesterday." So, I had already described the incident as an "interesting experience", and I had not accused anyone of anything. In response to this brother's challenge, I could say only that I had no idea whether or not the receptionist was racist, and that I really couldn't care less. What I did object to was the way she had carried out her duties. My complaint was that she did not know how to be a good receptionist. I did not know if this incompetence related solely to black visitors or if she treated everyone with the same lack of consideration. My guess would be that her problem *was* race-related. Her reactions during our subsequent discussion also supported this conclusion. But it could be that she was just having a bad day, or that she did not like my briefcase, and sent anyone with a briefcase like mine to the basement toilets. Actually I was more annoyed by my friend's reactions than I had been by the original incident. I found my black brother's reaction more difficult to understand and to accept than the bad manners of the white sister receptionist. And at least the sister had apologised.

I had another very interesting experience in Canada, which this time challenged my own values and preconceptions. I met a woman who belonged to one of the original settler families in Western Canada. It was a chastening experience and it gave me a good insight into how prejudice and preconceptions work. I had only ever encountered settlers in history books, and in movies, so my perceptions were based entirely on my knowledge of their historical role and my current understanding of Canadian politics. One of Peter's uncles had migrated to and settled in Canada and died without ever returning to the UK. It was his wife, who was in her eighties when I met her in Calgary, who I later discovered was a direct descendant of one of the original settler families.

We spent an afternoon together at her home. She had an Alsatian dog, which was the first dog I'd seen in Calgary. I was so scared of it that it had to be locked outside in the garden. I was glad that it was still summer, because my hostess explained that the absence of dogs is due to the harshness of the Calgary winters. I mentioned how much I liked Canadian homes with their large basements, and through remarks like this I learnt about the origins of this building design. I even got to see a copy of a book written by one of my hostess's relatives, documenting the opening up of Western Canada by its early settlers. It had drawings and photographs of their first dwellings, and I could see that these had been quite literally holes in the ground. I learnt that in the winter they made very deep holes, more like bunkers, as shelter against the bitter cold.

In the summer they continued to live in these holes as they built their houses over the top. In this way the "holes" were converted into basements. From this lady I also learnt a lot more about the lifestyle of the early settlers, and found it an education in living history. I forgot all my prejudices and preconceptions about "settlers", as I listened, fascinated and enthralled by her stories. Seeing the human face of a historical event changes things. While acknowledging this I also have to accept that some things never change: the social and economic conditions resulting from wars and famines, the economic exploitation and racism that force people to become "settlers", immigrants, or refugees. This was as far as I dared go in my effort to reconcile my own feelings with both the historical facts and the social reality reflected in one woman's story.

In the meantime with NAFTA, Canada seems set to become even more of an economic satellite of the USA, while the French Canadians fight for their own state, with the native Canadians forever left out in the cold.

The American way: plantation values plus space age technology

In the Caribbean society in which I grew up, to emigrate to the USA was everyone's big dream, rather like today's Hong Kong residents seeking to escape Chinese rule. Britain came a poor second or third even to the USA and Canada. Wherever you go in the world today you can be sure to be exposed to American cultural domination. The American way seems to be all-pervasive, but in my view not uplifting. I have read in the newspapers that if General Colin Powell's Jamaican parents had emigrated to Britain instead of the USA, he would never have had the brilliant military career he has enjoyed. Much the same has been said about the golfer Tiger Woods, the first non-white American Masters champion.

My parents, or strictly speaking my mother, as she took the initiative in most things, did try to emigrate to the USA, but I am pleased to say did not succeed. In 1958, as a raw teenager with what would now be called "attitude", I decided that I wanted to study Caribbean history as my special subject for the "A"-level history course. This was because I wanted to know more about my own country and region. Mr Cameron Tudor, who was my history teacher, checked the syllabus and came back with a negative. The exam board did not offer a paper in Caribbean history. Could I try another exam board then? He had already checked on this, and it was the same with all the exam boards – the nearest I could get would be American history, from the war of independence to the civil war. There was one more thing – I would have to do the paper on my own, as there was no teacher at the Modern high school able to teach it. So it was that every Thursday afternoon saw me in the reference section of the Barbados public library, reading and note-taking. I enjoyed my first stab at independent study, and I also managed to pass the exam.

My interest in American history and society is of long standing. I read indiscriminately, so that I am familiar with the work of most major American writers. Richard White was my introduction to American literature. In spite of the Plymouth Brethren and their prohibition against music and the cinema, I did discover rock 'n' roll and American popular music during my adolescence. It was a much longer time before I found jazz. There is a lot in American literature, scholarship and music that I like and admire. I am not totally anti-USA. The roots of the society, based as it is in such terrible crimes as the theft and despoliation of the land, and slavery, leave me with a sense of unease and discomfort. I am never really comfortable in the USA. Even though Canada is so close, and the two countries are very alike in so many ways, I don't feel the same level of discomfort in Canada. Just as I did not wish to get used to the crippled children of Calcutta, so I do not wish to "get used to it" the American way. There are things that one should never get used to.

That is why I have never had any wish to share in the American dream. While many of the world's people beat a path to America's door in response to the (now very muted) call to "Give me your tired, your poor, your huddled masses yearning to breathe free… "; I am happy to be the exception, and know that this is a very minority point of view in Barbados and the Caribbean. A lot more common are the views expressed in an editorial inthe *Nation* newspaper (29th April 1997), under the title "Special bond with the US". The writer of this article denounced the "brainwashing" that had led Barbadians to prefer a British to American education, and welcomed the changes that had led to more Barbadians now undertaking their education in US universities. The article continued thus:

> We are in many respects more culturally identified with the United States than with the UK. Cricket and our parliamentary and judicial institutions apart, we do not currently identify with the English as much as we do with the Americans… in

music we are so culturally identified that American artists find a ready and enthusiastic audience within our island. We identify with American boxers, writers and inevitably with the black American experience.

The writer goes on to refer to an article in the London *Times*, in which a former editor of that paper explained that "the Tiger Woods phenomenon" could not have occurred in England because of reasons of class and colour. The article concludes with a recommendation to Barbadians that as the US president prepares to visit our Barbados, "we ought to recognise the ever-deepening special relationship between our two countries."

So now we know. The truth of the matter is that there is no special relationship or deep bond between little Barbados and the giant USA – except of the kind that Goliath had with David. At the Atlanta conference, which was held during the week this editorial appeared, a US government representative apologised for the overbearing and insensitive way the USA often dealt with small Caribbean states. As to the observation that Barbados is more culturally similar to the USA than to Britain, except for cricket, the parliamentary and the judicial system – didn't these three things practically determine a way of life? Wherever American pop stars go they receive an enthusiastic welcome. Does that mean that they are culturally similar to, say, Japan, India, Singapore? Popular music is global entertainment, part of global youth culture, which lives quite happily alongside local cultures. Instead of threatening each other, they actually feed off each other.

The *Nation* editorial was a simple currying of favour to ensure that local journalists were not pushed aside during President Clinton's visit. This is confirmed in a story the paper carried the following week (2nd May 1997), reporting on the US ambassador's visit to the newspaper to brief the editor on arrangements for the presidential visit. "She [the US ambassador] also promised that the regional and international press would be given equal treatment by the United States officials during the visit." No doubt this was the editor's reward for his paper's leading article on the "special relationship"!

To return to that editorial in the London *Times*, about the young golfing champion, the Tiger Woods phenomenon. Is it really true to say that for reasons of class and colour Britain would never have a non-white golf champion, or a professional soldier of the rank of General Colin Powell? In my view this is too simplistic an analysis, even if a former London *Times* editor had made it. Firstly the population of black people in the USA and in the UK are not equivalent. Tiger Woods has actually described himself as a mixture of several different ethnic groups, including African-American, native American and Asian-American – a classic example of the US melting-pot society. In each of these different ethnic groups, with the possible exception of the native American, there is now a considerable middle-class, with middle-class values, middle-class money and middle-class aspirations.

The size of the UK black population does not compare with the size of the African-American population. Added to this are other complicating factors, such as the tendency among upwardly-mobile Caribbean people in the UK to emigrate to, yes, the USA and Canada, together with an increasing tendency towards outward migration of Caribbean people from Britain back to the Caribbean. These include not only young professionals seeking their fortunes in their parents' countries, but a range of people from all sorts of backgrounds. When I am in Barbados, hardly a week passes without my meeting someone who falls into the category of "UK returnee". Among these are the businesswoman who came on holiday, fell in love with her mother's country and decided to stay, and the coconut vendor who preferred selling coconuts in Barbados to drawing the dole in London.

A third factor affecting the profile of the black British population is the mobility of the Caribbean professional, who targets North America, the Caribbean and parts of Africa as suitable destinations to live and work. Many Caribbean people have family ties with North America, and many intellectual Africans from the Diaspora view Africa as their spiritual home. Apart from this, Caribbean people have always travelled and moved around in search of work, throughout the world. This travel, this search for work and life in other people's countries, is a characteristic of Caribbean people, and any analysis of black British people that ignores this factor has to be very deeply flawed, such as that of *The Times* editorial. Unfortunately the kind of one-sided analysis represented in this writing is very attractive to some people, for while they continue to pity black people as victims, they never have to consider us as fellow-citizens. That one-dimensional view of black people angers me, and I am particularly concerned when black people embrace the victim role. To me, in doing so, we forfeit our right to be in control, and put ourselves always at the mercy of others, always reacting, never initiating.

Now I want to return to my analysis of the social characteristics of

Britain's black population. These social factors that I have outlined above are unique to the African-Caribbean population in the UK. The other sizeable non-white British population, from the Indian sub-continent, does not experience these "pull" factors in relation to their countries of origin, though in common with people of the Caribbean they also migrate from the UK to North America. In the Indian sub-continent there continues to be political instability, high levels of corruption, poverty, wars and communal problems that impact on everybody's quality of life. In general most of these things are absent or considerably less in the Caribbean. This means that there is a constant drain of people and talent from the British black population, thus decreasing the likelihood of the emergence of the odd general or admiral.

As for golf, that is a special case. There was an instance in the south of England where a golf club refused to allow an adopted child to compete in a tournament, on the grounds that he was not the natural child of his parents. I can't see many African-Caribbean or English working-class people wishing to penetrate the stuffy oppressive world that is English golf. In Scotland, the home of golf, they do things differently, for there almost everyone plays. Maybe Scotland will be lucky enough to throw up a British Tiger Woods.

So the situation is more difficult and more complex than the London *Times* or the Barbados *Nation* will have it. In another earlier edition of the same newspaper (The *Nation*, 12th April 1997) there is an enormous headline, NO QUEEN, and beside it a smaller caption reads, "Arise Sir Fred!" with a picture of Sir Fred Gollop being knighted. The irony inherent in the two opposing headlines was apparently missed by the editor, or maybe not. In my own personal experience, of having lived all my childhood in Barbados, and most of my adulthood in England, I would say that Barbados is more culturally British than it is American. I would also strongly contest the notion that the emergence of top black golfers and army generals in the USA is an indication of the absence of class and race as significant social factors.

In my experience as a black woman, the USA is a more overtly racist and oppressive society than the UK. I have attributed this to the history of slavery and to the fact that the USA was a slave society in a way that Britain was not. The collective memory of slavery and the experience of the plantocracy still exerts subtle and not so subtle influences on American life today. I am not going to write a treatise on this. I will give but one example. During the Second World War black American GIs were welcomed to the UK by ordinary people, to the outrage and indignation of their white American colleagues. This is not to suggest that the British forces were open and tolerant, as this was clearly not the case, but as I have already said the picture is difficult and complicated by many factors. The simplistic analysis presented in *The Times* editorial fails to address this complexity, and falls into the usual white liberal trap of being able to see black people only as victims.

The British working-classes were not part of the empire in the same way that the upper- and merchant-classes were, but it is among the working-class that Her Majesty's former colonial subjects have come to live. There are varying degrees of racial tensions in the UK, racially motivated, attacks, arson, and even murders. The public inquiry into the way the Metropolitan Police handled the murder of Stephen Lawrence testifies to the degree of racial prejudice and indifference towards a section of the community, which is intolerable. While all this is true, at the same time there is a degree of social mixing as more black people enter the middle-class. In the USA the black middle-class is not accepted on an equal basis with the white middle-class: race is always the critical factor. In general, for the majority of the population, the UK is a much kinder, gentler society than the USA.

The writer of that London *Times* editorial should have asked whether an O J Simpson-type case could ever happen in the UK? I suggest that, faced with an equivalent scenario, the black British population would not be polarised along racial lines in the way as happened in the USA. For example (and not wishing anybody any harm) one of our black British athletes or boxers (who is married to a white British woman) killed his wife. I cannot imagine any section of the British public seeking to make racial capital out of such a tragedy. This suggests a healthy and better functioning, though far from perfect society.

Let me continue with some stories gleaned from my experiences and knowledge of life in the USA. In the 1980s, in middle America, I was invited to dinner at the home of a professional couple. The husband was originally from England, and the wife Jamaica. They lived in what seemed to me to be an area pretty much like the part of Surrey in which we were living at that time. The lady of the house told me that the day after she moved in, her next door neighbour, a white woman, had sent her maid, a black woman, with a note telling her that she (the maid) had been sent to befriend her. She replied, thanking her neighbour, saying she would choose her own friends, which might or might not include the maid. Twenty-five years had passed since that exchange of notes, and the two families had never ever exchanged as much as a word. In my own experience of living in an equivalent part of England, people are either polite or they ignore you.

In the mid-1990s a young English executive, someone known to me, was posted to the USA, and with him went his black British wife and their three children. In the USA they found themselves in a no-man's-land. The primary schools were fine, but the high schools were racially segregated, a situation they had never encountered in middle-class England. It was decided that the teenage child would be sent back home to England to a boarding school. This was the only way his parents could see of getting around the racial problems that they encountered in the US school system. In the same vein, an English woman on a visit to the USA decided to attend a Martin Luther King memorial day service. She was amazed to find herself the only white person in a congregation of hundreds of black Americans. It was only then that she realised that Martin Luther King day is clearly not at all an all-American day, but a black American day. Many white Americans do not acknowledge it even.

I know of at least one English academic who turned down a job in the USA because his wife said that she could not live in such a racially divided society. This was her experience over many years of visiting university communities there. In England, she was completely free to have anyone as a guest in her home, but she knew that in the USA she would not have the same freedom. Over many years of visiting, she had observed the racial divide, and she simply did not want to be part of it. Her fears were based on her experience of life among academics and intellectuals in some of America's leading universities and research institutes.

I once almost became involved in the racial politics of a US university when I was asked for advice concerning the performance of an African-American woman student whose research work was giving cause for concern. The person raising the matter was herself a non-white academic. In-depth discussion revealed that the problem was not academic at all but racial, in that the supervisors were too scared to discuss problems with the student for fear of being branded racist. Black and other academics who were "people of colour", as they put it, were afraid of being seen as "Uncle Toms" if they were too critical of the work of black students.

This conversation took place in 1994, and took me back to an experience I had during a visit to Boston, Massachusetts, a few years earlier. One of the hot topics in education in Boston at the time was the practice of universities awarding sports scholarships to students, most of whom were black, and most of whom were also more or less illiterate. The teaching profession was arguing for a minimum performance level before any student could be awarded a scholarship of any kind, including a sports scholarship. But the black teachers I talked to felt that the issue was being used to cut off black access to sport and to universities. The whole thing was extremely convoluted and I eventually gave up any attempt to understand it. It seemed to me that the real cause for concern was that, in the end, it was the student, the black community and the country itself that would lose out.

As a black woman academic I have had my fair share of actual or potential racist experiences, and while I refuse to be controlled by racism, I don't consciously downplay or ignore its significance and its cost. Once a white male colleague tried to lumber me with the task of discussing a problem with a black woman student whose performance was not quite up to scratch. My colleague explained to me that, as I was a black woman, "it would be easier for you to tackle this one." My response to this was straightforward. I said: "Okay, and in future I will send you all my difficult white students." I heard no more about that. Had the student's problems been of the kind to benefit from my help I would certainly have helped, but to be lumbered with every problem black student was a different matter, one to be speedily nipped in the bud.

I sense that in the racial politics of the US campus, this would not have been an option for me. It is possible that black academics in the UK have had experiences closer to the American kind, and if so they will have to tell their stories. I can tell only my own. Saying that reminds me that I did once turn down a senior academic post at what is now the University of the South Bank in London. I did not have a good feeling about the place and I sensed a high level of racial politics. My rejection of the post was made easier when the appointment committee took its time before offering me the job. I also did not like the fact that my office would be on the fifth floor, and that I would either have to use a lift or walk up and down five flights of stairs. So I took an equivalent post at Plymouth Polytechnic, now also a university.

I am supposed to be writing about the USA, and I must say that for me there are two main indicators of the effect of racial politics and racism there. Racism calls the tune to which black Americans dance. They do not set their own agenda, but react to the agenda of others. This strikes me as the values of plantation society adapted to a later century. It seems to me that African-Americans today are still controlled by those same values. The rise of the nation of Islam is the first main indicator of this reactive process. The second indicator of the damage racism has inflicted on the African-American psyche is the reaction of that community to the trial of O J Simpson, a black American, for the murder of his white American wife.

The hijack of a private tragedy to make racial and media capital was an essentially American thing. What I personally found most distressing was the way the black community reacted to the result of the criminal trial. Somehow, the acquittal of a man accused of the brutal murder of a woman he married becomes a cause for racial triumphalism. It seemed to me that the African-American community surrendered its moral judgement, and that racism was the real victor. When a people become unable to make independent moral judgements, whether they realise it or not, they are truly under the control of others. They are allowing the values of the white plantocracy of slavery to control the behaviour of black people at the end of the twentieth and at the start of the twenty-first century.

The nation of Islam and the Rev Farrakhan are above all a reaction to American racism. The flight by black Americans from Christianity to Islam solves nothing in terms of racial identity. Will the black Muslims be happy to share their paradise with their white Muslim brothers and sisters? As Malcolm X found out, Islam is as much a white religion as is Christianity. Islam and Christianity are both proselytising religions and they convert people wherever they go, process undertaken by the word or by the sword, or with both. For this reason both Islam and Christianity have adherents from all backgrounds and all races. As far as black history is concerned Arab Islam is as tainted as European Christianity. The worst thing about a movement that comes about as a reaction and continues as such, is that it remains limited and controlled by the same forces that gave it birth.

For me a truly creative movement would have developed new ideas and ways of doing things, and its energies would be directed at creating something new, not reacting to something old. It is possible, but very doubtful that this may yet happen with the nation of Islam in the USA. Doubtful, because religion generally, and modern Islam in particular, have shown themselves to be inherently conservative and reactionary. This means that the ideas of the plantocracy continue to control the thoughts and actions of black and white Americans, even in the twenty-first century. This is not a cause for celebration.

What I like best and enjoy most in the USA are the natural features of the country. I would like to walk the Florida Way, all 2,000 kilometres of it. The first river I ever saw was the Thames in London, which looked very big to me. Then I went to India and saw the Ganges, which was even bigger. Then I went to the USA and saw the Mississippi, and that was bigger again. Barbados would be nothing but a tiny island on the vast Mississippi! For someone like myself, who is used to walking along the Thames, a real disappointment with the Mississippi is the absence of footpaths. I can't imagine what the Amazon must look like – are there any footpaths on the Amazon? (Just asking.) We did walk a bit of the Florida Trail, about 8 kilometres, with only about another 2,000 to do.

We walked that little bit of the Florida Trail in 1990, after Peter and I spent a cold, wet Christmas in Houston and had then driven to Miami, stopping off along the way. In a small town by the Swannee River in Georgia we stayed for the night. I was driving, so Peter got out and went to book a room. Soon he came back with the key and we installed ourselves. I was tired and lay down to watch TV, while Peter went off to explore. Then, just as I was about to nod off, there was a knock on the door. In response to my invitation to come on in, a white woman entered the room. It was the hotel manager, who explained to me that she just wanted to make sure that everything was all right, and to check whether there was anything we needed. I thanked her, and replied that we were fine, everything was fine. She smiled, said goodnight, and left.

Later that same year, in Ramsey's bar in Speightstown, Barbados, we met an American man who hailed from Georgia. We told him of our car journey from Houston to Miami and he said he hoped we didn't have any trouble, because some of those people could be very stupid. Then to my surprise Peter told him that yes, we did have a bit of bother. I heard for the first time that when he had returned from his walk the hotel manager had been waiting for him. She told him that had she known he was travelling with a black person she would never have allowed us to stay. To that he had replied, "That is too bad," and walked out. When I heard this story for the first time, I was quite angry that it had been kept from me at the time. But Peter knew that I would have wanted to leave straightaway, and where would we have gone? There was no old man waiting at the bottom of the drive to invite us to share his humble abode. This was not Trinidad.

Uncle Sam calling Barbados

In the late 1960s, during one of my return visits to Barbados, I went for a stroll along some streets familiar to me from my childhood walks or bike rides as a teenager. It was around dusk, about 5.30. A young girl of about fifteen was walking the same route and we soon fell into step, greeting each other, then chatting about this and that. After a while she asked me if I was "from away", by which she meant was I living abroad. I admitted that I was, and she then went on to tell me, with something akin to desperation, how much she too wanted to "live away", her preferred destination being the USA. I did not try to change her mind, or to tell her any awful stories about the American way of life. But I did say that I did not think Barbados was that bad. She agreed that it wasn't, but it was "too small", and everything was "small, small". I could not disagree with her about that. I vividly recalled myself feeling exactly the same way at her age. By this time we had come to the parting of our ways. We said our goodbyes, and I wished her luck.

I still sometimes think of that young girl and wonder whether she got to the USA, and what she made of it. In 1997 I was reminded of her again when I saw a letter by a young Bajan girl in the *Nation* newspaper. I reproduce it in full, because for me it demonstrates the kind of change that has taken place in Bajan young women in the intervening years. It just so happens that it almost exactly sums up my own views and feelings towards the US government's role in the Caribbean. Here it is, it exactly as written.

I'm with you all the way, Arthur

As a young citizen of this country, I find it at my disposal to air my views on the Shiprider Agreement dilemma as it is bound to affect me in some way, sometime.

Let me applaud Mr Owen Arthur for not signing the "thing" in the first place; maybe he sees what I and all Barbadians see: the United States trying to own every small country she can get her hands on.

Why would America want to help us if she can't help herself. Mr Clinton needs to clean up the street corners of the big cities of the United States and reduce crime by at least 50 per cent before he can even think about helping others.

As small a country as Barbados is, you will agree that we have our drug trade under control and for years we have been doing it without the help of America.

Do we really need a number of FBI and CIA agents running around our paradise trying to catch drug mules? Hell no! If anything the United States should be begging the Task Force for help.

The other Caribbean countries who signed the agreement have my deepest sympathies, for you were too eager to be in an agreement with America you felt you had to sign it.

Mr Arthur you are doing a great job not signing the agreement and Barbados is backing you all the way 100 per cent and remember what the song says: "Our country – if we don't nourish it and cherish it somebody else gine come and take it".

Rasheda Marshall, 'Letters', from
The *Nation* (2nd May 1997)

Walking in America

American cities are hostile to walkers, and African-American walkers are in particular danger. In the summer of 1998 a black American hitch-hiker was murdered by white supremacists while trying to get a ride on the highway. I have walked in many of Europe's cities without ever feeling that I was taking my life in my hands, but when walking in America I have often felt that I was never really feel safe. The Americans take walking very seriously, at least in theory. There has even been a presidential commission on walking, established no doubt to see how many Americans are still capable of doing it! On a visit to Houston I found myself alone, with time to spare, so I decided to go for a walk. When my host telephoned to arrange to pick me up and did not get an answer he got very worried. The idea that anyone would brave the Houston traffic to go for a walk never occurred to him, so he came straight back to see what had happened to me. By the time he got there I was safely back in the house, having discovered that his part of Houston was not suitable for walking.

In some parts of Houston walkers are provided with little circular trails where people walk for exercise. On another visit to Houston, this time with Peter, we set out for a walk along the bayou, which was quite like walking along a canal in England. On the way back we decided to walk away from the bayou and through the cityscape. It was Christmas, 1989, the winter when Houston froze. There were burst pipes and water gushing out everywhere, and there was panic in the city. As usual Peter was our navigator as we walked back to Windsor Village, but I soon became a bit concerned because I could not recognise any landmarks. As I'd been in that part of the city many times before, I felt that I *should* recognise some familiar sights. Eventually I said to him that I thought we were heading in the wrong direction, but he had worked out the route and would have none of it. According to him we were on the right road. One hour later and we were still no closer to our destination, so I decided to ask the way. In common with most of the male species Peter is totally against asking directions, and I sometimes think that he would rather be lost forever than ask the way. On this occasion I did not wait for his agreement, I simply asked. The information we got confirmed that we were indeed heading in the wrong direction. We turned around and headed back the way we had just walked, Peter putting it all down to sun having been "in the wrong place". He had based his calculations on its being in one place and instead it was somewhere else! Walking with Peter is such fun.

Once I had a very frightening experience in upstate New York. It was February. I was staying in Yonkers, and one afternoon I set off for a walk in very sunny, if somewhat cold weather. A bus came along and I took it on spec, as it were. It turned round at the White Plains cinema complex, where the movie *Wall Street* was showing. I decided to go in and see it. When the movie finished, the February sun had gone and it had become very, very cold indeed, with the temperature at thirty degrees below. Once the cinema closed there was no one about, so I waited at the bus stop expecting a bus to show up any minute. No bus came, and there seemed to be no way of finding a schedule. Eventually I asked a passing cyclist and discovered that no bus was expected for at least an hour and a half, and that there would be no more buses direct to Yonkers until the next day. I walked up and down trying to stay warm and calm, for by then everything around me had taken on a sinister and threatening aspect. I felt that if I did not freeze to death, something or someone else would "get me". Somehow the ninety minutes passed without my freezing to death, and the bus did come. I got on and studied the faces of the people, looking for anyone I could safely approach for help, as that I needed in order to find my way back to Yonkers.

There were some odd-looking characters on that bus, men without socks, wearing thin cotton shirts, apparently oblivious to the biting cold. I do not normally feel cold much myself, but after standing so long on a street covered in snow and in below-freezing temperatures, my feet were as hard as rock. No wonder I marvelled at these oddballs on the bus, which was all very well but I had to do something about my immediate problem. I knew that I would have to get off at some point, either to change to another one or telephone for help. I felt that I had to be very careful about where I got off. Suppose it was in a very rough neighbourhood. To a woman alone at night, anything could happen. After much thought I approached a very motherly looking black woman, who literally took me under her wing and sorted out my transport problems. I made it back to Yonkers safe and sound. When I told them that I'd been to White Plains, the lady of the house remarked that after more than twenty years of living in this area she had never been there herself. I didn't think it wise to burden them with the full details of my trip.

In January 1990 Peter and I completed a car journey from Houston to the Florida Keys, enjoying many stops and many walks along the way. In the February we left the USA for Barbados, and returned to England in April. In May Peter had an emergency bypass operation to save his life. At the time when we were travelling across the southern USA and walking by the banks of the Swannee and Mississippi rivers, we had no idea of the trouble that was developing in his chest.

Driving in Miami was hell! So, whenever we visit Miami nowadays, we always travel by public transport, bus or train. We feel safer and it helps us to get to know the city that much better. My very first visit to the USA was as an in-transit passenger on my way to India in 1962. At the airport I saw policemen with guns in their holsters, and this was in fact the first time I had ever seen a gun. I could not help staring! I have since visited the USA on many occasions, and I can see that, compared with the weapons that Mexican policemen and security guards carry, US police guns are really quite small.

New England is a good place for walks. I have had some good ones in Vermont, as this is good walking country, and around Putney where I was staying there are many old bridges, such as the bridges of Madison County. It is also good country for movie making. Connecticut is another place for walks, as I discovered one weekend there. I like best the natural features of the USA, the Florida everglades and the Mississippi river, but there is still a lot to see and lots of walks to be done. I can say with Robert Frost that I still "…have promises to keep and miles to go before I sleep… ". And I also have a few more stories to tell about my American experiences.

The boy who did not take his medicine

In the summer of 1968 a twelve-year-old boy, a member of my extended family, came from the USA to visit us in Shepperton. His mother brought him to us, and she also brought a bag full of medicines, which were supposed to control his behaviour. I was informed that my little cousin was hyperactive and a chronic bed-wetter, and that he was to be our guest for the summer! His mother instructed me that on no account was he to miss taking his drugs, and she suggested that if he did dire consequences would follow. But on the day she left our house I took the bag full of the drugs and threw it right to the back of my wardrobe, on the highest shelf. I didn't want it to be too accessible, too easily reached.

Having put the drugs away I sat with my little guest to discuss our situation. Before going on let me explain something. When I did not know any better I used to think that the Food and Drugs Administration (FDA) was an organisation for administering food and drugs to the people of the USA. This also helped me to understand why there were so many fat people in that country, and so many enthusiastic drug-takers. I was also aware of the drug culture among American doctors, who sanctioned the prescription of drugs to children and young people in order to control something called "hyperactive behaviour". I had actually stayed in my home with my little cousin and I knew that he was no more hyperactive than I was – which may not be saying a lot, but it did mean that, like me, he too might be able to get along without drugs. But the bed-wetting was a real problem, and I did not propose spending my summer tied to a washing machine.

I explained this to my young guest. I told him that he would be provided with a potty and I pointed out that the toilet was just outside his bedroom door. We reached an agreement whereby he would receive 50p every morning the bed was dry, and at the end of a fortnight he would receive a bonus of £10. If he wet the bed once he would miss one payment, but more than once and he would have to start again from scratch. This was quite a generous arrangement for 1968, but I had worked out that the saving in time, labour, and electricity justified it. I have to admit that I was not very hopeful that this approach would work, but I felt that it was worth a try.

At the end of the two weeks he collected his payment in full. I told him that he had done it to help me but that from then on he should do it for himself. He stayed with us the whole summer without incident. He made friends with local boys of his own age and spent time visiting them. He joined us in lazy days by the river canoeing, at which he turned out to be very skilled. At the end of the summer he left us, and I have never heard a word from him since, though through other family members I heard when he married and also when he had his first child. In 1977, when we were moving from Shepperton, I found the bag full of medicines at the back of my wardrobe. It took me a while to figure out what it was. For the first time I read the labels and saw what they were, and also noted that they had all been prescribed by a paediatrician – the American way with child care.

Writing on the hoof

During my visit to Boston I met an American academic who, at the time, was very preoccupied with a book that he was writing. He carried the manuscript about with him and never missed a moment to add to it. Even at the petrol station, while the car was filling up, he would add a few lines. The night in question, he had taken me with him to a meeting of one of the local school boards, and we were on our way back to the city. I had been specially invited to get a glimpse of the way the American school system worked. I had found the whole experience very educational indeed. The local National Association for the Advancement of Coloured People representative was present, and all the issues raised seemed to be race-related. I was surprised to find that bussing was still one of the big issues. Boston had just installed its first black education supremo and it seemed that that white establishment was waiting, watching, and ready to pounce at the first suggestion of incompetence.

We discussed the board meeting as we made our way back to where I was staying, and I asked him whether it had been typical. My guide for the evening replied "pretty much", and had just started explaining the behind-the-scenes dynamics when an accident happened. We were on the inside lane of the roundabout when a car came from the right and banged straight into us. Luckily the impact caught the tail end of the car and not the front where I was sitting. But it was a close call. One minute we were driving along chatting, then I looked up and saw a car hurtling towards me with the clear intention of wiping me off the face of the earth.

After the two drivers had completed the usual formalities we continued on our way home. We were both very shaken, and had quite lost interest in school board politics. I was surprised to notice how very worried and concerned my host was about the damage to his car, so I said, "Surely the insurance will take care of that, won't it?" It was then that he told me that he was not insured, because, as he put it, "I never have accidents." He said this a few minutes after I had almost been killed in a car that he'd been driving. His comment simply added to the bizarre nature of the whole evening's experience.

In the morning, when we discussed the events of the previous night, we hardly mentioned the board meeting. Things got quite difficult as his wife considered aloud what her future might have been as a young widow. I decided to inquire about the progress of the book, and I also took the opportunity of asking about its subject. Up to then I'd been so fascinated by the writing process itself that I'd forgotten to show any interest in what was actually being written. The idea that someone could write on the hoof, adding a few words at traffic lights, a few sentences at petrol stations, and whole paragraphs at railway stations, left me speechless. In answer to my first question I learnt that the book was progressing well, and in reply to the second that the book was to do with the use of English in India. The thesis rested on the idea that India's failure to progress was due to the continued dominance of the English language.

Both husband and wife wanted my opinion, and they both invited me to comment. Somewhat reluctantly I said that India has such a multiplicity of languages that without English and Hindi people across the country wouldn't be able to communicate. Therefore English and Hindi were the common languages uniting India, which was quite apart from the benefits of English as the international language of industry and commerce. The writer did not welcome these comments at all. "Are you saying that my theory is rubbish?" he asked, with barely concealed hostility. I did not need to speak as his wife's voice broke the silence that followed his challenged to me. She advised her partner to listen to my views. "After all," she told him rather pointedly, "Maureen has lived in India, and you haven't." In the circumstances this was not a helpful comment and her husband simply responded that he had gone too far to start thinking again. I had seen him writing on the hoof, I knew the level of commitment to his book, and that was why I had been reluctant to make any comment. I'd known from the outset that he would continue as he had begun. Another example of the American way!

Journey to Cape Cod

The day I visited Cape Cod there was a congress of lesbian doctors, and the place was full to overflowing with beautiful women making a very public display of their undying love. I recall two such beauties, both blondes with long, flowing hair, lying on top of a statue entwined in each other's arms. It was a very touching picture, but it still left me wondering whether a congress of lesbian doctors was any different from any other boring conference. And why did lesbian doctors want their own conference? I will never know the answers to these questions, and I mention them only now because as I write about Cape Cod, those questions and that image of those lovers are the ones that come to mind.

That and the memory of the drive back. But let me start at the beginning. My friend and I had been up half the night talking about old times, bringing each other up to date about the present and generally enjoying each other's company. We did not go to bed until the early hours, and looking back now I can see that the decision to drive to Cape Cod was not a wise one. We woke up at six anyway, and thought, why not? By seven we were on the road. Before we left the house I suggested that we should stay the night, but my friend said that she could not leave her cats unattended. Even so I was still hopeful that she might change her mind once we got to the Cape. I knew that the return journey would take us at least ten hours, and this seemed to me a very long way to go only to turn around and drive back.

Our route included quite a few towns and built-up areas, and we made quite a slow pace. It was around 2.30 in the afternoon when we arrived at the Cape. We must have stopped en route, but I don't recall – all I know is that I was very glad to get out of the car and unwind my legs. We went for a short stroll along the beach, and that was when I saw the notice about the congress and the entwined lovers. After our short stroll we went to a restaurant, and as soon as we had finished our meal we set off on the return journey. Before leaving, I again suggested staying the night, and pointed out that there were several hotels nearby.

322

My suggestion met with the same blank refusal. We had to get back, the cats could not be left alone, and any night away from them must be properly planned. So we set off, planning to spend about an hour or so at Cape Cod.

On the way back the roads were clearer and we made much quicker progress. At some point I must have dozed off, or to put it more accurately "we" must have dozed off. Suddenly I was aware of the car swerving and skidding out of control, and once more I faced the prospect of a premature end on an American road. But my time had not yet come. Neither had the drama of the night reached its end, for about one or two kilometres from the house the car screeched to a halt and the driver got out. We were on a long lonely country road, and it was past midnight. What could be the matter?

"I thought I saw one of the cats," my friend said as she got back into the car. "False alarm?" I asked, without any hint of the irritation I felt. "Yes, false alarm," came the reply, and she added, "they're probably at home waiting for me." But they were not. Cats don't stay at home waiting for people. There was no sign of them until the next morning, so we could easily have stayed the night at the Cape and have avoided our near-accident. I know about Cape Cod from what I have read in *Encarta*, 1997, not from having actually visited the place. In fact my most vivid memories of that visit are of entwined lovers and another close shave with death.

A walk in middle America: "Tears, idle tears"

The summer of 1992 saw me once again in the USA, and this time I was visiting New England. My first stop was in Connecticut where I had arranged a meeting with a professor of engineering, whose advice I was seeking. I had done some research on risk assessment and child protection, and I wanted to see if it was feasible to develop an interactive training programme using both the research findings and the model of risk assessment that we had developed in Surrey. I had met the professor socially in England before he had moved across the pond. I asked a mutual friend to approach him on my behalf, to ask if he would be interested in talking to me about the project, and to advise me on the feasibility of my proposal. The reply came back in the affirmative, and it was arranged that I would stop off in Storrs, Connecticut, on my way from New York to New Hampshire.

When the bus arrived at Hartford on the Saturday afternoon, there was no one to meet me. After waiting a while, I rang the house, and the professor's wife answered and told me he was on his way. I waited, but I had already started to have misgivings. I started looking around and soon noticed that there was a hotel across the street. I was just considering going across to check it out when my host arrived. On the drive to his home he told me that they were all going to a barbecue later on, and that I could come if I wanted to. I hastily declined, explaining that I was very tired and that I would be quite happy having a quiet evening on my own. There was no sign of his wife when we arrived at the house, and during the time I was there I saw her once, very briefly, as I was leaving the next day.

The feeling of unease that had started at the bus stop grew, and I began ask myself what I was doing there. Even in the short time we'd been together I had been able deduce that the professor was not interested in my project. So I was on a hiding to nothing, and my visit was a pointless exercise. Once I began to think about it, I could see that it never really had anything going for it. The professor had not asked me to send any papers or provide any information ahead of my visit, so clearly there was no possibility of his giving me any real help and advice. I must have been on a high back in England, and I had failed to think through the matter properly.

So, sitting on a bed in a small room in Storrs, Connecticut, on a Saturday afternoon in June, I considered my predicament. My feelings were a pale reflection of those I had had on my arrival in Calcutta in 1962. I had the same sense of being lost, or disoriented. I was among people I hardly knew, and it seemed that my visit was a source of problems or conflict between the husband and wife. "Oh God!" I sat on the bed thinking about what I should do, as I was due to be collected the following day at about noon. I didn't see that I had any option but to stay overnight, as planned. My mind and my feelings were in turmoil, and although I was very tired I could not rest. So, surprise, surprise! I decided to go for a walk. The house was deserted except for one small boy watching TV. "I'm just going for a walk, to have a look around," I said as I was leaving. "See you later." He barely lifted his eyes as he replied, "See you later!" and continued watching TV and drinking his Coca-Cola.

It was about 3.30 when I left the house. It was a beautiful New England summer's day. I walked alongside a river that was bordered by very tall trees – oaks and cypresses, I think – though they were much larger than similar species in Europe. I began to relax and enjoy the scenery, and as I walked I tried to identify markers for the return journey. Storrs is a university town, and as well as the main university there are several colleges and other related institutions dotted about the place. I took careful note of my location as I went my way. I had been out for about an hour when I began to be very thirsty. I have a problem with thirst, because with me it doesn't seem to develop gradually – I go from feeling fine to desperately thirsty, when I simply must have a glass of water! I was at this point when I saw a café or restaurant of some kind, on the other side of the road. This was not a Houston highway – just the type of road one might find anywhere in Europe. I dashed across, ran up the embankment, but slipped and fell. And what a fall it was!

I landed quite safely, but using my hands to break the fall most of my weight fell onto them. That was okay, except that one of the fingers got twisted. My whole body went limp, as wave after wave of excruciating pain swept over me, and somewhere deep inside me tears began to well up. Lord Tennyson wrote of tears:

> Tears, idle tears, I know not what they mean,
> Tears from the depth of some divine despair
> Rise in the heart, and gather in the eyes.

The poet might not have known what his tears meant, but I knew very well what mine were to me. I knew that once I started crying I would not be able to stop. I would cry for all the pain I'd been through: not just the physical pain of the finger (which could well be broken), but all the other, deeper pains – tears of sorrow for my dead son-in-law, my widowed daughter, my mad son, my sick husband, and my unhappy friend. And there were tears of anger and frustration for the situation I'd got myself into. I felt that they would overwhelm me and wash away my last reserves of strength, and could begin to see men in white coats gathering around me. So, although my tears rose in the heart, they were not allowed to gather in the eyes. I blinked them back, pulled myself up, dusted myself off and headed for the café.

A few minutes later, having had a drink of water, I was tucking into vegetable moussaka and reading the papers. No one could tell from looking at me that I'd just experienced a major life crisis. I returned to the house to find the boy sitting in the same place, still glued to the TV. "Hi," I said, to which he greeted me in like fashion, "Hi" – and continued to watch the TV. I went on with "Well, I think I'll go to bed now – good night." The boy wished me good night in return and I went to bed. I was asleep in no time, but I very soon woke up. I listened to the radio and heard a lot about something called "commencement". Commencement seemed to be the American way of university graduation – only with a lot more speeches. The next morning I was up early, had a cup of tea, then went with the professor to a field to watch him cut up trees into logs, in a very North American way. On the return journey we chatted briefly about my project, but it *was* just chat, for we both knew that I'd wasted my time coming there. It was at this point that we passed by a wood and I decided to walk back.

After that walk, everything looked brighter. Mrs Professor had surfaced and my friend had arrived and was waiting to take me away. A few days later, in New Hampshire, for reasons that I cannot now recall, I wrote a poem about crying in the bath, something along the lines of that as the only place where it is safe to lament. Immersed in bath water a few idle tears wouldn't make much difference – and wouldn't show.

9

LOOSE ENDS: WALKING, TALKING, GETTING LOST, BEING SCARED

Lone women travellers are often perceived as participating in something abnormal... . At the same time they are also heralded as very brave ambitious people who exemplify the heights to which women can rise in achieving that which is normally expected of men.

Hall, D, Kinnaird, V, *Tourism: A Gender Analysis*

IN AN earlier chapter I wrote about my long-standing fascination with Guyana, the country where my father originated, and I mentioned that all my life I have been perplexed by the question of how he came to be born there. Had it been a matter of pure chance, I wondered. Had my itinerant grandmother been passing through Guyana when my father decided to be born, or did she have a more permanent attachment to the place?

Through asking myself these questions, it slowly dawned on me that I am, in fact, from a line of black women travellers. I am in no way original. The one thing I know for sure about both my grandmothers is that they were travellers.

In the Barbados of my childhood it was very rare for adults to engage children in conversation. Although my mother was different in this respect, in that she talked a lot to me, she didn't like to talk about her background. I think she felt uncomfortable with the fact that she was not a legitimate child. The word "bastard" had very strong negative connotations for her. As for my father, he hardly spoke about anything at all, except to bark orders of one kind or another. It was as if by osmosis that one absorbed things, and in this way I came to know that my mother's mother had travelled around the Caribbean islands, transporting and selling fruit and vegetables. My grandmother's family owned land in Grenada, and it must have been the produce of it that she took to sell in the other islands. I have no idea why my paternal grandmother travelled to Guyana and other places. Both my grandparents died when their own children were very young, and my parents were both raised in their respective islands, my mother in Grenada and my father in Barbados, by childless aunts.

Another thing I also know for sure is that my grandmothers travelled for very different reasons from me, and I have no idea whether they enjoyed their journeys or whether it was simply a way of earning a living. I also do not know whether these two women ancestors of mine went out on the road alone or with others, but I suspect that they got to know people and were probably part of a regular group of island travellers. I myself have often been "a lone woman traveller", and as such I have, from time to time, attracted some interesting comments. Men wonder that my husband "allows" me to go off on my own, while other women are often simply envious. Many travel books often have special sections for women travellers, with warnings about dressing appropriately for particular cultures and strategies to avoid the attentions of "local men". In my view most travel books, and especially those for women, are written for a completely white audience. Non-white women are by definition "local", hence that widens the gap between the female tourist/traveller and local women.

Without the benefit of travel books I have, over the years, developed my own survival strategies, and so far things have worked out. Where dress is concerned I see what the local women are wearing and follow them. In Malawi, Dr Banda banned women from wearing trousers, so skirts it was. In East Africa I was quite surprised to find most women dressed in the Muslim style, with their heads covered, and so on. I was taken around Mombassa by a Muslim woman who drove around with her head scarf in her lap, which, whenever we passed through certain areas of the town, she would hurriedly throw over her head. We had a few scary moments! She told me that the "fundamentalists" were on the lookout, and if they saw her without her scarf her husband would get into trouble for not controlling her. The problem of "appropriate dress" may also be an issue not only for "local" women, but female visitors and tourists. In these circumstances most women can feel oppressed at having dress codes imposed on them (while men may well be free to dress as they choose).

Where men are concerned, I try to anticipate potentially embarrassing situations and take avoiding action. Travelling alone in Africa, I was met by a male colleague who promised to spend some time with me and show me around. As we sat drinking on the balcony of my hotel room I began to think of possible complications. Very early on I mentioned that I had brought some presents for his children and asked him when I was going to meet his family. The next day he took me to his home, where I met his wife and children and became a friend of the family. Sometimes I get help from unexpected quarters. Once I was hiking with a large group of people in the English countryside, when I found myself in a group of three – a young man, a not so young single woman, and me. The young man and I were having quite a chat. He wanted to know about my interests, how I spent my time, what I did for a living, and so on. Our female companion decided to come to my assistance and announced in a loud voice, "She is a grandmother, she has grandchildren to keep her busy!" I laughed and said, "Only one grandchild, actually" – then I increased my pace and left the young man to her tender mercies. In Africa the status of grandmother confers respect and deference, so I am always happy to proclaim my status there.

On another occasion, when I was being shown round a mining town in the interior of Guyana, my guide, one of the miners, informed me that the best time to visit the "Landing", the area that passed as the town centre, was at night. He told me that the whole place came alive then, with music, dancing and lots of people about. He was really surprised when I replied that I spent my evenings reading and writing notes. As the conversation progressed he became even more amazed to learn that I was a married woman. He said that he would not allow his wife to go off on her own. When I inquired where his wife was, he told me that she was in New York, and saw no irony in that. Yet, to me, New York seemed a much more threatening and dangerous place than the jungle of Guyana, and I felt that he had more reason to worry about his wife's safety than my husband had about mine. Adrian Forsyth, in his book *Tropical Nature: Life and Death in the Rain Forest of Central America*, published in 1984, remarks that

The streets of a large American city and the inside of the tropical rain forest might seem to have little in common even though both are regarded as jungles.

He continues,

They [the city jungle and the tropical jungle] share at least one common denominator: an ability to induce vague unease, if not outright fear in the souls of those who venture out after dark.

Need I say more?

As to the process and means of travelling, my life in that respect has gone through several stages. My first experience of travel was by aeroplane, when, in 1962, I left Barbados for India via London. At that time I took air travel in my stride, and if anything enjoyed it. So it was for many years. Then for no reason that I could understand, things changed and I became terrified of travelling by aeroplane. I found it difficult to believe that I was the same person who had once blithely boarded a four-seater for a destination with a beach for a runway, and uncertain tides. Somewhere along the road of life I had developed this terror of air travel, and I endured this torture for many years. Every time I booked a flight I would convince myself that I was going to be okay "this time", only to find myself reduced to a quivering wreck when I actually boarded the plane. I somehow managed to appear outwardly calm, but inside was turmoil, as my pulse and heart rate skyrocketed and my palms became clammy with sweat. I would look around at all the other people behaving normally: chatting, sitting quietly, and reading. I would tell myself, "If all these people can travel on a plane without fear, so can I!"

It was no use, and panic invariably set in. Over the years I developed what I called my "calming routine". This began with my rather feeble attempts at relaxation by breathing deeply and "letting go". Then I would move on to a book or anything that I could read as a means of distraction. Once I had managed to convince myself that I was not on a plane, things settled down, and as long as I did not think about flying I would be all right. But if I forgot and allowed the reality of things to slip into my conscious mind, I would once more be overwhelmed by panic and have to start my calming routine all over again. This torture went on for many years, then it went just as suddenly as it had come.

Travel by plane once more became just another means of transport.

During the time when I was afflicted by this fear I never made an issue of it. I did not talk about it to anyone, even to Peter. I just tried to accept it as the price I had to pay for the speed, comfort and comparative safety of air travel. It was only after I got over it that I felt free to talk about it, for I think that I was afraid that talking about it would make it a "problem" in a way it had not been before. As things were, I knew that once I got off the plane, my problem was at an end, and talking about it would only prolong my agony. In any case, what could I say? I had no explanation for the origins of my plane-phobia, if that was what it was. After almost twenty years of fear-free air travel it had simply come on, and so I lived in the hope that just as it had come, it would go, which is exactly what happened. Although I am okay with air travel now, it is not my preferred mode of transport. I generally prefer to travel by bus – and indeed, I have travelled around on most things that move, including an ox-cart. Some of these means will feature in the stories that follow.

Bus travel – some experiences and some characters

In 1993 my husband Peter and I spent a couple of months visiting Bhutan. We went via Calcutta, and as our Australian friend refused to travel on an Indian bus we went by plane to Thimpu, the capital of Bhutan. When it was time to leave Bhutan we had no constraints on our choice of transport, so the bus it was. The roads were not bad and we were lucky to have a very careful driver.

Our friends the park rangers, who had saved us from death by hypothermia on a weekend mountain trek, saw us off at the bus station. We waved and waved, we were sad to be leaving Bhutan, with its monks and its mysteries, its prayer flags and prayer wheels, and the violence of war throbbing underneath all these symbols of peace. I had learnt about the tensions between Bhutan and Nepal, and something called the greater Nepalese movement, which was intent on incorporating Bhutan into Nepal. Every now and again one heard or read in the papers about some outburst of violence, and of refugees and other indications of unrest. A few days after visiting a Dzong (or monastery), there was a picture in the newspapers of the body of one of the monks, lying covered in blood, with his throat slit. Visiting that monastery had been such a unique experience. It was so peaceful and so remote. I had never felt so far removed from the world, the flesh and the devil. However, as the picture of the dead monk showed, I had been deceiving myself. In seeing peace and perfection in the Dzong, I was looking for nirvana – and the photo brought this home to me. Even so, I loved Bhutan and I was sorry to be leaving.

Time to return to the bus ride to Calcutta. During that journey I fell into conversation with an undercover Christian who had been in Bhutan converting people. I had heard about this movement that, like the early Christians, held their meetings in each other's houses, with frequent moves to avoid detection. I think he rather fancied himself as the Indian equivalent of St Paul among the early Christians. I could not see any reason why he should want to change the people of Bhutan from Buddhism to Christianity. I thought that they were just fine as Buddhists, but I decided to keep my views to myself, and listened with the silence he took for approval, as he related his experiences in Bhutan.

St Paul invited me to a meeting in Calcutta and I accepted, thinking that I would then have the opportunity of learning more about this undercover movement, and also hopefully have more freedom to express my own views. We did in fact meet up in Calcutta, but I was unable to go with him to the meeting. He came on the day I had to go the police station in connection with the theft of my bag. He was very disappointed, but promised to pray for the safe return of my belongings. Unfortunately his prayers were not answered. My meeting with this modern-day St Paul was a very interesting encounter, which would never have occurred on a plane. Air travel is far too expensive, and out of the reach of ordinary people, especially in the so-called developing world. I know that in order to become acquainted with any country and to meet ordinary folk, two modes of transport are highly recommended: by foot and by bus. This combination never fails.

Very different was my experience of bussing it in Australia. Travel from Cairns to Darwin was by that means, but the bus had been converted to provide space and comfort for young people who were looking for a novel way to see the country. The advertised age range was eighteen to thirty-five, but nothing daunted, and being "young at heart", we booked ourselves on the trip. We did not have any problems due to our age or anything else, and as the bus was less than half-full the owner-driver was hardly going to miss the chance of increased revenue by rejecting us. Every evening, as dusk approached, we stopped at a campsite and pitched our tents. During much of the day we sat in the bus and watched as the endless miles of Australia passed by. We stopped for lunch and to explore tourist traps, but apart from that we sat in a state akin to stupefaction, induced by the landscape. The outback was not really an "outback", as all the campsites were extremely well appointed, with every convenience (including telephones). Peter and I came in for a lot of good-natured teasing every evening when we pitched our little tent for two. When he booked us on the bus Peter had forgotten to ask about the sleeping arrangements. He was therefore extremely unhappy when on the first night it became clear that we would all be sharing one big tent. This experience would include both communal sleeping and communal living. This type of thing was completely outside Peter's experience and he spent a very disturbed first night. At breakfast everyone noticed his bleary eyes: remarks were made, an explanation was called for, and, as usual, it fell to me to find something appropriate to say. As a result of my explanation, a Dutch couple lent us their tent, as they were used to communal sleeping and had no need of it. After that first night, the group pitched two tents, one large for everyone else, and a second small one "just for you and Peter".

The pitching of the tents always gave rise to much amusement and much speculation as to the reasons why we had to have our own. We were on this bus for ten days, and we had an enjoyable time travelling in the company of these young people, and they did not seem to mind when we opted out of their more risqué games. We were okay with football and volleyball, but we drew the line at their version of "touch" or whatever. There was a particularly good feeling among the women, and I remember us all sitting together under a tree somewhere in the Australian outback, and talking woman talk. That and the women's communal pee sessions will stay with me always, and that ten-day bus journey from Cairns to Darwin remains for me one of the highlight of our visit to Australia.

From Australia we move to South America and a bus ride from Guatemala to Mexico City. This was surely a ride to remember, different in every respect from any other long-distance bus journey I have ever made. Generally speaking I/we have been fortunate with coach/bus drivers, but this was to be the exception. We had booked and paid for our tickets in advance. Peter always reads and follows the instructions in the travel guides, and this was what the *Rough Guide* had advised: "Book in advance to be sure of your seat." Joke. The bus left on time, full to capacity with passengers who, like us, had all bought tickets and paid the full fare, even without reading the *Rough Guide*. Within minutes of leaving the bus depot the bus driver was soliciting for passengers, even though there was standing-room only. He was a reckless driver and drove very fast, with one hand on the steering wheel and the other gesturing to people along the road, beckoning them to come with him. People crammed in, money changed hands, more people crammed in, and even more money changed hands. Where would it end? How many people would they cram onto the bus before it broke down?

I tried to be socially conscious and to think that without this bus these people might have to wait in the sun for hours or walk very long distances. But I was still concerned about it breaking down under the load, or toppling over, or something. None of this happened. Our speedy progress to Mexico was hindered when we came to major road works with traffic stretching back for miles and miles. We had an enforced break here and were allowed to get off the hot, crowded bus and stand about on the hot empty road. After an hour and a half of this we were boarded and the bus crawled along behind an extensive line of traffic. The good thing was that for a while the driver was forced to drive more or less slowly and more or less safely. Added to that there was simply no opportunity for soliciting passengers. Excepting the men working on the road, there were no people around.

Once we cleared the road works and the delay, the driver was back to his old tricks, speeding and soliciting. How we got to the Mexican border in one piece I will never know. The driver was happy, his pocket was bulging with his share of the profits, and he was all set to make the return journey that same night. He was clearly set on making as much money as he could in what would almost certainly be a short life. I was very glad to get off his bus and to be free of the driver from hell!

From lorry to ox-cart – encounters of a challenging kind

Of all the forms of transport I have ever used, travelling at the back of a lorry is the least to be recommended. Not only is it uncomfortable, it is also very dangerous. However, in the absence of anything else, travelling in the back of a lorry is most welcome. If one survives it can be talked about forever after. Having travelled down Lake Malawi for two nights and three days we alighted at a small village near the border with Tanzania. Peter and I stayed with the luggage and our German student companion went off in search of transport. After twenty minutes or so he returned smiling. Transport had been arranged, and we would be going by lorry to the next village, which was right on the border. What about a place to stay? No problem. He had been told there was a hotel at the village.

We gathered up our luggage and followed him to the spot were the lorry was parked. We waited and waited, as this kind of travelling does involve a fair amount of hanging around. The three of us had assumed that the lorry was on its way to the village and was simply giving us a lift, for which of course we would pay. We were told to get in, and did so – but so did a hundred others! The back of that lorry was as crowded as it was possible to be, as this was the one and only means of transport in the area. People sat on our luggage, people sat on each other. Luckily we did not have to travel for very long before the first passengers started to dismount, and it was about half an hour or so after departing that the lorry made its first stop and people got off – enough that the remainder of us could almost breathe. This was the first of several stops until the lorry was almost empty, except for us three foreigners, the German student, Peter and me, plus the driver and the guy who had collected the fares.

By this time the African night had set it, and we were surrounded by complete and total blackness. The three of us began to feel a bit nervous. Where were we? Why were we the only passengers left out of all the many that had started off from the village? None of us said anything, but we knew that our thoughts were the same. Then I spoke: should we check once more that there was a hotel or guesthouse around? We agreed that we should. The driver's mate (otherwise fare collector) assured us that there was a hotel and that we were heading for it. We wanted to believe him, and we wanted to trust him, for we really had no choice. But all our previous experience of hotels had been associated with roads, roads with street-lighting, electricity. Here we seemed to be in a wilderness, no lights, no streets, and only the dirt track on which the lorry was driving along. We wondered who would build a hotel in a place like this?

The three of us were at the point of giving up and accepting that we would be the next set of "disappeared" travellers, when the lorry swung into a compound. We all saw the motel sign at the same time. The manager received us, and told us that due to a cancellation there was one vacant room. If we accepted it we would have to pay a slight premium because of some reason or other. We accepted the room with joy! And we offered our student companion sleeping room on the floor but he declined, and booked a space in the campsite. During the night he was robbed of his passport and most of his money and had to return to Lilongwe. It was then that I decided to check my store of hidden cash, only to find that most of it had been stolen. Still, at least we were safe and sound in our lovely motel room, and had much to be thankful for.

The next day we were able to look around and see the beauty and tranquillity of our location. We were by the side of Lake Malawi, the motel had only recently been built, and it was very well appointed. The owner-manager told us that he had built it for international travellers, because there was no accommodation available where people could stay if the border was closed, or, if like us, they arrived too late to reach the border. This same man also very kindly arranged a lift for us on an oil tanker, which was heading for the border and Tanzania. We travelled in the tanker for one and a half days, staying overnight in one of the lodging houses that the tanker drivers used. There were four of us, the driver, two Peters – the driver's brother was also called Peter – and me. The roads were unbelievably bad and the going was extremely slow, but our driver had been this way many thousand times before, so it was not surprising that we reached the railway station with time to spare.

It is back to South America for my next ride in the back of a lorry, and this was in the Guyana interior. The first time I'd been in Africa with Peter we were heading for a train to take us to another country, but this time I was travelling by myself, on a day tour with a group on a visit an Amerindian village. The people who ran the tourist lodge where I was staying had arranged the tour. First we would visit the family of our Amerindian hostess, then would go to see some of the local "development" projects in the surrounding area. Except for the roads being just as bad, this lorry ride in Guyana could not have been more different from the East African one, which we have just looked at. For a start the lorry was there primarily for the benefit of the three visitors: a couple from Manchester, England, and myself. The manager told us that he would be taking the opportunity of our excursion to collect wood from the forest, during the course of the day. He hoped that we would not mind. We didn't.

I had forgotten just how uncomfortable riding in the back of a lorry could be – even with lots of space. It was the start of the rainy season, and the potholes were big, very big, and the going was slow, very slow. It took us almost two hours to travel twenty-five kilometres, all the while being tossed and shaken about and trying to convince oneself that it was a worthwhile exercise.

In fact, it was very worthwhile. It was especially good to visit an Amerindian village, which we were told had been there since the beginning of – ? Well, of everything. We visited two projects, the first of which was a women's farming co-operative where we saw the women hard at work, preparing cassava in the timeless fashion of the Amerindians. The second project was concerned with developing an index of local knowledge on plants and trees with medicinal value, and also drying and exporting for sale samples. These two visits were by way of reward for enduring the rigours of travel by lorry, but there was also a downside to that day, and to tell of this I must go back and start at another time and place.

I had two reasons for visiting Guyana. One was to visit my father's birthplace, and the other was to see the Great Kaieteur Falls. I wanted to do a hiking tour, but time and money did not allow for this, so I settled for a day tour by plane. Among my fellow day-trippers was a couple from Manchester, England. It was a small plane – just ten passengers, the pilot and the tour guide. The lady from Manchester sat next to me, and I soon learnt that she was terrified of flying. I understood this, so I sympathised, and we continued to chat off and on during the flight. Later, as I sat in silence near the falls, just looking and drinking in its terrible beauty, the Manchester lady came and sat down beside me and started chatting away. I really would have preferred to be alone and quiet. Instead I decided to be polite and joined in, so I mentioned that I had wanted to hike down to the falls. This led us on to a general discussion about walking and hiking, then the lady mentioned that she loved walking in the Lake District, and I said that I did too! The amazement that greeted this innocuous bit of information was truly astounding: "What you? You know the Lake District? You have walked in the Lake District?" Without waiting for a reply she continued to exclaim and to throw questions at me in quick succession. Eventually she paused and I said, in a very matter-of-fact voice, that I had walked in the Lakes many times in the past, and hoped to do so many times in the future.

Well, the lady simply could not get over this. Fancy that, where else in the UK had I been? Had I ever been in Wales? My reply, as casual as ever, was "Yes, many times, Wales is nice for walking, I love walking in Wales." I was beginning to take a perverse pleasure in her obvious confusion. We sat in silence, while she tried to make sense of what she'd heard. At least that is what I guessed she was doing. Then it was time for me to ask her some questions, so I said, "Why are you so surprised that I should have visited the Lake District? Surely the Lake District is a big tourist attraction with visitors from all over the world. So what's the big deal about my having been there?" My comments and questions caused her to become quite flustered, and she denied that she had been surprised, but we both knew that she was lying and we both knew the reason why. This lady from Manchester had never in her tiny mind associated walking in the Lake District with black people. This information was therefore deeply disturbing to her sense of order, and the expectations she had of "her world".

A few weeks after this conversation, on a Sunday morning hike in Barbados, I walked with the international field officer of the Duke of Edinburgh award scheme, a black Caribbean man, who had not only hiked for years in the Lake District, but had also run numerous training courses there. My other companion on that hike, a black sister from the Bahamas, had fond memories of a long damp week spent walking in the Lake District during her student days in England. People like these two would send the lady from Manchester into the intensive care unit. Black people don't hike, and we certainly didn't hike in the English Lake District.

The Manchester lady was not alone in her view and perceptions of who should be where doing what on this earth. The incident in Guyana called to mind something similar at the Mona campus of the UWI, during my one and only visit there in 1976. It happened at the dinner table in the senior common room. I was sharing a table with a number of other people, including an English professor, a scientist and Fellow of the Royal Society (FRS), no less. As he sipped his soup he made the usual polite conversation by asking me where I was from. When I replied "Surrey", his spoon stopped in mid-air, and his mouth fell open. "Surrey University?" he repeated, with no attempt to hide his astonishment, I might even say dismay. I confirmed that he had got it right first time. I asked him, as I was to ask the Manchester lady almost twenty years later, "Why the surprise?" He said that he had expected me to say that I was from the University of Ghana, or somewhere like that. He had not been expecting to hear Surrey University. So, I apologised for being from the wrong university, and as this exchange had been overheard by the rest of the table there was now a somewhat heavy silence.

It was a Caribbean colleague, a historian, who broke it, with the words, "It's not her fault that she is not from the University of Ghana!" The FRS looked suitably chastened, and smiled bravely, then normal conversation resumed.

There are English, British, European academics in universities all over the world, and there is nothing remarkable about that. That is as it should be. But a black woman in an English university – surely some mistake? Whoever heard of black people walking in the English Lake District or teaching in English universities? I wonder if the same incident would occur today, and I suspect that it could. I have to say that I have had my fair share of surprises to do with other people's lifestyles. I was introduced to a young woman in Bhutan, who wanted to know where I was from. I assumed that she meant where I was born and replied, "Barbados, in the Caribbean – do you know where that is?" Her reply made me realise just how small the world really is. "Yes," she replied, "I know the Caribbean very well – we have our holiday home in the Bahamas." I was certainly not expecting that response from her. In fact it was the last thing I expected to hear, but I immediately expressed my delight at this news and we chatted on about life in the Bahamas.

I did not have any firm views about where rich Bhutanese ladies should have their holiday homes, and I had not invested a lot of thought or feeling on this topic. I had not consciously or unconsciously formed views as to their place in this world. I could therefore assimilate information of this kind without undue reactions. Therein lies the difference between the way I reacted to the Bhutanese lady's news and the reactions of the Manchester lady and the FRS to what I told them about myself. That was disturbing to them because it upset and challenged their world-view. There were more than twenty years between those two encounters, and there were major differences between the lady from Manchester, who described herself as "uneducated", and the university professor and FRS – but as far as I was concerned they might have been twins.

The problem for these people is that I just can't seem to learn my place! It probably stems from my mother's stubbornness in not sending me off to be a maid. When I meet people who think that I *should* be a maid, I tend to avoid them if possible.

It is time to return to the story of the day-trip to the Kaieteur Falls. After our little talk about walking and such, I did my best to avoid the company of the Manchester lady, but in spite of this, as we parted in Georgetown, she said, "Hope to see you on the Rupunnuni!" I dismissed this as polite chat, and promptly put it out of my mind. But when I arrived at the resort the following week I heard that two more guests were expected, a couple from "Manchester, England". As there was to be no escape I decided to make the best of it and set out with the owner's son to the Rupunnuni, to meet them off the boat. It was a two-hour hike, through mud that at times threatened to reach up to my waist, so I was very glad that we would be returning by ox-cart, which was slow and very bumpy. I tried to recall whether I had ever been in an ox-cart before, and had vague memories of doing something like it in an Indian village during my student days, but I couldn't be sure.

We sat three abreast, and watched uncomfortably as the girl in charge whipped the poor oxen in a bored and routine fashion. There was no way they could increase their speed, so why was she whipping them? It was just the routine.

For something to say I remarked that the owner of the resort was a friendly, genial type, and very welcoming. The resort was owned and managed by an Englishman, and his son, the young man with whom I had walked to meet the new guests, was of English and Amerindian parentage. This young man was also in the cart, sitting in front of us, beside the girl with the whip. After my comments about our host, the Manchester lady pointed at the lad and half-stated, half-questioned, speaking slowly but loudly, as if a toddler just learning to talk, "And this – is his son?"

This information clearly belonged in the same realm as black people walking in the Lake District. She had the greatest difficulty taking it in. She must have also thought that the young man was deaf; either that or she was totally indifferent to his feelings.

I decided to make no further attempt at conversation. We continued our slow journey to the resort, and as soon as we got there I decided to have a much-needed rest, and went directly to my room, thereby missing lunch. I then decided to miss dinner as well, as I was feeling very tired, and was not sure if I was sickening for something or just sick of the company. Either way I was not feeling hungry. I had no appetite, either for food or company.

Our lorry journey to the Amerindian village, the home village of the wife of the proprietor of the resort, took place the next day. Having back-tracked to the Kaieteur Falls and UWI, I will now return to the events of that day. We were nearing the end of our day-trip, and we had been well entertained by the parents of our hostess. We were now about to complete our last stop before returning to the resort. This final stop was a visit to our hostess's eldest sister, who was also the village health worker. We all climbed down from the lorry and walked towards the family, who were gathered together under an awning in the garden of their home. There were many children milling about. Suddenly the Manchester lady started pointing at one of the children and shouting out, "Look at her! Look at her! She is blonde!" She grabbed our hostess by the arm and turned her towards the child, all the while pointing and inviting all present to observe the blonde child: "Look at that one, she is blonde!" Everyone was trying very hard to ignore her and to pretend that nothing was happening. But I could not bear it so I intervened, and I hissed into her ear something along the lines of "Stop embarrassing us, you just can't come into people's homes and make comments about their children, and carry on like that." She stopped her idiotic comments at once, and after that she remained unusually subdued.

As we sat in the garden of the Amerindian family, our English host led us into a discussion in the course of which it became evident that the Manchester pair were fundamentalist Christians. I had to remind them of the genocide and theft of land that Christians had inflicted on the ancestors of these Amerindians, only to be told, quite categorically, that "Christopher Columbus was not a Christian". We had already touched on the evolution versus creation debate, and had established no common ground. I therefore returned to the lorry, and waited for the return journey to begin. I found that the best position was to sit or lie on the floor of the lorry. Mercifully, the journey back was a bit quicker, and for the first time ever I saw a macaw in the wild. From the back of a lorry it was possible to see it very clearly, when from a car or bus I couldn't be that sure – perhaps I would have missed it, or got only a quick glimpse. Travel in the back of a lorry has some compensations, but I was very glad to see the lights of the resort beaming their welcome home.

I had a very small dinner and went early to bed, and lying there wondered about the make-up of people in a fundamentalist heaven. Would there be any young men with English fathers and Amerindian mothers? Would there be any black women walkers? Would there be any blonde children from an Amerindian village, deep in the rain forest of Guyana? Or perhaps there would be room only for white people from Manchester, England. There was one thing I was sure of: even if there was room for me, I would have to say, "Thanks, but no thanks." I had found it very difficult to endure this type of company for a day, but to be stuck with them for eternity was unthinkable – but I know I needn't worry about that.

Travelling here and there by boat

My travel experience with boats is an echo of my travel experience with planes: to begin with I travelled quite happily on them, then, for no reason at all, I started being seasick. The only difference is that whereas I seem to have overcome my plane sickness, I still suffer acutely from seasickness. This means that for me travel by boat can sometimes be pure hell.

My worst boat journey ever was from Swanage in Dorset to the Scilly Isles, off the west coast of England. It was a beautiful summer's day, the sun was shining, the birds were singing, or at least swaying about in the breeze, we were on holiday in Dorset, and the Stone family were on a day-trip to the Scilly Isles.

Almost as soon as the boat left the quay I started to heave, and this went on for the two hours that it took to complete the journey to St Mary's Isle. I do not eat breakfast, so I had very little food to vomit up, and the result of this was a dreadful retching and heaving on an empty stomach. Trying to be sick but unable to bring up anything but bile, in addition to a constant and profuse sweat, I became so weak and dehydrated that I had to be helped off the boat. I stumbled to the beach and collapsed. Peter brought me some water, I drank my fill, then I fell into a deep sleep. Peter and the children went to explore St Mary's and also to visit another island very nearby. When they returned I was more or less myself. We talked about whether I should return by helicopter, as Peter had got the schedule and price. It seemed that everything was agreed, and that I would indeed return by helicopter.

Then, as I began to feel better, I had my doubts. I began to feel that to go by helicopter would mean the end of boat travel for me. I thought of my friend who had been in a swimming accident, in which three out of four had drowned. He had been the only survivor, and the next Saturday he went back to the same beach, for his usual afternoon swim. He told me that had he not gone then he would never ever have returned, and like me, he loved the sea. I decided to chance it. The return journey was much smoother, and I was glad that I had made this decision. But every time I go on a boat journey, I remember that trip, and I feel faint as I wonder whether what awaits me will be anything like that. So far I have not had a repeat of that experience.

During the round-the-world trip of 1992–93, I went on a visit to the Great Barrier Reef. The weather was bad and the sea was quite choppy. Several passengers were unable to return by boat, and a helicopter came for them. I am pleased to say that I was not one of these. I also managed to go whale-watching in New Zealand without being seasick, even though a young American girl sitting behind me was either throwing up or retching most of the time. I have even been fishing with my fisherman friend in Barbados, his boat little bigger than a large bathtub – and that didn't make me seasick. The condition is unpredictable, enough so that I approach each sea journey in the hope that this time I will be okay. In Norway, travelling by cruiser in the North Sea, I had no problem, but travelling in a Norwegian boat that now plied the waters of the Caribbean I was very, very seasick. I'd been on the *MV Windward* twice before without incident, and I was beginning to believe I may have conquered the problem. Unfortunately I was wrong. So much so that I am beginning to doubt whether I will ever have the courage to face that sea journey again. I now know that no amount of sickness will stop me going to sea, for even as I write this I am in the process of arranging a sailing holiday in the Bahamas for the summer (of 1998).

I did not start off my sea journeys by being sick. When I first travelled by boat in 1967, I had experienced no problem at all. Peter and I went with our six-months-old baby daughter from Barbados to Grenada on one of the boats that had been given to the defunct federation of the West Indies by the Canadian government. The two boats were called the *Federal Palm* and the *Federal Maple*. I think it was on the *Maple* we travelled. The boat was very overcrowded, very smelly and dirty. It was neither a pleasant nor enjoyable journey, and we were all glad to get off that boat – but I was never seasick. From Grenada we went on a little inter-island schooner to Trinidad, much to the embarrassment of my snobbish cousin, who felt that she would never live down the disgrace! "Why can't you travel by plane like everyone else? And you married to an Englishman and behaving like poor people!" We were not bothered by such considerations. The sea was rough, and that too did not bother me at all. I thought that this was normal, so I do not know why this suddenly changed and I began to suffer.

The year of my return to Barbados was 1967, after having left for India in 1962, and that was also the year Peter first visited the Caribbean. Since that time I have travelled quite extensively in the region by various methods, including boats, sometimes with Peter and the children, often on my own. In 1978 we all had a very enjoyable boat trip to Dominica, calling at other islands on the way – including St Vincent and St Lucia. We travelled in the MV *Stella*, a cargo boat with one large cabin, which suited us fine. The boat sailed at night and docked in the day, so we always had at least a day in port. We would find a hotel, and leave it in time to rejoin the boat for the next stage. When we reached Dominica we stayed for a week or so and waited to be picked up by the boat on its return. After that first visit to Grenada, in the *Federal Maple*, we never went there again by boat, but followed my cousin's advice and took the plane like everyone else. On one occasion we went from Grenada to Carriacou on one of the small schooners that ferry people and goods between the islands. Carriacou is a tiny island in the Grenadines, which is part of Grenada. I remember it as being as near to paradise as anything, but that was in 1973.

During that visit to Carriacou, Peter had a birthday and his treat was a visit to an even smaller island, called Robinson Crusoe Island. One of the local boatmen took us in his boat, under sail. We all loved the deserted island, and dreamed of staying on, but too soon it was time to leave. During the return journey the boatman began to tell us about the boating festival and regatta that had just passed, where vessels from the surrounding islands had competed, and our boatman had won the race for fastest boat. Peter used to sail, so he was very interested in all this, and soon the two of them got to talking non-stop about it. This led to the boatman demonstrating just what he and his boat were capable of. He increased his speed and the boat began to tilt on its side. I became very concerned for the safety of the children and for myself. Here we were with two youngsters in the open, almost certainly shark-infested seas, in a tiny boat, with no other in sight. Back home in Surrey our children were not allowed near the Thames without life jackets, yet here they were, on the open seas, totally unprotected. Somehow I did not feel that these were the conditions in which to marvel at anyone's sailing skills, and I made this quite clear and demanded to be returned to the safety of land. But Peter and the children really enjoyed the excitement and the danger, and none of them could understand why I had to be such a spoil-sport.

I have been frequently across the English Channel by ferry and hovercraft, but I am happy to switch my loyalty to the channel tunnel. I have lain prostrate on bunks on too many ferries. Things are different on sailing boats. Mad fishermen apart, I enjoy them, and at one time we actually belonged to a sailing club on the Thames, where I did an occasional bit of crewing. I've done a bit of sailing/cruising around the Solent in the south of England, and once, a long time ago, in the Scottish isles. We went from Tanzania to Zanzibar by cruiser, and we even considered sailing by dhow from Zanzibar to Mombassa, but decided against it when we found that it could take as long as three weeks if the wind fell. The thought of being stuck for so long on a small, crowded boat, without sanitation of any kind, just did not appeal. The plane journey took about two hours, so we did that. We did have an afternoon sailing/cruising on a dhow in the waters round Mombassa, and that was good. If the wind fell they simply turned on the engine! There was no waiting around, becalmed!

Our visit to the Bahamas presented us with many unusual and interesting experiences, not least boat travel to outlying islands. This came about due to our friendship with the local doctor. I say "local", but actually he was from the Philippines. His work took him on visits to patients in other smaller islands, travelling by boat from Abaco. He travelled by cruiser, and we were fortunate to be invited go with him on several of these visits. For me it was an amazing experience. On one occasion we arrived on a tiny islet at about three o'clock in the afternoon. There was no one about, and the houses were shut up and seemed deserted. Why had we come to an apparently uninhabited island? Well, it wasn't anything of the kind! Slowly people began to emerge, windows opened up, and very gradually the place came to life. We had arrived at the end of the afternoon siesta, and everyone seemed half-dazed as they walked slowly up the street to the doctor. They also seemed very, very pale – even for Caribbean whites, who put a lot of effort into preserving their paleness. I was told that this was due to inbreeding. The people were polite but distant, and I was glad to leave, as there was something sad and strange about these paradise islands, apparently suspended in time.

Our trip to the real Paradise Island, in search of the bird of paradise, was a really unique and memorable experience. It came about thus. It was 1989 and we were in Tobago, staying in an idyllic village call Charlotteville. We had read about Paradise Island and the elusive bird of paradise, which very few people had ever seen. (Sorry, but I have only just realised that this is another fisherman story, but please don't be put off.) Peter and I were fascinated by what we'd heard and we began to think about going to the island in the hope of seeing the bird. We must have mentioned our interest to people in the village, because very soon we had an offer. One of the fishermen offered to take us. We agreed a price, and agreed to meet him by the beach at five the next morning. Five o'clock found us waiting, as arranged, but no boat, and no boatman. Word was sent, and by 5.30 a somewhat sleepy fisherman arrived and the three of us got into his very small boat. We were soon well out to sea, when he announced that he had forgotten to "walk with the anchor!" – to "walk with" as in "to carry", "to bring" etc.

There we were, two middle-aged people, still unable to swim properly, and dependent on a man who had forgotten to bring an anchor with him. It was best not to think about what could go wrong. The boat tossed about like a cork in the huge waves, and we held on as best we could, trying to ignore the absence of anchor and life jackets. Then the boatman had an idea: "Why don't you two do some fishing?" We protested that we didn't know how to fish. His memory might have been faulty but his psychology was perfect! He advised us that this is a good time to start, and pushed a bag containing hooks and lines towards us. He had clearly not forgotten to walk with the fishing gear! He instructed us in the art of setting the bait and soon we were ready to begin fishing. At first we threw the fishing rods rather listlessly into the water, expecting nothing to happen. But fish began to bite and soon we are hauling them in and fishing for all we were worth – so much so that the time passed very quickly and soon we were approaching Paradise Island.

We saw the tourist boat just ahead of us, churning along, looking very staid and almost regal in the water. I began to wish that on this occasion at least I had been more of a tourist and less of a traveller. I felt sure that the tourist boat, with its American customers, would always have a built-in anchor and life jackets. We landed at the same time as a pair of American tourists off the tourist boat. We exchanged words of greeting and the hope that we would be lucky enough to see the bird of paradise. Peter and I spent the next two hours or so exploring the island, but we did not see any trace of the bird – in fact we didn't see that many birds at all. Soon it was time to leave, and I had by then decided against a repeat of the boat journey. Even our success at fishing was not sufficient to tempt me back into the boat, and I was going to walk back. First, I had to reach land. As a first step in this direction I suggested a drink at the hotel just opposite the island. Without an anchor the boatman could not leave his boat, so he dropped us off at the hotel, and sat in the boat waiting in the shallow water.

Peter waded out to the boat with a beer for him, then the two of us sat on the hotel veranda drinking and looking out at the boatman. I took a deep breath and announced to Peter that I was going to walk back. I was surprised to hear him say, "I will join you." How to tell the boatman? Simple, just call out and tell him what we were doing and wave him goodbye as we departed on foot. It was about one o'clock when we set off on our walk back to Charlotteville, and we arrived at our cottage at about half past three.

Not long after getting back, I saw from the safety of our cottage window the boatman sail around the bend and approach the sea front.

After tying up he brought us the fish. We told him how glad we were that he had returned safely, and he laughed and said that there had never been the slightest danger. He also told us that by abandoning him we had shown that, after all, we were "just tourists", but this did not stop him from accepting our invitation to dinner. That meal was going to be quite an international affair with Scots, English, Caribbean and American people all present. The party came about in a curious way. After leaving Paradise Island, and having had our drink at the nearby hotel, when we went to settle the bill we were dismayed to find that they did not take credit cards, and we had no cash. In the event we were saved from doing the washing up by a young American couple from Martha's Vineyard, whom we'd been chatting to. They agreed to pay the bill, and we invited them to our cottage so that we could repay the debt, and also to join us for dinner, and enjoy the fish that we had caught earlier that day.

After all this excitement I was glad to set off on a nice quiet walk back to the cottage, but this was not to be. Instead, I spent most of that time in the company of a Scotsman, whom I had met in a most interesting way. I've mentioned before that I am afraid of dogs, and I wrestle constantly with this fear. Sometimes I win, and make friends with a dog, but mostly I lose. On this occasion I passed a white man walking with a stick and a dog – or so I thought. The dog began to give me a lot of attention and I began to get scared, so I more or less ordered him to keep his dog away from me. Smiling sweetly, he replied in a soft Scottish accent, "He is not my dog, but you are welcome to walk along with me if you are scared." I admitted that I was scared and we walked along together. By this time the terrain was quite hilly, and Peter was some way behind us. It turned out that the Scotsman was married to an English painter, who was somewhere busily painting.

He walked me back to the cottage, and after a drink he left with a dinner invitation for himself and his wife. Soon after he left the Americans turned up. They had checked out of the expensive hotel and wanted a bed for the night. We had a spare room, so that was a problem solved. They helped to prepare the meal, and some time later the Scottish/English pair arrived, and last of all came the boatman. Everyone agreed that fish had never tasted so good. That boat trip to Paradise Island left me with some of my most memorable and enjoyable experiences.

For me boat travel has meant very different experiences depending on whether I was at sea or on a lake, river, or canal. My journeys at sea have often been spoilt by sickness, but I have always enjoyed river travel, and cruising about on a lake can be quite fun – provided it is not too long, like Lake Malawi. Three days on an overcrowded boat there is not my idea of pleasure cruising. A day and a half on Lake Kariba is just about right. During the trip down Lake Malawi we spent the entire time on the deck. We had been told that it would be easy to rent a cabin, but the few cabins there were had all been booked in advance, so we slept in chairs on an open deck for two nights. Peter lost his voice, but still says that he really enjoyed the journey, mainly because during the day he could pretend to be Michael Palin.

As for river travel, the Thames was the first real river I ever saw. In Barbados we'd talked about River Road and Constitution River, but when I saw the Thames I knew that this really was a river. If I can't be near the sea or in the mountains, then I must be near a river, and it was by the Thames that I first realised how important being by the water is to me. I've always enjoyed walking by the Thames in a way I don't like walking anywhere else in the world. Old Father Thames will always be special to me. When I first came to live in England, and for many years every summer, we went for river trips up and down it. I can remember breast-feeding my son on a boat in the shadow of Windsor Castle, attracting many disapproving stares. Before this I had been introduced to the Ganges, or the Hoogly as it is known in Calcutta, with boat trips one of the more pleasant aspects of life in Calcutta. When I returned there in 1992, I just had to go by the river. One afternoon, I slipped away by myself and did just that. It seemed to me that nothing had changed, for even the bathers seemed identical to the people who had been there thirty years before. The river seemed to me to be the only unchanged part of Calcutta – for better or worse, it was just the same. Then we went to southern USA, and visited St Louis, and here I saw the mighty Mississippi. We took a river trip on it in the *Mississippi Queen*. I was amazed at the width of that waterway, and I was overawed by its size. It was even wider than the Ganges, and so wide in fact that the Thames was a stream by comparison.

In the summer of 1997, during that visit to Guyana, I went for cruises on two rivers – the Essequibo and the Berbice. The trip across the Berbice was very short. On another occasion I took my friend for a day out on the Essequibo, exploring the river from the island resort that was our base. We were in a party of about ten people, plus three tour guides, and were at the gold-mining town of Bartica, when we went ashore to look around. In Guyana, at every port, airport and bus terminal, wherever people are on the move there are transport touts, begging and cajoling travellers to take their minibus, taxi, boat or whatever – and so it was with us. We were soon approached by one with "Are you travelling?" This is their opening bid for your custom. My Guyanese friend replied: "Yes, but we are on the tourist boat." He did not even try to hide his amazement as he repeated after her, "You are in the tourist boat?" We nodded. He was left in no doubt that we were two black women who had both the time and the money to travel tourist-style. We were not transporting food into the interior for our husbands or brothers, we had not come to collect or deposit our children or to check on our mothers, and we had not come to buy jewellery for resale. We were simply spending a day on the river, travelling for pleasure. What was the world coming to? He walked away with a very puzzled look on his face.

Part of our Essequibo experience was shooting the rapids in the cruiser that had been imported from the USA for that purpose. Our tour guides were really pleased with themselves for exposing us to such thrills. But to somebody who had been white-water rafting on the Zambezi it was very tame stuff. When we got back to the resort I asked one of the guides whether he had ever heard of the Victoria Falls? He replied that the only falls he'd ever heard of were the Kaieteur, and asked me in all seriousness if the Victoria Falls were in Barbados! I told him they were in Zimbabwe, in Southern Africa, though he didn't seem very interested. So, I did not mention anything about white-water rafting down the Zambezi, with the river in full flood and at its greatest speed. I thought that such a story would be wasted on a person who thought that the Victoria falls are in Barbados, and that white-water rafting could be done in a cruiser.

As I said, I love being by water, the sea, the river, or by canals. Canals are always associated with walking, but in the summer of 1971 we spent a week in a long boat on the Llangollen canal in North Wales. We always meant to go back, but never have.

Just a note about horses

Next to walking, horses probably provided people with the earliest form of transport. In most parts of the industrialised world horses no longer do provide transport, or work for their living, in the countryside or in the towns. Sometimes, walking alongside canals in England, it is still possible to see horses pulling canal boats, pretty much as they did in the great days of canal travel, but this is a comparatively rare sight. Not so in Guyana. In Georgetown, the capital, in 1997, it was surprising to me to see horse-drawn carts transporting wood around the city. This was an everyday occurrence and a common sight. I found it really interesting, as horses are not a regular part of my life, though I find them beautiful and fascinating creatures. I am also a bit in awe of them. The very first time I ever went on horseback was the summer of 1963, in Kashmir. I had joined one of the day trips to Pahlgam. We were picked up in Srinager and taken to a spot where there were men and horses waiting for us, and were told to mount the horses. I had very grave misgivings, but as there seemed to be no alternative I did as I was told. When we returned to Srinager at the end of that day, I had the greatest difficulty in walking – indeed I could hardly stand upright. Since that time I have been on horses, ponies and even on a donkey – and I can tell you that the world looks different from the back of an animal.

So, wherever I travel now, I always welcome the chance of exploring the countryside from the back of a horse. Moreover the only pleasant memory I have of my encounter with the Manchester lady (see above) is of an afternoon we spent horse-riding in the savannah. After the ride, in my effort to become more at ease with horses, I began to pat and talk to them in what I hoped was a friendly voice. We had already been told that the horses did not have names, so it was a matter of "good horse, nice horse" and such like nonsense. I noticed something about the black horse's ear. What was that? We looked closer. The ear was swarming with tics, to the extent that we could not distinguish between the two. My feeling of nausea promptly returned. Without discussing it we both called out to the Amerindian horseman to "come and see this!" – whereupon we showed him the horse's ear. "Yes," he said, "tics." He did not seem at all bothered. So the two of us decided to go and see the owner about it. We were at one over the horse, where there had been no common ground where people were concerned.

In the spring of 1998 we made our second visit to Venezuela and headed for Merída in the Andes. The summer before, back in England, when we were planning this trip, Peter proposed that we take the tram up and spend the day walking to the nearest village, where we would spend the night, returning to Merída by taxi the next day. The taxis commute between the villages daily. According to his guidebook, the walk was very easy and should present no problems. Talking about it in England was one thing, but facing the possibility of a 20-kilometre hike, high up in the Andes, with a man who'd had triple bypass surgery, and

350

was feeling none too well, filled me with dread. There was only one way we would do this journey, and that was to exclude walking, so this was one time when it wasn't on my agenda. We went by jeep and returned by pony, a journey that I have written about elsewhere.

Small railway journeys

I've described my railway journeys as "small", in order to contrast them with the great railway journeys of notable people. They are small in the sense of being insignificant, as rail travel has not figured very much in my mode of transport. I've been on three rail journeys that have been memorable: The Canadian Pacific from Calgary to Toronto, the East African Railways from Mybea to Dar es Salaam, and through the Copper Canyon in Mexico.

I have already given an account, in a different context, of a railway journey my son and I made across Canada in the summer of 1983. In February 1992 Peter and I crossed the border from Malawi into Tanzania, having hitched a lift on an oil tanker, with a driver who not only took us to the railway station at Mybea, but also waited to see us safely on the train to Dar es Salaam. The first thing we learnt on boarding was that we would not be allowed to travel together. In Tanzania passengers are segregated according to gender, men and women having to occupy separate compartments. Peter shared a compartment with a Chinese engineer, and I was in one with two women – one of them turned out to be from the Caribbean. She was married to a Tanzanian and was returning home after being away in the USA. I could not enjoy this train journey, and I spent most of the time lying down, and feeling very fragile. I recall how Peter and I came together from time to time, and on one of these occasions we went to the bathroom to filter some drinking water for me. I could only hope that we had not left it too late to do this, for by that time I'd had diarrhoea for almost three weeks.

The train passed through two national parks, and I stirred myself to see if I could spot any wildlife, and did in fact see the odd elephant. Viewing wildlife from a speeding train was not very rewarding, so I soon gave up. Anyway I was feeling really ill most of the time. The lady from Guyana recommended a doctor in Dar. I wrote down the name and address, but when I got to Dar I could not find the bit of paper. However, my condition improved and I decided to wait until we got to Mombassa, and see a doctor there. After a few days we set off by boat for Zanzibar, where we had to show our passports and go through customs, even though Zanzibar is supposed to be part of the republic of Tanzania.

Zanzibar has my record for being the most expensive place in the world from which to make an international phone call or send a fax – in fact I decided that a one-page fax, at £31, was a bit too much. I think it was the sugar-cane drink that I could not resist, or it may have been the aubergines from the roadside stall, but whatever it was my condition worsened and I was back to square one again. By the time we reached Mombassa the diarrhoea was very bad, and once again I was feeling quite poorly. The images I carry in my mind of that rail journey across Tanzania are very much bound by the four corners of the compartment and the toilet. This was not a good time for me.

Mexico and our railway journey though the Copper Canyon was, I am pleased to say, a very different experience. Our journey took us from Los Moches to Pasada Barrancas and then on to Creel. It was done like this to maximise enjoyment of the canyons, and unlike the Tanzania experience I was fit and well, and able to enjoy the trip very much. I have written elsewhere about my experience of hiking in the Copper Canyon, but as for the train journey itself I have two outstanding memories. The first is of a young American white man with one leg. We were in the same part of the train for most of the day before I realised that he had only one leg – and that was because he was wearing shorts. I have a friend, who had recently started wearing a prosthesis, having lost a leg due to diabetes. The difference between him and this young man, who literally ran around the train, hopping off and on at every stop, could not have been greater. I wondered about that difference – was it just in the technology, and that the young man's artificial leg was as good as a real one? Or was it the age at which the limb had been lost? The American was in his early twenties, and my friend just was a bit older than I, about fifty-five. Or was it simply a difference in attitude, with a difference in coping strategies?

On that train in the Copper Canyon I reflected on this, all the while aware of the two men sitting just behind us, a couple of old men from Alabama. I had never met anyone from Alabama, and nothing I had heard about that place made me want to – least of all two old white men travelling on a train in the Copper Canyon. Things have a way of happening. I knew their story before I met them, for they had been coming on the same trip for many years, each year with their wives. Their wives were now dead, but out of habit they continued the custom, even though they admitted that without the women it wasn't the same.

Although they were travelling together, they still seemed lonely for other conversation. Every now and then one or the others would approach another traveller and begin to chat. As I observed the various reactions, some welcoming, some cold, I felt quite safe in my blackness, and was sure that two men from Alabama would not want to engage me in conversation. I was wrong. My turn came. Not only did I get into conversation, we were invited to share in their lunch. What was I to make of this? Were they just two nice old men, or were they retired, or even active members of the Ku Klux Klan? I would never know, just as I would never know the reason for the difference between my friend with the missing leg and the young man on the train. The ride through Copper Canyon was fantastic, and I think I needed to reflect on these human problems in order to stop myself from being overwhelmed by its scale and grandeur.

Lost in Africa

My most interesting experience of being lost while driving a car was Gaborone, the capital of Botswana, in Southern Africa. I had been invited to a cocktail evening by the couple I was staying with, but I was not really a party person so I opted instead to attend a meeting of writers and journalists at a nearby hotel. For transport, I was offered the use of the spare car, and as the distance was so short I gratefully accepted. The house where I was staying was on a new middle-class estate that could have been located in Surrey, except that the streets had no names and the houses no telephones. I could see that it was very important for me to be able to find my way safely back after the meeting. It started at six p.m. and was only a block or two away, so I left the house just after five, in order to have a good look round and establish some markers for the return journey. I drove very slowly and noted the exact spot to turn off the main road into the estate, then into the road where the house was located. It seemed very straightforward, and I felt that I had everything well under control. I had no doubt that I would find my way back with little trouble.

I was wrong – very wrong. I did okay on the first turn, but after that nothing was where it should have been. It did not help that there was no street lighting at all, so I couldn't see the markers I had noted. I drove round and round. I considered going back to the hotel and staying there for the night, but my friends did not have a phone, so I would be unable to tell them where I was. Although my friend's husband worked for the Botswana telephone company, after more than two years they were still waiting for a phone of their own. As I could not check into a hotel, I decided to wait by the road and hope I could see them as they came back from the cocktail party, though I really did not know if they were already home. I waited for about half and hour, then saw a car with a woman driver, with children. As the car turned into the road where I was parked, it slowed down, and I quickly jumped out of mine and asked the way to my friend's house, desperately trying to describe its location. Unfortunately, like me the car-driver was also a visitor. She was from Zimbabwe and had no real idea about the geography of the place. She offered to take me to where she was staying, and felt sure that someone there would be able to help me. I thought "any port in a storm", and I duly followed her to a house a few streets away. Here, we both explained my predicament, and another young lady volunteered to take me in her car to look for my friend's house. Once we had found it we would return for the car.

I gratefully accepted this suggestion and the two of us set off in search of the house. At this point I was fairly confident of being able to recognise it and the street, but I stopped being sure of anything after I'd got it wrong about five or six times. I was about to give up any hope of ever finding it when I saw one of my markers – a white garage door – signalling the turn into my road. This time I *was* really sure, and this time I was right. The ordeal was over. It had taken us almost an hour to find a place that was a five-minute car ride away. We returned to the lady's house and collected the car. She insisted on following me back, just to make sure that I did not get lost again. After she'd seen me safely home, she accepted my invitation to lunch the next day. The next morning, as I walked round the estate, it seemed impossible that I could have been so hopelessly lost in such a small place.

The previous night, when we were driving round in our search, my rescuer told me of a visitor from the USA, a cousin of hers, who had been lost trying to find her house. He had ended up staying the night in the police station. He had been unable to contact his mother, for again there was no telephone. She worked herself into such a state that she suffered a stroke and had to be admitted to hospital. After she heard about my adventure, my friend (the one I was staying with) told me of a similar experience she'd had. Apparently, not very long after moving to the estate, she had been unable to find her own home and had walked round for about an hour in broad daylight, carrying a toddler on her back and her shopping in both hands. She had got off at the wrong bus stop and had been totally disoriented. I felt slightly comforted by these stories, and at least I had not ended up at the police station, and with me it had been pitch-black night and not the middle of the bright sunny day. Even so, this experience left me feeling deeply mortified.

Lost in Venezuela

Another quite expensive experience of being lost was in Venezuela, in South America. Peter and I had travelled by boat to Margarita, a small island off the main Venezuelan cost, where we spent a few days before leaving by plane for Caracas. We planned to travel around and explore until it was time to meet the boat, then we would head for a location near the port and stay overnight, to be within reach of the boat on the day of our departure for Trinidad. Things were going well, and there were no thefts, no losses. On the day before we were due to meet the boat we headed for the port of La Guaira, booked into a hotel and decided to spend the day relaxing.

We were required to re-confirm our booking, and as my Spanish was not quite up to this I asked the hotel receptionist to do it for me. He telephoned the shipping company and a long discussion followed. Something was happening and it smelt of trouble. It took some time for the story to unfold, but after he had finished speaking with the booking clerk the receptionist asked me how we planned on getting to the boat. I said by taxi. He told me that it would take two days by taxi. I told him we had passed the port on the way to the hotel, and it was just up the road. He said: "That is not the port you want; your port is 350 miles away." His English was very good, I understood him perfectly, and we were off course by the margin he'd said.

Peter was upstairs on the roof garden relaxing by the swimming pool, and I decided that as a visual aid was required he would have to come down to reception so that I could explain the situation fully. Reluctantly he dragged himself away. There was a big map of Venezuela in the hotel foyer. We went up to it, and I pointed and said, "We are here and we should be there, and the difference is approximately 350 miles." That was the distance between La Guaira and Guiria. We were in the former, but we should have been in the latter. We decided to return to Caracas airport early the next day. Option number one was to fly to the town nearest the port where we should have been, completing the journey by taxi. Failing this we would get a plane direct to Trinidad, and forget about the boat.

Option number one came through, and we got to see a lot more of Venezuela than we had planned. We arrived at the port with hours to spare, but with no money to pay the taxi man, who would not accept traveller's cheques, and impounded our luggage in exchange for his fare. The shipping agents saved the day by opening up their office and changing the travellers' cheques, and only then did we recover our luggage. The fare we had been charged was exorbitant, but we were in no position to argue. We never did count the cost of this little episode, but I know that getting lost can sometimes be very expensive and also very stressful.

On a bicycle made for one

As a means of individual transport, next to walking I like cycling best of all, and one of the joys of living in Dorset is to be able to ride along miles of cycle paths. I once got lost on a weekend bike ride in East Sussex, in the Seven Sisters park.

I still can't figure out how it happened, as I have walked that park in all weathers at all times of the year, and thought I knew it very well. The only difference was the mode of transport. Every time I thought that I was on the cycle path I would end up on the footpath, and when I tried to find the cycle path again I would end up practically in the sea. This was quite early in the morning. I had set off from the YHA hostel just after seven, and there was virtually no one around. I decided to stop trying to find the cycle path, and instead cycle on the footpath, all the while keeping a look out for park wardens and the like.

The only problem was the condition of the terrain and frequency of stiles. The terrain was rough and at times very steep, not ideal for cycling. At each stile I had lifted my bike and rucksack over, before climbing over myself. There are seven hills and a lot more than seven stiles on this trail, and it was very hard work. Luckily it was too early for wardens and I had almost reached the park exit before I saw the first group of hikers, by which time I had found the proper cycle path, so no worries there. From the Seven Sisters I rode on to Eastbourne, and spent the afternoon in the sauna and swimming pool, before taking the train back to Surrey. It had been an interesting, but very tiring weekend.

There were two memorable things about that weekend cycling in Sussex. As well as constantly losing my way along the cycle path, there was an encounter on the bench outside the YHA. Although the YHA has made many concessions to the market place, their hostels still do not open before a set time, usually 5.30 in the afternoon. I had arrived well before that, and was sitting on a bench, quietly enjoying the views. After about ten minutes I was joined by a man who was obviously a hiker, as he was well kitted out and carrying a lot of gear. We started chatting and he told me that he was spending a week cross-country walking. He had been planning it for a long time, and although he was still recovering from a recent illness, he had persisted with his plans. He did not look well. He seemed exhausted, and very relieved to have reached the hostel. Then he wanted to know what I was up to? I told him I was spending the weekend riding from Hastings to Eastbourne through Seven Sisters Park. He reacted to this information in a very strange, almost hostile manner, asking me if I was sure I knew what I was doing, riding about the countryside on my own? My own reaction was equally curious. I became very confused as I tried to explain and justify myself. I don't know why I responded to this strange white man in this way, at whose patronising, almost insulting questions, I would normally have told him to mind his own business. Well, it was a good learning experience, and since that time I have not been on a weekend ride.

On being a vegetarian traveller – food and drink

One of the forms I had to complete in the process of being allocated a place at an Indian university requested information on my diet. I had to say whether or not I was a vegetarian. I was completely unfamiliar with the word and had to look it up before responding with a very firm "no". This was in 1961. By 1976 or thereabouts I not only knew what the word meant, I had become a partial vegetarian, eating no meat of any kind but still eating fish. In 1995, when we were travelling in Central America, I decided to cut fish out of my diet, and I have not felt the need for it since.

Those who are vegetarian by religion are often confused by my attitude towards meat-eating. I have no problem cooking and serving meat and fish, I just do not want to eat it myself. I also do not have any strong feelings about animal rights and things like that. I try to explain to people who are vegetarian by religion, i.e. vegetarians from conviction, that my being one has nothing to do with religion or morals and everything to do with taste and aesthetics. I went off meat firstly because of the taste. Once I began thinking about it I realised that the poor taste was due to the way the animals were reared and the way in which meat was being produced and processed. I found that I could live a reasonably healthy life without meat, and as I had ceased to enjoy it, why bother?

I do not like people making a fuss over the fact that I do not eat meat or fish. I have never seen a meal prepared where meat and fish were the only items on offer, and I operate on the basis that there is sure to be some non-meat/fish foods being served. No one ever sits down to a meal consisting only of the flesh of dead animals and fishes. In hotels and restaurants I do not object to paying the same price as meat-eaters, provided I get an equivalent meal, and not a limp lettuce leaf and a stale slice of cheddar or a salad for lunch, tea and dinner. This type of thing used to happen quite frequently when I first cut meat out of my diet. That was twenty years ago, but things have improved, and almost anywhere in the world one can now find a vegetarian item on most hotel and restaurant menus.

"Most" does not mean all. And one can still be penalised for not eating meat or fish. One of the worst Christmas lunches I've ever had was in Costa Rica in 1996. We had left San José, the capital city, where there were lots of vegetarian restaurants, to spend Christmas in Quepos, on the Atlantic coast. As soon as we arrived I went down with flu. Our apartment had no hot water, very little of anything, including cutlery, kitchen utensils etc. Although the weather was hot the water was very cold, and bathing in it did me no good at all. I spent most of the time shivering or sweating or both. Hoping I would recover in time to enjoy a Christmas lunch Peter set out in search of a suitable restaurant, with a good view and a menu that catered for vegetarians. It took him a while but eventually he returned very pleased with himself, his mission accomplished. So, on Christmas day we went for our lunch to a restaurant with a spectacular view overlooking the sea, but when I went to order something vegetarian I got a very odd look. We were told in no uncertain terms that they were serving only turkey and ham, as this was their Christmas menu. But what about the assurances that had been given to Peter?

No one had an explanation, and the person who Peter had dealt with was nowhere to be seen, and all they could offer me was an omelette. By this time I had completely lost any interest in food, and did not care what I ate. So I accepted the omelette, which was served with carrots and cauliflower, all of which was very tasteless. I thought of the beauty and variety of the vegetables in any Costa Rican market and wondered what possessed them to serve watery carrots and cauliflower on Christmas day. When the bill came we were amazed to find that we had to pay a hefty excess for my "special dish", almost twice as much as for Peter's turkey and ham.

Because I once used to be very fond of meat, when I changed, many of my family and friends found it very hard to accept. After more than twenty years of not eating meat I was recently invited to lunch by a friend who had cooked a chicken dish especially for me! I said to her, "You know I haven't eaten meat for ages!" Her reply was that she thought she'd tempt me, knowing how much I'd liked that particular chicken dish. On a visit to Barbados, soon after changing my diet, I was invited to lunch where pig trotters had been specially prepared for me. Even as a meat-eater I had never ever eaten pig trotters, so it was a very awkward lunch. I was left in no doubt that I had not been a good guest, who had not appreciated the effort that had been made for me. A few years later, when I went to dinner at this home, one of the sons of the family was going through his Rasta stage and was not eating meat, so I was no longer such an oddity or a difficult guest. In Barbados in the spring of 1998 I went shopping for avocados in Speightstown. I told the market woman that I wanted good avocados because they were an important part of my diet. She looked up at me and exclaimed: "You vegetarian! I going that way too, slowly… my body can't tek too much meat… too much chicken… I turnin' more an more to de vegetables and fruits… an ma daughter too, she is coming along wid me." This conversation, especially in this context, really surprised me, as Barbadians have one of the highest rates of chicken consumption in the world.

I have never been a big eater and since becoming fully vegetarian I think that my life has become much simpler. The first time I visited Zimbabwe I did have a problem. We were away from shops and restaurants and there was virtually no fruit or vegetables on offer. The main dish was a kind of corn meal served with meat and gravy, though without the meat and gravy it was almost impossible to eat the corn meal. I lost a lot of weight during those three weeks. In India during my student days I had been introduced to curries of all kinds, including meat and fish, and I had enjoyed them very much. In those days I knew very few people in Calcutta who were truly vegetarian, and even on the so-called meatless days it was always possible to get a meal with meat in Calcutta.

It was in Delhi where I first tasted tandoori chicken, and the experience lives in my mind to this day. My American friend and I were on our return journey from Kashmir to Calcutta via Delhi. We had arrived by bus, and we were tired and hungry. A shower lifted the tiredness, and we changed and went to find the restaurant that had been recommended as serving the best tandoori chicken in India. I can't recall the name of it but I believe it is still functioning and still serving the best tandoori chicken in India. That night we ordered one whole chicken and two nans (unleavened bread) and we did not stop eating until, as toddlers say, it was "all gone". I thought the taste of the chicken exquisite, and I had never tasted anything like it. This was a unique experience. I do not think I would ever have become vegetarian if all meat tasted like the chicken we had that night.

In Kenya, after returning from the Serengeti, we took our hostess for dinner at the Carnivore restaurant. This was famous for its advertisement: "You've seen the animals of the Serengeti, now eat them!" They do not have any vegetarian dishes on their menu. You might say there was no call for them, and you'd be right. So, they were thrown into confusion by my request for a non-meat dinner. They had all the exotic animals of the Serengeti on offer, including giraffe, elephant, ostrich, and crocodile – but nothing for a vegetarian. In the end I settled for the inevitable salad, while the other two stuffed themselves with every kind of flesh.

I have been told that all Chinese cooking is done with pig fat – so as a vegetarian I should not eat in a Chinese restaurant, though I am unable to become very exercised over that as an issue. I know that anywhere in the world where there is a Chinese restaurant I can find something to eat. A typical one will always have a menu with a very wide variety of vegetables, as well as different types of noodles and rice dishes. But, on occasions, Chinese food is served in a way calculated to deaden the appetite of such as me. In Hong Kong I attended a banquet in honour of some visiting American academics. Adorning the centre of the table was a huge chicken complete with head and feet. I found it very difficult to ignore the chicken, and my eyes kept returning to *its* eyes even as my stomach heaved. A colleague sitting next to me had a similar reaction and decided he would become vegetarian for the duration of that meal. Our Chinese hosts obviously did not share our weak dispositions. Apparently, there is a Chinese saying that sums up their attitude to food: if it has legs and it is not a table, we eat it; if it flies and it is not an aeroplane, we eat it; if it swims and it is not a boat, we eat it. This almost certainly explains why there are not many Chinese who are vegetarian.

Although my being vegetarian is not based on any moral philosophy or values, I have found that being one can present problems and dilemmas of that kind. Take bananas. I have always loved bananas, and until I went to Australia I was totally unaware of the politics behind them. I had heard the phrase "banana republic", used to describe some countries in Central and South America, but I never gave it much thought. Now I know that like the Latin American drugs industry the banana industry was established and protected by US interests. The banana industry generates massive pollution, and massive profits.

In Costa Rica the banana industry is associated with massive environmental pollution, and ill health in its plantation workers. Male sterility results from exposure to pesticides, and there are birth defects in children born to banana plantation employees. In Costa Rica concerns have become so great that the government has set up a commission of inquiry to examine the role of bananas in the economy. The profits are so big that a Chiquita banana grown in Central America and exported to Australia can be sold for less than a locally grown one – and still make a profit. The USA government and Chiquita bananas are threatening the small, improvised eastern Caribbean states with bankruptcy over the preferential treatment their bananas receive from the European Union (EU). However, I try not to think too much about the politics, otherwise I might be tempted to start eating beef! (Not really, only joking.)

Enough about food. Let's talk about drink, or to be precise, water. When travelling this is my main problem, and on several occasions I have been very ill as a consequences of drinking, or otherwise ingesting, contaminated water. So now I am careful to the point of tedium, and drink only filtered, boiled or bottled water. When I was growing up in Barbados I thought all water tasted as good. On my way to India in 1962 I visited England and found the water tasted awful, though from there I went to India and found that it was often not available at all, or when it was it was both foul to drink and dangerous to one's health. When I left India in 1965 and came to live in England, at first I could not get used to the fact that to get a drink of water all one had to do was turn on the tap. From time to time I would turn it on just to see the miracle of safe, running water. Today in Barbados you get the same horrible taste of water as anywhere else in the world – full of chlorine and pesticides, but safe to drink. In Costa Rica the taste is very nice, but in spite of what the guide books may say, it is not safe to drink – or at least not safe for me to drink (as usual Peter came to no harm).

Once in Costa Rica we were renting a casita (a little house) in the grounds of a much bigger one. One of the things that had attracted me to it was its location, which was at the top of a hill with spectacular views. The only trouble was the ascent up this steep hill. The taxis didn't want to drive there because of the multitude and depth of the potholes. There was a bus that went at unpredictable times, but stopped halfway up. We stayed in this cottage for a whole month while we went to school to improve our Spanish. Every morning at eight o'clock we set off down hill, with our books and our bags, to catch the bus into Escazu. And every afternoon we did the return journey, except that with each passing day the walk up became harder, not easier, as the hill seemed to become only steeper. One afternoon I returned to the casita alone, as Peter had gone into San José. I had just completed the walk and was standing outside the landlord's house waiting for the key. Peter had taken ours with him, and so I had to borrow the spare. There I was, standing admiring the flowers, and the next thing I remember was lying on the ground with the landlady holding up my head and telling me to lie still. I had passed out.

Medical examination and tests established that I was heavily infected with water-borne bacteria. Unlike other, similar occasions, this time I'd been struck down without warning. I had been happily drinking the water, and because I showed no signs of illness I assumed it to be safe. So, from now on, I vowed to stick to filtered or bottled water forever after, though I knew that one day somewhere in the world I would come back from a long walk, and without thinking pick up a glass of water and drink. Only when the diarrhoea and sickness started would I remember my vow. If my experience in Mombassa is anything to go by, one day it might well be my last glass of water. Such is life.

The word "transport" has different meanings in different parts of the world. In urban metropolitan societies the word is often used in connection with sophisticated systems and massive movements of people. In poorer countries the word is used more for something on a much smaller scale. In Dominica, as you walk along or stand about, you may be asked if you want transport. No one ever says, "Do you want a lift?" or "Have you got a car?" It was always do you want transport or have you got transport? In Guyana one is always being asked, "Are you travelling?" This means exactly the same thing as, "Have you got transport?" In the process of travelling and being transported, I have met fellow-travellers, made new friends, and perhaps new enemies too. My involvement with and observation of other travellers have not led me to believe that travel broadens the mind. I have learnt that, depending on each individual, it is as likely to broaden the mind as it is to confirm existing prejudices, and to create new stereotypes.

During my travels – by whatever means – I have sometimes lost my way, and as a consequence have had unexpected and sometimes interesting encounters. Travelling or not, food and drink are essential to life, and I have found that being on the road has become less risky and more enjoyable since I decided to stop eating meat and fish. This does not solve the problem I have with water. In the industrialised world the supply and delivery is fast becoming just like any other industry. Water is no longer taken for granted, and the worse it tastes the more it costs. But at least it is relatively safe to drink. In the rest of the world water is very often contaminated by human and industrial waste, and pesticides used in agriculture. For many millions of people water, which should be the source of life, becomes the reason for ill-health and often of death. Too often, the availability of transport and my wish to travel make me one of those millions.

On being "packaged"

I have been visiting Spain since 1965, but it was only in the summer of 1997 that I experienced a package holiday to that country. Only then did I realise what a gap this constituted in my knowledge and understandings of travel and mass tourism.

Within a day of my return from Barbados to Dorset, in June 1997, Peter was in hospital suffering from chest pains. The remainder of the summer was spent in worry and anxiety. Not only was Peter's health not good but his mother had moved to Dorset, which only increased our worry-quota by one hundred per cent! As our thirty-second wedding anniversary approached I decided that we simply had to get away. But on this occasion I did not feel confident enough to travel independently, so I turned to Thomson's holidays.

Actually, for us being packaged wasn't that bad. We spent just one afternoon lying on the beach, and the rest of the time we were off walking and exploring as usual. My fears about Peter's health proved groundless and we had some lovely walks, and even had our very first swim in the Mediterranean. We travelled by bus to outlying villages in the Sierra Nevada, and on one such journey I could have sworn that I had wandered into one of Pedro Antonio Alarcón's stories. There was an old peasant talking about country life, and although I did not get all that he said, his tone and manner of speaking came straight out of Alarcón. We also spent an afternoon cycling, visiting a nature reserve about ten kilometres from where we were staying. We hired a car and went to Granada for the day. I had waited a long time to get there, and it was worth it. I looked into the possibility of a trip to Cadiz, but had to decide against it. We were delighted to find that we were free to organise our time as we pleased and that there was no pressure to "join in".

For me the worst thing about a package holiday was being penalised for being a vegetarian. It was a case of water everywhere and not a drop to drink – except that it was food everywhere that could not be eaten, at least by me. We were on what is called half-board – breakfast and evening meal. These were served buffet-style, and one could eat as much as one wished. This approach to mass catering seemed to offer people the opportunity of practising how to be starving refugees. There was not much for me to practise on, as the caterers had a meat/fish obsession, even added meat or fish to the vegetable soups, pastas and rice. No dish was complete without it. Only a few of the salads and vegetables were spared, so there was very little that I could have. However, I have to admit that I did once over-indulge – when I had two helpings of spinach!

Apart from the amusement of watching people stuff themselves, this experience of being packaged brought home to me the fact that Europe has benefited most from mass-tourism. In 1997 30,000,000 people visited Spain – and we were two of them! Although I already knew something of the sociology of mass tourism, I found it necessary to be packaged in order to appreciate its full implications. Thirty million is an awful lot of people, so just think what that means in terms of beds, linen, food, transport. Where would the Spanish economy be without its tourist industry? Where indeed!

I doubt whether this kind of scale is matched elsewhere in the world, and the movement of people on this magnitude must profit the European economy as a whole. Airlines must depend on this trade for a substantial portion of their revenue. Manufacturing industry must also be tied into building, servicing and maintaining the infrastructure, to meet the demands and the wear and tear of so many people. I begin to understand for myself that it is not the poor countries of the south that have benefited. The tourist industry in poor countries is almost always owned, controlled and managed by people from Europe and

North America, and the profits flow from poor countries to rich ones. Therefore the rich countries of the north are the main beneficiaries of developing tourism in the poor countries of the south. Apparently, Spanish money and know-how control the development of tourism in the Dominican Republic, in the Caribbean, so it stands to reason that in this case most of the profits are vacuumed away from poor to rich. The local economy will count itself lucky with the crumbs.

On the visit to Southern Spain I saw another side to the water problem, and this was in relation to tourism. Neither at the hotel nor on the beach was there any word of warning or any suggestion that the water was anything other than plentiful. All the beaches are peppered with showers, which never fail to dispense water in abundance. So imagine our surprise when we saw a notice in English in the entrance to the Almeria museum, asking visitors to conserve water. This was the one and only reference to conservation that we saw during the two weeks we spent there. In the visitor's centre at Cabo de Gata I learnt that Southern Spain is in a perpetual struggle not to become a complete desert, though there are large areas where the desert has already won. Even so the fight for the tourist money must take precedence over the fight to save the land. So be it. And now for something completely different.

Walking dangerously

> I shall be telling this with a sigh
> Somewhere ages and ages hence:
> Two roads diverged in a wood, and I—
> I took the one less travelled by,
> And that has made all the difference.
>
> Frost, Robert, from "The Road not Taken", in
> *The Road not Taken*, Gramercy Books, NY

There is danger in walking, just as there is danger in just about everything. Of the many involved in walking, I find myself ambivalent about getting lost. Why? Well, if I am truly honest, I have to admit to the delicious excitement that often goes with being lost, and the relief and sense of achievement that comes with a happy ending. However, underlying each such experience is the very real fear that this one may *not* have a happy ending. A walker might end up lost for days, to be attacked by man or beast, or might simply die of exposure to the cold or heat, or of hunger and thirst. A walker can be killed by a car or bus, or drop down dead from exhaustion, just because her time had come. Walking/hiking is just the same as living, and the dangers and the risks are as many and varied as the people involved.

There are lots of walkers, especially men, who like Peter never travel without a map, but *still* manage to get lost. I can barely map-read myself, and of course I get lost too. As I said, this can be a positive experience, extending one's knowledge not least of one's self. It also adds danger, excitement and adventure to what might otherwise be mundane. Even so, getting lost is not to be recommended, especially for lone women hikers. For us there is an increased risk of being robbed, raped or killed. I've had many experiences of losing my way, becoming disoriented, or simply taking the long way round to my destination.

These include losing myself on a walk in a wood in New England, in the USA, but becoming completely and utterly disorientated while driving a car in Botswana, in Southern Africa, is quite another matter. I think that I have now come to regard getting lost occasionally as part of the experience of travelling and hiking, and I accept that I will probably always have occasional experiences of this kind, however careful or well prepared I try to be. Of course, there are times when I am neither careful nor well prepared: my walk in New England was an impulsive action – I saw a footpath and wanted to explore it, and simply gave in to the urge to walk.

But in Botswana I'd planned my journey meticulously, and even did a dry run and marked my route very carefully, though that was in the light of day. In the blackness of night all of my markers vanished and I was left totally confused and disoriented. I have given a full account of this episode earlier in the chapter, so I will continue here with some other instances of getting lost.

Many years ago, while on holiday on the Isle of Skye, my two children and I went for a little walk and somehow ended up in a field of barley – or was it oats? The farmer came out shouting and carrying on, and in my haste to escape his fury I ran and twisted my ankle. I then had to walk about three kilometres back to the cottage, in great pain and carrying a toddler. By the time we reached it my ankle was very swollen and for the rest of the holiday I was able only to limp around on my bandaged foot. As I said before, walking can be very dangerous. If I had not twisted my ankle I might have ended up being shot by an irate farmer.

I also recall with a mixture of feelings the Sunday I spent with a friend on the Ridgeway, when the two of us became hopelessly lost. Map in hand, we wandered around for hours, covering about forty kilometres instead of the sixteen we had intended. We had planned our walk very well, two women out for a day's hike, and we had no thought of losing our way. The problem was that we used "the Gallops" sign as our marker, without realising how many hundreds of these there were on the Ridgeway. The two of us were chatting as we walked along, and not taking much notice of our surroundings, and by the time we started to take note of our location in relation to where we had parked the car there was hardly anyone about. We were well and truly lost. We were the last people to leave the Ridgeway that Sunday afternoon, and when at last we found the car I could not disguise my gratitude to the inventors of the internal combustion engine. I do love walking, but a masochist I am not.

Lost in darkest Sussex

For the many years Peter and I have walked in the English countryside, we have mostly followed the recommended walks. But sometimes we go on an unknown route. Peter has map in hand, and we set off to explore a bit of the English countryside. So it was on this particular Sunday in the spring – the year I can't remember. We drove down towards Brighton, and just past a stables, near a pub with a "footpath" sign nearby, we stopped and parked. I am not going to try to describe the English countryside in spring – anyone interested should read the English Romantic poets – let me just say it was a lovely day. Peter led the way, with the help of his ordnance survey map, and I simply enjoyed the walk.

Then the weather changed. It started to rain while we were up on a hill in an open field. Here I began to show an interest in our location – for where were we? "Well, according to the map we should be here [pointing], but… " In fact we were lost, but luckily the sky was clear and it had only been a mild shower. We continued walking, but soon I started getting thirsty, tired and irritable. "What's the good of all this map-reading if we're going to get lost anyway?" A stony silence greeted this outburst.

Eventually we descended near a small hamlet, by which time it was around 1.30 p.m., and in those days all pubs closed at 2.00. I felt as if both starvation and dehydration were staring me in the face. That couldn't be so, and we were probably a couple of hours from home, once we actually found the car. I decided to knock on one of the doors and ask the way, though Peter was dead against this – not only because like most men he hates asking, but it was quite likely we would be disturbing the family at Sunday lunch. I did not let this thought deter me, for as the good book says, "Knock and it shall be opened unto you, seek and ye shall find."

Peter held back, but I went forward and knocked on the door, and indeed it was opened unto me, and we were pointed in the direction of the nearest public house. The lady I spoke to behaved as if she regularly answered her door to black women hikers asking the way to the nearest pub. I would never have done this in the USA, as I would have been too afraid of being shot (there was a Japanese who was killed by an American householder when, in very similar circumstances, he approached a house to ask for directions).

A Sunday morning in Connecticut

I was once lost on a hike in the USA, but I am pleased to say that I did not approach a householder for directions, and so was not shot dead. Nor did I try to hitch a lift, and so avoided the possibility of being lynched. In recent years both of these things happened to two non-white male walkers in that great democracy. Having said that, it is only fair to say that when I was walking – in New Hampshire – people kept offering me lifts. Eventually I did accept one into town.

In the bookstore the lady in charge told me that she had walked in Europe, and regretted that there was nothing like that here in the USA. In the video store I got into another conversation about walking, and a female customer started telling me about some nice walks in the area. She offered to take me in her car and show me one. I accepted my second lift of the day and as we drove along she told me that, as a youngster, she and her friends used to do a lot of walking, and this one up the hill was one of her favourites. She went on to say that it had been years and years since she'd been up there.

I was dropped at the side of the road and shown a path that, I was told, led up to the summit. So, I just kept walking onward and upward until I reached the top. At the top there was a splendid view, which I sat and enjoyed, in splendid isolation. Then I retraced my steps, went into town and got a lift home. I promised my friend that I would show her the walk, but when we went to find it at the weekend the path had completely disappeared. I searched and searched but couldn't find it anywhere. I began to have a strange feeling that my friend thought I'd made the whole thing up, because, as she said, she'd lived in Vermont for more than twenty years and no one had ever shown her their favourite walk. As far as she knew no one ever walked. What could I say? Anyway, all this is just a little aside, a glimpse of another version of the USA, because I must return to the story I am supposed to be telling. It is set in Connecticut and not in New Hampshire.

I was spending a miserable weekend in Storrs, Connecticut, and on the Saturday I'd fallen and injured one of my fingers, which was swollen and very painful. On the Sunday morning I went with the man of the house to watch him cut up some trees into logs for his winter fuel. As we were driving back to the house, I spotted a footpath leading into some woods. I was overwhelmed by the urge to walk, so I asked about it and was told that it would come out not very far from the house. There was no stopping me then! But to be on the safe side, I asked for more directions, and was told that all I had to do was keep walking straight ahead. Then there was no way I could get lost. So, I got out of the car – which immediately sped away and was soon out of sight. Once in the wood I saw that there were several paths, and very soon I had lost any idea of which direction was straight ahead.

Unlike the poet, I took the road "most travelled by", and hoped for the best. Several times I went up blind alleys, and more than once I ended up by a river – but was it the same river? I had no idea, and I was not going to ask any of the fishermen quietly fishing, as this would be too much of a give-away – first that I was a stranger, and second I was lost. So, I would pause by the water and look around, before moving on. I tried to keep walking roughly in the direction that I understood to be straight on, but after so many diversions this was pure guesswork. I must have guessed right, for at last I emerged from the wood and found myself on the outskirts of the town. When I got back to the house I agreed with my host that it had been a nice walk, though I made no mention of the many doubts and diversions that I had experienced along the way.

Oslo in the spring and France in the summer

In Norway I went the long way back to the YHA hostel – this was on the outskirts of Oslo. I was travelling by bus and had got off at the wrong stop. It was April, but still very cold, and as the night began to close in I got worried. I was getting colder and colder, but then I saw a young male jogger dressed in a tracksuit coming towards me. I decided that I had no option but to ask him the way – either that or I'd freeze. I stopped him and asked him whether I was on the right road for the hostel. As I suspected, I was not – I had already passed the turn-off. The young man told me that he was going my way and offered to walk with me, and needless to say I accepted. We walked and talked for about ten minutes.

Of course, he told me his story. He was a schoolboy, a refugee from the Croatian war. He liked Norway but wanted to return to Croatia after the war. He spoke excellent English (I find that most Eastern Europeans do – and these are ordinary people such as taxi drivers, not an educated elite). It seemed to me that whatever else communism did, it left behind an educated people, well able to speak the international language of the modern world. I cannot help but compare this with the very misguided attempts of African-American and Caribbean "educators" to restrict poor black children's access to English, by making local dialect the medium of instruction in school. But that was not the same for them or their own children, for who would do the TV and radio interviews!

Let me get back to walking. One summer in France Peter and I got lost in a wood. We walked around in circles until we came upon a group of butchers having their annual picnic. It was an amazing scene – there were tables piled high with food and a very large pig on a spit! There were lots of very happy Frenchmen drinking wine. They smiled at us, and we smiled at them. They said bonjour, and we replied likewise. We did not stop to ask the way. French footpaths are very well signed, but we somehow always managed to venture off them, though invariably came upon a restaurant, bar or café, which is a reward for having been lost, and for finding the way again.

Caribbean escapades

In the 1970s the Stone family group got lost in Dominica, because Peter put absolute faith in his map. When much against his will I asked someone the way, we found out that the map was ten years out of date and we had been looking for a non-existent road!

In 1996, during one of my many visits to Trinidad, three of us went for a walk – my son and one of my friends. The other two got tired and wished to rest, but I wanted to walk up to the ridge. My friend told me to follow the path, which I did. I reached the ridge and was soon walking among pine trees and admiring the splendid view below. When I thought I'd walked long enough I turned to retrace my steps, only to find myself confronting a myriad of paths! I had no idea which was the right one, so I took the one that seemed to me well travelled. It was the wrong one and I ended up completely lost.

I decided to run, but this made me very thirsty and I began to panic. I realised that running was out of the question, but I still had an impulse to do so, so I tried to calm myself down, persuading myself to keep on walking purposefully. So that's what I did, but every now and then I would burst into a spontaneous bout of running. Soon I would become exhausted and would return to walking again. All the while I was hoping against hope that the path would lead me to a road or village. At long last I did come out near some houses, on the edge of a settlement or suburb.

By this time I had been lost for about two hours, and had been running or walking for all this time. There was blood on my legs and arms, inflicted by razor-sharp leaves. I was covered in sweat, and my boots were very muddy. I was not a pretty sight, but when I saw a lady outside a house I approached her and asked for a drink of water. She asked me, as though she knew me, "Where are the others?" I replied that there were no others. "You mean you have been in the forest alone?" She looked at me in amazement, and I was forced once more to consider the terrible fate that could have befallen me. Rather soberly I walked back to where the car was parked, and waited for the other two to turn up. That was one time when getting lost had not been any fun at all.

Lost down under

My last story in the dangerous walks theme concerns a hike in New South Wales, Australia. Peter and I were staying at my then friend's beach house in Bateman's Bay. One weekend my friend came to visit and to take us on one of her walks. The house backed on to a national park and we were to walk through this to the beach, and back via a different route. We were told it would be a twenty-kilometre round trip. I should have known that it was likely to be "one of those walks" when things began to go wrong for me, right from the start. Instead of walking to one of the proper entrances the three of us decided to clamber up the side of the ridge, into the forest. The other two managed fine, but for some reason I started slipping and sliding, lost my balance and almost fell off, much to their amusement. I didn't find it funny at all. I wasn't hurt, but I was a bit shaken, and began the walk in a somewhat chastened mood – though this didn't last long.

It was June, the middle of the Australian winter, and a very good time for walking, and we were well into our stride. After a couple of hours we came to a more or less deserted campsite. Although I am not averse to the forest as a toilet when necessary, I was happy to see a real WC and wasted no time in using it. But I was soon to learn that I had breached one of the sacred mores of Australian social life, using other people's toilets without permission. "But there was no one to ask!" I protested. "Then you should not have used it," came the stern reply. Suitably chastened for the second time that day, I decided to cheer myself up with a swim. Peter dipped one reluctant finger in the sea and stated that it was far too cold for him, but I jumped right in and started swimming vigorously. Soon my friend, who used to be a champion swimmer, joined me in the water, and began teaching me how to belly-surf. Things were going very well.

Swimming always makes me hungry, and soon it was time for our picnic lunch. We were sitting on the beach eating our meal when a large kangaroo joined us. I know very little about roos, as the Australians call them, but I remember a TV show in a which I saw one that refused to do anything his trainer had arranged, and, turning the studio up-side-down, had to be hastily removed. This behaviour was said to be very uncharacteristic of that animal in particular, and of roos in general. All I can say is that it must have been the same roo on the beach that day. He was an extremely aggressive and demanding beast, who tried to take one of our sandwiches. At that we gave him one, but that was not sufficient. Soon he was badgering us for more. Then he tried to snatch one, literally out of my friend's mouth. At this point we gave him all we had left, packed up and moved away, and as everything was now trussed up we decided to start our return journey. This was where the fun started.

This was 1993, a year in which several visitors to Australia had disappeared in mysterious circumstances. We were always being told about this and warned to be extra careful. No thought of it was in my mind as we set out. We had been this way before, and we were with a native and experienced walker who knew the area well. "No worries, mate!" We'd be back at the house in no time. We set off at around 2.00 in the afternoon, assuming that as per the earlier schedule we would be back at about 4.00 or 4.30. In fact it was closer to nine when we eventually reached the house.

"What happened? What happened? I'm coming to that!" (With apologies to W H Auden.) All went well for the first hour or so. I was confidently walking ahead, when a somewhat timid voice called me to a halt. "Someone had blundered." We were lost, and perhaps at that point did not know that we were really lost – just thought of ourselves as a bit off the route. We retraced our steps, looking for landmarks, though I'd been there before and knew it was pointless doing this in the forest. We would have to find our way back to the campsite and start all over again. By this time we'd found the main road. It was getting dark, and we had been walking for at least three hours. We decided to try to get a lift. Several cars passed us, ignoring our turned-up thumbs. I began to doubt whether anyone would ever stop.

It was getting cold, we had no water, no food, and no warm clothing of any kind. How would we cope if we had to spend the night in the forest? I was just beginning to work on this problem when a car, with two young men in it, stopped for us. Gratefully the three of us squeezed into the back seat, with me in the middle. We told them our destination. No worries, they knew the area very well, and although they were not actually going past the house they could drop us nearby. We could not thank them enough. Then things changed. The driver swung the car off the road and into the forest itself. Where were we going? We were surrounded by total darkness, except for the beam of the car's headlights, which cut a swathe through the line of trees ahead of us. The forest, in which we had taken so much delight when we we'd been hiking, became a hostile and threatening place. I could barely make out the trees, which seemed to float past us like giants.

I began to think about the people who had disappeared, and to feel that a night under the stars might have been a safer alternative after all. When I could contain myself no longer, I asked whether this was a quicker route than by the main road. We'd already told them the reason we'd been walking and trying to hitch a lift. One of the men then explained that they were beekeepers, and that they had hives in the forest, which they visited regularly. There was no question of getting lost. I wished that I could believe them. I tried to catch Peter's eyes, but he was staring fixedly ahead. I turned to my friend, who looked nervous and apprehensive, her smile weak and watery. There was no comfort there.

I decided to take a closer look at our rescuers. One had his leg in a plaster cast. "You've hurt your leg?" "Yeah, it's broken." Some comfort there, as a man with one leg in plaster should not pose too big a problem to an able-bodied woman. What about the other one? Tall and thin, he was not exactly your typical Australian macho-man, though his driving was impressive enough, as he bobbed and weaved the car through the forest as if on a racing circuit. At times it seemed that we had come to a dead end, but then right at the last minute he would make a sharp turn and we would be on another path. I began to plan my survival strategy. Then it occurred to me to ask myself the question, "What if they are armed?" Fortunately I did not have very long to dwell on that possibility, for just then the car emerged onto a main road, with other cars and light and people! Whoopee!

Grateful thanks were expressed and the car with its two beekeepers sped off into the night, while the three of us slowly walked the three or so kilometres to the house. Of course, we talked about our experience, and I learnt that my friend's smile had been meant to hearten and encourage. She'd felt safe and wanted to convey this feeling to me. I laughed as I told her that it had quite the opposite effect. Peter didn't say anything, but I knew that he'd been as worried as I. A few days on in Canberra I was talking about the weekend and began describing the look of desperation on my friend's face. Hasty consultation with her reminded me that I was under strict instructions not to talk about this incident in front of her husband. Under no circumstances was he to know that we'd been lost in the forest.

It seems that when my friend was setting out to join us, her husband, who was not coming with her, had expressed anxiety about her map-reading skills, and great foreboding about her ability to take us on a forest walk and back without getting lost. And she, of course, had dismissed these fears – with the contempt they deserved. So, I never did get to finish my account of that weekend walk, and I've had to wait until now to tell the full story. In the meantime that friendship has long since ended, and I can hope only that the husband won't bother to read this book.

Well, that is the end of my "loose ends" and all that. I am sure that it looks as if I do some foolhardy things, and take unnecessary risks. I wondered about defending myself against this charge, but decided instead to tell two stories of female deaths. The first is of a black girl who was sent to the USA from Haiti by her mother to escape from the drugs and violence of her native country. She had been there only about a week when she was caught in the crossfire of a shoot-out between drug gangs, and was killed. She had gone down the street to buy an ice cream. She was eight years old. The second story is from a *Crime Watch UK Special*, (BBC, 13th October 1998), which reported the murder of a middle-aged English woman, killed as she walked a few metres from her home at 4.30 on a summer afternoon. The murder, which was carried out by a passing motorist, was described as a completely random, motiveless crime. One might think that a woman would be safe walking on a main road, near her own home, in broad daylight, but one would be wrong. Given the uncertainty of life and the arbitrary nature of death, is it not best to simply get on with living, travelling, walking and talking? As for tomorrow, why, as the poet (Fitzgerald) wrote:

> tomorrow we may be ourselves with yesterday's seven thousand years

> Fitzgerald, E (1942) (translator), *The Rubaiyat of Omar Khayaam*, Walter J Black, NY

PostScript

The uncertain and arbitrary nature of life was brought home to me in December 1997, when just a few days before Christmas whilst sitting in my car in a traffic jam, a car skidded into mine. Both cars were wrecks, and so was my back. The accident brought an end to my academic career, and seemed at first to threaten my hiking and walking activities, but almost four years on, in January 2002, although not back to long-distance walking, I can now at least enjoy a moderate hike – even if I have to pay for it later.

Given the uncertainty of life and the arbitrary nature...

REFERENCES

Hall, D and Kinnaird, V (1996), A note on women travellers in Kinnaird and Hall (eds) *Tourism, a Gender Analysis*, Wiley, London

Chapter One

Barbados National Trust, Duke of Edinburgh Award Schemes (1994), *Hike Barbados! Guide*, Barbados Heart Foundation, Barbados

Campbell, F (1994), *On Foot Through Africa*, Orion, London

Collins, M (1985), "The Walk" in *Collection of Short Stories*, Rain Darling, London

Davies, M, Longrigg, F, Montefiore, L and Jansz, N (eds) (1986), *Half The Earth Women's Experience of Travel Worldwide*, Pandora/Rough Guide, London

Enloe, C (1989), *Bananas, Beaches and Bases: Making Feminist Sense of International Politics*, Pandora, London

Green, E, Hebron, S and Woodward (eds) (1990) *Woman's Leisure – What Leisure?*, Macmillan Education, Basingstoke, UK

Hall and Kinnaird, *Tourism, a Gender Analysis*

Harris, Trudier (1982) *From Mammies to Militants*, Temple University Press, Philadelphia, USA

Heart and Soul: Health and Fitness Magazine for African-American Women (May 1997), Rodale Press, PA, USA

HMSO (1995) National Survey Data, London
Morris, Jan/James (a) (1954) *Journey*, OUP, Oxford, (b) (1992) *Locations*, OUP, Oxford

Momsen, J (1994), "Tourism, Gender and Development in the Caribbean" in Kinnaird and Hall (eds) *Tourism a Gender Analysis*

Rungano, Kristina (1984), "The Woman" in *A Storm is Brewing*, Zimbabwe Publishing House, Harare

Samuels, R (1998), *Island Stories: Unravelling Britain*, Verso, London

The Ramblers' Association (Spring 1997), *Rambling Today, Magazine of the Ramblers' Association*, London

United Nations Statistics 1979, United Nations, NY
Wong, Judy Ling (1997), "Just Like Us", article in *Rambling Today*

Chapter Two

Collins, M (1985), *Short Stories*, Rain Darling, London
Duck, S (1983), *Friends for Life: The Psychology of Close Personal Relationships*, Harvester Press, Sussex, UK
Faderman, L (1985), *Surpassing the Love of Man: Romantic Friendship and Love Between Women*, Women's Press, London
Jung, A (1997), *Breaking the Silence*, UNESCO, Paris
La Pierre, D (1988), *City of Joy*, translated by K Spink, Arrow Books Ltd, London
Mellor, M (1992) (ed), *Breaking the Boundaries*, Virago, London
O'Connor, P (1992), *Friendship Between Women: a Critical Review*, Harvester Wheatsheaf, NY
Orbach, S (1997), *Between Women: Facing up to Feelings of Love, Envy and Competition in Women*, Arrow, London
Seth, Vikram (1993), *A Suitable Boy*, Phoenix, London
Stacey, J (1985), *Big White Sister Needs Help – Sexuality and Racism in the Women's Movement*, Women's Studies Occasional Papers: number 7, University of Kent, Canterbury
Walker, Alice (1992), *Possessing the Secret of Joy*, Vintage Books, London
Wharton, E (1995), *The Mother's Recompense*, Virago, London
Wilson, M and Russell, K (1996), *Divided Sisters Bridging the Gap Between Black Women and White Women*, Anchor Books, NY

Chapter Three

Barbados National Trust
Barrow, C (1996), *Family in the Caribbean – Themes and Perspectives*, James Currey Publishers, Oxford
Clarke, E (1957), *My Mother Who Fathered Me*, George Allen and Unwin, London
Collins, M, "The Walk"
Harris, T, *From Mammies to Militants*
Heart and Soul (May 1997)
Morris, Jan/James, *Journey*
Momsen, J, "Tourism, Gender and Development"
Robinson, J, *Women: A Guide to Women Travellers*

Rungano, K (1963), "The Woman"
University of Bournemouth: Department of International
Communications (1995), *Spanish Self-Learning Course Stage Four,*
Bournemouth, UK

Chapter Four

Burns, G (1998), *Happy Like Murderers – The West Case,* Faber and Faber,
London
Naipaul, S (1992), *Unfinished Journey,* Penguin, London

Chapter Five

Gibbons, R (1995), "Syncretism and Secretism in the Manifestation of
African Spirituality" in *At the Crossroads: African Caribbean Religions
and Christianity,* Caribbean Council of Churches, Jamaica
Mphahlele, E (1974), *The African Image,* Faber and Faber, London
Richburg, K (1998), *Out of America – A Black Man Confronts Africa,* Harper
Collins, New York
Rodney, Walter (1972), *How Europe Underdeveloped Africa,* Bogle
L'Ouverture Publication, London
Rushdie, S (1993), *Midnight's Children,* Penguin, London
Spong, Bishop (1998), At the Lambeth Conference of Bishops,
Lambeth, London
Stringer, C and McKie, R (1997), *African Exodus: The Origins of Modern
Humanity,* Pimlico, London

Chapter Six

Alfred, Lord Tennyson, from "The Princess" in *The Oxford Library of
English Poetry,* vol III (ed) John Wain, OUP, Oxford
Beckles, H (1996), *Black Masculinity in Caribbean Slavery,* WAND
(Women and Development Unit) Occasional Paper 2/96, UWI,
Barbados
Braithwaite, E K, *Mother Poem,* OUP, Oxford
COIP – Caribbean Organisation of Indigenous Peoples (1996),
Conference Report, Carib Council of Dominica, Commonwealth of
Dominica
Ffrench and Bacon (1992) *Nature Trails of Trinidad,* revised and edited
by Dr Victor Quesel, rev. ed. SM Publications, 1992, Trinidad

Government of Guyana National Development Strategy Georgetown Guyana

Haniff, N, (1996), *The Stereotyping of East Indian Women in the Caribbean*, WAND (Women and Development Unit) Occasional Paper 1/96, UWI, Barbados

Melédez and Duncan (1972), *El Negro en Costa Rica*, Editorial Costa Rica, San José, Costa Rica

Purcell, T (1993), *Banana Fallout – Class, Color and Culture Among West Indians in Costa Rica*, Centre for Afro-American Studies, UCA, Los Angles

Rossi, A (1997), *La Loca de Gandoca*, ESUCA San José, Costa Rica

Springer, Pearl Eintou (1977), "Bois" in *Shades of I-She – Every Woman's Story in Poetry*, The Collective, Diego Martin, Trinidad

Wrangham, R and Dale, P (1996), *Demonic Males – Apes and the Origins of Human Violence*, Bloomsbury, London

Chapter Seven

ACT Teacher (1993), *Rebutting Mabo Myths*, Canberra, Australia

Khilnani, S (1997), *The Idea of India*, Hamish Hamilton, London

Koestler, A (1960), *The Lotus and the Dragon*, Hutchinson, London

Metha, V (1962), *Walking the Indian Streets*, Faber and Faber, London

Naipaul, V S (1964), *An Area of Darkness*, Penguin, London

Reanney, D (1991), *The Death of Forever: A new Future for Human Consciousness*, Souvenir Press, London

Rushdie, S (1990), *Midnight's Children*

Smith, V (1958), *The Oxford History of India*, OUP, Oxford

Chapter Eight

Stone, M (1990), *Young People Leaving Care – A Study of Management Systems Service Delivery and User Evaluation*, Royal Philanthropic Society, Redhill, Surrey

Stone, M (1996), book review in *British Journal of Social Work*, June

Swift, K (1995), *Manufacturing Bad Mothers – a Critical Perspective on Child Neglect*, University of Toronto Press, Toronto

Chapter Nine

Fitzgerald, E (1942) (translator), *The Rubaiyat of Omar Khayaam,* Walter J Black, NY

Frost, R (1992), "The Road not Taken" in *The Road not Taken,* Gramercy Books, NY

Hall and Kinnaird, *Tourism, a Gender Analysis*

INDEX